The Contemporary Keyboardist

by

JOHN NOVELLO

The Contemporary Keyboardist

by

JOHN NOVELLO

SOURCE PRODUCTIONS

Toluca Lake, California

SOURCE PRODUCTIONS
10415 Sarah Street
Toluca Lake, California 91602

ISBN 0-9614966-0-6

Edited by Daveda Lamont
Cover Design by Michael Bayouth and John Novello
Artwork, Design and Illustrations by Peter Green Design
Cover Photography by Jim Hagopian
Music Copying by Suzanne R. Gaffney

Printed in the United States of America by
Delta Lithograph Co.

To Menga, John and Patti
and Gloria
and to
Zara

ACKNOWLEDGEMENTS

I would like to express my special thanks to Daveda Lamont, whose superb editing helped transform my raw manuscript into a concise and flowing communication; to Tony Cohan, for his encouragement and invaluable advice on the mechanics of manuscript preparation and publishing; to Chick Corea, whose friendship and creations are a constant source of inspiration; to Ron Moss, whose overall support, business assistance and friendship have been invaluable; to Evelyn Brechtlein for helping out with all the little important details that go into publishing a book; to Michael Bayouth for his imaginative front cover concept; to Jim Hagopian for his creative photography and friendship; to Charlie Banacos for his incredible insight into jazz improvisation and the art of teaching it; to Basil Ronzitti, whose teaching and example inspired my whole musical career; to Dr. Paul Martin, whose instruction in serious composition opened up new universes for me; to Berklee College of Music and its staff for providing the concentrated atmosphere which allowed me to immerse myself in the art of playing and creating music; to Terry Trotter for his uncompromising viewpoint on technique and musicality; to Vidal Garcia for his assistance in editing and copying all the music examples; to Peter Green Design for literally putting this book together; to Suzanne Gaffney, who did the final music copying; to my incredible family—Menga, John and Patti—whose love and support made this book possible; and to Gloria, whose love and companionship bring joy into my life.

I would also like to express my very deep appreciation to all the great artists who took off valuable time from their busy schedules to share their insight and expertise in their interviews; to students everywhere whose quests for musical advancement have actually inspired this manual; and to L. Ron Hubbard, whose technology on life and livingness is priceless.

Grateful appreciation also to the Yahama International Corporation, Fender Musical Instruments, and Europa for their support.

The author would like to express his grateful appreciation to the artists interviewed for generously giving their time and allowing him to publish their valuable insights and experience. He would like to emphasize that the philosophical, religious and musical concepts and views expressed or quoted in the book by himself and these artists are those of the individual expressing them alone, and do not necessarily reflect the views of any other artist interviewed, or the author. It is through this diversity of ideas that the author feels the purpose of the book can best be accomplished.

CONTENTS

IMPORTANT NOTE

In studying this book be very, very certain you never go past a word you do not fully understand.

The only reason a person gives up a study or becomes confused or unable to learn is that he or she has gone past a word or phrase that was not understood.

If the material becomes confusing or you can't seem to grasp it, there will be a word just earlier that you have not understood. Don't go any further, but go back to BEFORE you got into trouble, find the misunderstood word and get it defined.

*Excerpted from study technology
developed by L. Ron Hubbard*

Foreword

The <u>Contemporary Keyboardist</u> is the most up-to-date, diverse and complete book on keyboards and keyboard playing I've ever seen.

John has taken the time to pass on through the written word seemingly every inch of his own keyboard playing experience with an entertaining, down-home delivery that keeps you interested.

So many music books I've seen stay pretty much on the level of technique. It's therefore refreshing to come across a book on playing music that keeps the reader constantly oriented towards the truth that the spirit, talent, and abilities of the player are forever senior to any of the techniques he might employ.

Thus, in addition to using it as a text, many keyboardists will probably want to keep <u>The Contemporary Keyboardist</u> on hand and use it as an ongoing reference guide in the same way they would an encyclopedia.

My hat's off to John and <u>The Contemporary Keyboardist</u>.

Chick Corea

Prelude

My main intention for writing this manual was to contribute something of importance back to a subject that has been so rewarding to me. As I have always enjoyed helping others, there seemed no better way, then, to make the path easier than by organizing and writing down the vast body of knowledge and information that I had accumulated as a student (which I'll always be), composer, musical director, multikeyboardist, producer, and teacher.

Although I had found a few good books that covered specific topics such as technique, improvisation, harmony, and so on, there appeared to be nothing available that put the whole music game into perspective for the contemporary keyboardist. Except for those who can attend one of the few fine schools that exist, most up-and-coming musicians study a little here and and a little there and then try to put it all together themselves. Possibly that's what you've found yourself doing. Well, I have news for you! The music scene is so diverse and competitive that if you approach it glibly, the odds are definitely against you. The "overnight success" stories are the exception, not the rule.

So what I felt was needed was a comprehensive self-study manual that sufficiently prepared and oriented a keyboardist to the current scene--a survival manual, if you will, or book of basics. After three years of exhaustive work and research, The Contemporary Keyboardist was the result.

This manual is unique in several ways--first, in the scope of information covered, and second, in the organization, evaluation, and application of this information: I've put it into what I feel is the optimum learning sequence; I've tried to select and emphasize the most important information; and I've given drills, exercises, and music examples that I think you will find helpful in developing your abilities.

Thus this book was designed to be of value to you whatever your current level of expertise and whatever your individual musical goals.

Best of luck!

How to Use This Book

This book is divided into four sections. The first, "A Philosophy of Music," deals with abilities that I believe are senior to the mechanics of music. Thus communication, cause-effect principles and practice disciplines are discussed insofar as they relate to the game.

The second section, "Mechanics," which takes up most of the manual, covers the basics of keyboard music and playing (notation, harmony, improvisation, sight reading, multikeyboards, etc.) as well as their applications.

The third section, "The Business Scene," contains some valuable guidelines and advice concerning the business of music as it affects the contemporary keyboardist.

And the last section, "Interviews," lets you hear what some of the most successful keyboardists and composers on the contemporary scene have to say about themselves, their art, and playing.

If you are an advanced student, you may wish to scan through the Contents and turn directly to what interests you, whether it be the artist interviews, advanced improvisation, sight reading, cause-effect principles, or any of the other chapters.

But if you are a beginner or intermediate keyboardist, you will obtain the best results by studying this manual from beginning to end, making sure you do all the drills and exercises within each chapter as you go along, as well as the assignments at the end. For it is in this manner--as a comprehensive self-study manual--that The Contemporary Keyboardist functions best. I believe that in today's music scene it is optimum, if not imperative, for a keyboardist to be well trained. When you are, your work potential, and thus your ability to survive and continue in the game, is greatly improved. Translated into English, this means you have a better chance to make a good living, enjoy the art, and maybe be ready for that big break that is always possible in the music game!

Part One

A Philosophy
of Music

Chapter 1

Art and Communication

Before I get started, you might ask what art and communication have to do with playing keyboards and making music. Well, my answer to that is nothing--and everything! Nothing, if your goal is to play mechanically, with no communication or emotional impact--and everything, if you wish to communicate with some soul. The latter is what "good players" do, whether they know it or not. They communicate a little bit of themselves with enough expertise to produce some kind of emotional response.

So what is art? And how good does a work of art have to be to be good? Since I believe the answers to these two questions are important, even critical to good performances, let's pursue this a little further--okay?

In the Art Series, a series of essays by L. Ron Hubbard, can be found answers to many of these questions. The Art Series is a brilliant clarification of basic artistic principles, and I highly recommend this series to anyone who wishes sanity on the subject. Basically, Hubbard defines art in this way:

"ART is a word which summarizes THE QUALITY OF COMMUNICATION."*

Quality refers to how good the technical rendition is, while communication refers to the message. Hubbard also says this about art:

---

* L. Ron Hubbard, Art Series (Los Angeles: Bridge Publications, 1983), "Art," Art Series 1, p.1. (See "Recommended Reading" at the end of this chapter for the publisher's address.)

"Seeking <u>perfection</u> is a wrong target in art. One should primarily seek communication with it and <u>then</u> perfect it as far as reasonable."*

This is simple but powerful stuff! This is the secret of what the true professional constantly does. He or she always obtains communication with the art form at the minimum sacrifice of technical quality. Someone who directs his or her efforts only toward perfection of the technical aspect does so as a result of past failures to communicate, according to Hubbard.** Now think about that for a while!

In response to the question of how good a work has to be to be good, Hubbard answers that a work of art has to have--

"TECHNICAL EXPERTISE ITSELF ADEQUATE TO PRODUCE AN EMOTIONAL IMPACT."***

So the whole purpose of your technical expertise is to produce an emotional impact so your communication rockets through. It's that simple!

Have you ever been in the presence of a great artist and been simply mesmerized by how effortlessly he or she performs the most difficult of tasks? Well, that's the emotional impact of his or her technical expertise that Hubbard is talking about. Stay around for the rest of the performance so you can get the message too!

This is so important that I would like to drive it home even further, using language as an example. In language, the technical expertise would be your knowledge of words--vocabulary--and their usage. Once anyone learns a basic vocabulary, they <u>immediately</u> begin communicating. If they then run into some difficulty speaking or writing, they simply need to learn the necessary words and their usage to be able to complete their communication. The

---

* Hubbard, <u>Art Series</u>, "Art," p.2.
** Hubbard, <u>Art Series</u>, "Art," p.3.
*** L. Ron Hubbard, <u>Art Series</u> (Los Angeles: Bridge Publications, 1983), "Art, More About," Art Series 2, p.3.

point here is you don't study every word in the universe before attempting communication. On the other hand, the more command you have over the language (the technical expertise), the more accurate and effortless your resultant communications. John F. Kennedy is a well-known example of a man who communicated with enough technical expertise to produce an emotional impact as well as a message.

It also follows that if you had a very limited vocabulary, your communications might be limited to things like "See Spot run" or "Look at the cat"--hardly enough technical expertise to produce an emotional impact, but nevertheless a communication! That's why art is not simply defined just as a communication:

"ART is a word which summarizes THE QUALITY OF COMMUNICATION."*

--L. Ron Hubbard

---

* Hubbard, Art Series, "Art," p.1.

Chapter 1

ASSIGNMENTS

_____ 1. Define art and give ten examples of it.

_____ 2. Explain, in your own words, the relationship of communication to art.

_____ 3. How much technical expertise should one strive for?

_____ 4. What's more important in a musical performance, the resultant communication or the technical rendition?

_____ 5. Write, in your own words, how this data on art and communication might apply to you as a contemporary keyboardist.

SUGGESTED READING

Hubbard, L. Ron. _Art Series_. Los Angeles: Bridge Publications, 1983. For information on obtaining the _Art Series_, write Bridge Publications, Inc., 1414 N. Catalina Street, Los Angeles, California 90027.

Chapter 2
CAUSE-EFFECT PRINCIPLES

What makes a great performance? Why do some artists communicate better than others even though their technical expertise is comparable? What does playing "mechanically" mean? What do people mean when they say a particular performer "cooks" or has a lot of "feeling" or "soul"? Well, in order to intelligently discuss the answers to these questions, one must understand the whole in relation to its parts.

The first step toward this understanding would be to identify the actual players and components of the music game, defining our terms as we go along. Many of the phenomena I wish to discuss were accurately named, described, and defined for the first time by L. Ron Hubbard. The definitions enclosed in quotation marks in the following text are his. (Several related meanings or senses are given for some words, and in these cases each meaning is set off individually in quotation marks.)*

The Player

Who or what actually is it that has this impulse to create and play music (or participate in any art form, for that matter)?

Well, you and me--of course! But for our purposes, we need to be a little more exact. Hubbard uses the word thetan to describe what we're after here:

A thetan (taken from the Greek word theta, meaning "thought" or "life" or "the spirit") is "the being who is the individual and who handles and lives in the body."

----

* The definitions enclosed within quotation marks in this chapter are taken from the Dianetics™ and Scientology® Technical Dictionary, by L. Ron Hubbard (Los Angeles: Publications Organization United States, 1975). Dianetics and Scientology are trademarks owned by the Religious Technology Center and are used with its permission.

The thetan is "the person himself--not his body or his name, the physical universe, his mind, or anything else." It is "that which is aware of being aware; the identity which is the individual. The thetan is most familiar to one and all as <u>you</u>."

And: "The spirit is not a thing. It is the creator of things."

You often hear people refer to "life force" or "life energy." Hubbard uses the word <u>theta</u> to describe this concept. <u>Theta</u> is "thought, life force, <u>elan vital</u>, the spirit, the soul, or any other of the numerous definitions it has had for some thousands of years." Theta is "the energy peculiar to life which acts upon material in the physical universe and animates it, mobilizes it and changes it."

What is the exact relationship of the thetan to the body? Hubbard describes a body as "a carbon-oxygen engine which runs at 98.6° F. It runs on low combustion fuel, generally derived from other life forms." He says further, "The theta being (thetan) is the engineer running this engine in Homo Sapiens." Homo Sapiens is "an animated vegetable guided by the life force (thetan). By itself the body would live, walk around, react, sleep, kill, and direct an existence no better than that of a field mouse, or a zombie. Put a theta being over it and it becomes possessed of ethics and morals and direction and goals and the ability to reason; it becomes this strange thing called Homo Sapiens."

These ideas may be familiar to some and foreign to others. But whether or not you have a subjective reality on them, you will see, as you keep reading, that we're leading to some important, practical points that can put you in much greater control of your music <u>and</u> your overall career.

A Game

Hubbard has said, "Life can best be understood by likening it to a game."*

---

* L. Ron Hubbard, <u>Scientology, The Fundamentals of Thought</u> (Los Angeles: Publications Organization United States, 1956).

So if we view the various activities and endeavors we engage in as games or parts of a game, the physical universe can be considered as the playing field and all the various physical universe objects--from keyboards to even our bodies--as the tools and instruments we use to play them.

This is how I would sum it all up: Thetans, following individual purposes and for the sake of a game, interact with the physical universe. These interactions result in many interesting phenomena, music being just one.

Creation

What is the process of creation? How do we arrive at these desired effects and interactions?

First let's look at the concept of the spiritual universe, or "universe of theta." Hubbard defines it very simply. The spiritual universe is "thought matter (ideas), thought energy, thought space, and thought time combined in an independent universe analogous to the material universe."

To cause something to happen, a person first postulates it in the spiritual universe. To postulate is "to conclude, decide or resolve a problem or to set a pattern for the future or to nullify a pattern of the past." (Example sentence: He postulated that he would be a good sight reader.)

The word is also very useful as a noun: A postulate is "a self-created truth"; "an expected end result"; "causative thinkingness." (Example sentence: His postulate to become a good keyboardist was realized.)

Another word with a special meaning defined by Hubbard is mock-up. As a noun, mock-up means "a self-created object which exists as itself or symbolizes some object in the physical universe. It is an imaginary picture of a real or potentially real physical universe 'something.'"

Examples of mock-ups could be a painter's idea or mental picture of how a planned painting will look, or a musician's concept of how a piece will sound when he plays it.

Mock up as a verb means "to get an imaginary picture of." (Example sentence: Mock up a new keyboard setup.)

Now, once you have created a mock-up or postulated some end result--what happens next?

Cause and Effect

Let's look at how a thetan postulates or causes a desired mock-up to flow from the spiritual universe into the physical and back into the spiritual with regard to the music game.

As you will see, communication plays a vital part here. The first thing we need to understand is exactly what communication is. Here are several of the ways Hubbard defines communication:

1. "The interchange of perception through the material universe between organisms or the perception of the material universe by sense channels."

2. "The interchange of ideas across space."

3. "The consideration and action of impelling an impulse or particle from source point across a distance to receipt point with the intention of bringing into being at the receipt point a duplication and understanding of that which emanated from the source point."

4. "The FORMULA of COMMUNICATION is: CAUSE, DISTANCE, EFFECT with INTENTION, ATTENTION and DUPLICATION with UNDERSTANDING."

In order to help you understand how the above principles of communication and cause and effect can be applied to the creation of music, I've created the following diagram, "The Music Macrocosm." The arrows show the direction of the communication flows as they relate to a musical performance.

THE MUSIC MACROCOSM

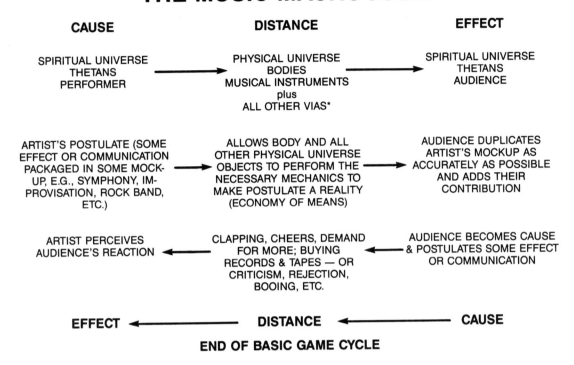

CAUSE	DISTANCE	EFFECT
SPIRITUAL UNIVERSE THETANS PERFORMER	PHYSICAL UNIVERSE BODIES MUSICAL INSTRUMENTS plus ALL OTHER VIAS*	SPIRITUAL UNIVERSE THETANS AUDIENCE
ARTIST'S POSTULATE (SOME EFFECT OR COMMUNICATION PACKAGED IN SOME MOCK-UP, E.G., SYMPHONY, IMPROVISATION, ROCK BAND, ETC.)	ALLOWS BODY AND ALL OTHER PHYSICAL UNIVERSE OBJECTS TO PERFORM THE NECESSARY MECHANICS TO MAKE POSTULATE A REALITY (ECONOMY OF MEANS)	AUDIENCE DUPLICATES ARTIST'S MOCKUP AS ACCURATELY AS POSSIBLE AND ADDS THEIR CONTRIBUTION
ARTIST PERCEIVES AUDIENCE'S REACTION	CLAPPING, CHEERS, DEMAND FOR MORE; BUYING RECORDS & TAPES — OR CRITICISM, REJECTION, BOOING, ETC.	AUDIENCE BECOMES CAUSE & POSTULATES SOME EFFECT OR COMMUNICATION

EFFECT ← **DISTANCE** ← **CAUSE**

END OF BASIC GAME CYCLE

*__via__, via means a relay point in a communication line (Hubbard, *Technical Dictionary,* under "via"). A person communicates his musical message by means of his body, hands, and instruments (among other things). Thus these can be seen to be means — vias — by which he relays the communication that he orginates.

As the diagram shows, the basic game can be reduced to just one ingredient--COMMUNICATION!

So let's recapitulate, because this is most important! <u>You</u>, the spirit, life force, cause-point, awareness unit, thetan, artist, do the following:

1. Postulate or mock up a message to communicate--feelings, emotions, sensations, desires--whatever you want to communicate.

2. Guide the physical universe vias (one's body, instruments, etc.) until the desired postulate or mock-up is realized. Through "economy of means" (the correct mechanics) and technical expertise, the artist performs the act in the physical universe medium.

3.   Observe if the audience has received, duplicated, and understood your mock-up.

4.   Accept audience's acknowledgment, whatever it may be, and continue playing the game.

As the diagram shows, the communication becomes two-way when the effect-point (the audience in this case) becomes a cause-point (see diagram). This, of course, is the desired result. Hubbard says, "When a work of painting, music or other form attains two-way communication, it is truly art." And, "True art always elicits a contribution from those who view or hear or experience it. By contribution is meant 'adding to it.'"*

So if the audience cannot contribute to the performance in some way, you're doomed. If there is a law that should be chiseled in stone, this is it!

Now, the true test of any knowledge is its workability. In other words, how does this help you, the contemporary keyboardist? How can this data be applied to synthesizers, electric pianos, clavinets, sound reinforcement, effect devices, etc? Okay, give this step-by-step procedure a try. I have had much success with it.

I.   Research and Development (R & D)

    A.   Decide what kinds of sounds you like best to create. If you don't already know, then you have to do some research. This is accomplished by checking out other artists' creations, experimenting on your own, and so on. It takes as long as it takes, so be patient.

    B.   Research what type of keyboard setup would best respond to your demands. (Chapter 18, "Multikeyboards," contains features and advantages of multikeyboard setups as well as guidelines for choosing them.) Are your mock-ups--the music or effects you want to create--so complex as to warrant a full multikeyboard laboratory, or will just an acoustic piano do the trick? Get the idea?

---

* L. Ron Hubbard, Art Series (Los Angeles: Bridge Publications, 1983), "Art and Communication," Art Series 5, p.1.

C. <u>Get as familiar as possible with your setup,
    what it can or can't do.</u> If it falls short of
    producing what you "hear," then add to it, sub-
    tract from it, modify it, do whatever to it
    until you feel comfortable with it. If you com-
    promise with <u>your</u> reality of how it should be,
    your attention will get stuck on mechanics and
    you'll fall short of your intended communica-
    tion, believe me!

II. <u>Game Cycle</u>

Although the following game cycle is accomplished
rather rapidly and subliminally by the professional,
I have found that breaking it down into its component
parts facilitates understanding.

A. <u>Performance Cycle</u>

    1. Postulate the desired effect, mock-up, or
        sound you wish to communicate into the
        physical universe.

    2. With as much enthusiasm as possible, guide
        the body, instruments, or whatever with an
        <u>easy</u> intention toward the desired effect.

    3. End of performance.

B. <u>Post-Performance Critique Cycle</u>

    1. Critique: Compare resultant physical uni-
        verse sound with what was intended. If it
        falls short of the mark:

    2. Adjust resultant sound to likeness of your
        intended sound.

    3. Improve your mental postulate or mock-up if
        necessary!

    4. Now do your thing!

Repeat the above Game Cycle as necessary until you're
able to effortlessly do in the physical universe what you
intend or postulate.

Thus, as you can see, poor performance in any coordinated muscular activity is due to a poor postulate or mock-up. A poor postulate could be one which was wrong to begin with, incomplete or unclear, has counter-intention (doubt, self-invalidation) in it, or too much attention on mechanics (as opposed to communication).

In fact, the actual need for repetitive training itself seems to result in the first place from an incomplete or unclear postulate by the performer. It can be viewed as a sort of conservative backup plan or a substitute for failure to use a very powerful native ability. In other words, ideally, at a very high level of operation, one wouldn't need to practice at all!

This concept of putting one's attention on the desired result is not brand new. I know of two other viewpoints on this subject. In his book, The Pianist's Art,* Powell Everhart calls this principle the "Intention-Corroboration Principle." Luigi Bonpensiere, in his book, New Pathways to Piano Technique,** refers to it as the science of "idio-kinetics." Although both books are incredible and definitely recommended reading, their explanations of this cause-effect principle are unclear as to who, or what, is ideating* these end results--whether it's "nature," your "will," your "mind," or just what.

But because of the discoveries and clarifications of L. Ron Hubbard, we are able to perceive this distinction between spirit and body. So it is you, a spirit, who runs the show. You postulate these effects and demand results from the body, instruments, etc. It is you who wills the "will," minds the "mind," and nurtures "nature"!

As stated before, this is extremely important. You can see that one does have to do something. One does not simply sit at his instrument and wait for his postulate to happen. You must do something! You, as distinct from your body and mind, are the conductor. The orchestra plays when and how you direct it. If you direct it with a clear easy intention, with certainty, and with enthusiasm, you'll get its best performance. If, however, you direct it with an unclear intention--with lots of effort or strain--with uncertainty--with lack of enthusiasm--you'll get its worst performance!

---

* Powell Everhart, The Pianist's Art (Atlanta: Powell Everhart, 1958).
** Luigi Bonpensiere, New Pathways to Piano Technique (New York: The Philosophical Library, 1953).

* ideate, to form an idea of; imagine; conceive.

So, in summary, your instruction and study should concern itself with the following:

1. Improving your ability to postulate the desired effect and demand its fulfillment in the physical universe.

2. Enhancing this process with the necessary mechanics--technique, ear training, harmony, improvisation, etc.

Ultimately, as I see it, the gig is this. Increase your potentials as an individual spirit and to that degree your postulates will become more effective and powerful. I highly recommend the technology of Scientology applied religious philosophy, researched and developed by L. Ron Hubbard, as an extremely valuable and workable means to this end, especially for artists.* In Hubbard's own words:

> Scientology is the study of the human spirit in its relationship to the physical universe and its living forms. It is a science of life. It is the one thing senior to life because it handles all the factors of life. It contains the data necessary to live as a free being.**

So if you wish to add some sanity to your artistic career, check it out. It works.

I hope this chapter has given you some workable insights into the philosophical side of the game as I see it. Now go back and see if you can answer the questions we posed in the first paragraph of this chapter!

------

* Scientology is a trademark owned by the Religious Technology Center and is used with its permission.
** Hubbard, Technical Dictionary, under "Scientology."

Chapter 2
ASSIGNMENTS

_____ 1. In your own words, explain the difference between playing "mechanically" and playing with feeling, or with "soul."

_____ 2. Why is it important to research and develop the right keyboard setup? What is the guiding factor in determining the right setup?

_____ 3. When you are performing, what should your attention be on, and why?

_____ 4. Discuss what you would do if there was a vast difference between your intended effect and the actual effect you created while playing.

_____ 5. If your keyboards were to end up not sounding like you "hear" them in your own mind or universe, describe what you would do. Would you just cope, or what?

_____ 6. Describe the ideal communication cycles at a performance. What is the difference between a one-way communication and a two-way communication?

_____ 7. Describe in your own words what all musical instruction should concern itself with and why.

SUGGESTED READING

Bonpensiere, Luigi. New Pathways to Piano Technique. New York: The Philosophical Library, 1953.

Corea, Chick. Music Poetry. Los Angeles: Litha Music, 1980.

Everhart, Powell. The Pianist's Art. Atlanta: Powell Everhart, 962 Myrtle Street, Northeast, Atlanta 9, Georgia, 1958.

Chapter 3
Practice Disciplines

During my many rewarding years as a teacher, I have observed that the students who progress the fastest and the furthest are those who understand how to practice. Therefore I make it standard procedure to thoroughly orient a student to the "ideal scene" of practicing in order that we (the student and I) both reap the best results. "I didn't practice this week because--" is simply not accepted and missing a lesson without a makeup is instant dismissal. Although this might seem a little harsh, it produces incredible results and separates the serious from the glib!*

Before we look at a standard operating procedure for practicing, there are a few terms that we need to define:

1. Pre-practice, the period right before actually practicing where you set the goals for the session.

2. Practice, the actual "doingness," where you are trying to achieve a certain ability through repetition, evaluation, attention to detail, reevaluation, comparison to the ideal scene--in general, a time for "think"!

3. Post-practice, the time for comparison of what you have just done in the practice session with what you intended to do, so as to determine what the next session's content should be.

4. Playing, is simply playing! It is using whatever technical expertise you have to express yourself to the audience. If there is any kind of "think" going on, then to that degree you are not playing.

---

* glib, superficial; insincere.

5.   <u>Objective Self Criticism</u>, becoming self-sufficient at
     being your own critic. This ability allows the stu-
     dent to eventually dispense with his or her teacher
     and free him or herself as an artist!

     After making sure you've understood these defini-
tions, you should read and carry out the following steps
for organizing practice sessions:

1.   Form an honest conviction toward achieving your goal
     or goals--for example, to be a great studio musician.

2.   Decide to set aside a minimum amount of time each day
     for practice. Start low and gradually increase the
     amount of time per day.

3.   Each day, graph your "honestly done practice hours"
     in order to keep an accurate record. This is impor-
     tant because you'll want to know if your statistics
     are rising, staying consistent, or falling. If
     they're falling, you'll need to quickly reorganize
     your time! (See illustration below.)

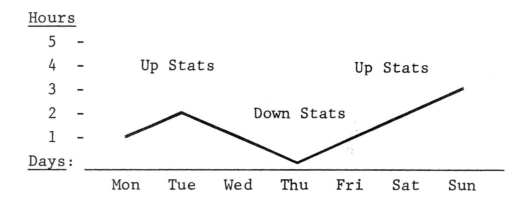

4.   <u>Create</u> your day the night before. This simply means
     to plan a time schedule of your whole day and in-
     clude, of course, <u>your practice time</u>.

If you have a straight job, your schedule might look like this:

```
7:30 AM  -  8:30 AM . . . Up, shower, breakfast
8:30 AM  -  9:00 AM . . . Travel to work
9:00 AM  -  5:00 PM . . . Job
5:00 PM  -  7:00 PM . . . Dinner
7:00 PM  -  8:00 PM . . . Relax
8:00 PM  -  8:15 PM . . . Pre-practice reflection
8:15 PM  -  9:30 PM . . . Practice
9:30 PM  -  9:45 PM . . . Post-practice reflection
9:45 PM  - 11:00 PM . . . Leisure
11:00              . . . Bed
```

If you're a fulltime musician, your schedule might look like this:

```
10:00 AM - 11:00 AM . . . Up, shower, breakfast
11:00 AM - 11:15 AM . . . Pre-practice reflection
11:15 AM -  1:15 PM . . . Practice
1:15 PM  -  1:30 PM . . . Post-practice reflection
1:30 PM  -  2:00 PM . . . Lunch
2:00 PM  -  3:00 PM . . . Promote career
3:00 PM  -  6:00 PM . . . Rehearsal for gig
6:00 PM  -  7:00 PM . . . Dinner
7:00 PM  -  8:00 PM . . . Travel to gig and set up
8:00 PM  -  1:00 AM . . . Night gig
1:00 AM             . . . Home and bed
```

Doing this each day starts you on the road to being cause over your life instead of effect, thus increasing your chances for success. Eventually you'll find yourself creating weeks at a time and more!

The above four steps allow you to organize and create time so you can get on with the business of practicing. What follows, therefore, is a standard procedure for practicing:

Practice Procedure

1. If possible, leave your problems outside the practice room. If that is not possible, then it's probably better that you handle whatever it is your attention is on and _then_ practice: otherwise the practice session might be very glib--in other words, you might not really get anything from it, but just be going through the motions.

2. Shift your attention to the goals you have created for the session, and when you feel ready to start, then say out loud:

3. "START!" I have found that most students never _really_ start the practice session. Simply sitting down and playing around the piano is not practicing. Therefore, giving yourself a verbal start makes the session a little more real and important.

4. Organize your allotted time by practicing the most difficult things first, when you're fresh, and the easiest things last. Also make sure you cover everything you planned--especially if you have a limited amount of time. If you don't cover everything, mark your place and begin there at your next practice session.

5. Be aware of your emotions, for they can get in the way. Boredom, anger, depression, grief, etc., can take the "attack" out of the session. If you become aware of negative emotions, get up and take a five-minute break and then resume. Enthusiasm is the emotion necessary for successful practice sessions. If you take your time and practice things gradiently--that is, progress gradually--you won't stir up these negative emotions.

6. When you've either completed your targets or your allotted time, end the practice part of the session and give yourself a "well done" (mentally or out loud). But there's still one more very important step--

7. Now PLAY! Play anything! It may or may not be related to your lesson, but just play. Always play after you practice because that's what you're practicing for--remember? Now, playing has no "think" associated with it--no evaluation or consideration of how you're doing. That part of the session is over.

Just imagine you're playing for an audience and simply play! Don't stop, even if there are mistakes. Playing is the real thing and a professional performance means you're in control. If you ever get a chance to ask a great artist what's going on while he's performing, you'll find that he usually can't explain it. That's because there's <u>nothing</u> going on. If the artist is prepared--meaning he's done his homework--then the only thing going on is "playing"-- so play on, maestro!

If applied honestly, the above practice procedure will pave the way for the student to advance rapidly and therefore realize his or her potentials in a relatively short time. It is false data that it has to take eight to ten hours per day and twenty years to become a real professional. With good guidance and diligent, organized practice, one can become quite adept in a relatively short time.

Chapter 3
ASSIGNMENTS

_____ 1. Explain in your own words the difference between practicing and playing.

_____ 2. Of what value are the pre- and post-practice reflection periods?

_____ 3. Define objective self-criticism. How does one attain this ability and why is it so important?

_____ 4. Why do you think it's important to have a goal before you get on with learning?

_____ 5. What edge, if any, does scheduling your day the night before give you in relation to practicing consistently?

_____ 6. On paper, create or mock up a possible practice session (1-1/2 hours long), using all the data in this chapter.

_____ 7. Why is practice considered the door to realizing your potentials?

_____ 8. What might be the reason for simply playing after a heavy practice session?

Part Two

Mechanics

Chapter 4
THE BASIC BASICS OF MUSIC

The goal of Part One was to clear up some of the mystery associated with the mental aspect of creating music. Part Two, however, deals with the essential mechanics any keyboardist should master in order to increase his or her survival potential. Contrary to what some people will say, understanding these mechanics won't make you "mechanical" and won't make you lose your "soul." If you understand the principles in Chapters 1 through 3 and you feel good about them, all the knowledge in the world about music and keyboard playing won't stifle you. On the contrary, it will help. When you need it, you'll have it. It's just that simple.

The only way being trained can hurt you is if you lose sight of why you're getting trained. So let's put that falsehood to rest. Playing "mechanically" is not the result of knowledge: it is the result of incorrect <u>application</u> of knowledge!

Now, what are these basic-basics? They are <u>rhythm</u>, <u>melody</u>, <u>harmony</u>, and <u>orchestration</u>.

RHYTHM

Rhythm is the organization of music with respect to time. Time and rhythm were duplicated by primitive man long before melody, harmony, orchestration, or other decorations were even sensed, let alone understood. Rhythm, therefore, holds first place as the basic expressive factor. It is the core of the blended activity of the entire playing mechanism. It is the sum total of pulse, meter, tempo and groove.

Pulse is the recurring basic equal beat which may be explicit or implicit (that is, heard or not heard, but there nonetheless). Meter is the organization of pulses into units. These units constitute the time signature. Tempo is the space or length of time between each pulse. Ah, and last, but definitely not least--groove!

How many musicians didn't get the gig or session because their groove wasn't quite right? Well, groove is the "feel" or interpretation of the basic rhythm. It's the right feel, dictated by the musical style, and it enables one to produce the desired emotional impact. It makes it possible for the audience to listen easily, without confusion. Stated another way, groove is the rhythm superimposed over the tempo which helps project the musical idea. No matter how complicated the details of the music, the groove, or "rhythm of form," as Abby Whiteside calls it, is what sweeps the audience off its feet and makes for an inspired and professional performance.

A metronome, for example, has good time, or tempo, but make no mistake about it--it doesn't groove! It is just a pulse counting device which is awaiting a groove! So time (pulse) and rhythm (groove) are not synonymous. Time is but the orderly recurrence of pulse. It is possible to maintain time without having recourse to rhythm, as I stated above in discussing the metronome--but the converse is not true. Rhythm must employ time as a frame for its "feel"--and feel is accomplished by characteristic volume contrasts (dynamics), syncopation, orchestration, etc.

Translated into English--a musician could conceivably have good time and not have good rhythm--but not usually vice versa. You can put this performer under the domination of the rhythm of a good group or orchestra and he'll be swept along inside the current of their rhythm and have an inspired performance. But alone, his performance is uninspired and unemotional--he concentrates largely on details, or mechanics, making it difficult for the listener to understand. Well, he is ignorant of the principles covered in Part One and he is the victim of bad practicing habits. All practicing should be, in the end, concerned with preparing for an inspired and emotional performance--as discussed earlier, one that communicates! Details are a necessary evil--but, once learned, they are sublimated into the "rhythm of form" or groove!

That is why solo piano playing separates the amateurs from the pros. Great performers always command the situation and never do anything but create music, whether with a great orchestra or group, or without. They all exhibit this tremendous rhythmic force--they are saturated with it and consequently we, the audience, receive a truly professional and exciting performance. All great musicians, athletes, actors, etc., have a fundamental rhythm which makes for an astounding, effortless performance. In other words, "It don't mean a thing if it ain't got that swing..."!!!

MELODY

Melody is a succession of single notes or tones (Example 1). Although Example 1 fits the definition of a melody, it has no rhythmic activity and is rarely found. More often, melody is contoured and animated by strong rhythmic interaction (Example 2). Furthermore, most melodies suggest harmonies (Example 3). Some, however, are nonharmonic, consisting of only one chord or key color (modal) (Example 4a), or are very angular, meaning their intervals challenge harmonic interpretation (Example 4b). Some melodies suggest or outline harmonies other than those designated in their accompaniment (upper structure harmony) (Example 5). Some just about defy any classification--they simply exist (Example 6). Some melodies interweave with each other and create what is known as counterpoint--the combination of two or more independent melodies (Example 7). Johann Sebastian Bach's compositions are great examples of this style.

EXAMPLE 1:

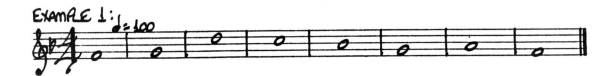

Now, what makes a melody great? A succession of tones does not necessarily make for a great melody. Well, a melody is a succession of tones grasped by the mind as a significant pattern. For the average uneducated listener, to group or understand this melody really means to perceive the relationship of the beginning to the middle, of the middle to the end. Just as we grasp the single complete thought of a whole sentence instead of just the words, we apprehend the whole melodic statement instead of just the single notes. Heard in this way, the melody comes to life and takes on meaning, clarity and direction. It produces that emotional impact we talked about earlier.

To produce this effect in the listener, the melody must have movement, tension, and variety.

If you wish to further study the devices that have evolved to help the listener apprehend melodies, I suggest you study the craft of composition, for only by composing many melodies will you truly understand the art.

HARMONY

Harmony, in the modern sense, means the structure and function of chords and their relationship to each other. A chord is normally three or more notes sounded simultaneously (Example 8), although these notes may be sounded one at a time (Example 9).

The distance between any two notes in a chord is called an interval. There are two types of intervals: harmonic--notes struck simultaneously (Example 10), and melodic--notes struck in succession (Example 11). Later in this manual we shall study intervals in detail, as they are the basic building block of chords and melodies!

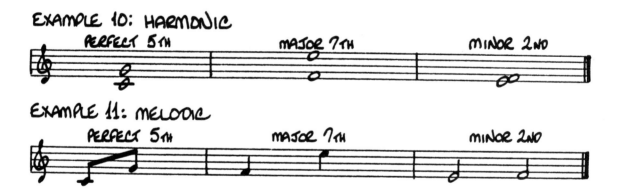

Harmony almost always has a melodic aspect: first we tend to hear the upper voices of a chord progression, and then the bass, or lower, voice (Example 12). Sometimes, however, this is reversed, depending on a variety of factors that will be discussed later. The inner voices are less likely to be heard. But the inner voices as well as the outer voices influence the chords, for we hear a chord not only as a vertical structure but also as the consequence of all its voices. In other words, the linear or horizontal movement affects the vertical, and vice versa. As a matter of fact, good voice leading (smooth movement of all voices) can make even a weak chord progression sound great! (Example 13). Bill Evans was noted for his impeccable harmonic voice leading on the piano.

ORCHESTRATION

Orchestration, the fourth basic element of music, is considerably more important than is generally realized. In its traditional sense, orchestration simply meant writing music for the instruments in the orchestra--strings, brass, reeds, flutes, percussion and piano. In its contemporary and expanded sense, orchestration means using whatever instrument or instruments are necessary to enhance the basic music. That may include all the traditional instruments plus the contemporary ones--electric piano and organ, synthesizers, etc. It requires, therefore, considerable knowledge of all musical instruments: their method of sound production, their range, their capacities and limitations, their positive and negative points. It also requires a well-developed aural imagination and memory, which means possessing the ability to imagine and recall sounds of various instruments, both singularly and in combination. Lastly, it requires an ability to match the melody, harmony, and rhythm to the correct instruments--those instruments which best carry the communication of the music to the audience.

Orchestration is not just for the serious composer. The contemporary keyboardist is expected not only to play a multitude of keyboards well, but also to arrange and orchestrate music for all types of instrumental combinations. The keyboardist who simply plays one keyboard is basically unheard of today, unless he is a genius and unique stylist! And the keyboardist who knows nothing of other instruments will be closing the door to a very rewarding and profitable segment of the musical industry--arranging and composition.

The main ability gained from studying orchestration is that one learns how to emphasize the essentials and suppress the nonessentials of the components of melody, harmony, and rhythm. Doing this allows the total intention and meaning of the music to get through to the audience. Orchestration, then, enhances communication. It is music's paper garment!

Chapter 4
ASSIGNMENTS

_____ 1. Define the following:

a. Rhythm

b. Melody

c. Harmony

d. Orchestration

_____ 2. Why would a thorough grounding in all of the above basics be helpful to you as a keyboard-ist?

_____ 3. What is the difference between <u>time</u> and <u>groove</u> and how are they related?

SUGGESTED READING

Dallin, Leo. <u>Techniques of Twentieth Century Composition</u>. Dubuque, Iowa: Wm. C. Brown Co. Publishers, 1957.

Machlis, Joseph. <u>Introduction to Contemporary Music</u>. New York: W. W. Norton & Company, 1961.

Russo, William. <u>Jazz Composition and Orchestration</u>. London: University of Chicago Press, 1968. chaps. 1-4.

Chapter 5

Symbols and Nomenclature

The key to real understanding of any technical subject is its symbols and nomenclature. Once these are duplicated and understood, the door is opened and the subject can now be understood and then applied. Before you continue reading, make sure you have read the "Important Note" on study at the front of the book.

I will make no attempt to cover all musical symbols and nomenclature in this chapter, for there are excellent manuals already written on the subject. I will, however, explain the basic symbols and terms, as they are extremely important and are the ones most often misunderstood.

1.   <u>Time Signature</u>, a fractional sign placed just after the key signature whose denominator (bottom number) indicates the kind of note (half, quarter, eighth, etc.) that gets one count, and whose numerator (top number) indicates the number of these per measure.

The formula for a time signature is as follows: x/y, where <u>x</u> equals the number of counts and <u>y</u> equals what kind of note gets one count.

<u>Examples</u>:

3/4   =   three quarter notes per measure, and a quarter note gets one count

5/2   =   five half notes per measure, and a half note gets one count

4/4   =   four quarter notes per measure, and a quarter note gets one count

6/8   =   six eighth notes per measure, and an eighth note gets one count

There are two types of time signatures--simple and compound:

(a) <u>Simple Time</u>, a signature whose numerator uses as its top number the figure 2, multiples of 2 (other than those which are also multiples of 3), and the figures 3, 5 and 7. Therefore, 2/x, 3/x, 4/x, 5/x, 7/x and, rarely, 8/x, where <u>x</u> is any one of the eight note values, are simple time signatures.*

(b) <u>Compound Time</u>, shows as its numerator only multiples of 3 beginning with 6. Therefore, compound time signatures arrive at their true rate of speed (tempo) by dividing their top number by 3. The quotient (result) shows the correct number of divisions in the measure. Therefore, 6/x, 9/x, 12/x, and 15/x are really, respectively, 2, 3, 4, and 5 divisions to the measure with the values indicated by their denominators grouped into three.**

<u>Examples</u>:

6/8   translates into 2/4, or two sets of eighth note triplets, and a quarter note gets one count.

9/8   translates into 3/4, or three sets of eighth note triplets, and a quarter note gets one count.

The only musical advantage, then, of compound time signatures is to suggest or indicate the proper feel. So a signature of 12/8, if used correctly, should indicate an eighth note triplet feel or variation thereof; otherwise the composer should have used 4/4!

Last, there is wide misunderstanding of the symbols C, and ₵ which I'd like to clear up. At present C means <u>common time</u>, or 4/4, and ₵ means <u>cut time</u>, or 2/2. Since they are used this way, one should know them. However, knowing the original meaning of these symbols and terms may help clarify the entire subject of time signatures for many. (As a matter of fact, if one could find and clear away all the <u>false</u> information and data from past subjects he or she has studied, his or her learning rate and ability to apply what was learned would increase tremendously.

---

* Powell Everhart, <u>The Pianist's Art</u> (Atlanta: Powell Everhart, 1958). chap.4, p.49.
** Everhart, <u>Pianist's Art</u>, p.49.

For more information on this subject, check out "False Data Stripping," an essay by L. Ron Hubbard that can be found in the Organization Executive Course book, <u>Management Series</u>, Volume 1.)*

Our present system of music notation developed from the notation of early times, when music was written by Christian clerics. Thus it is no wonder that religious connotations accompany the nomenclature of notation. In ancient music, a small circle was placed at the beginning of the score to indicate "<u>tempus perfectus</u>"--which was later translated to "perfect time." Perfect time was understood as being triple in meter, or having three even divisions to each measure (3/x). It derived its name from the Holy Trinity--a composite spiritual being in three identities, symbolically represented by the "perfect" circle, which has no beginning or end.

Eventually vernacular music** began influencing ecclesiastical music*** just prior to the Reformation, and one new practice was the increased use of <u>duple</u> time. Scores then began appearing with part of the circle omitted to designate "<u>tempus imperfectus</u>," or "imperfect time"--time with two even divisions of the measure. The resultant symbol was the broken circle, "C," which we still use--but it has evolved to mean 4/4, or <u>common time</u>, today. When cut through by a perpendicular line, "¢," it means 2/2--<u>cut time</u>, or <u>alla breve</u>.

2. <u>Note and Rest Values</u>. Following is a table of note and rest values as they relate to different time signatures.

---

* L. Ron Hubbard, <u>The Management Series</u>, Vol. 1 (Los Angeles: Bridge Publications, 1982), p.262.

** <u>vernacular music</u>, nonreligious music; secular music.

*** <u>ecclesiastical music</u>, religious music; music of the church.

TABLE OF THE EIGHT NOTE AND REST VALUES

# OF BEATS				NOTE SYMBOLS	NAME	REST SYMBOLS
x/16	(x/8)	x/4	x/2			
16	8	4	2	1. ○	whole note	▬
8	4	2	1	2. ♩	half note	▬
4	(2)	1	1/2	3. ♩	quarter note	∤
2	1	1/2	1/4	4. ♪	eighth note	⅞
1	1/2	1/4	1/8	5. ♬	sixteenth	⅞
1/2	1/4	1/8	1/16	6. ♬	thirty-second	⅞
1/4	1/8	1/16	1/32	7. ♬	sixty-fourth	⅞
1/8	1/16	1/32	1/64	8. ♬	one hundred and twenty-eighth	⅞

Here is an example of use of this table: a time signature of x/8, where x, let's say, is 3, means there are three eighth notes per measure, a quarter note gets two counts, and a quarter rest gets two counts silence. The indicated values are circled.

3. Tie, a curved line joining two notes of the same pitch into a continuous sound. Therefore, a half note tied to a quarter note in 4/4 time means that pitch or note receives three counts and is sounded as one note. Any of the eight note values may be tied to a like value or to a different value, to another tied note, or to any dotted note (see next section for dotted notes). Rests are never tied! They are written as needed to show the duration of silence.

4. The Dot, a dot placed to the right of a note is simply an abbreviation of one of the eight time values discussed under the section on note values: A dotted note is held for the count value of the printed note plus the count value of the next descending note. A double dotted note simply means hold for the count value of the printed note plus the note values of the next two descending notes.

Example in 4/4 time:

𝑂	dotted whole note	$= 𝑂 + 𝄐$	=	6 counts (4+2)
𝑂..	double dotted whole note	$= 𝑂 + 𝄐 + 𝄐$	=	7 counts (4+2+1)
♪.	dotted eighth note	$= ♪ + ♪$	=	3/4 count (1/2+1/4)
♪..	double dotted eighth note	$= ♪ + ♪ + ♪$	=	7/8 count (1/2+1/4+1/8)

A dot, therefore, is an abbreviation for a tied note. A whole note tied to a half note is abbreviated as a dotted whole note. So a dot means the printed note is tied to the next descending note value.

Trouble with dots is caused by muddled thinking and making unnecessary computations. The customary practice of teaching one to think of dots as representing half of preceding values forces one to think in reverse--that is, to refer back to something prior. This is what you do when you figure that a dot is half of the original value of the note, or that two dots means half of half of the original value, etc. Although the formula is mathematically correct, having to slow down or stop to do these calculations in the middle of a creative flow and the reverse thinking that they require are disruptive of the cause-effect process discussed earlier (which consists of creating and postulating the future, and performing with no need for attention on anything in the past).

So this is another example of something that works in theory, but not in actual practice. Instead of needing to refer back to another value to calculate time, you should simply learn the eight descending note values, considering each one an entity unto itself. Once you have, you will automatically and instantaneously know what any dotted or double-dotted note means. So--if you are making calculations while playing, you haven't learned dotted notes!

As an important comment here, problems with duration and time mean that the rudiments of duration and time aren't fully understood. That is why the symbols and nomenclature in this chapter are so important for you to learn before you go on to the nitty gritty of playing. Many technical inhibitions thought of as physical limitations are actually due to confused or muddled thinking resulting from misunderstood or not-understood words or symbols--something never to forget!

5. Equal Temperament, the tuning of keyboard instruments in such a way that all the semitones (the smallest interval in Western music) are equal--in other words, so that the octave is divided into twelve equal parts. This has the effect of putting all the intervals except the octave slightly out of tune. The advantage of the system, which is now universally accepted, is that intervals have the same value in all keys--for example, a major third is a major third no matter what key it's played in. Any other system of tuning favors some keys at the expense of others and makes modulation (changing keys) difficult outside a restricted range.

6. Semitone, the smallest interval in Western music. Referred to as a half step. A semitone or half step upward in pitch means the very next note, white or black, to the right. A semitone or half step downward in pitch would be the very next note to the left.

7. Whole tone, a whole step, consisting of two semitones.

8. Accidentals, a comprehensive term for sharps, double sharps, flats, double flats, and naturals prefixed to a note in a composition:

sharp   (♯)   raises a note by a semitone or
                      half step

double sharp   (X)   raises a note by a whole tone or
                      whole step

flat   (♭)   lowers a note by a semitone or
                      half step

double flat   (♭♭) lowers a note by a whole tone or a whole step

natural   (♮) neither sharp nor flat: it is the character or sign placed on any degree of the musical staff to nullify the effect of a preceding sharp or flat.

9. Key Signature, the sharps and flats placed at the beginning of a composition to indicate it is to be played in one of the fifteen written major scales (tonalities) or their relative minor scales. Key signatures are also a shortcut to having to write out recurring accidentals within a composition. For example, the key signature of the key of A has three sharps: F-sharp, C-sharp and G-sharp. The key signature thus signifies to the player that all F's, C's and G's are sharp unless prefixed by another accidental such as a natural (♮) or double sharp (✗) sign.

The following is a table of the fifteen key signatures.

KEY SIGNATURE CHART

Number of Accidentals	Key	Order of Accidentals	Key Signature
7 sharps	C♯, A♯ min.	FCGDAEB	
6 sharps	F♯, D♯ min.	FCGDAE	
5 sharps	B, G♯ min.	FCGDA	
4 sharps	E, C♯ min.	FCGD	
3 sharps	A, F♯ min.	FCG	
2 sharps	D, B min.	FC	
1 sharp	G, E min.	F	
0 sharps & flats	C, A min.	none	
1 flat	F, D min.	B	
2 flats	B♭, G min.	BE	
3 flats	E♭, C min.	BEA	
4 flats	A♭, F min.	BEAD	
5 flats	D♭, B♭ min.	BEADG	
6 flats	G♭, E♭ min.	BEADGC	
7 flats	C♭, A♭ min.	BEADGCF	

Although there are twelve actual sounding keys, there are fifteen written keys, since three keys have two different "spellings." This is called <u>enharmonic</u> spelling (e.g., C-sharp and D-flat, F-sharp and G-flat, C-flat and B). A convenient way of visualizing these keys is known as the <u>circle of fifths</u>. Clockwise on the circle are the sharps, while counterclockwise are the flats. Every key is a perfect fifth apart--hence, circle of fifths. The subscript number following each key refers to the number of sharps or flats. (See illustration.)

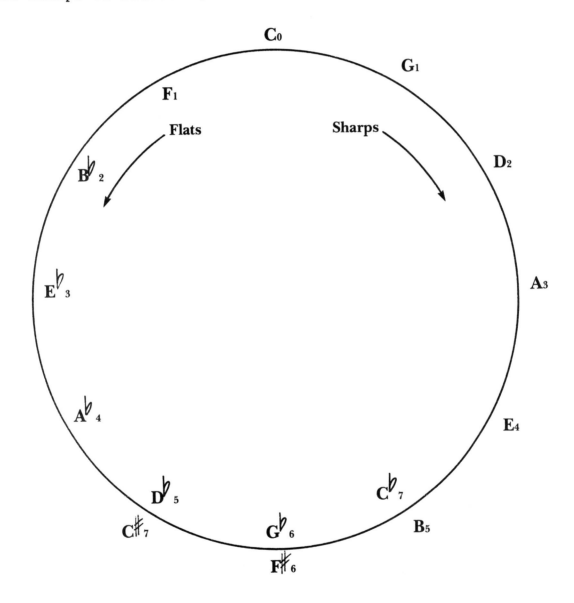

Summary: There are fifteen written keys: one natural, seven sharps, and seven flats.

10. <u>Grand Staff</u>, 11 lines in number, the treble clef today being the upper five, the bass clef today being the lower five, and middle C being the actual middle, or 11th, line. (See illustration.)

```
——————————————————————————————————————— F ———
————————————————————————————————— D ———————
———————————————————————————— B ———————————
———————————————————— G ———————————————
———————————————— E ———————————————————
———————— Middle C ———————————————————
—————— A ———————————————————————
———— F ———————————————————————————
—— D ———————————————————————————————
— B ———————————————————————————————
— G ———————————————————————————————————
```

Because the original grand staff was so confusing to read, resulting from the optical illusions created by so many lines, it was later split literally in two. What resulted were the present-day treble and bass clef staves--two sets of five lines plainly separated from each other.

Clef signs (clef is French for "key") were then created to point out certain C's and F's as guide notes to help clear up the confusions. A clef sign has no connotation of piano key, however. It is simply the "key" to the location of named tones on the staff and on the keyboard. These clef signs, now associated with the five lines of the split staff, are movable. Their location on the staff indicates where middle C (thus any note) is found (see Example 14). There are, in all, seven clef signs--treble, bass, soprano, mezzo-soprano, alto, tenor, and baritone.

EXAMPLE 14: MOVABLE CLEFS

The middle line of the piano score of today is still middle C, as it was on the grand staff, but this line is now omitted and has been replaced by a <u>ledger</u> line (a short line that shows an upper or lower extension of the staff).

The top staff is called the treble or G-clef, and the bottom is called the bass or F-clef. On piano scores, middle C occupies the ledger line below the treble staff or the ledger line above the bass staff. Also, middle C is so called because of its place on the grand staff, not because it appears in the middle of the piano keyboard (Example 15). The middle of the acoustic piano is actually E above middle C!

EXAMPLE 15:
PRESENT DAY PIANO STAFF

11. <u>Tempo Markings</u>, give the rate at which specified note values are to be played. They can be approximations like "Adagio" or "Allegro," or exact metronome markings like ♩ = 90. Traditional composers used Italian names, while present-day composers may and usually do use anything they wish, such as "lively," "quick," etc., or a metronome marking along with an adjective--which is by far the most optimum (♩ = 72 medium swing). Since one doesn't always have a metronome handy, I advise learning some fixed marking, such as a quarter note = 60 (1 beat per second). From this all other tempos can be approximated. Any memorized tempo marking will obviously suffice.

Although the traditional tempo markings are used mostly in "serious" music, they are occasionally still used by composers in jazz and some commercial music. The following is a table of the most often-used traditional tempo markings.

TABLE OF TEMPO MARKINGS

	Grave	- solemn, very very slow
	Largo	
SLOW	Adagio	
	Andante	
	Andantino	

	Allegretto	- moderately quick
	Moderato	
FAST	Allegro	
	Vivace	
	Presto	
	Prestissimo	- greatest speed possible

12. <u>Dynamics</u>, degrees of loudness and softness in a musical performance. The degrees are usually indicated by certain abbreviations or signs:

<u>Sign</u>	<u>Word</u>	<u>Meaning</u>
ppp	pianississimo	extremely soft
pp	pianissimo	very soft
p	piano	soft
mp	mezzo piano	medium soft
mf	mezzo forte	medium loud
f	forte	loud
ff	fortissimo	very loud
fff	fortississimo	extremely loud
fp	forte piano	loud and immediately soft
sf & sfz	sforzato and sforzando	heavily accented attack literally, forced
$<$	crescendo	gradual increase in volume
$>$	decrescendo, diminuendo	gradual decrease in volume
	sempre crescendo	continual increase in volume
	crescendo poco a poco	increase volume little by little
	decrescendo poco a poco	decrease volume little by little

13. Articulation, refers to the types of attacks and releases of notes. Articulation helps make music clear and concise. There are two basic interpretations of articulation: classical and jazz (Examples 16-23).

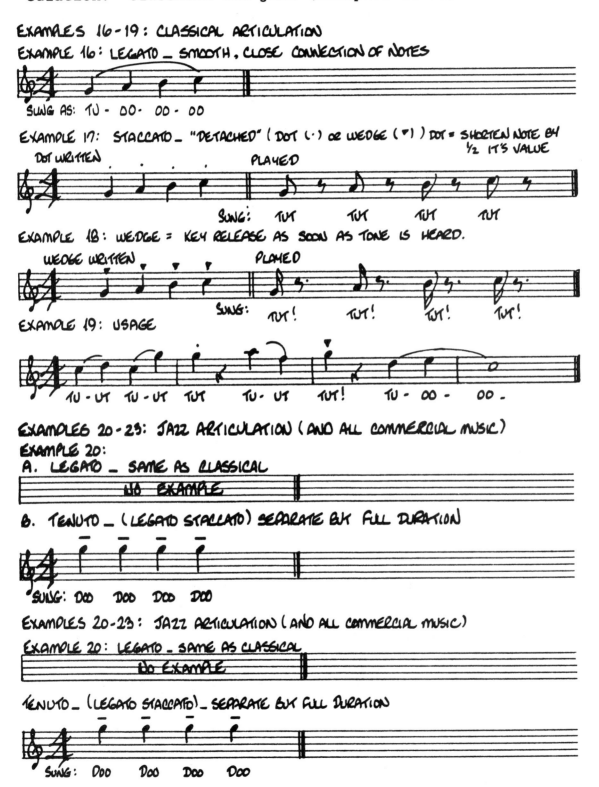

EXAMPLES 16-19: CLASSICAL ARTICULATION

EXAMPLE 16: LEGATO — SMOOTH, CLOSE CONNECTION OF NOTES

SUNG AS: TU - OO - OO - OO

EXAMPLE 17: STACCATO — "DETACHED" (DOT (·) OR WEDGE (▼)) DOT = SHORTEN NOTE BY ½ IT'S VALUE

DOT WRITTEN   PLAYED

SUNG: TUT   TUT   TUT   TUT

EXAMPLE 18: WEDGE = KEY RELEASE AS SOON AS TONE IS HEARD.

WEDGE WRITTEN   PLAYED

SUNG: TUT!   TUT!   TUT!   TUT!

EXAMPLE 19: USAGE

TU - UT TU - UT TUT   TU - UT   TUT!   TU - OO - OO -

EXAMPLES 20-23: JAZZ ARTICULATION (AND ALL COMMERCIAL MUSIC)
EXAMPLE 20:
A. LEGATO — SAME AS CLASSICAL

NO EXAMPLE

B. TENUTO — (LEGATO STACCATO) SEPARATE BUT FULL DURATION

SUNG: DOO   DOO   DOO   DOO

EXAMPLES 20-23: JAZZ ARTICULATION (AND ALL COMMERCIAL MUSIC)

EXAMPLE 20: LEGATO — SAME AS CLASSICAL

NO EXAMPLE

TENUTO — (LEGATO STACCATO) — SEPARATE BUT FULL DURATION

SUNG: DOO   DOO   DOO   DOO

14. <u>Caesura</u> ("tracks"), ⌒‖ , a type of cutoff (Example 24).

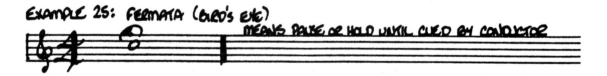

15. <u>Fermata</u> ("bird's eye"), 𝄐 , pause or hold until cued by conductor (Example 25).

EXAMPLE 25: FERMATA (BIRD'S EYE)   MEANS PAUSE OR HOLD UNTIL CUED BY CONDUCTOR

16. <u>Accents</u>, > , lean on the attack (Example 26).

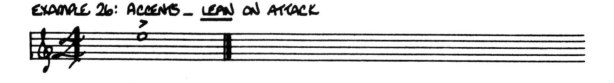

17. <u>Rubato</u> ("robbed"), implies that what is taken
from the time element at one point of the phrase must be
repaid in another. This then would create a slowing down
and a resultant speeding-up of notes to compensate, and
vice versa. However, in this day and age it is quite
common to never repay what one has stolen, and thus rubato
has evolved to mean simply <u>free time</u>--slowing down and
speeding up as desired. But technically, rubato and free
time are different, and you should be aware of both meanings.

18. <u>Accelerando</u> (accel.), increase speed gradually.

19. <u>Ritardando</u>, <u>Rallentando</u> (rit. and rall., respectively), becoming gradually slower.

20. <u>A Tempo</u>, return to the original tempo.

21. <u>Double Time</u>, play twice as fast as previous
tempo.

22. <u>Double Time Feeling</u>, music is written to sound
as fast as double time but the tempo is really the same.

23. <u>Slur</u>, a curved line that connects different
notes (ties connect notes of the same pitch). The notes
under the slur are to be played closely connected, or
legato. The last note under the slur is treated as if it
were almost staccato (Example 27).

EXAMPLE 27: SLURS_ DELINEATE CERTAIN PHRASES BY SHORTENING LAST NOTE IN SLUR.

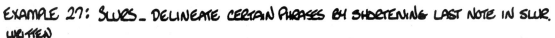

24. <u>Da Capo</u> (D.C.), literally "from the head," or go back to the beginning of the piece and play it again.

25. <u>Del Segno</u> (D.S.), literally "from the sign," or go back to the point in the music marked with the sign and play again from that point forward.

26. <u>Coda</u> (⊕), literally "tail"--a passage, long or short, at the end of a piece which brings the music to a satisfying conclusion.

27. <u>D.C. al</u> ⊕, go back to the beginning of the music and when you see the coda sign (⊕), jump to and play the coda (⊕).

28. <u>va</u> and <u>vb</u>:

    (a) <u>8va</u>, play an octave higher in pitch than written.

    (b) <u>15va</u>, play two octaves higher in pitch than written.

    (c) <u>8vb</u>, play an octave lower in pitch than written.

    (d) <u>15vb</u>, play two octaves lower in pitch than written.

29. <u>D.S. al</u> ⊕, go back to the sign (𝄋) and play the music until you see the coda sign (⊕) and then jump to and play the coda.

30. <u>Loco</u>, literally "place"--means in the normal place. Used to contradict or override a previous 8va sign by indicating that the music is to be played at the normal pitch written.

31. <u>Simile</u>, literally "like." Used as a direction to continue a formula which has been indicated, such as the arpeggiating of chords, etc.

32. <u>Repeats</u>, a repeat from the beginning of a composition is indicated by :‖ --double bar and two dots. The repeat of a section is indicated by ‖: at the beginning and :‖ at the end of the section.

33. ∥ , means repeat the previous measure. When it is used to repeat the previous two measures, it is written as ∥ (Example 28).

EXAMPLE 28:

REPEAT PREVIOUS 2 MEASURES

There are many other signs and symbols, sucn as ornaments (mordents, trills, grace notes, etc.) and electronic music and avant-garde notations, that I have not discussed. I have, however, listed some excellent books on these symbols in the bibliography at the end of the book. Those discussed in this chapter are the ones most used and it is very important that you understand and know them before going on.

51

Chapter 5
ASSIGNMENTS

_____ 1. Define time signature and explain the following signatures:

   a. 3/4
   b. 4/4
   c. 5/8
   d. 7/4
   e. 3/2

_____ 2. If compound time signatures can be reduced to
simple time signatures, what is the reason
for having them? Give an example.

_____ 3. a. Write down by memory the eight note
values and their corresponding rests,
making sure you start from largest and go
to smallest.

          b. Does the time signature have anything to
do with the values of notes and rests?
Give examples if so.

_____ 4. What is equal temperament? Why might knowing
this data be important to you as a keyboardist and composer?

_____ 5. What is the difference between a <u>tie</u> and a
<u>slur</u>?

_____ 6. Write out the key signatures of the fifteen
major and minor keys, showing the correct
placement of accidentals.

_____ 7. Name the seven clef signs and indicate which
ones are used today.

_____ 8. What is the value of ledger lines?

_____ 9. Explain the value that tempo and dynamic
markings contribute to the overall performance of a composition.

_____ 10. Define and gives examples of the following:

   a. Legato
   b. Tenuto
   c. Staccato
   d. Jazz staccato

_____ 11. Explain rubato and how it might be used in jazz and commercial music.

_____ 12. Define the following: (a) Caesura, (b) Fermata, (c) Accents, (d) D.C. al⊕, (f) A Tempo, (g) Double time, (h) 8va.

_____ 13. Why is nomenclature so important in learning a technical subject? Recall subjects that were difficult and reflect on the effect that misunderstood or not-understood nomenclature might have had on your learning them.

_____ 14. Read through music scores to check your understanding of basic music notation. Whatever you don't know, look up in this chapter. If it's not covered in this chapter, it will most probably be explained in any music dictionary, unless it is electronic music notation, avant-garde, etc. In that case, each specific composer tends to have his own approach and will usually explain the notation at the beginning of the composition.

SUGGESTED REFERENCE BOOKS

Ammer, Christine. Harpers Dictionary of Music. New York: Barnes & Noble, 1972.

Boehm, Laszlo. Modern Music Notation. New York: G. Schirmer, 1961.

Britannica Book of Music. New York: Encyclopedia Britannica, 1980.

Randel, Don. Harvard Concise Dictionary of Music. Cambridge: Harvard University Press, Belknap Press, 1978.

Westrup, J.A., and F. Harrison. The New College Encyclopedia of Music. New York: W. W. Norton & Company, 1960.

Chapter 6

Basic Harmony

INTRODUCTION

There are two types of harmony--<u>intervallic</u> and
<u>chordal</u>. Intervallic harmony usually occurs in counter-
point--the art of combining melodic lines (Example 29).
Since melody is senior to harmony in contrapuntal composition, the chords that are sometimes expressed are very
unlike chords expressed in chordal harmony. They are
often incomplete and ambiguous. But through such chords
the opposite of intervallic harmony--chordal harmony--was
evolved.

In chordal harmony, chords are entities all to themselves, capable of behaving according to their own
harmonic laws independent of melodic and intervallic
considerations. The harmony of jazz and commercial music
is chiefly chordal, and usually preestablished. Example
30 is a standard blues progression which has been and
still is the framework for many jazz, rock and blues
compositions. Chordal harmony, then, is harmony waiting
for melody and rhythm--it serves as their framework;
intervallic harmony is a coalescence of melodies and
rhythms.

EXAMPLE 30:

If you wish more expertise in intervallic harmony, there are many excellent books available on counterpoint that you can study. At present, however, we will concern ourselves with chordal harmony--hence, chords!

The first step in understanding chords is understanding intervals, since they are the basic building block of all chords.

INTERVALS

The unit of harmony is the interval. The name is most accurately used to describe the "distance" between two tones. As discussed in a previous chapter, there are two types of intervals: harmonic, in which tones are sounded together (Example 31a), and melodic, in which tones are sounded consecutively (Example 31b). The tones which form the interval are drawn from the scale--of which there are three main types: major, minor (with its harmonic and melodic forms), and chromatic.

EXAMPLE 31 A: EXAMPLE 31 B:

Very shortly we will learn these and other scales in all keys, as they are important tools in improvisation.

It is customary to refer to the scale tones or degrees by Roman numerals as well as the following names:

I.   Tonic (the key note)

II.   Supertonic (the next step above tonic)

III.   Mediant (halfway from tonic to dominant)

IV.   Subdominant (as far below the tonic as the dominant is above it)

V.   Dominant (actually dominant element in the key)

VI.   Submediant (halfway down from tonic to sub-dominant)

VII.   Leading tone (with melody tending toward the tonic)

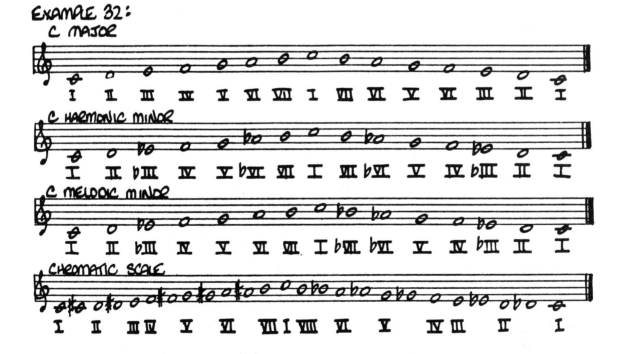

EXAMPLE 32:

The classification of intervals is as follows:

Unisons to eighths are <u>simple intervals</u>--less than an octave.

Ninths to fifteenths (two octaves) are <u>compound intervals</u>--greater than an octave.

EXAMPLE 39: SIMPLE INTERVALS

COMPOUND INTERVALS

Compound intervals may be reduced to simple intervals by subtracting the octave (seven extra tones) from them.

<u>Example</u>:   Major 10th - Major 3rd
               (10 minus 7 = 3)

               Perfect 12th - Perfect 5th
               (12 minus 7 = 5)

The use of compound intervals will be discussed in Chapter 8, "The Basics of Improvisation."

Altered intervals are ones whose top notes are lowered or raised by a half step. The following rules apply to altered intervals:

1.   Major intervals made a half tone smaller become minor.

2.   Minor intervals made a half tone larger become major.

3.   Major and perfect intervals made a half tone larger become augmented.

4.   Minor and perfect intervals made a half tone smaller become diminished (Example 34).

EXAMPLE 34:

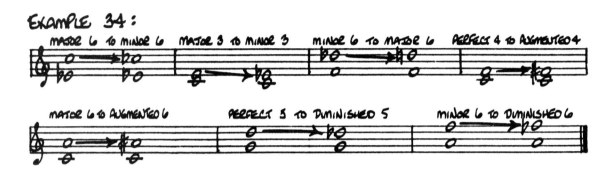

INVERSION

Mirror inversion, means the original interval and its inversion are of equal size but extending in opposite directions (Example 35).

EXAMPLE 35.

Harmonic inversion, the notes simply reverse position, the top becoming the bottom and the bottom becoming the top, resulting in a new interval (Example 36).

EXAMPLE 36:

TABLE OF HARMONIC INVERSION

(Formula: subtract interval from nine)

Perfect Unison	becomes	Perfect Octave
Major 2nd	becomes	Minor 7th
Major 3rd	becomes	Minor 6th
Perfect 4th	becomes	Perfect 5th
Perfect 5th	becomes	Perfect 4th
Major 6th	becomes	Minor 3rd
Major 7th	becomes	Minor 2nd
Perfect Octave	becomes	Perfect Unison

CONSONANT AND DISSONANT INTERVALS

A consonant interval is one which sounds stable and complete, whereas a dissonant interval is "tense" and wants to resolve into a consonant one. In general, the following classification of consonance and dissonance holds true:

Consonant	The perfect intervals and the major and minor 3rds and 6ths
Dissonant	Augmented and diminished intervals and the major and minor 2nds, 7ths and 9ths
Exception	The perfect 4th is dissonant when there is no tone below it (Example 37a).
	The perfect 4th is consonant when there is a 3rd or perfect 4th below it (Example 37b).

EXAMPLE 37 A: 37B:

60

Although the above classifications are admittedly open to subjective and evolutionary interpretation, they still hold true most of the time and are good guidelines.

ENHARMONIC INTERVALS

Enharmonic intervals are intervals in our tempered scale system that sound the same when played on the piano-forte even though they sound slightly different in an un-tempered situation. An example is the augmented second and the minor third (Example 38). Unless these intervals are heard in their harmonic context they sound exactly the same. However, in an untempered situation, say in a string orchestra, they do sound slightly different. A good string player will play the G-sharp in Example 38 much closer to the A a half step above, and the A-flat much closer to the G a half step below, to indicate more accurately the interval's tendency toward resolution. In fact, some string players find it very disturbing playing with a piano because of its inability to "stretch" its intervals!

EXAMPLE 38:   SAME SOUND ON PIANO BUT DIFFERENT SPELLING

ROOT DETECTION

To understand a chord fully, one must be able to determine its root. A root is the fundamental note upon which a chord is constructed by superimposing intervals (for example, thirds, fourths, fifths, etc). In order to determine the root of a chord, we must be able to determine the root of an interval, since intervals stacked upon each other make chords. In Example 39 the intervals are listed in the order of their vertical importance or strength. The augmented fourth, or tritone, really has no root and is consequently the weakest interval. It is, however, a very important sound, as we shall see later.

EXAMPLE 39:

To find the root of a chord, then, find its strongest interval per the order given in Example 39. The root of the strongest interval will be the actual root of the chord, regardless of what the chord symbol says. (Many people name chords incorrectly--by their appearance or shape rather than their function.) (See Example 40.)

EXAMPLE 40:

In Example 40e, there are four strong perfect fifth intervals. In this case, the lowest one takes precedence due to the acoustical phenomenon that a low note exerts more harmonic influence than a high one.

Some chords, however, constructed of identical intervals, really have no stable root, such as chords built in perfect fourths (Example 41a), chords built in major thirds (Example 41b), and chords built in successive minor thirds (Examples 41c and d).

EXAMPLE 41:

Now, why is it so important to know the root of a chord? Because the truth is the truth! The <u>true</u> root will sound whether we want it to or not--whether or not the alphabetical symbol (C maj.7, etc.) is correct. If you limited yourself to traditional, time-tested chord progressions, you might have little need to know root detection. But if you dare to get creative and move into chord progressions of your own construction and get involved in composition, arranging, orchestration, etc., knowledge of root detection and progression is a must. The root progression supports the whole composition. It is heard, even if subliminally, almost as another melody, as it determines the tonal basis of the music. And without a sound knowledge of the tonal basis of a piece, improvisation, theme construction, and orchestration can be tricky business!

There are drawbacks to this method of root detection, but only in traditional progressions where the real roots are more than obvious. This method is most helpful in creating and using chords which are not built in thirds (nontertial chords).

<u>CHORDS</u>

A chord is a combination of two or more intervals. A triad is the simplest of chords. A triad is a chord of three tones obtained by superposition of two thirds (Example 42a). Despite numerous contemporary developments, the triad is still the basis of our whole harmonic system and should therefore be fully understood. The following table shows that, in addition to root position, a triad has two other forms or inversions.

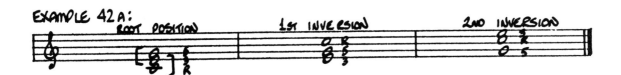

EXAMPLE 42A:

root position   -   root on the bottom

1st inversion   -   third on the bottom

2nd inversion -   fifth on the bottom

Chord inversions are discussed in more detail a little later in this chapter.

Diatonic major harmony, or harmony proper to a major scale, begins with the superposition of thirds from the major scale to form triads (Example 42b).

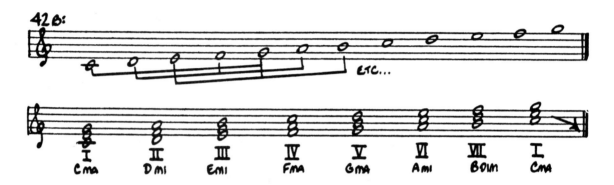

Diatonic minor harmony, or harmony proper to a minor scale--in this case harmonic minor--begins with the super-position of thirds from the minor scale to form triads (Example 43).

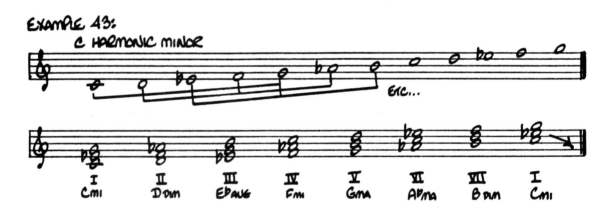

Since triads on these different scale notes differ in interval structure, there exist four major "qualities" of triads (Example 44).

EXAMPLE 44:

	Scale Tones	Intervals
Major Triad	(R 3 5)	or Major 3rd and Perfect 5th
Minor Triad	(R ♭3 5)	or Minor 3rd and Perfect 5th
Dim. Triad	(R ♭3 ♭5)	Minor 3rd and Dim. 5th
Aug. Triad	(R 3 ♯5)	Major 3rd and Aug. 5th

The major and minor chords are consonant chords because they contain only consonant intervals, while the augmented and diminished triads are dissonant because of the presence of the dissonant intervals Aug. 5th and Dim. 5th.

A chord is identified by the Roman numeral of the scale degree that the chord is constructed upon as a root, whether it is in root position or inversion.

So that means the following:

Roman Numeral	Major Mode	Minor Mode (Harmonic Minor)
I	Major Triad	Minor Triad
II	Minor Triad	Diminished Triad
III	Minor Triad	Augmented Triad
IV	Major Triad	Minor Triad
V	Major Triad	Major Triad
VI	Minor Triad	Major Triad
VII	Diminished Triad	Diminished Triad

DIATONIC SEVENTH CHORDS
(Tetrads - 4-Note Chords)

The same procedure as was used for the triads is used to construct the diatonic seventh chords. The result is the diatonic seventh--major mode (Example 45), and the diatonic seventh--minor mode (Example 46).

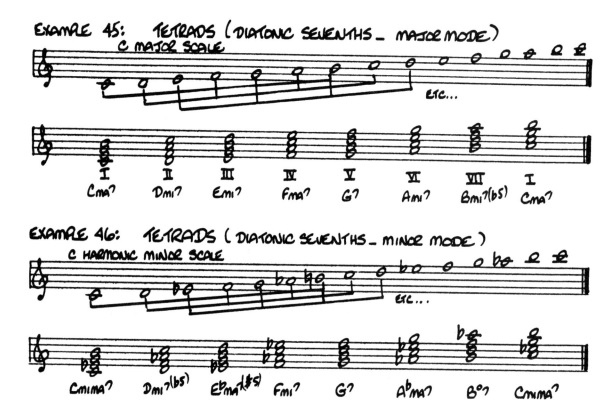

Translated into English, this means the following:

Roman Numeral	Major Mode	Minor Mode
I	Major 7th	Minor Major 7th
II	Minor 7th	Minor 7th($\flat$5)
III	Minor 7th	Major 7th($\sharp$5)
IV	Major 7th	Minor 7th
V	Dominant 7th	Dominant 7th
VI	Minor 7th	Major 7th
VII	Minor 7th($\flat$5)	Diminished 7th

Although the most effective vertical minor sounds are derived from the harmonic minor, the use of the flat sixth in the bass line destroys familiar patterns such as the I - VI - II - V progression, etc. To avoid this, minor jazz harmony has evolved as follows:

1. The bass line is the ascending melodic or tonic minor scale.

2. The inner voices are all harmonic minor.

Example 47 shows what happens to the diatonic seventh chords combining the above two elements. The only difference, then, is the VI chord which, if based on the harmonic minor scale, was A♭ maj.7 but now becomes A min.7(♭5) if based on the above elements. This allows progressions incorporating the VI chord to function, yet still be in the minor mode. "Angel Eyes" and "Yesterday" are examples of tunes involving minor jazz harmony.

EXAMPLE 47:

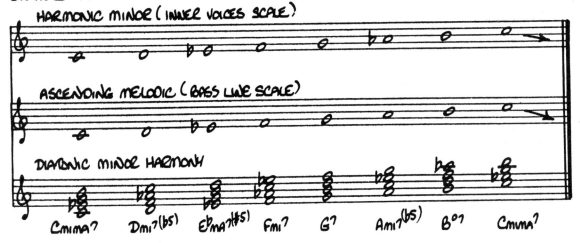

THE DIMINISHED SEVENTH CHORD

One seventh chord that does not appear naturally in any key is the diminished seventh chord. It can be formed on any note on the keyboard by building an interval combination of a minor 3rd, a diminished 5th, and a diminished 7th from the root, or simply by constructing three minor thirds on top of each other (Example 48). This chord and its uses will be discussed in detail later on.

EXAMPLE 48:

We have now covered the six basic <u>qualities</u> or families of chords, from which all other variations are somewhat derived:

Chord	Scale Degrees	Intervals
Major 7th	(R, 3, 5, 7)	M3, P5, M7
Minor 7th	(R, ♭3, 5, ♭7)	m3, P5, m7
Dominant 7th	(R, 3, 5, ♭7)	M3, P5, m7
Minor 7th(♭5)	(R, ♭3, ♭5, ♭7)	m3, °5, m7
Diminished 7th	(R, ♭3, ♭5, ♭♭7)	m3, °5, °7
Minor Major 7th	(R, ♭3, 5, 7)	m3, P5, M7

ALTERED DIATONIC SEVENTH CHORDS

Since jazz and commercial harmony are to a large extent chromatic, it is important to be able to build any of these chord qualities on any scale degree. This requires altering the scale-tone diatonic seventh chords to other chord qualities. So, for example, even though the II chord in the key of C major is D min.7, one must be able to build and use the other chord qualities such as D maj.7, D7, D min.7(♭5), D dim.7, and D min.(maj.7) (Example 49).

EXAMPLE 49:

Not only can diatonic seventh chords be altered to produce other kinds of chords, they can also be raised or lowered chromatically by sharping or flatting each note in the chord a half step. Thus, in Example 50, the II chord in the key of G, which is A min.7, can be raised or lowered by indicating ♯II or ♭II--which translates to A♯min.7 or A♭min.7 respectively. If the II chord has already been altered, for instance, to A min.7(♭5), then the ♯II or ♭II would translate to A♯min.7(♭5) or A♭min.7(♭5) (Example 51).

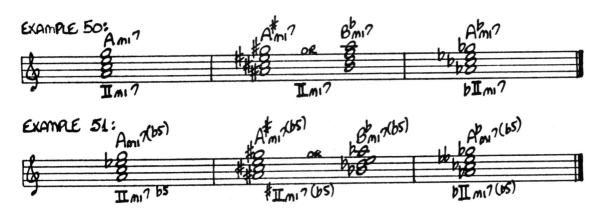

These devices of alteration and chromaticism are essential to jazz and pop harmony and should be mastered in all twelve keys.

CHORD INVERSIONS

Every chord, whether a triad or a tetrad (chord of four tones), may have a note other than the root as its lowest tone. When this occurs, the chord is said to be in an inversion.

When the root is in the bass (bottom note), we have first position or root position; if the third is in the bass we have second position or first inversion; if the fifth is in the bass, we have third position or second inversion; if we have a four note chord (tetrad), then we may have the seventh in the bass voice and thus have a fourth position or third inversion. Example 52 shows the six chord qualities of C and their respective inversions.

EXAMPLE 52:

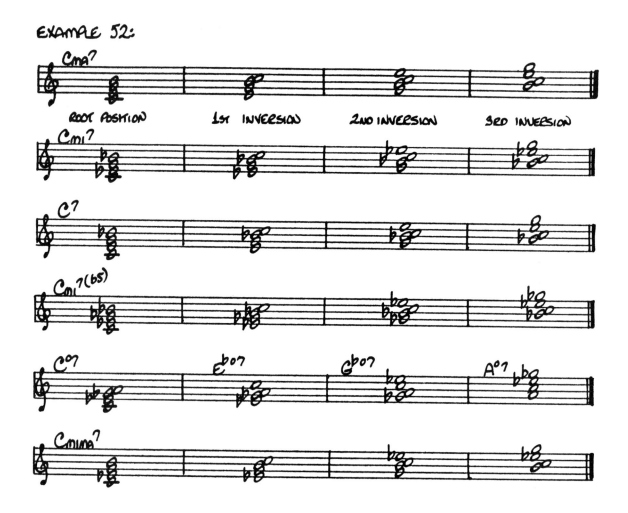

It is important to note here that because of the symmetrical properties--all minor thirds--of the diminished chord (triad or tetrad), its inversions are really other diminished seventh chords in root positions. The diminished chord will be discussed in detail in Chapter 12, "Advanced Harmony."

THE 216 FUNDAMENTAL CHORD SYSTEM

Now that we have studied the six basic chord qualities, it is time to study their variations or subqualities--seven more tetrads in all. Add to this the four basic triads and one variation called the suspended triad and we have a total of eighteen fundamental chords per key, or 216 chords (18 x 12 = 216)! The following is a

complete breakdown of all eighteen fundamental chords and
their respective chord symbols and formulas. They should
be learned in all keys (Example 53).

EXAMPLE 53:

THE 18 FUNDAMENTAL CHORDS

Chord	Scale Tones	Intervals	Symbols
1. Major triad	1, 3, 5	M3, P5	C, C maj., CM, C ma
2. Minor triad	1, $\flat$3, 5	m3, P5	C$^-$, C min., Cm, C mi
3. Diminished triad	1, $\flat$3, $\flat$5	m3, $^\circ$5	C$^\circ$, C dim.
4. Augmented triad	1, 3, $\sharp$5	M3, +5	C$^+$, C aug., C^{+5}
5. Sus triad	1, 4, 5	P4, P5	C sus, C sus^4
6. Major 7	1, 3, 5, 7	M3, P5, M7	C maj.7, CM^7, C$^{\Delta 7}$, C ma^7
7. Major 7($\sharp$5)	1, 3, $\sharp$5, 7	M3, +5, M7	C maj.$^{7(+5)}$, C$^{\Delta 7(+5)}$, C ma$^{7(+5)}$
8. Major 7($\flat$5)	1, 3, $\flat$5, 7	M3, $^\circ$5, M7	C maj.$^{7(\flat 5)}$, C$^{\Delta 7(\flat 5)}$, C ma$^{7(\flat 5)}$
9. Major 6th	1, 3, 5, 6	M3, P5, M6	C6, C maj.6, CM^6, C ma^6

10. Minor (major) 7th	1, $\flat$3, 5, 7	m3, P5, M7	C^{-}(maj.7), C$^{-\Delta}$7, C min.(maj. 7), C mi(ma^{7})
11. Minor 6th	1, $\flat$3, 5, 6	m3, P5, M6	C^{-6}, C min.6, Cm^{6}, C mi^{6}
12. Minor 7	1, $\flat$3, 5, $\flat$7	m3, P5, m7	C^{-7}, C min.7, Cm^{7}, C mi^{7}
13. Minor 7($\flat$5)	1, $\flat$3, $\flat$5, $\flat$7	m3, °5, m7	C$^{-7(\flat5)}$, C$\emptyset$, C mi$^{7(\flat5)}$
14. Diminished 7th	1, $\flat$3, $\flat$5, $\flat\flat$7	m3, °5, °7	C°^{7}, C dim.7
15. Dominant 7th	1, 3, 5, $\flat$7	M3, P5, m7	C7, C dom.7
16. Augmented 7th	1, 3, $\sharp$5, $\flat$7	M3, +5, m7	C aug.7, C^{+7}, C7(+5)
17. Dominant 7(sus.4)	1, 4, 5, $\flat$7	P4, P5, m7	C$^{7(sus.4)}$, C$^{7sus.}$
18. Dominant 7(flat 5)	1, 3, $\flat$5, $\flat$7	M3, °5, m7	C$^{7(\flat5)}$

As we progress into improvisation and advanced harmony, we will see how these chords are used, for through
application only will these chords be fully understood.

Chapter 6
ASSIGNMENTS

_____ 1. Define interval. Explain the difference between simple and compound intervals.

_____ 2. Identify the following intervals, writing them in the spaces provided.

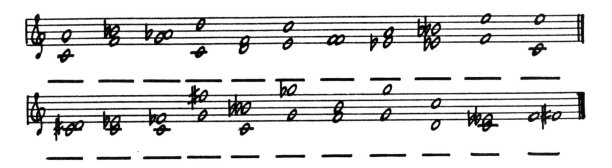

_____ 3. Invert the following intervals:

    a. Unison
    b. Min. 2nd
    c. Perfect 5th
    d. Major 3rd
    e. Minor 7th
    f. Minor 6th

_____ 4. Give some examples of enharmonic intervals.

_____ 5. Identify the roots of the following chord structures using the technique discussed in this chapter.

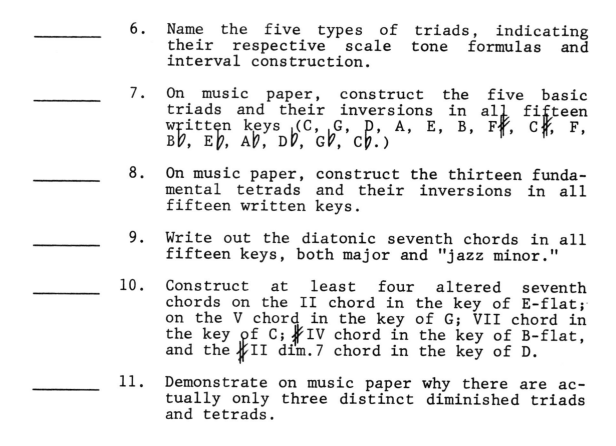

_____ 6. Name the five types of triads, indicating their respective scale tone formulas and interval construction.

_____ 7. On music paper, construct the five basic triads and their inversions in all fifteen written keys (C, G, D, A, E, B, F♯, C♯, F, B♭, E♭, A♭, D♭, G♭, C♭.)

_____ 8. On music paper, construct the thirteen fundamental tetrads and their inversions in all fifteen written keys.

_____ 9. Write out the diatonic seventh chords in all fifteen keys, both major and "jazz minor."

_____ 10. Construct at least four altered seventh chords on the II chord in the key of E-flat; on the V chord in the key of G; VII chord in the key of C; ♯IV chord in the key of B-flat, and the ♯II dim.7 chord in the key of D.

_____ 11. Demonstrate on music paper why there are actually only three distinct diminished triads and tetrads.

SUGGESTED READING

Hindemith, Paul. The Craft of Musical Composition. New York: Associated Music Publishers, 1941.

Piston, Walter. Harmony. New York: W. W. Norton & Company, 1969. chaps.1-4.

Russo, William. Jazz Composition and Orchestration. London: University of Chicago Press, 1968. chaps.1-9 especially.

Chapter 7
Fundamental Scales and Chords

Before we ease into the creative world of improvisation, it would be helpful to acquire some facility with fundamental scales and chords. Although this chapter is not a thesaurus of scales and chords, it contains the basic ones. Learn them and you'll be more than on your way.

You should use the following scales and arpeggios as a reference when doing the drills. All drills should be played with both hands and in all keys until mastered. I strongly suggest you use a metronome for purposes of time and motivation. Above all, practice with intention, attention, patience, persistence, and enthusiasm. Try to make all drills as musical as possible. If I hear a boring drill, I immediately know the student is bored. Emotions originate from beings, not drills and exercises! One gets little benefit from this type of practice and is probably better off doing something else. So apply the appropriate data from Chapter 3, "Practice Disciplines," if you have difficulty of any kind.

MAJOR SCALES AND ARPEGGIOS

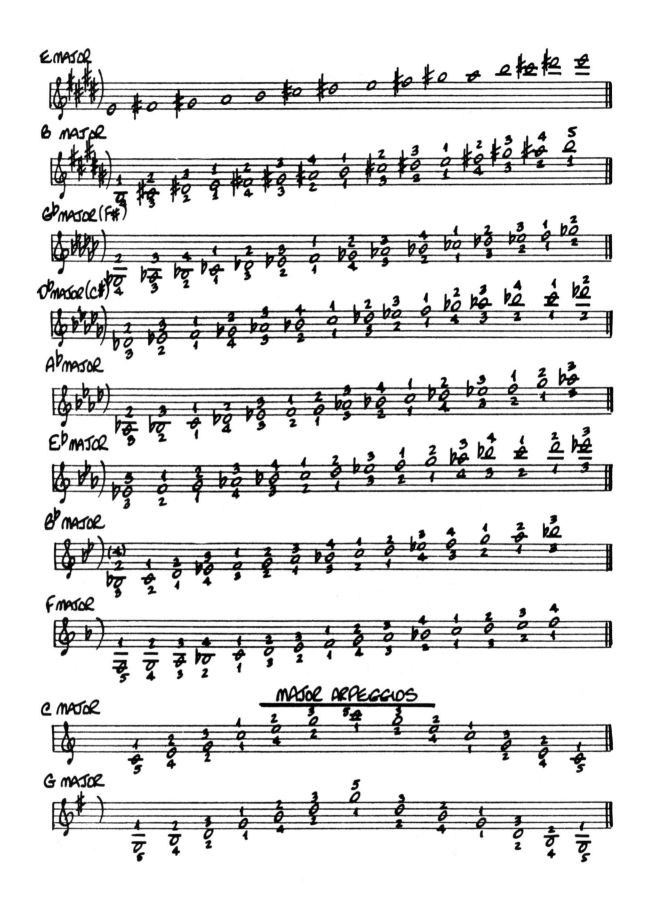

There are actually seven different types of minor scales:

    1. Dorian
    2. Phrygian
    3. Aeolian
    4. Locrian
    5. Harmonic Minor
    6. Melodic Minor (Traditional)
    7. Jazz Minor (Melodic Minor
        Ascending)

Since the first four types are basically derived from the major scale and are discussed in Chapter 14, "Modality," and since melodic minor (traditional) is not important at this time, we will concentrate on harmonic minor and jazz minor.

MINOR SCALES AND ARPEGGIOS

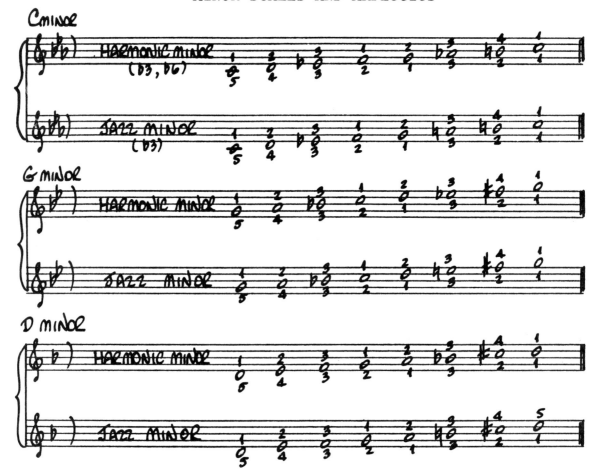

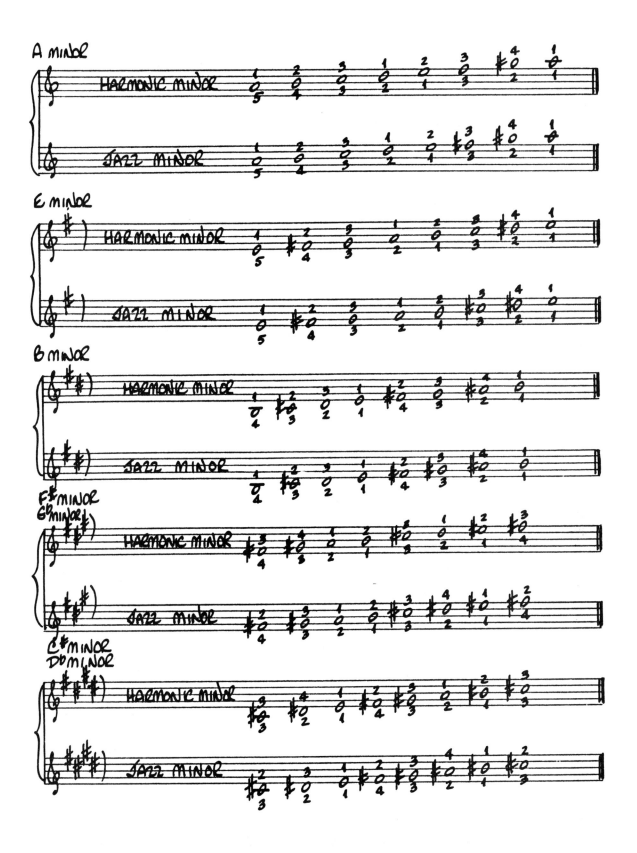

The Key Regimen Drill

I refer to this drill as the "Key Regimen Drill" as it constitutes a systematic way of acquiring facility and flexibility in all keys. I have written it out entirely in the key of C. You should, of course, transpose it to, and learn it in, all other keys as well. All scales should be played over at least two octaves, hands separately and together, preferably with a metronome. Remember, though, the purpose of this regimen is not velocity! It's just to get you acquainted with the important musical elements of every key. So play smoothly and evenly and with certainty.

4. DIATONIC PROGRESSION

5A: DIATONIC CIRCLE OF FIFTHS (PARALLEL)

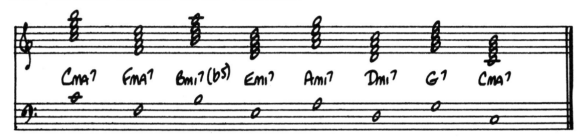

5B: DIATONIC CIRCLE OF FIFTHS (VOICE LED)

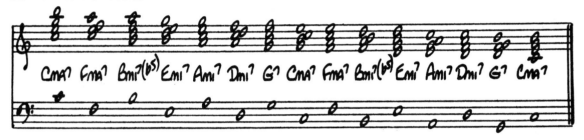

The Constant Structure Drill

The purpose of doing thi drill is to acquire facility in moving the basic tetrads around in the circle of fifths. Although each example starts out in root position, be sure to practice it in all inversions. The drill should be practiced in two ways:

1. The left hand plays the root or bass note while the right hand plays the chord quality.

2. Both hands play the chord quality.

CONSTANT STRUCTURE DRILL (CIRCLE OF FIFTHS)

MAJOR 7THS

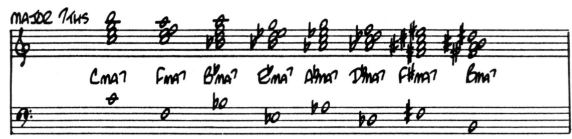

Cma7   Fma7   B♭ma7   E♭ma7   A♭ma7   D♭ma7   F#ma7   Bma7

Ema7   Ama7   Dma7   Gma7   Cma7   ALL KEYS, ALL INVERSIONS

MINOR 7THS

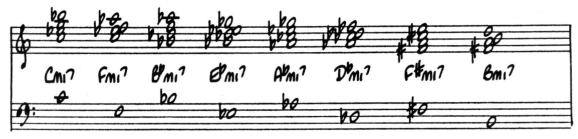

Cmi7   Fmi7   B♭mi7   E♭mi7   A♭mi7   D♭mi7   F#mi7   Bmi7

Emi7   Ami7   Dmi7   Gmi7   Cmi7   ALL KEYS, ALL INVERSIONS

Dominant 7ths

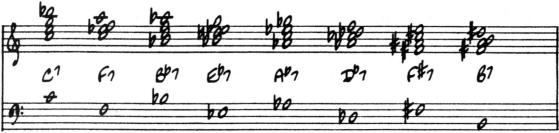

C7 F7 Bb7 Eb7 Ab7 Db7 F#7 B7

E7 A7 D7 G7 C7 ALL KEYS, ALL INVERSIONS

Minor 7 (b5)

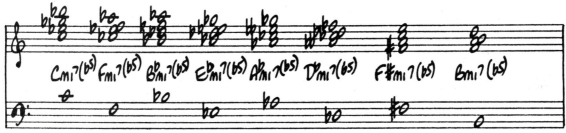

Cmi7(b5) Fmi7(b5) Bbmi7(b5) Ebmi7(b5) Abmi7(b5) Dbmi7(b5) F#mi7(b5) Bmi7(b5)

Emi7(b5) Ami7(b5) Dmi7(b5) Gmi7(b5) Cmi7(b5) ALL KEYS, ALL INVERSIONS

DIMINISHED 7THS

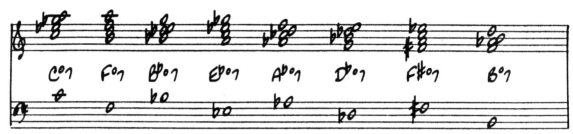

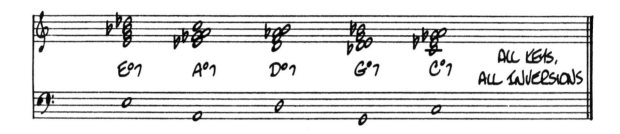

MINOR MAJOR 7THS

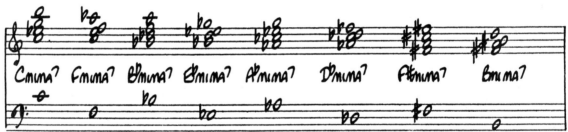

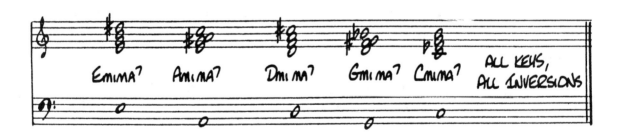

The Chromatic Chord Quality Drill

The purpose of doing this drill is to acquire facility in moving the basic chord qualities chromatically up and down. As above, this drill should be played in two ways:

1. The left hand plays the root or bass note while the right hand plays the chord quality.

2. Both hands play the chord quality.

Chapter 7
ASSIGNMENTS

_____ 1. Is there really such a thing as a boring drill or exercise? Explain what you would do if you suddenly found that you were bored while practicing an important drill.

_____ 2. Practice the major scales in all keys, making sure to use the indicated fingerings.

_____ 3. Practice the major arpeggios in all keys, making sure to use the indicated fingerings.

_____ 4. Practice the minor scales (harmonic minor and jazz minor) in all keys, making sure to use the indicated fingerings.

_____ 5. Do the Key Regimen Drill in all keys, as indicated:

    a. scales
    b. triads
    c. tetrads
    d. diatonic progressions

_____ 6. Do the Constant Structure Drill as indicated. Be sure to try all inversions.

_____ 7. Do the Chromatic Chord Quality Drill as indicated. Be sure to try all inversions.

SUGGESTED READING

Cooke, James Francis. Mastering the Scales and Arpeggios. Bryn Mawr, Pa.: Theodore Presser Co., 1913.

Slonimsky, Nicolas. Thesauras of Scales and Melodic Patterns. New York: Charles Scribner's Sons, 1947.

Stuart, Walter. Innovations in Full Chord Technique. New York: Chas. Colin, 1956.

Chapter 8

The Basics of Improvisation

Improvisation is the art of creating music spontaneously. There is nothing mysterious about the process, as some would have you believe. Mystery is proportional to unknowingness. If you change unknowingness to knowingness, there's no mystery. It's really that simple! So once you are familiar with certain basics, you will be able to improvise, and the more you improvise, the better you'll get. The process is very similar to learning how to speak. A child learns a few basic words and phrases and begins using them to communicate. As these new words and phrases become second nature, he assimilates more and more and gradually increases his vocabulary. Between having others speak the language constantly and his own language studies, the child becomes quite fluent very quickly at improvising the language.

This exact process is the one I apply in teaching musical improvisation. One simply becomes familiar with the vocabulary of music (chords and scales) and begins the cycle of communication--in this case, chords and scales are used instead of words and phrases. As the student improvises more and more, and listens to more and more improvisation by other keyboardists, he will surely become quite fluent at improvising and eventually develop his own style.

I would like to acknowledge Charlie Banacos, with whom I studied, for his incredible insight into and clarification of this least-understood area--jazz improvisation. This chapter and its organization were in large part inspired by his instruction in the following basics.

A AND B VOICINGS

The A and B voicings (chord structures) make up the basic textural sound of contemporary jazz and are important for you to learn before we get into improvising. They will provide the necessary left hand support while the right hand begins improvising. Once improvising with the right hand becomes second nature, we will then explain other left hand techniques.

These voicings will initially be studied within the framework of the II-V-I progression, which is the basic cadence of all jazz harmony. They are formed by adding certain tensions (9s, 11s, or 13s) to basic chord qualities and voicing them as shown below.

The A form voicings are as follows:

Key of C:

II^{-9}	$-\flat3, 5, \flat7, 9$		D^{-9}	$-$ F, A, C, E
V^{13}	$-\flat7, 9, 3, 13$		G^{13}	$-$ F, A, B, E
I^{9}_{6}	$-$ 3, 5, 6, 9		C^{9}_{6}	$-$ E, G, A, D

(See Example 54.)

Since these voicings are being considered for the left hand, it will suffice to learn the A voicings in the six keys (C through F). If this particular voicing was continued up (F-sharp through B), it would become too thin sounding and get in the way of the right hand. To handle this problem, the B voicings should be learned in keys F-sharp through B.

The B voicings are as follows:

II^{-9}	$-\flat7, 9, \flat3, 5$		$A^{\flat-9}$	$-$ G$\flat$, B$\flat$, C$\flat$, E$\flat$
V^{13}	$-$ 3, 13, $\flat7, 9$		$D^{\flat13}$	$-$ F, B$\flat$, C$\flat$, E$\flat$
I^{9}_{6}	$-$ 6, 9, 3, 5		$G^{\flat9}_{6}$	$-$ E$\flat$, A$\flat$, B$\flat$, D$\flat$

Assignment:

    1.   Fill in the remaining A and B voicings (Examples 54 and 55).

EXAMPLE 54: MAJOR (A & B VOICING)

EXAMPLE 55:

2. Learn all A and B voicings by practicing them in the following manner:

    a. Left hand plays the root, right hand plays voicing.

    b. Left hand and right hand play the voicing (one octave apart).

After these major A and B voicings have been mastered, you should learn the minor A and B voicings.

The A voicings in C minor are as follows:

$II^{-7(\flat 5)}$ — $\flat 3, \flat 5, \flat 7, R$ $D^{-7(\flat 5)}$ — F, A$\flat$, C, D

$V7^{\flat 13}_{\flat 9}$ — $7, \flat 9, 3, \flat 13$ $G7^{\flat 13}_{\flat 9}$ — F, A$\flat$, B, E$\flat$

I^{-9}_{6} — $\flat 3, 5, 6, 9$ C^{-9}_{6} — E$\flat$, G, A, D

The B voicings in G minor are as follows:

$II^{-7(\flat 5)}$ — $\flat 7, R, \flat 3, \flat 5$ $A^{-7(\flat 5)}$ — G$\flat$, A$\flat$, C$\flat$, E$\flat\flat$ (D)

$V7^{\flat 13}_{\flat 9}$ — $3, \flat 13, \flat 7, \flat 9$ $D^{7\flat 13}_{\flat 9}$ — F, B$\flat\flat$ (A), C$\flat$, E$\flat\flat$ (D)

I^{-9}_{6} — $6, 9, \flat 3, 5$ $G^{\flat -9}_{6}$ — E$\flat$, A$\flat$, B$\flat\flat$ (A), D$\flat$

As with the Major A and B voicings, do the following drills:

1. Fill in the remainder of the A and B voicings (Examples 56 and 57).

EXAMPLE 56: MINOR A & B VOICINGS
FORM A:

EXAMPLE 57:
FORM B:

2. Learn all minor A and B voicings by practicing
    them in the following manner:

    a. Left hand plays root, right plays voicing.

    b. Left hand and right hand play voicing.

TENSIONS

The following is a tension chart that indicates the available tensions with respect to the chord qualities. In general, a <u>tension</u> is really any tone that enriches a basic chord sound without destroying its basic "color." The following tensions are traditionally the most agreed upon and the most successful. Be sure, however, to experiment with your own ideas, as tensions can be very subjective. Remember, rules were created and are still being created by people such as yourself!

EXAMPLE 58: TENSION CHART

Chord Quality	Tensions					
Major Triad, Major 6th, Major 7th	9	♯11	13			
Minor Triad, Minor 7th	9	11	(13)			
Dominant 7th	♭9	9	♯9	♯11	♭13	13
Minor 7th(♭5)	(♭9)	9	11	13		
Diminished 7th	9	11	♭13	♭15		
Minor 6th, Minor Major 7th	9	11	(♯11)	13		
Aug. Triad, Aug. 7th	9	♯11				
Aug. Major 7th	9	♯11	13			
Dominant 7th(sus.4)	♭9	9	♯9	♭13	13	
Major 7th(♭5)	9	11	13			

The circled tensions in the chart are used less often, but are nevertheless <u>very</u> available. Try them out and see for yourself. Whenever there are questions about available tensions, consult this reference chart. Although these tensions should be memorized, they won't become real to you until you actually hear them in real musical situations. At that point, you will simply be able to <u>use</u> them as your "ear" dictates! In Chapter 11, "Advanced Improvisation," a more in-depth analysis of these chords and their respective chord scales appears.

Assignment:

1. Using Example 58 as a model, write out the remaining chords and tensions in the other eleven keys.

2. Get familiar with each chord and its tensions by simply playing the chord in your left hand and then sounding the tensions one at a time with your right hand.

THE IMPROVISED LINE

The improvised line can, for learning purposes, be broken down in the following manner:

Chord tones (c.t.)   R 3 5 7

Passing tones (p.t.)   scale tones that connect two adjacent chord tones

Approach tones (ap.t.)   notes that embellish or approach chord tones from above or below. For now, these will be defined as chromatic from below (half step) and scale step from above.

Tensions   9 11 13

Using C min.7 as an example, study Example 59.

EXAMPLE 59: THE IMPROVISED LINE

In Example 60 I have written a solo over some traditional changes (chord progression). Notice that every note in this solo falls into one of the above categories. We will explore this thoroughly after we do a few exercises.

EXAMPLE 60: IMPROVISED LINE ANALYZED

Assignment:

    Using the appropriate A or B left hand voicings, play the following exercises (Examples 61 and 62) in all twelve keys. Always play exercises with some kind of tempo, even if it's slow at first. Speed comes later!

    Note: If you have trouble hearing the root motion of the progression, play the root in the left hand and the given melody in the right. Then play the appropriate left hand voicings. This applies to all other similar exercises.

THE CONTEMPORARY KEYBOARDIST

104

TRANSPOSE ALL THE ABOVE EXERCISES TO ALL 12 KEYS

ANALYSIS OF "AUTUMN LEAVES"

The following is a complete analysis of the old standard, "Autumn Leaves" (Example 63). Although this tune is considered to be in G minor, note that the first four measures are in B♭ major, the next four measures are in G minor, and so on. What this means to the improviser is that a lot of tunes have <u>key centers</u> that shift. The improviser needs to know about these key centers to be able to improvise correctly and easily. In fast improvising, using key centers is a very natural process. Knowing and applying key center improvising can make a seemingly complicated song into a simple one. Have you ever experienced playing with a musician who can improvise over a set of changes simply by ear without even knowing them? The answer is a sensitivity, either natural or developed, to key centers. Once one develops this ability, he is ready for more advanced concepts and techniques such as intervallic playing, modal playing, "outside" playing, etc.

AUTUMN LEAVES:
Autumn Leaves (Les Feuilles Mortes) English Lyric by Johnny Mercer. French Lyric by Jacques Prevert. Music by Joseph Kosma. © 1947, 1950 Enoch Et Cie. © Renewed 1975, 1978 Enoch Et Cie. Sole Selling Agent for USA (Including Its Territories & Possessions) & Dominion of Canada: Morley Music Co. by agreement with Enoch Et Cie. International Copyright Secured. All Rights Reserved. Used By Permission.

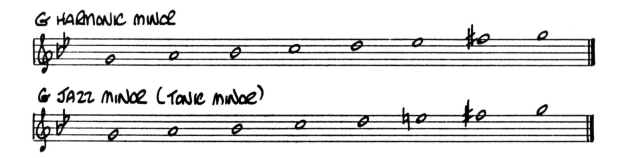

The following drills and exercises are therefore very important and should be done honestly and completely. I refer to this section as the "wall of keys," since all exercises must be done in all keys in order to get the maximum benefit possible and the necessary flexibility in all keys. Now remember, it takes as long as it takes, but by the time you get to the eighth or ninth key you'll be starting to cook if you've practiced sincerely and with purpose.

Exercise 1

Using the A and B voicings previously learned, learn the changes to "Autumn Leaves." The rhythm indicated is just a suggestion to get you started. You may comp* however you want once you feel at home with the changes, as long as it doesn't interfere with your right hand improvisational exercises. Make sure you play all exercises as musically as possible. This means groove!

* comp, is musical slang for accompany. It means to play changes in order to support a melody, solo, etc. It implies ad-libbing harmonically and rhythmically.

Exercise 2

    With the left hand only, play the appropriate A and B voicings for all the changes in "Autumn Leaves."

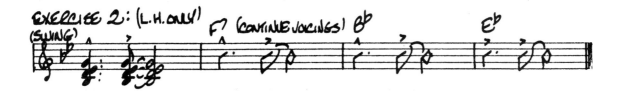

    Now that the left hand changes have been explored, it is time to explore the improvised line with the right hand. The left hand, if honestly learned, will act as a solid bed or track over which the right hand will perform exercises closely related to improvising. Initially this might present an independence problem because one has to put attention on the left hand changes and rhythm and the right hand exercise simultaneously. Shortly, however, with practice, the left hand will become second nature and a lot of attention may be put back on the right hand. Although in more advanced playing the left hand is not necessarily confined to this "support" role, I have found that one should have the support of a strong left hand while learning how to improvise.

    So in Exercises 3a and b and the others following, comp the changes of "Autumn Leaves" with the left hand and perform the given exercises with the right hand. Exercise 3a has been completely written out as an example. Note how the root, 2nd, 3rd, 4th, and 5th of each chord must also correspond to the given key center or scale of the moment. Exercise 11, the "Tension Exercise," has also been completely written out. This exercise is invaluable for learning the upper part of chords, as it concentrates on the 7, 9, 11 and 13.

    Notice what tensions go with what chord qualities and review the tension chart given earlier in the chapter, if necessary. You'll find these exercises quite powerful in that they will help you shorten your road to "improvisational freedom"--the reason being that they, and other exercises to follow, focus primarily on training the almighty ear! Once the ear is happening, look out! (Exercises 3 through 11.)

JAZZ SOLOS

Earlier in this chapter we broke the improvised line down into four possible categories: chord tones, passing tones, approach tones, and tensions (Example 59). It is now time to acquire some valuable experience by creating our own solos, using these categories, over the changes of "Autumn Leaves." The only rules or guidelines are the following:

1.   The solo must consist of notes only from the four categories (chord tones, passing tones, approach tones, tensions).

2.   Use tensions sparingly. If they are used, they must be preceded or followed by an interval skip of at least a minor third or a rest. This is to ensure that they *function* as tensions and not passing or approach tones. For example, a D resolving upwards to an E♭ on a C min.7 chord is not a tension 9. It is an approach note to a chord tone. Get it?

Extended duration of a note (1-1/2 or more beats) may also be used to reinforce the note as a tension.

Although I have provided an example of how these jazz solos should be written (Example 64), it is very important to realize that these solos are individual creations and as long as the guidelines are followed, anything goes. Also, these solos should be done away from your instrument, simply using your "mind's ear." Don't worry if you have no idea how they sound. These exercises are supposed to be done intellectually in order to explore improvisational possibilities that the ear might never hear.

So the assignment is to write at least seven jazz solos per key (one a day). At first it may take you a while to write a solo, but the more you do, the quicker you'll get. There are twelve keys, so you have 144 jazz solos. Have a nice trip!

"GIANT STEPS"

The next tune we will explore is John Coltrane's legendary "Giant Steps." Because of its fast tempo and different harmonic progression, this tune has a reputation for being quite difficult. We will therefore explore an approach to it somewhat different than the one we used with "Autumn Leaves."

Example 65 is a complete analysis of "Giant Steps." Notice that this composition consists of three tonal areas--B major, G major, and E♭ major. The exercises that follow simply give you experience at changing tonal areas at fast tempos. Exercises 1 through 12 each consist of two motifs or "patterns."

GIANT STEPS:

Giant Steps by John Coltrane. © 1974 Jowcol Music. Used By Permission.

Pattern (a) is a two-beat pattern and is used on all two-beat chords. Pattern (b) is a four-beat pattern, to be used on all four-beat chords. These exercises should be practiced in all keys and immediately at a fast tempo in order to gain experience and insight into the problems of "light speed" playing--they have no real value at slow tempos. It is said that these are some of the same exercises Coltrane actually practiced before he made his famous recording. The trick to fast playing is relaxation, and perception of the overall basic rhythm instead of every little beat. So push yourself to play at fast tempos, no matter how difficult it seems. Eventually, if you persist, you'll begin to relax and become used to the tempos.

Example 66 shows how Exercise 1 should be practiced. Relax and have a ball!

INTERCONNECTING SCALES

This is a simple but useful concept that can be applied to any tune or progression. It simply means practicing moving from one tonal area, or key center, to the next by connecting their corresponding scales. "Giant Steps" is the perfect tune to begin using this technique on because of its three clearly defined major key centers: B, G and E♭.

You simply begin on count 1 of the first measure on any note diatonic to the key of B and begin playing an ascending line, let's say in eighth notes, at a slow tempo until you get to the next key center. Then you simply make the appropriate scale alteration or transition to the next key center and continue this process while moving upwards on the keyboard until you reach the top of the piano. Then change directions and continue the process, going as low as possible without interfering with your left hand (Example 67).

This first step is considered done when you can move up and down your instrument at a fast tempo without any effort, "think," mistakes, or lags.

Step 2 would simply be changing directions at will (Example 68).

Step 3 would be skipping notes at will instead of playing note after note (Example 69).

Step 4 would simply be adding rests (Example 70).

EXAMPLE 70:

Now remember, these are just drills that will help
you become familiar with the changes. Once this familiarity is accomplished, anything goes--tensions, approach
notes, passing tones, chord tones, scales, elbow smears,
burning the piano--whatever. It's your personal creation!
Just know when to do what so you don't get fired!

STANDARD OPERATING PROCEDURE FOR IMPROVISATION

When tackling a new tune or set of changes, it helps
to have an organized approach. I have developed a common-
sense sort of operating procedure that I use whenever I
feel uncomfortable with a song or progression:

1. Play melody with R.H. (right hand) while singing
    it; play bass or roots with L.H. (left hand).

2. Play melody with R.H. while singing it; comp or
    play L.H. voicings.

3. Play voicings or chords with R.H.; play bass
    with L.H.

4. Play exercises with R.H. while L.H. plays:
    a. Bass
    b. Voicings

5. Solo or improvise with R.H. while L.H. plays:
    a. Bass
    b. Voicings

6. Freely improvise with both hands--whatever you
    "hear" is what you do.

Every player, after a lot of experience, develops his
own procedures. The above is meant only to be a workable
guideline for the beginner.

Also, the improvisational techniques described in this chapter are geared toward jazz lines and jazz harmony because I feel that most of the basics are naturally inherent in this idiom. Once you understand the basics, learning any particular style is just a matter of listening to records and actual playing experience. Later in this book we will discuss more advanced improvisational techniques, as this chapter was meant simply to ease you into a very uncodified and creative field. Play on!

Chapter 8
ASSIGNMENTS

_____ 1. Do the "Autumn Leaves" exercises on at least ten songs or chord progressions of your choice. Try and pick songs in different keys.

_____ 2. Do the "Giant Steps" exercises on at least ten songs of your choice.

_____ 3. Do the interconnecting scales exercise on ten songs of your choice.

_____ 4. What types of notes make up the improvised line, and what are their functions?

_____ 5. Describe the improvisational process in your own words.

SPECIAL NOTE

For more information on Charlie Banacos's personalized correspondence courses in jazz improvisation (basic, intermediate and advanced), you may write to him at 27 Flume Road, Magnolia, Massachusetts 01930 USA.

Chapter 9

Ear Training

What is <u>ear training</u>? Why is it so important? What's the ear's relationship to the eye (sight-visio), touch (tactile), and what is the relationship of all three (ears, eyes, touch) to your mind and to you?

Well, actually they are your <u>antennae</u> and are hooked up to your brain--switchboard--through which you, the operator, call the shots according to the information received. In other words, the eye looks, that you may see; the ear listens, that you may hear; the fingers touch, that you may feel.

Now, although all three senses are important, which is the most important? Yes, that's right--the <u>ear</u>!

The ear is the judge! Educate the ear and problems with key location, technique, improvisation, etc., simply fall by the wayside.

The ear is both receptive and directive. It receives sound images from within (the creative faculties of the imagination) and actual sounds from instruments without. With this data the ear can direct the eyes and playing mechanism. So educate the ear and you'll be happening!

Now, in reality, it's not the ear we're training, it's <u>you</u>--you the individual, the spirit, the operator. But, as explained above, the ear is the conduit or receiver for most of this information--hence the term <u>ear training</u>.

The goal of ear training is to enable you to simultaneously identify, differentiate, and process certain levels of musical information primarily sensed through the ear (melody, harmony, rhythm and dynamics, to name a few), resulting in the composite skills and actions of performing (playing, singing, improvising, etc).

The ability to hear these levels simultaneously is a basic prerequisite for effortless performances and the mark of a natural and confident player. The following exercises are designed to zero in on them and improve your musical sensitivity. So the drills should not be regarded as an end in themselves, but as a means to attain this sensitivity.

I hope this puts into perspective the importance of the ear--the judge!

Definitions

Perfect Pitch or Absolute Pitch, the ability to determine a note from its frequency or rate of vibration alone, along with the ability to sing or name a note asked for.

Perfect Relative Pitch, given a note, the ability to identify any other note. This is done by being able to hold a key center and identify intervals.

Exercise 1 - Perfect Relative Pitch

Given any note--in this case C--be able to identify any of the other eleven notes (twelve if you include C).

Procedure:

1. Mock up C mentally by playing it on the piano until you can sing it, as well as "hear" it in your mind. Playing a stock progression such as the I - IV - V - IV - I will definitely help define the key center if you're having problems.

2.   Either by closing your eyes or turning your back to the piano, hit any note, preferably in your vocal range for now, with the eraser end of a long pencil. By comparing the just-struck note with the one that's hopefully still in your head, you should eventually be able to identify the interval and thus the note. Your answer should pretty much occur within two seconds. We're trying to develop the intuitive response. Too long a time and too much "think" is no good, even if you get the note right. Dig! If you don't know, make a guess. You might be surprised how many you'll get right this way. Intuition, "gut feeling," "going for it"--whatever one calls it-- sometimes seems elusive, but is <u>always</u> very powerful, once developed!

This should be done a few minutes every day until you can do it consistently. It takes as long as it takes. After all, you're only trying to develop perfect relative pitch--give yourself a break! Six months to a year to develop this ability is not uncommon.

Exercise 2 - <u>Reverse Relative Pitch</u>

Given a note--in this case C--be able to sing any other note.

<u>Procedure</u>:

1.   As in Exercise 1, get C in your mind.

2.   Point to any note within your vocal range and sing it.

3.   Check to see if you're right by sounding the note.

4.   Repeat Steps 1 through 3.

The difference between this exercise and Exercise 1 is that in the first exercise, you are trying to identify a sound after hearing it, while in Exercise 2 you are asked to sing a sound on command. Since these abilities, along with creativity, are what playing is all about, you'll find these exercises very helpful.

Exercise 3 - Half Step Whole Step

Given any note, be able to sing a half step up or down, and a whole step up or down. Although this exercise can be done with any interval, half steps and whole steps are the most beneficial.

Procedure:

1. Play note (staccato).

2. Sing desired note (staccato) a half or whole step up or down.

Exercise 4 - Basic Triads

Given any note, be able to sing any basic triad.

Procedure:

1. Play or locate any note.

2. Sing any one of the four basic triads up and down:

   a. Major
   b. Minor
   c. Diminished
   d. Augmented

Exercise 5 - Basic Tetrads

Given any note, be able to sing any of the six basic tetrads.

Procedure:

1. Play or locate any note.

2. Sing any one of the six basic tetrads.

   a. Major 7th, major 6th
   b. Minor 7th
   c. Dominant 7th
   d. Minor 7th($\flat$5)
   e. Diminished 7th
   f. Minor major 7th, minor 6th

Exercise 6 - Scale Duplication

Given any note, be able to sing the following scales:

    a. Major
    b. Harmonic minor
    c. Melodic minor ascending
    d. The Modes (Ionian, Dorian, Phyrgian, etc.)
    e. Whole tone
    f. Symmetrical diminished
    g. Altered dominant

Procedure:

1. Play or locate any note.

2. Sing any one of the above scales up and down.

These scales and their uses are discussed in detail in Chapter 11, "Advanced Improvisation." The ability to accurately hear these scale colors is very useful when improvising.

Exercise 7 - Intervallic Duplication

Given any harmonic interval, be able to identify it simply by its sound.

Procedure:

Either by using a prerecorded tape of random intervals, or by striking the piano using two pencils, identify the sounded interval.

Exercise 8 - Basic Chord Recognition

Given any of the basic triads and tetrads, be able to identify them simply by their sound.

Procedure:

The best approach to this drill is either to make a tape of random triads and tetrads or have a qualified friend play the chords. Whichever way you decide to do it, do only triads first and then tetrads. Once your ear is happening, you may mix triads and tetrads. It is very valuable to be able to recognize the basic chord qualities by ear.

Exercise 9 - The Duplication Exercise

This exercise is incredibly valuable in developing one's ability to duplicate musical notes, phrases, and dynamics. Mozart was known and highly respected for this ability.

Procedure:

On count one of a measure, play a note of any duration and dynamics (volume and touch) and then duplicate it on count one of the next measure.

This exercise is best done with two people. One person plays and the other duplicates. However, you can prerecord a tape using a metronome, playing the first measure while leaving the second measure blank. You then try to duplicate the sounds of the first measure during the blank second measure.

Start off simple, trying to duplicate one note at first as to pitch, duration, and dynamics. Then try two-note, three-note and four--or more--note phrases. Memory is your only limitation.

This drill can be very demoralizing, so hang in there! (See Example 71.)

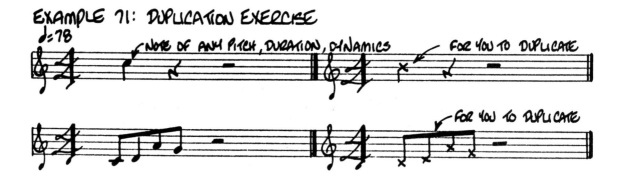

EXAMPLE 71: DUPLICATION EXERCISE

Exercise 10 - Melodic Duplication and Transposition

To help develop the ability to be able to <u>play</u> what you clearly hear mentally.

Procedure:

Pick a melody that you can <u>accurately sing out loud</u>. The quality of your voice is unimportant. Using two hands, play the melody by ear, starting on different notes at random. Play slowly and in time, trying all kinds of melodies. Christmas carols, nursery rhymes--whatever you can sing well--are the types of melodies you should start off with. Eventually you can graduate to more difficult melodies, but make sure you can sing what you're attempting to play.

Exercise 11 - Ear Accuracy

To further fine-tune the ear.

Procedure:

Sing each line of every Bach Two-Part Invention separately. Because of the extreme linear makeup of these lines, the ear is forced to be accurate.

This exercise may be difficult at first, but stick with it--with diligent practice, you'll get it, and the results will be extremely beneficial.

RECORD COPYING

Definition:

<u>Record Copying</u>, actually means duplicating, analyzing, understanding and playing material from other respected artists' recorded works (records and tapes).

For example, many piano players copy Charlie Parker solos in order to get his viewpoint on improvising and phrasing. Or let's say you want to learn how to play authentic blues piano. You might buy the recordings of Dr. John and other artists like him and begin doing record copies until you assimilate the style to your satisfaction. So unless you're creating a brand new style, anything you want to learn is probably somewhere on records and tapes waiting to be appreciated--gospel, rock & roll, jazz, rhythm and blues, fusion, new wave, pop, avant-garde--whatever.

A basic knowledge of musical notation, harmony, improvisation, and rhythm, although not necessary, is important in order to facilitate the take-down process.

Now let's take a look at a standard operating procedure for record and tape copying.

Record Copying Procedure

1. Locate material to copy that's (a) not too advanced relative to your present level of musical understanding, and (b) interesting and valuable to you musically.

2. You need a record player or tape machine (reel-to-reel or cassette) to use in the take-down process. The tape recorder or record player should preferably have a variable pitch so it can sync to your keyboard, as well as a slow speed for closer observation of fast licks. Now, although record copying can obviously be done just on a mental level, committing the material to memory as you go, it's best to also write it down so you can refer to it later.

3. Start the take-down process:

    a. Listen to the chord progression first, paying attention to the bass and its harmonic rhythm. Once this is duplicated, try to determine the chord qualities of the progression. Then you may determine the exact voicing as to tensions, etc.

    The above process is done over and over, always comparing what you think the sound is to the original until it perfectly matches. You may have to do one chord at a time until the entire progression is figured out.

    b. Next, begin taking down the other parts, whatever they may be--solos, vocal lines, counterlines, fills, etc. Never overwhelm yourself. Short phrases are easier to retain than long ones. Sometimes you have to shut the tape or record off after one or two notes, before you actually hear it.

In extremely fast lines or chord progressions, it may be necessary to slow the tape or record down to half speed, if your machine is capable of it. Although this drops the recorded material down an octave, it helps tremendously, and after you get it, you can transpose the phrase back up an octave.

c. Once you've finished copying the phrase, chord progression, song, symphony, or whatever, you can begin playing along with the record or tape to see if you're on the money. As the ear sometimes plays tricks on you, you'll probably discover a few spots that need another listen.

d. If you're satisfied you've duplicated the material, then now it's time to learn it as closely as is possible with your present level of expertise. This is the fun part!

e. Note: duplication is different from understanding. Duplicate what's on the record or tape exactly at first; then afterwards you can analyze for understanding. Mixing both processes at the same time may lead to your "intellectualizing" what you're hearing (thinking something was played that really wasn't and/or vice versa) rather than hearing what's really there.

f. Although the whole process is slow at first, you will become better and better and eventually be able to simply listen to "sounds" and know what they are--that's what it means when somebody says someone has "good ears"!

I have included a couple of record copies I did of two of my favorite keyboardists, Oscar Peterson and Chick Corea. Check these solos out. If your "chops" are ready for the challenge, try learning them!

PUT ON A HAPPY FACE:

PUT ON A HAPPY FACE

OSCAR PETERSON

THE CONTEMPORARY KEYBOARDIST

136

PUT ON A HAPPY FACE

OSCAR PETERSON

PUT ON A HAPPY FACE   OSCAR PETERSON

SPAIN

C. COREA
POLYDOR

SPAIN   C. COREA

Chapter 9
ASSIGNMENTS

_____ 1. Describe in your own words the role of the ear in regard to music.

_____ 2. Define:

   a. perfect pitch
   b. perfect relative pitch

_____ 3. Do all the indicated exercises in this chapter.

_____ 4. Do a record copy of one of your favorite artists' compositions, or of something in your favorite musical style, following the procedures outlined in this chapter. Now practice what you've copied until you can play along with the record or tape. Do another, and another, and another!

_____ 5. Locate Oscar Peterson's Put On A Happy Face album (Verve Records) and Chick Corea's Light As A Feather album (Polydor Records). I've included record copies of "Put On A Happy Face" and "Spain" from these albums at the end of the chapter. Listen to each tune while watching the score. Do this many times. Try learning these solos if your technique is up to it. You may also want to do your own record copy of the comp (left-hand) part, as this will give you added insight into the right-hand improvisation.

SUGGESTED READING

Edlund, Lars. Modus Novus, Studies in Reading Atonal Melodies. New York: Alexander Broude, 1963.

Fish, Arnold, and Norman Lloyd. Fundamentals of Sight Singing and Ear Training. New York and Toronto: Dodd, Mead & Company, 1972.

Mason, Thom David. Ear Training for the Improviser, A Total Approach. Studio City, Cal.: Dick Grove Publishing, 1981.

Chapter 10

Rhythm

In Chapter 4, "The Basic Basics of Music," we took a look at the role of rhythm as it relates to the performer and audience. In Chapter 10 we shall look at ways to increase our rhythmic awareness. It might be beneficial at this time to review the section on rhythm in Chapter 4 as an orientation.

Basically there are three types of rhythms in music:

1. <u>Regular</u> - a rhythm with an evenly stressed beat (Examples 72a and b).

EXAMPLE 72A: (EVEN — NO ACCENTS)   72B:

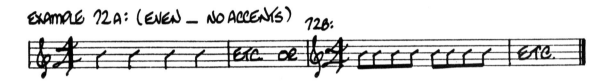

2. <u>Syncopated</u> - displacements of the normal accent by transferring it from a strong to a weak beat or from a strong to a weak part of a beat.

    Syncopation has stresses which do not agree with the normal metrical stresses. These are accomplished by accents, and accents are made by contrasts in volume, note duration, pitch, and timbre (tone color), as well as rests and changing meter (Examples 73a-g).

EXAMPLE 73A: (ACCENTS BY VOLUME)   73B:

EXAMPLE 73C: (ACCENTS BY DURATION)

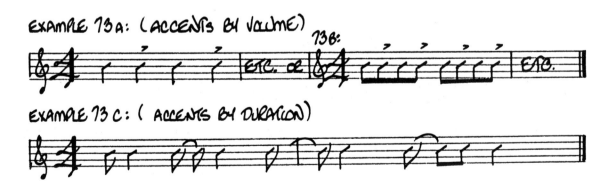

EXAMPLE 73 D: (ACCENTS BY PITCH)

EXAMPLE 73 E: (ACCENT BY TIMBRE)

*BEATS 2 + 4 WILL SEEM ACCENTED BECAUSE OF THE DIFFERENT TONE COLOR OF THE TRUMPET COMPARED TO THE FLUTE EVEN THOUGH THEY ARE PLAYING THE SAME NOTES!

EXAMPLE 73 F: (ACCENTS BY RESTS)

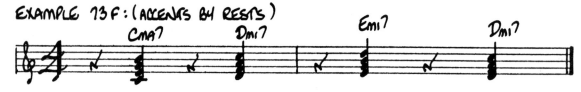

EXAMPLE 73 G: (ACCENTS BY CHANGING METER)

3.   Free Time - rhythm in which the durations of the notes and rests are not fixed fractions or multiples of a common unit of duration.

Although difficult to grasp until experienced, free time is a flow of movement through time with simply no restrictions as to tempo, groove, etc. It is a movement from one stressed important point to another stressed important point by way of unstressed transitional points, usually with no steady tempo. Within free time, however, there may be certain regular or syncopated rhythms, accelerandos, rests, or whatever feeling of movement the player or composer desires. Free means no rules. Do what you like! Play the indicated passage or musical phrase as you wish! (No example.)

These three rhythmic feels can be combined to produce many complicated rhythms and can be applied harmonically as well as melodically (Example 74).

THE NINE BASIC RHYTHMS

Now, before we proceed to advanced syncopations, odd meters, polyrhythms, etc., it is necessary to understand and apply the following nine basic rhythms:

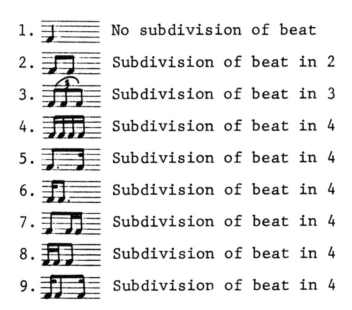

1.   No subdivision of beat

2.   Subdivision of beat in 2

3.   Subdivision of beat in 3

4.   Subdivision of beat in 4

5.   Subdivision of beat in 4

6.   Subdivision of beat in 4

7.   Subdivision of beat in 4

8.   Subdivision of beat in 4

9.   Subdivision of beat in 4

As you can see, these nine rhythms are simply different ways to subdivide a <u>beat</u>! In actual fact, there are really only four subdivisions: rhythm 1 has no subdivisions; rhythm 2 is division of a beat in half; rhythm 3 is division of a beat in thirds; rhythm 4 is division of a beat in fourths, and rhythms 5 through 9 are basically permutations of rhythm 4--so are still considered subdivisions in 4. There are, of course, subdivisions of a beat in groups of 5, 6, 7, 8, and so on, which we will study later, but for now it is better that we learn these basic nine and their applications.

The following exercises will help increase your rhythmic awareness as well as improve your sight reading. When doing any rhythmic drill, one should have a fixed time base such as a metronome, click track, or drum machine. An important point to remember, though, is never to play <u>to</u> the metronome, play with it! Use it as a guide to a particular tempo, then <u>duplicate</u> the tempo mentally and simply do what the metronome is doing. Too much dependence on an external fixed time base can produce "stiff" time (good tempo but no groove). So by doing what I suggest, you eventually won't need the metronome or whatever. You will have developed your own sense of accurate tempo plus still be able to groove!

<u>Exercise 1</u>

By either clapping or playing a single note on the piano, play each basic rhythm as indicated until it is accurate, effortless, and in time. Use a metronome setting of about ♩ = 72 and count each rhythm out loud as indicated.

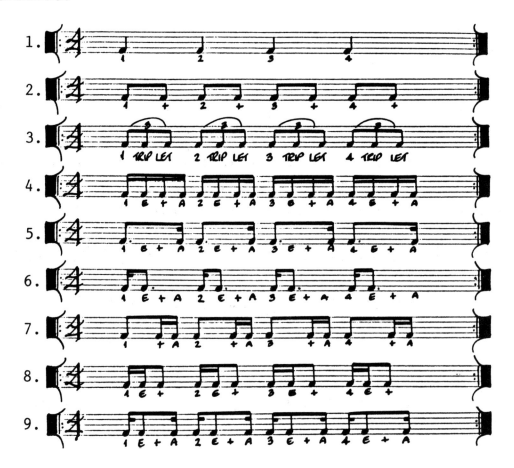

Exercise 2

Practice transitioning at random from one basic rhythm to another without losing the tempo or rhythm. The most difficult transition is going from a division of three (rhythm 3) to a division of 2 or 4 (for example, ♫♩ to ♫ , etc).

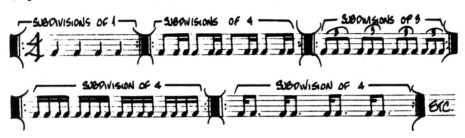

It helps to recognize in advance what subdivision you're transitioning to. Knowing if it's a subdivision in 1, 2, 3, or 4 and how to count it is the key to learning any rhythm. Once learned, however, you'll simply hear subdivisions and consequently be able to play them without counting.

Exercise 3

Write at least seven full pages of "rhythm etudes"*-- more if necessary--using the nine basic rhythms. Use a time signature of 4/4 and be as creative as you like. Try all kinds of possible combinations but do not, in this exercise, use any ties or rests. Using metronome marking ♩ = 72, practice each etude until you can clap each rhythm accurately without stopping. Be as musical as you can!

---

* etude, French for "study," hence a piece of music designed to give practice in some branch of instrumental technique (excerpted from The New College Encyclopedia of Music, by J.A. Westrup and F. Harrison, under "etude").

Although you'll find this takes a lot of determination to conquer, it's an invaluable exercise for getting your time and rhythmic reading together. Once this is accomplished, confronting different pitches and chords is a little easier.

Exercise 4

Same as Exercise 3, except add ties at <u>random</u> to your etudes! You'll soon discover that the basic rhythms can evolve into many complex rhythms!

Exercise 5

Same as Exercise 3, except add rests at random to the basic rhythms (no ties). I have again used the same example so you can see how the rests were added.

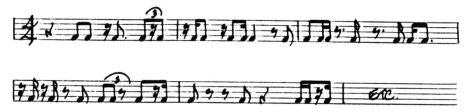

Exercise 6 - Combination Etude

Now let's see what you're made of. Add ties and rests, put the metronome on really slow to begin with (♩ = 58), and clap through all your new rhythm etudes. You'll find that once you've mastered this exercise, you'll not again easily be fooled by any rhythm pattern!

ADVANCED RHYTHMS

Now that you've mastered the nine basic rhythms, it's time to look at more advanced subdivisions of the beat, namely subdivisions in 5, 6, 7 and 8. Following are basic rhythms 10, 11, 12 and 13:

10. 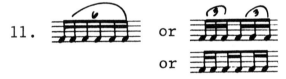 means each sixteenth note gets 1/5 of a beat or five notes per one click of the metronome.

11.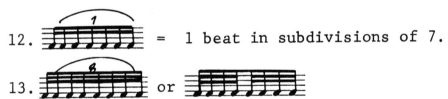

= 1 beat in subdivisions of 6.

12. = 1 beat in subdivisions of 7.

13. or = 1 beat in subdivisions of 8. These notes are now referred to as 32nd notes. Therefore, eight 32nd notes equal one quarter note equals one beat.

Although theoretically we could go on and on, it's practical to end here since subdivisions of 9, 10, 11, etc., are less frequent and can be dealt with individually when encountered. To gain facility with rhythms 10 through 13, you should again do all of the same exercises as were done with rhythms 1 through 9. (Exercises 1-6-- the rhythm etudes, etc.) Keep on cookin'!

ACCENTS

An accent over or under a note () simply means the note should be given more emphasis by playing it with more stress, pressure, or velocity. Since accents can change the feel of rhythms, it is important to practice our basic rhythms with different accents to acquaint our ears with the resultant sounds.

The following exercises are to be practiced to develop facility in emphasizing internal accents in any of the previous basic rhythms. Again, they may be practiced by either clapping your hands, or playing a note or chord on the piano. Use your imagination!

Although the above exercises do not exhaust all the possibilities, you'll find yourself well prepared and inspired!

POLYRHYTHMS

Rhythmic Independence, the ability to hear and perform two or more rhythms at the same time. Two or more rhythms played simultaneously are called polyrhythms. They may be thought of as two different meters (time signatures) played against each other.

Polyrhythms are usually very difficult to confront because of incorrect practice procedures. For best results, I suggest using this practice procedure with the polyrhythm exercises on the next few pages:

Practice Procedure

1. Use a metronome in order to keep the basic beat or meter absolutely consistent while you concentrate on the counterrhythm. The counterrhythm may be clapped, sung, played on an instrument, or whatever.

2. It is extremely important to count the exercise as indicated in order to fully understand it.

3. Continue using the above procedure until the relationship of the rhythmic patterns is fully heard and felt. You will then be able to use your own groove without the aid of the metronome.

4. Once duplicated, you should memorize the sound of the particular polyrhythm for quick future use.

The following exercises cover only what I feel are the most essential polyrhythms. If you desire to explore polyrhythms further, there are many manuals (especially for drummers) which delve extensively into this interesting area.

Finally, after you feel you've gained sufficient confidence and understanding with a certain polyrhythm, you can try using the right hand to play a melodic line corresponding to the counterrhythm while the left hand plays the basic pulse in either chordal or single line accompaniment. The daring may try vice versa!

The Polyrhythms:

    1.   Two against one (Example 75)

    2.   Four against one (Example 76)

    3.   Three against one (Example 77)

    4.   a.   Three against two (Example 78a)

b.   Six against four (Example 78b)

As an exercise, play each of the above rhythms separately before going on to the following etude.

<u>Drills:</u>

Play the rhythmic etude in Example 79 with the
metronome at varying tempos. Then compose your
own etudes and learn them until the basic
polyrhythms are easily played.

5.   Now by adding eighths, triplets, and sixteenths to 3
against 2 and 6 against 4, we get the following
results:

a.   eighths (Example 80)

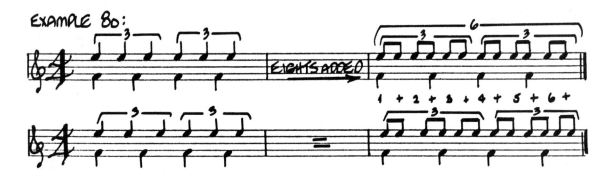

b.   triplets (Example 81)

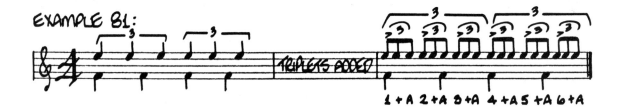

c.   sixteenths (Example 82)

<u>Drills</u>:

Play the etude in Example 83 with the metronome
at varying tempos. Compose your own etudes
until these new polyrhythms are easily played.

EXAMPLE 83:

Well, I hope you're still with us, because we have a few more--but only for the daring!

6. Half note triplets (3 against 4) (Example 84). Now, as before, this polyrhythm can be subdivided into quarters, eighths, sixteenths, and triplets.

EXAMPLE 84: (3 AGAINST 4)

7. 3 against 4--adding quarter notes (Example 85). It is important to count

$\overset{>}{\underline{1}}$ and $\overset{>}{\underline{2}}$ and $\overset{>}{\underline{3}}$ and

making sure you stress the accents. Don't count 6, even though it appears to be the same polyrhythm. In order to keep the "3 against 4" feel intact, you must stress the accents!

EXAMPLE 85: ADDING QUARTERS

8. 3 against 4--adding eighths (Example 86). As in the above example, stress the accents by counting

$\underset{>}{\underline{1}}$ e and a $\underset{>}{\underline{2}}$ e and a $\underset{>}{\underline{3}}$ e and a

EXAMPLE 86: ADDING EIGHTHS

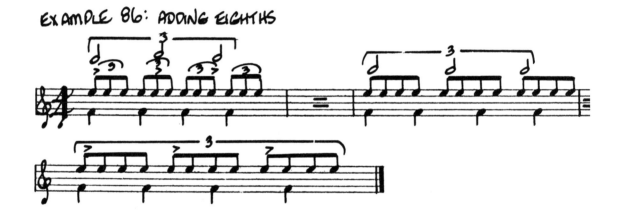

9. 3 against 4--adding sixteenths (Example 87). As before, stress the accents. This polyrhythm is obviously difficult to play fast, so slow it down.

EXAMPLE 87: ADDING 16THS OR 8THS DOUBLED

10. 3 against 4--adding triplets or 9 against 4 (Example 88).

EXAMPLE 88: ADD TRIPLETS _ 9 AGAINST 4

Drills:

    a. Learn the "3 against 4" etude (Example 89). Make sure you don't count any measures in 6. Remember, the basic polyrhythm is 3 against 4.

EXAMPLE 89: ETUDE

b.   Compose your own etude and learn it.

11.   4 against 3 (Example 90). In this example the basic
       pulse is 3 instead of 4. Once the 4 is learned, make
       sure you count 4 against 3! Now, using the same pro-
       cedure as before, we can subdivide 4 against 3 into
       added eighths and sixteenths--which I'll let you do
       on your own if you're still with me. Now play the
       etude in Example 91.

In Conclusion

        Although you might be thinking I've already gone too
far into polyrhythms, there really are more. The cultures
of Africa and East India have helped shape and advance the
rhythmic sensitivity of the western musical world. I have
only touched upon some of the basic polyrhythms. There
exist many others, such as 5 against 4, 7 against 4, 11
against 4, and 13 against 4, to name just some. If you're
sincerely interested and have the patience, there are many
books--especially drum books--devoted to these more advanced polyrhythms.

I will also leave you with the concept of poly-metrics, or polytime signatures--the juxtapositioning of two or more different times. I wrote a composition dedicated to Bela Bartok a few years ago which is in 8/8 over 9/8! Although the downbeats of each time start off the same, they don't come together for 72 more beats (1 beat = an eighth note). Both times together seemed to create a whole new third time, or feel, which I found very stimulating.

Well--enough food for thought!

ODD TIME SIGNATURES

Time signatures whose numerators are 3, 5, 7, 9, 11, etc., and whose denominators may be 2, 4, 8, 16, etc., are called odd time signatures. Although tricky to feel at first, odd time signatures can become second nature with practice. Example 92a is an excerpt from "Take Five"--one of the most famous odd time tunes ever written.

CHANGING METERS

When a meter within a tune or composition changes periodically, instead of staying a constant 3/4, 4/4, or whatever, we have changing meter. This may or may not happen frequently within a composition, depending upon the composer's intentions. Example 92b is a composition I wrote called "Modal Moods" which demonstrates changing meters while still hanging on to musicality.

MODAL MOODS

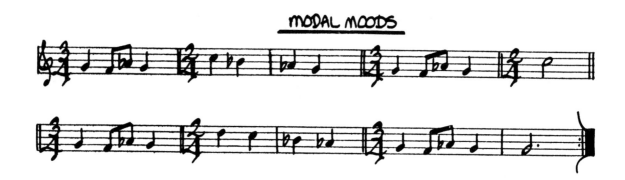

Since the use of odd and changing meters is nowadays common practice, it is advisable to gain some confidence, as well as competence, with them. Since there are many great texts and drum books that cover them thoroughly, I will not treat them in detail. I will, however, recommend a procedure to get you started:

1.   Read Alan Dawson's drum book and Louis Bellson's Odd Time Reading Text and "woodshed"* all exercises daily.

2.   Either by yourself or with other players (or both), do a lot of jamming with odd times and changing meters. Learn as many tunes in this bag as you can until the effort in playing them disappears. Stay with it. Living on a 4/4 planet has probably taken its toll!

---

* woodshed or shed, to practice purposefully and intensively.

RHYTHMIC AILMENTS AND CURES

1.   <u>Bad or unsteady time</u> - Stems from not being <u>cause</u> as a player, but <u>effect!</u> The player has probably been depending upon other players for the time instead of "putting it there" himself. The solution is to play with some fixed time apparatus such as a metronome or drum machine until you can comfortably <u>co-create</u> <u>with</u> these devices, not <u>to</u> them! Then play without these aids and see if you can create the time all by yourself. Then make it a habit to play with good players as much as possible. Remember, good effortless time is part of the magic of music!

2.   <u>Rushing or dragging</u> - Although a player may have good overall time, he may rush or drag phrases on occasion. This usually stems from an inability to subdivide beats properly in one's mind into eighths, triplets, sixteenths, etc. The solution is an exercise: play quarter notes with your foot or hand or whatever and mentally sing the nine basic rhythms one at a time, adding accents until you notice which subdivision is uneven. Concentrate on these subdivisions until they're right on the money. Then just play, and maybe tape yourself to see if the problem is indeed handled. Continue the exercise until you're happening!

3.   <u>"Warp speed" playing</u> - Playing at fast tempos challenges the best of players. One must relax and think in long musical phrases, or forget it. The key here is playing at fast tempos daily until you are able--even at these seemingly difficult speeds--to relax, and the <u>effort</u> turns to <u>ease</u>.

4.   <u>"Tortoise" tempo playing</u> - Playing at super slow tempos can be just as challenging as fast ones since most players <u>rush</u> (speed up) a lot. The key here, as in (2) above, is to practice your subdivisions at the troubling tempos until you can mentally "prehear" them and thus have control!

THE CONTEMPORARY KEYBOARDIST

5.   <u>Losing "one"</u> - Player's time is weak to begin with and he's probably been either unknowingly or knowingly depending on other players for his time. He's therefore setting himself up for imminent disaster, for as soon as anybody does anything complex or unexpected, the downbeat, or "one," disappears! Now, since "one" really never changes or disappears, it's the player's perception of "one" which is the problem. The player must be confident enough to <u>create</u> the time by himself and then listen to the <u>total sound</u> in order to musically lock in with the groove! Depending on others, rhythm machines, click tracks, etc., puts one at effect, not cause. One creates from within. The player who has good time and groove is <u>constantly creating</u> good time and groove. The minute you stop creating these musical commodities, that's it-- they're gone. I hope this helps clarify the area.

Chapter 10
ASSIGNMENTS

_____ 1. Define <u>regular time</u>, <u>syncopated time</u>, and <u>free time</u> and give your <u>own</u> examples.

_____ 2. Write out the nine basic rhythms and their corresponding subdivisions.

_____ 3. Do Exercises 1 through 6 until mastered!

_____ 4. Write out the advanced rhythms 10 through 13 and their corresponding subdivisions.

_____ 5. Apply Exercises 1 through 6 to these advanced rhythms until they are mastered. Then write a combination etude including all thirteen rhythms and learn it.

_____ 6. Define an <u>accent</u> and give some examples.

_____ 7. Do the indicated accent exercises (1 through 5) until you feel good about accents.

_____ 8. What is meant by <u>rhythmic independence</u>? Define <u>polyrhythm</u>.

_____ 9. Do all the indicated polyrhythm drills, making sure you follow the step-by-step procedure. Don't be in a hurry--it takes as long as it takes!

_____ 10. List the common rhythm ailments and their cures.

_____ 11. What are <u>polymetrics</u>, or <u>polytime signatures</u>?

_____ 12. Define odd time signatures and changing meters and give examples of each.

SUGGESTED READING AND REFERENCES

Bellson, Louis, and Gil Breines. <u>Odd Time Reading Text</u>. Melville, N.Y.: Belwin Mills Publishing Corp., 1968.

Chapin, Jim. <u>Advanced Techniques for the Modern Drummer</u>. New York: Jim Chapin, 1948.

Corea, Chick. <u>Music Poetry</u>. Los Angeles: Litha Music, 1980. pp.10, 11.

Dawson, Alan. <u>A Manual for the Modern Drummer</u>. Boston: Berklee Press Publications, 1962.

Magadini, Pete. <u>Musicians Guide to Polyrhythms</u>. Vols. 1-2. Hollywood, Cal.: Try Publishing Co., 1968.

Mehegan, John. <u>Jazz Improvisation 2--Jazz Rhythm and the Improvised Line</u>. New York: Watson-Guptill Publications, 1962. pp.1-58.

Whiteside, Abby. <u>Indispensables of Piano Playing</u>. New York: Charles Scribner's Sons, 1961. chaps.2 & 10.

Whiteside, Abby. <u>Mastering the Chopin Etudes and Other Essays</u>. New York: Charles Scribner's Sons, 1969. pp.128-150.

Chapter 11
Advanced Improvisation

In this chapter we will look at various chords and their respective <u>chord scales</u>. Once a player can hear tonal (key) centers, as were discussed in Chapter 8, he or she is now ready for the chord scale approach--an approach which will simply give the player more tools to work with and thus allow the creative process to remain fresh and flowing. The more improvisational tools a player has, the less likely that that player will end up stuck with a stagnant "bag of licks." Before actually beginning this approach, however, you should familiarize yourself with the scales given in Example 93, in all keys (four octaves), both hands together. Work out your own fingerings! All examples are in C.

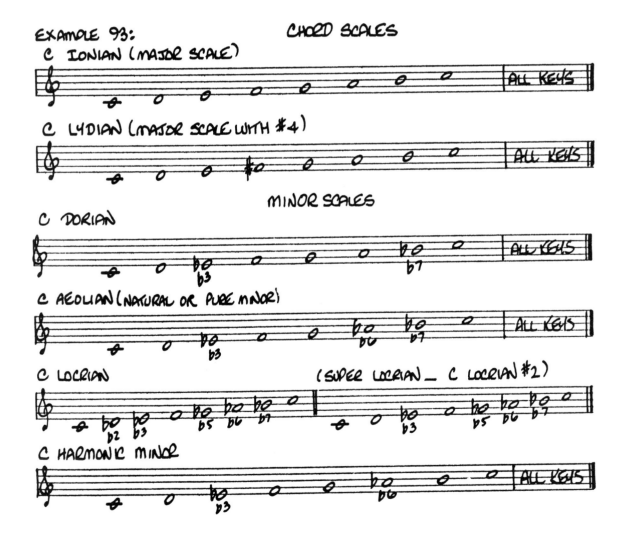

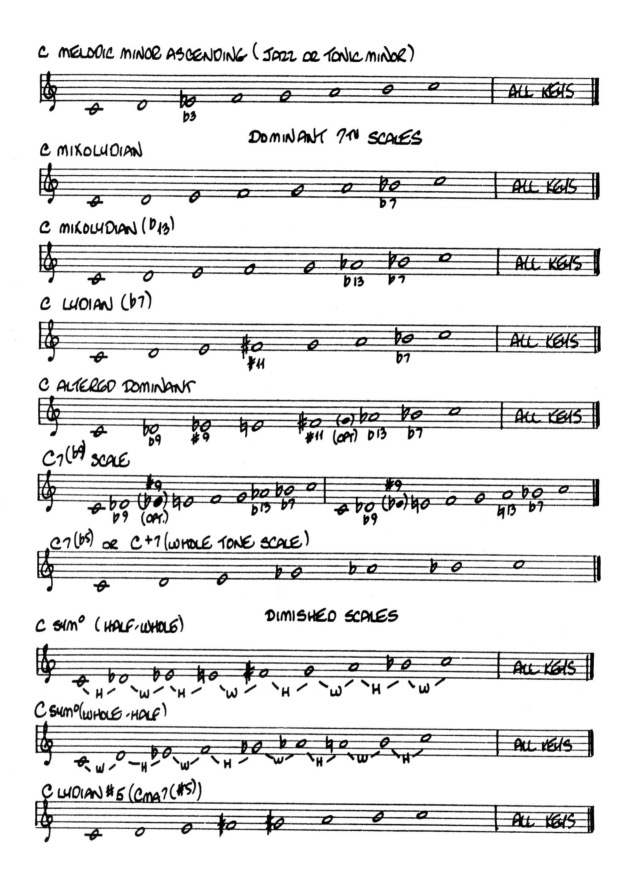

We are now ready to take a detailed look at the various previously discussed chord qualities and their respective scales from a linear or improvisational viewpoint. Each chord quality or family is broken down in the following way:

1. Chord tones

2. Tensions

3. Scale of key that chord usually functions in

4. Respective chord scale

5. Breakdown of chord tones, approach notes (chromatic and double chromatic), passing tones

Each quality (eleven in all) is in the key of C. Your assignment is to duplicate the examples in all fifteen keys:

Procedure

1. Write out the first chord quality (major 7th) in all fifteen keys. (Use Example 94a as a model.)

2. Arpeggiate chord tones and tensions on the piano in order to train the ear to the sounds.

3. With left hand playing chord tones only (R 3 5 7), play appropriate chord scale.

4. With left hand playing chord tones only, run through all remaining exercises (passing tones, approach tones).

5. Repeat procedure on next chord quality (Examples 94a-k).

EXAMPLE 94 H: Cma7+5 __ CHORD NAME
Ima7+5 __ CHORD FUNCTION

Cma7 +5

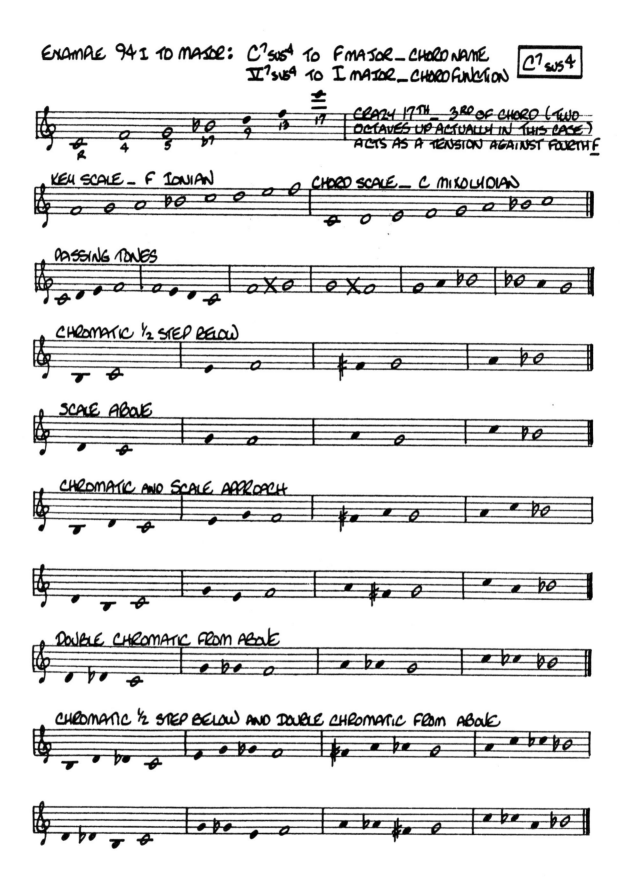

EXAMPLE 94 I TO MINOR : C⁷sus⁴ TO F MINOR
                        II⁷sus⁴ TO I MINOR

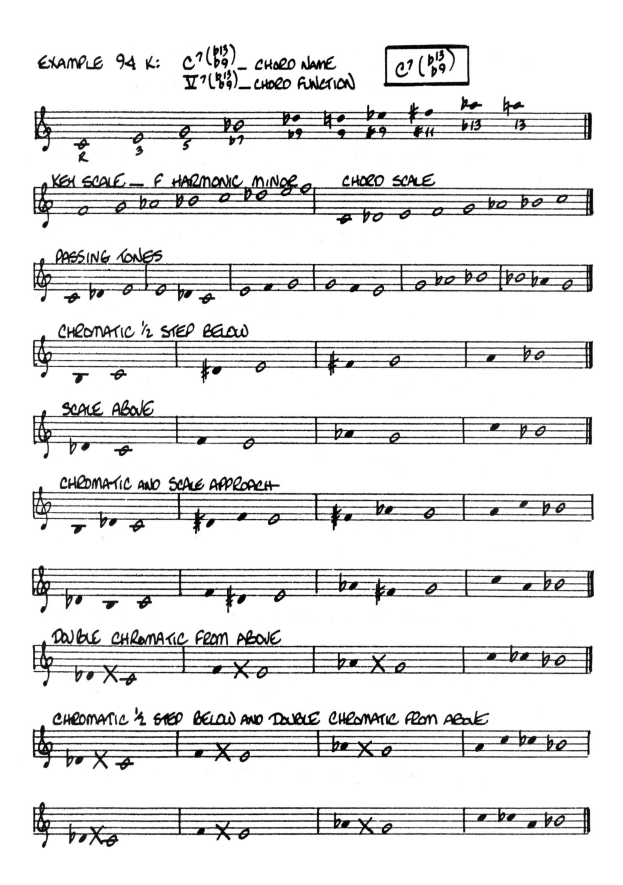

The goal of learning these scales and chord breakdowns is simply to facilitate the improvisational process by getting you very familiar with its component parts. Since the three most important communication channels used in any playing are aural (sense of hearing), visual and tactile (sense of touch), the clearer these images are in the mind before we actually play, the better the performance.

In other words, a player plays the best by prehearing, pre-seeing, and prefeeling his or her communication. So the more familiar you become with the component parts of improvisation (scales, chords, intervals, flows, dynamics, etc), the clearer these images become--the aural, of course, being the most important!

A blind pianist, for example, must out of necessity rely on a strong aural and tactile image, since the physical visual image is impaired. But remember, he or she can still see mentally! It is said that Beethoven wrote much of his famous Ninth Symphony quite deaf. Well, since he was trained and could obviously hear mentally (prehear), he just wrote it out! He just didn't get a chance to appreciate his composition performed in the physical universe. Get it?

Don't go on until these chord breakdowns are learned, no matter how long it takes!

Diminished 7th Chord

There are two types: secondary dominant* and chromatic or passing.

The secondary dominant diminished 7th chord functions as a secondary dominant 7th in first inversion. It definitely looks, sounds and functions like a secondary dominant (Example 95). The chromatic or passing diminished 7th simply connects two chords chromatically without acting as a secondary dominant to its target chord (Example 96).

---

* The primary dominant in any key is the V7 chord. Any dominant 7th built on any other scale degree is considered to act as a secondary dominant 7th chord (e.g., A7 is a secondary dominant in the key of C).

EXAMPLE 95:

EXAMPLE 96:

Now this relates to improvisation in the following way: a diminished chord, no matter how it functions, can always take a symmetrical diminished scale (whole-half). It may also take a type of diminished scale made up of its chord tones (R 3 5 7) plus the chord tones of its target chord (Example 97). This particular passing or nonsymmetrical diminished scale defines the function and key center more accurately than the symmetrical diminished scale, which tends to create a floating or <u>no key</u> area.

EXAMPLE 97: ♯I°⁷ SCALE

So to summarize--use the symmetrical diminished (whole-half) to create a floating or no key area, and use a passing or nonsymmetrical diminished to accurately define the key area.

<u>Drill:</u>

> Learn the passing (nonsymmetrical) diminished scales in Example 98 in all keys. Although it's not necessary to write these out in all keys, I do recommend it.

EXAMPLE 98:

Here are some tunes that incorporate diminished chords of this nature:

1. "It Could Happen To You"   3. "Call Me Irresponsible"

2. "Birth Of The Blues"   4. "Memories Of You"

184

STANDARD CHORD SCALE PROCEDURE

Now although most chords dictate an obvious chord
scale, some are, at first glance, hard to figure out.
But there are certain critical tones that give this away,
such as whether the 4th degree is natural or sharp;
whether the 2nd degree is natural or sharp; whether the
9th degree is natural, flat or sharp; and whether the 13th
degree is natural or flat. Where do you look for the
answers to these questions?

First:

The obvious place is the chord symbol or chord itself. If the chord is C7♭9♭13, you wouldn't ask yourself whether the 9th and 13th were natural or flat.
That's like asking who is in Grant's tomb! However,
the chord symbol may be wrong, so let's continue.

Second:

Look to the written melody over the chord in question. One or more of the above tones in question
might appear in the melody and thus give you the
answer. For instance, in Example 99a the D♭maj.7
and G♭maj.7 use a Lydian scale, because in the
melody the 4's are sharp (G natural on D♭maj.7 and C
natural on G♭maj.7). Also, in the last measure,
F min.7 takes Aeolian because of the natural 2nd and
flat 6th in the melody.

EXAMPLE 99 A:

Third:

If the answers still aren't apparent, look to the
tonal area preceding the chord in question. In Example 99b, although the melody tells us that the 4th
(11th) is sharp, we may still be unsure about the 9's
and 13's. However, if we look to the D♭maj.7 tonal
area (preceding tonal area), we find that the tones

in question are altered and thus the altered scale is the most correct scale (E♭, D♭, and A♭ are ♯9, ♭9, and ♭13, respectively).

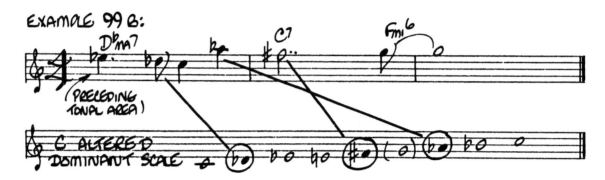

Fourth:

If all the above guidelines still leave you in doubt, look to the tonal area after the chord in question. In Example 99c, the first three techniques still don't tell us what minor scale to use (Dorian, Phrygian, Aeolian, etc). If we look to the following tonal area, we will find a B♭ and F, which tell us that Phrygian is the most obvious chord to the ear.

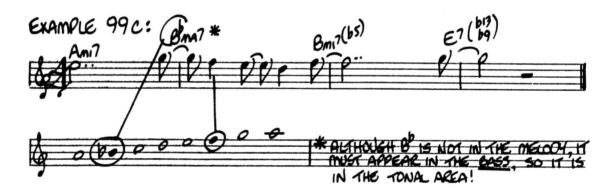

SUMMARY OF CHORD FAMILIES AND RELATED SCALES

a. ## Major Family

Ionian or Lydian, depending upon whether the 4th is natural or sharp respectively.

EXAMPLE 100A: MAJOR FAMILY — C, Cma⁶, Cma⁷

b.   Minor 7th Family

Dorian, Aeolian, Phrygian, depending upon 2nd, and 6th.

If natural 2nd and natural 6th: Dorian.
If natural 2nd and flat 6th: Aeolian.
If flat 2nd and flat 6th: Phrygian.

EXAMPLE 100B: MINOR 7TH FAMILY — Cmi⁷

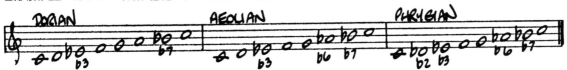

c.   Dominant 7th Family

Because of all the available tensions (9's, 11's, and 13's) in the dominant 7th family, there are about 25 dominant scales. This is so because of this chord's tendency to resolve--in other words, it's very tense! By using the standard chord scale procedure, steps 1-4, you'll be able to determine if the 9th is natural, flat, or sharp; whether the 11th is natural or sharp; and whether the 13th is flat or natural.

I have written out a few of the most historically used dominant 7th scales. Remember, all dominant scales must contain the root, 3rd, and flatted seventh, and all indicated chord tensions must become part of the scale. Also, the word "altered" written after a chord symbol (such as "C alt.") means that at least the 9th is flat or sharp and maybe the 13th is flat.

A final note here is that almost anything goes on this chord, for if you make a composite scale of chord tones plus all available tensions, you get an eleven note scale--the only note not available being the major 7th (B on a C7 chord)--and even that can be used as an approach note!

The rest of the dominant scales not written out
here are simply the remaining permutations available.
Check these out on your own!

EXAMPLE 100 C: DOMINANT 7TH FAMILY

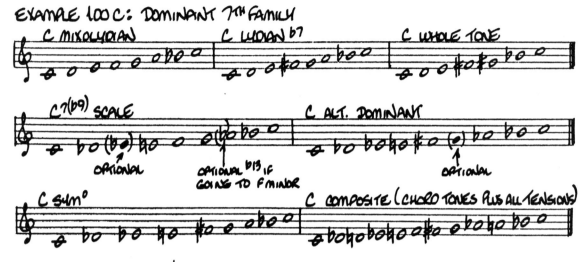

d. Minor 7th (♭5) Family

Almost always takes the Locrian scale. If the
9th is natural, however, it must take Locrian natural
2nd--sometimes called super-Locrian.

EXAMPLE 100 D: Cmi7(♭5) FAMILY

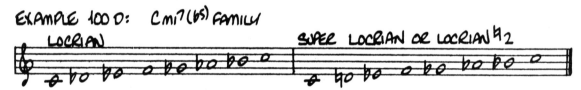

e. Diminished 7th Family

Symmetrical diminished (whole-half) or the
appropriate passing diminished scale.

EXAMPLE 100E: DIM7 FAMILY

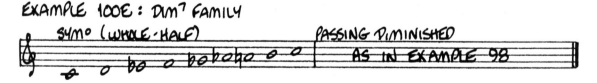

f. Tonic Minor

May take harmonic minor or melodic minor ascending. Check whether 6th is flat or natural!

EXAMPLE 100 F: TONIC MINOR — Cmi, Cmi6, Cmima7

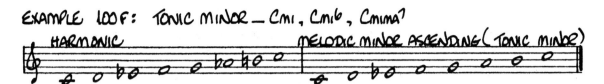

g. Augmented, or Augmented 7th (♮9)

Always takes whole tone scale.

EXAMPLE 100 G: C AUG. or CAUG7(♮9)

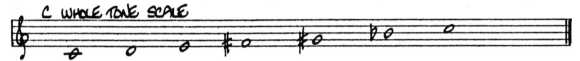

h. Major 7th (♯5) Family

Always takes Lydian with a raised fifth.

EXAMPLE 100 H: MAJOR 7 (+5)

i. 7th Suspended 4th Family

Takes Mixolydian most of the time, but on occasion it may take Dorian 2nd when the 9th is altered and Phrygian when the 9th and 13th are altered. This usually happens when going to I minor (Example: G7 sus.4 to C minor).

EXAMPLE 100 I: C7 sus 4 FAMILY

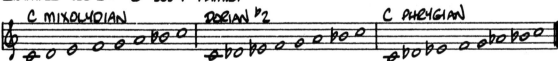

j. Major 7th (♭5) Family

Always takes Lydian because of the flat 5.

EXAMPLE 100 J: C ma7(♭5)

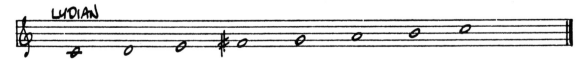

Now let's apply this and analyze a tune or two. Example 101a is a tune by Keith Jarrett called "The Fields We Know." Following is a measure-by-measure breakdown of the standard procedure for determining chord scales.

EXAMPLE 101 A:

THE FIELDS WE KNOW

K. JARRETT

Note: In measure 7 of Example 101a, there are actually a few dominant scale options available, but the altered scale is the most likely choice by the ear!

"THE FIELDS WE KNOW"

Keith Jarrett

MEASURE	QUALITY CHORD	CRITICAL TONES	WHERE FOUND	CHORD SCALE
1	Major 7	4	Natural 4 in Melody (E)	Ionian
2	Major 7	4	Sharp 4 in preceding tonal area (D♯)	Lydian
3	Minor 7	2 and 6	Natural 2nd in melody (G♯) Natural 6th in preceding tonal area (D♯)	Dorian
3	Dom. 7 (sus. 4)	2 and 6	Natural 2nd in melody (C♯) Natural 6th in melody (G♯)	Mixolydian
4	Dom. 7 (sus. 4)	2 and 6	Natural 2nd in preceding tonal area (D♯) Natural 6th in melody (A♯)	Mixolydian
5	Dom. 7 (sus. 4)	2 and 6	Natural 2nd and 6th in preceding tonal area G♯ and D♯	Mixolydian
6	Dom. 7 (sus. 4) to Dom. 7	2 and 6	Although the 2 and 6 are altered in the preceding tonal area, this measure should take Mixolydian because of parallel chord structures.*	Mixolydian
7	Dom. 7	9, 11, 13	♭13 in melody (D♭) ♯9 in previous area (A♯) ♯11 in following tonal area B natural	Altered
8	Major 7	4	Natural 4 in preceding tonal area	Ionian
9	Minor 7 (♭5)	2	♭2 in preceding tonal area (B)	Locrian
10,11,12	Dom. 7 (sus. 4)	2 and 6	Parallel structures	All Mixolydian

* *parallel chord structures*, means same quality chords in succession. By their very nature, they usually take the same type chord scale. Use your ear and decide for yourself, though, because you may want to get creative.

Example 101b, "Autumn Leaves," is chosen so you can see how the two techniques (key centers and chord scale) compare. In this tune, it's actually easier to think and hear the key centers than it is to think of each separate chord scale. You may want to try improvising while alternately thinking each way.

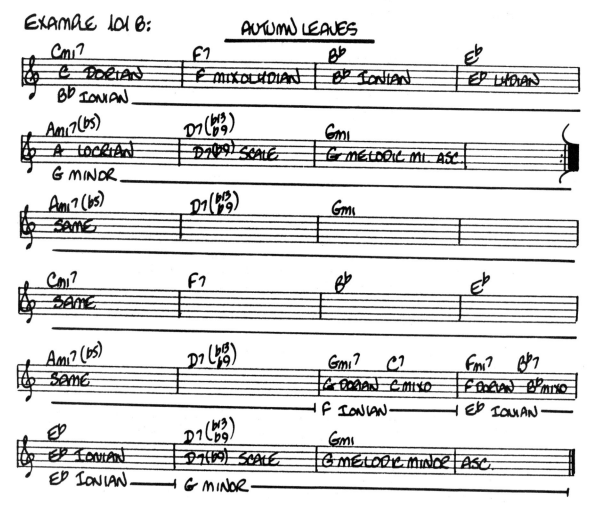

Chord Scale Drill

1. Use the techniques just discussed to analyze any tune for the correct chord scales.

2. Get familiar with each chord scale by exploring its possible intervallic permutations (L.H. comps while R.H. varies the scale).

3. Do the interconnecting scale exercise until you can play through the changes with no effort or stops.

4. Now just improvise by permuting the notes from each chord scale until you're cooking.

5. Now add the basic technology of approach tones, passing tones, chord tones, and tensions to the chord scale permutations (be-bop).

6. Now just play! Do nothing else. Don't think or apply any concepts; just create some sounds over the chords--do whatever you like. In other words, say something--anything! Play! Create! Cook! Burn! Smoke! Communicate! Get the idea?

ADVANCED TECHNIQUES

In order to keep our improvisations fresh and interesting, it's important to have some tools available to "stretch" our ears. Otherwise, we may find ourselves and our audiences getting a little bored with the same bag of licks. The following techniques are therefore very valuable in stimulating this type of creativity.

I would like to acknowledge Gary Burton for his valuable insight and inspiring instruction in this generally undefined area.

Since most of the techniques given will stretch the concept of key center, they can be considered to be "out of key," or, in street talk, "outside" techniques.

You must realize, however, that this is all relative, because "outside" means nothing except when compared to "inside." Inside techniques such as those we have been discussing will have to be mastered before outside techniques will readily work for you.

The following advanced techniques are divided into three areas: melodic, harmonic, rhythmic.

I. MELODIC CONCEPTS

A. Intervallic Playing

Means imposing the restriction of certain intervals
(e.g., perfect 4th, minor 2nd) over progressions.
Intervallic playing can be broken down into five
categories:

1. Strict
2. Altered and/or inverted
3. Connection with foreign intervals
4. Recurrent or repeated intervals
5. All of the above, or free intervallic playing

1. Strict Intervallic - Deciding on a certain
    combination of intervals, such as perfect 4th
    and minor 2nd, and playing strictly that! (See
    Example 102a.) These intervals will take us
    "out of key" at times, but by their inherent
    pattern, they still make melodic sense and add
    some color and tension.

EXAMPLE 102A: STRICT INTERVALLIC (P4 AND MAJOR 2ND)

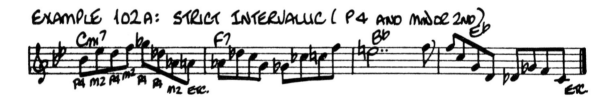

2. Altered and/or Inverted - Instead of, let's say,
    a strict perfect 4th and minor 2nd, using any
    4th (perfect or augmented) and any second (minor
    or major) as well as their inversions (perfect
    5th, diminished 5th, major 7th, minor 7th).
    This simply adds more variety to the above game
    (Example 102b).

EXAMPLE 102B: ALTERED AND/OR INVERTED

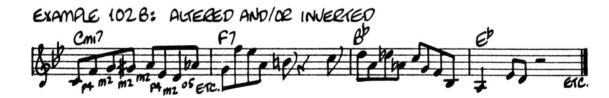

3.   Connection with Foreign Intervals - As in 1 and 2 directly above, except one occasionally gives relief to the intervallic pattern for various musical reasons (e.g., to land on a chord tone) and then resumes the pattern (Example 102c).

EXAMPLE 102C: CONNECTION WITH FOREIGN INTERVALS

4.   Recurrent or Repeated Intervals - Simply repeating the same interval in any pattern in or out of the tonal center (Example 102d). The interval can also be altered or inverted!

EXAMPLE 102D: RECURRENT OR REPEATED INTERVALS

5.   Free Intervallic Playing - Combination of all the above (Example 102e).

EXAMPLE 102E: FREE INTERVALLIC

Intervallic playing also works especially well over one chord and adds much needed color and tension (Example 103).

EXAMPLE 103:

Exercises

1. Write many solos over tunes of your choice in all five different intervallic categories and then learn them.

2. Practice spontaneous soloing in this style until it becomes a useful tool!

Here is a list of some players who use these techniques in some way, shape or form:

Cecil Taylor	McCoy Tyner
Alan Holdsworth	John McGlaughlin
Herbie Hancock	Chick Corea
Keith Jarrett	Don Mock
Mike Brecker	Gary Burton

B.   Scales Within Scales

Means building a strong scale on any note of another scale (Example 104a). In Example 104a the chord scale is C Lydian. We simply pick any note of the scale--let's say E--and build another scale on it, in this case E symmetrical diminished 7. Play the example.

EXAMPLE 104A:

C.   Scale Superimposition

Means instead of playing the proper chord scale, superimpose some other scale over the chord change. Now when the chord changes, simply change to another superimposed scale, and so on. This works best with strongly identifiable scales like whole tone, symmetrical diminished, pentatonic, blues, etc. (See Example 104b.)

EXAMPLE 104B: SCALE SUPER-IMPOSITION

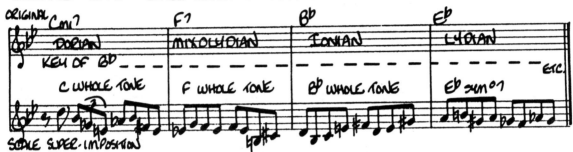

D.   Chromatic Playing (chord tone chromaticism)

Means simply varying the intervals of the chromatic scale. The chromatic scale states no tonality and clashes with none, but really adds a lot of color and variety. It works best, however, by starting on a chord tone, playing chromatically and then landing on some other chord tone. This keeps things musical! (Example 105.)

EXAMPLE 105: CHORD TONE CHROMATICISM

II. HARMONIC CONCEPTS

A. Same Quality - Different Pitch

In Example 106 the top line contains the original changes and the bottom line contains the changes we derive our scales from for improvising. Notice the quality doesn't change (minor 7th stays minor 7th, dominant 7th stays dominant 7th, etc), but the pitch does.

B. Same Pitch - Different Quality

Frequently called modal interchange because one simply changes modes (for example, minor 7th to dominant 7th, or, in other words, Dorian to Mixolydian) (Example 106b). In order for this to qualify as an outside technique, one must play the original chord change, but use the scale of the different quality for improvising. (For example, C Ionian over a C minor 7th chord will produce two "out" notes, E and B.)

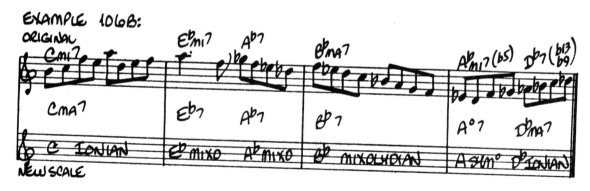

C.   Successive Quality Chords

In this technique, one simply uses successive chord qualities as a bridge to the next chord. Some interesting movements can be obtained with this technique! (Example 106c.)

D.   Chordal Melodies

The logical evolution of all the above harmonic concepts is to simply create an imaginary melody over existing chord changes and then harmonize every note with different quality triads and/or tetrads. Works especially well over stagnant changes! (Example 106d.)

III. RHYTHMIC CONCEPTS

A. Rubato Playing

This is simply "robbing" the time, or speeding up and slowing down, matching up with the original tempo at exciting moments. In other words, the rest of the group plays at one tempo while the soloist purposely either speeds up or slows down--and then matches up again at exciting moments. This works best when playing over one tonal area or color. (No example.) When there are a lot of changes, one can even speed up or slow down the harmonic changes, which can produce a very interesting effect. (No example.)

B. Uneven Subdivisions

Taking some of the polyrhythms we studied in Chapter 10 and applying them melodically, we can create some interesting feels.

Example 107a: 3 against 2

Example 107b: ♩. = new ♩ note of new time. This produces an illusion of a slower time within the original one.

Ultimately, rhythm is a flow. You can shape this rhythmic flow and do anything you like to it as long as you don't lose the <u>original</u> flow--that is, unless you intend to!

<u>Drill</u>:

> Over a stable rhythm--say one created by a metronome or rhythm machine--practice improvising with <u>free</u> rhythms, starting and stopping at will. Relax and play what you hear and hear what you play. Anything you create is all right--just don't lose the flow--unless you want to!

I hope these techniques have stretched your ear and given you some ways to keep your improvisations fresh. Now remember, in the heat of improvisation one just <u>plays</u>! These are practice techniques, not playing techniques. The only valid playing technique I know is simply...to play! The more you do it, the better you'll get!

Chapter 11
ASSIGNMENTS

_____ 1. Describe the differences and similarities of the <u>key center</u> approach to improvisation versus the <u>chord scale</u> approach. Which technique do people who play by ear use?

_____ 2. Do the eleven chord analyses in all fifteen written keys, making sure you follow the indicated procedure (Examples 94a-k).

_____ 3. Explain the symmetrical and nonsymmetrical diminished 7th scales as to what they are and when they may be used. Give examples.

_____ 4. What are the "critical tones" that guide the improviser in choosing the correct chord scales?

_____ 5. What is a workable procedure for determining the correct chord scale for any chord? Explain in detail.

_____ 6. Do the chord scale drill over as many tunes and progressions as necessary until it becomes second nature.

_____ 7. What does playing "outside" mean?

_____ 8. Define <u>intervallic</u> playing and give examples of its <u>five</u> variations. Do the indicated exercises until your understanding becomes the ability to play intervallically!

_____ 9. Define <u>scales within scales</u>, <u>scale superimposition</u>, and <u>chromatic playing</u> and give examples of each.

_____ 10. Name the four "outside" harmonic techniques and give examples.

_____ 11. In what ways can rhythm be used to create interesting improvisational effects?

_____ 12. Try creating your own devices or "games" for enhancing your improvisations. After all, these devices you have just studied were created by people just like you!

SUGGESTED READING

Corea, Chick. Music Poetry. Los Angeles: Litha Music, 1980.

Dallin, Leo. Techniques of Twentieth Century Composition. 2d ed. Dubuque, Iowa: Wm. C. Brown Co. Publishers, 1964.

Russell, George. The Lydian Chromatic Concept of Tonal Organization. New York: Concept Publishing Co., 1959.

Chapter 12

Advanced Harmony

Now that we're familiar with the basic triads and tetrads, along with their tensions, it's time to look at two other aspects of chords:

1. <u>Harmonic Progression</u>, the tendency of chords to <u>resolve to other chords</u> (the choice of a chord to follow a given chord).

2. <u>Voice Leading</u>, the procedure followed in connecting chords, in which each tone in a chord is considered a separate voice or melody and has certain tendencies of movement.

Now, since chords are primarily identified by their roots, chord progressions are best understood by their root progressions, and root progressions can be translated into Roman numerals representing a succession of scale degrees. Although we found in Chapter 6 that a variety of chord qualities may be built on these roots (e.g., C min.7, C maj.7, C7, etc.), this variety of chord colors does not alter the importance of the root relationships. In other words, changing the qualities of chords cannot remedy a weak root progression.

Although the following generalizations do not always hold true, they nevertheless are the tendencies of traditional diatonic root progressions which, if understood, will give an insight into contemporary harmony.

Root ⟶	Usual Tendency ⟶	Sometimes ⟶	Less Often
I	IV or V	VI	II or III
II	V	VI	I, III, or IV
III	VI	IV	II or V
IV	V	I or II	III or VI
V	I	VI or IV	III or II
VI	II or V	III or IV	I
VII	III	I	

The dominant-tonic relationship or progression is definitely the strongest and most traditionally satisfying--ask Haydn, Mozart, Beethoven, etc! (Example 108.) In general, any progression with root motion downwards in fifths or upwards in fourths has an analogous effect (Example 109).

EXAMPLE 108

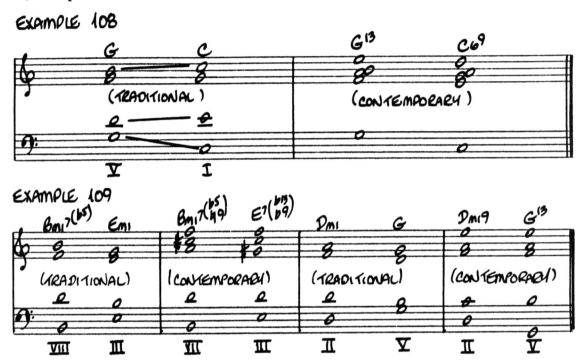

Root motion down a fourth or up a fifth is also very strong, but not as strong as a fifth down or a fourth up, and sounds distinctly different (Example 110).

EXAMPLE 110

Root motion up or down by scale step, although weak, has the interesting effect of producing a completely new harmonic color because it consists of a completely new set of notes (Example 111).

EXAMPLE 111

Root motion in thirds produces a weak but soft effect which is sometimes very useful (Example 112).

EXAMPLE 112

Drill:

At this point you should slowly and repetitively play through all of the above examples in order to acquaint your ear with the indicated root motions.

If one were to study traditional harmony further, the evolution of complex chromatic harmony from this simple diatonic harmony would become evident. Traditional harmony, however, is not the subject of this chapter, so now we will bridge into contemporary harmony and its applications in commercial music.

THE II-V-I PROGRESSION

Understanding the II-V-I progression and all its variations is like opening the door to the land of harmony,
so here goes!

The mechanics of communication in music have to do
with the application of tension and release techniques to
rhythm, harmony, melody, and orchestration. The rhythms
created by applying these techniques to harmony are called
harmonic rhythms. (Thus, a harmonic rhythm is the rhythm
resulting from the movement of chords, one to the next).
The whole reason why chords tend to move or stay at rest
in the first place is based on tension and release. The
less stable a chord is, the more it wants to resolve its
voices to another chord. Chords that tend to stay at rest
may be described as static in nature, while chords that
are unstable and want to move can be described as tense in
nature. Understanding this principle allows the performing musician, as well as the composer and arranger, to use
the best possible harmonies for the desired effect.

Let's begin by looking at the diatonic major progression (Example 113). Although each chord is an entity unto
itself, it can be further grouped into categories that
have specific qualities or behavioral patterns.

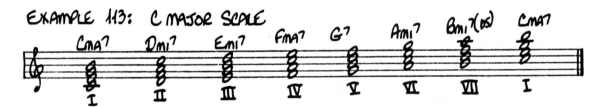

Categories	Chords	Qualities
Tonic (static)	I, III, VI	Stable, no real tendency to move on; release.
Subdominant (axis)	II, IV	Not very stable, tendency to resolve or axis (pivot) to another chord; tense.
Dominant (tension)	V, VII	Very unstable, strong tendency to resolve; very tense.

Later on we will see how this categorical thinking can facilitate reharmonization--the substitution of new chords or harmonies for the basic chords or set of changes.

Also notice that the II-V-I progression fulfills the requirements of all three categories:

II = subdominant = axis (moving)

V = dominant = very tense

I = tonic = static (very stable)

Progressions of this nature are known as cadences. A cadence may be defined as a harmonic progression which suggests a conclusion, if only temporary. The II-V-I progression is known as a full or perfect cadence because of its finality (Example 114). Other cadences derived from these colors or categories are the imperfect or half cadence--tonic to subdominant (Example 115); the plagal or church cadence--subdominant to tonic (Example 116); and the interrupted cadence, commonly known as the deceptive resolution--dominant to some chord other than the tonic (Example 117). Although these are traditional cadences, they--along with their many variations--still constitute to a large extent the basis of contemporary harmony.

EXAMPLE 114: FULL OR PERFECT CADENCE

EXAMPLE 115: HALF OR IMPERFECT CADENCE

EXAMPLE 116: PLAGAL OR CHURCH CADENCE

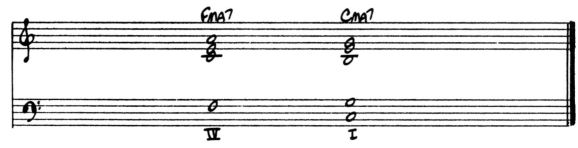

EXAMPLE 117: INTERRUPTED OR DECEPTIVE RESOLUTION CADENCE

THE FLAT 5 DOMINANT 7TH SUBSTITUTE

The most critical notes or voices of most chords are the three and seven. They are known as guide tones, as they actually define a chord's quality or color (major, minor, etc.) and thus lead or guide a chord to its next destination. Guide tones will be discussed in more detail in Chapter 13, "Voicings and Comping." The immediate importance here is in connection with the dominant seventh chord and its substitute. If you take a look at Example 118, you will find that the guide tones for G7 and D♭7 are the same but reversed as to melodic function. The third of G7 is identical to the 7 of D♭7 (B = C♭), while the seventh of G7 is identical to the third of D♭7 (F = F). The fact that the guide tones are identical along with the strong root motion of both progressions--V7 to I in case of G7 to C and ♭II7 to I in case of D♭7 to C--makes for the interchangeability of these two chords. The D♭7 is then known as the substitute V7 of G7 or sub V7/V7 (V7 of V7) (Example 118). Now, not only does this relationship permit substitution, but it allows the two related dominant seventh chords to be used in succession: V7-♭II7-I or ♭II7-V7-I (Example 119).

EXAMPLE 118

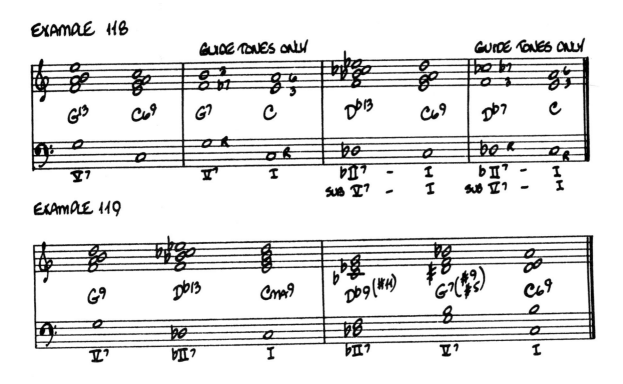

EXAMPLE 119

THE II-V PROGRESSIONS

We now have enough background data to evolve the following important II-V progressions and their permutations:

Progression A:

DOMINANT TO TONIC (V7 - I or G7 - C)

V7 of I Box

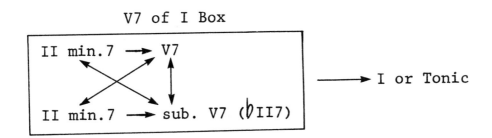

→ I or Tonic

Translated into English, this means that the following progressions are possible using the ♭5 substitute and related II min.7 chords preceding any dominant 7th chord.

The following box relationship is in the key of C for ease of understanding.

G7 to C Box

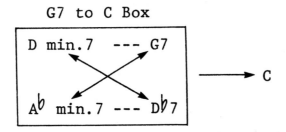

Notice the following progressions that can be derived from these simple relationships:

1. G7 - C
2. D♭7 - C
3. D min.7 - G7 - C
4. D min.7 - D♭7 - C
5. A♭ min.7 - D♭7 - C
6. A♭ min.7 - G7 - C

Drill:

> Write out the V7 of I box relationships, as just discussed, in all other keys and play the six possible resultant chord progressions using standard A-B voicings!

Progression B:

SECONDARY DOMINANT TO DOMINANT TO TONIC (V7/V7 - V7 - I or
D7 - G7 - C)

V7 of V Box

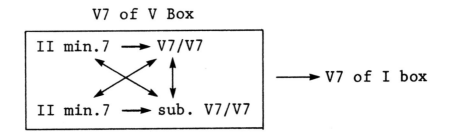

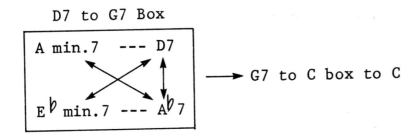

D7 to G7 Box

→ G7 to C box to C

Again, the above example is in the key of C. Since the progressions of this box flow to the previously dis-cussed V7 of I box, the possible progression variations are as follows:

1. D7 to all six progressions of the V7 of I box:

        D7 - G7 - C
        D7 - D♭7 - C
        D7 - D min.7 - G7 - C
        D7 - D min.7 - D♭7 - C
        D7 - A♭ min.7 - D♭7 - C
        D7 - A♭ min.7 - G7 - C

2. A♭7 (sub. V7 of D7) to all six progressions of the V7 of I box:

        A♭7 - G7 - C
        A♭7 - D♭7 - C
        A♭7 - D min.7 - G7 - C
        A♭7 - D min.7 - D♭7 - C
        A♭7 - A♭ min.7 - D♭7 - C
        A♭7 - A♭ min.7 - G7 - C

3. The four possible two-chord progressions of the V7 of
    V box coupled with all six variations of the V7 of I
    box:

    A min.7 - D7 to progress. 1 thru 6 of V7 of I box
    A min.7 - A♭7 to progress. 1 thru 6 of V7 of I box
    E♭ min.7 - A♭7 to progress. 1 thru 6 of V7 of I box
    E♭ min.7 - D7 to progress. 1 thru 6 of V7 of I box

Drill:

    Write out all the V7 of V box relationships to
    V7 of I box relationships as indicated in all
    keys using standard A-B voicings.

Progression C:

SECONDARY DOMINANT TO SUBDOMINANT (V7 TO II min.7) TO
DOMINANT TO TONIC (A7 - D min.7 - G7 - C)

V7 of II min.7 Box

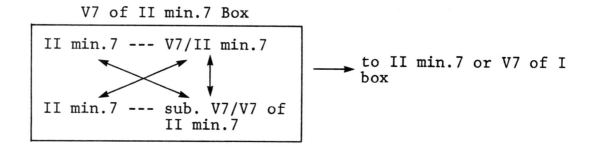

Translated into English this means:

A7 to II min.7 Box

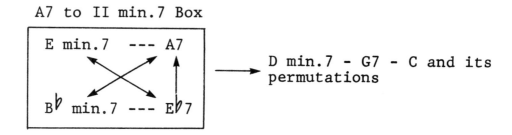

The possible progressions are as follows:

1.   A7 to Nos. 3,4,5,6 of Progression A
2.   E♭7 to Nos. 3,4,5,6 of Progress. A
3.   E min.7 - A7 to Nos. 3,4,5,6 of Progress. A
4.   E min.7 - E♭7 to Nos. 3,4,5,6 of Progress. A
5.   B♭ min.7 - E♭7 to Nos. 3,4,5,6 of Progress. A
6.   B♭ min.7 - A7 to Nos. 3,4,5,6 of Progress. A

Drill:

As before, write out the V7 of II min.7 box relationships in all keys and play all progressions using standard A-B voicings.

Now, to summarize all this madness, here is a diagram of all three progressions and all their possible five-chord progressions!

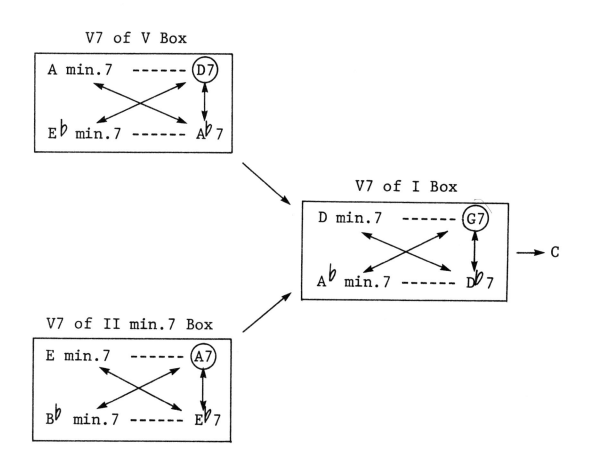

V7 of V Box

V7 of I Box

V7 of II min.7 Box

The chord in the upper right hand corner of each box indicates the name or function of that box. Thus the V7 of V in the key of C is D7, the V7 of II min.7 is A7, the V7 of I is G7. They are circled for easy identification.

There are 32 possible five-chord progressions per key using all three boxes! I have written these out below in the key of C in preparation for the next drill.

Possible five-chord progressions using the V7 of V to V7 of I boxes:

1. A min.7 - D7 - D min.7 - G7 - C
2. A min.7 - D7 - D min.7 - D♭7 - C
3. A min.7 - D7 - A♭ min.7 - D♭7 - C
4. A min.7 - D7 - A♭ min.7 - G7 - C
5. A min.7 - A♭7 - D min.7 - G7 - C
6. A min.7 - A♭7 - D min.7 - D♭7 - C
7. A min.7 - A♭7 - A♭ min.7 - D♭7 - C
8. A min.7 - A♭7 - A♭ min.7 - G7 - C
9. E♭ min.7 - A♭7 - D min.7 - G7 - C
10. E♭ min.7 - A♭7 - D min.7 - D♭7 - C
11. E♭ min.7 - A♭7 - A♭ min.7 - D♭7 - C
12. E♭ min.7 - A♭7 - A♭ min.7 - G7 - C
13. E♭ min.7 - D7 - D min.7 - G7 - C
14. E♭ min.7 - D7 - D min.7 - D♭7 - C
15. E♭ min.7 - D7 - A♭ min.7 - D♭7 - C
16. E♭ min.7 - D7 - A♭ min.7 - G7 - C

Possible five-chord progressions using the V7 of II min.7 to V7 of I boxes:

1. E min.7 - A7 - D min.7 - G7 - C

2. E min.7 - A7 - D min.7 - D♭7 - C

3. E min.7 - A7 - A♭ min.7 - D♭7 - C

4. E min.7 - A7 - A♭ min.7 - G7 - C

5. E min.7 - E♭7 - D min.7 - G7 - C

6. E min.7 - E♭7 - D min.7 - D♭7 - C

7. E min.7 - E♭7 - A♭ min.7 - D♭7 - C

8. E min.7 - E♭7 - A♭ min.7 - G7 - C

9. B♭ min.7 - E♭7 - D min.7 - G7 - C

10. B♭ min.7 - E♭7 - D min.7 - D♭7 - C

11. B♭ min.7 - E♭7 - A♭ min.7 - D♭7 - C

12. B♭ min.7 - E♭7 - A♭ min.7 - G7 - C

13. B♭ min.7 - A7 - D min.7 - G7 - C

14. B♭ min.7 - A7 - D min.7 - D♭7 - C

15. B♭ min.7 - A7 - A♭ min.7 - D♭7 - C

16. B♭ min.7 - A7 - A♭ min.7 - G7 - C

II min.7 - V7 Drill:

1. Write out all three boxes in all keys as per the example in the key of C.

2. Write out all the 32 possible five-chord progressions in each key.

3. Play all progressions using standard A-B voicings in the following manner:

    a. Left hand bass, right hand voicing (Example 120a).

EXAMPLE 120A:

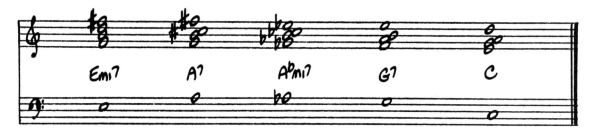

    b. Left hand voicing and right hand voicing an octave above (Example 120b).

EXAMPLE 120B:

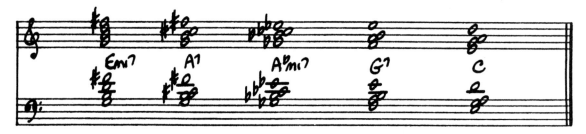

I hope these drills have shed some light on the importance as well as the possibilities of the II/V progression.

SUBDOMINANT MINOR

The subdominant minor category is simply the minor version of the axis or moving pole, as discussed earlier--subdominant. The subdominant minor category contains the following chords:

    II min.7♭5
    IV min.7, IV min.(maj.)7, IV min.6
    ♭II maj.7
    ♭VI maj.7
    ♭VII7
    ♭VI7
    V7 sus.4(♭9)

These chords all have the 6th degree in common (A in the key of C). Now let's look at all four poles or categories together, in the key of C, to put things in perspective. Notice that the subdominant category has been expanded to include the following nondiatonic chords:

    II7
    IV7
    ♭VII maj.7
    ♯IV min.7(♭5)

The reason for this is that these chords simply function as a subdominant pole or color.

Tonic		Subdominant	
I	- C maj.7	II, II7	- D min.7, D7
III	- E min.7	IV, IV7	- F maj.7, F7
VI	- A min.7	♭VII maj.7	- B♭ maj.7
		♯IV min.7(♭5)	- F♯ min.7(♭5)

Subdominant Minor

II min.7($\flat$5) - D min.7($\flat$5)

IV min.7 - F min.7

IV min.(maj.)7, IV min.6 - F min.(maj.)7, F min.6

$\flat$II maj.7 - D$\flat$ maj.7

$\flat$VI7, $\flat$VI maj.7 - A$\flat$7, A$\flat$ maj.7

$\flat$VII7 - B$\flat$7

V7 sus.4($\flat$9) - G7 sus.4($\flat$9)

Dominant

V7 - G7

VII - B min.7($\flat$5)

Categorizing chords in this manner, as to function or color, facilitates chord substitutions and reharmonizations, as we shall see later. However, let's continue by looking at other harmonic phenomena, which, if understood, will assist us in analyzing chord progressions:

OTHER HARMONIC PHENOMENA

1. Nonfunctioning Dominant Chords

These are dominant chords that don't obey the normal II-V or V-I type cadence. Categorically these chords function as axis or moving harmonies and therefore are subdominant in nature. Example: II7-IV-I; I-III7-IV.

2. Pivot Chords

These are chords that function in two tonal areas simultaneously and therefore act as a transition or pivot to a new tonal area.

For example:

/ E♭   / G min.7   C7 / F maj.7   / F min.7   B♭7 /
Key of E♭ -----------
                   Key of F ----------------

                   pivot
                   chord (G min.7):

                   Functions as III min.7 chord in the key of
                   E♭, and functions as II min.7 to V7 in the
                   key of F.

Pivot chords are very useful in making smooth musical transitions to new key areas.

3.   Diminished 7th Chords

As stated earlier, there are basically two types:

a.   Chromatic or Passing:

Simply connects two chords chromatically.   For example:

II min.7 - ♯II°7 - I6

(I6 means a chord in 1st inversion)*

IV - ♯IV°7 - I$\frac{6}{4}$

(I$\frac{6}{4}$ means a chord in 2nd inversion)*

See Example 121a.

_____

* These symbols are a musical shorthand, called figured bass, that was widely used by composers in the early 18th century. The Roman numeral identifies the root, while the Arabic numeral (e.g., 6, $\frac{6}{4}$, etc.) identifies the inversion.

EXAMPLE 121 A: CHROMATIC OR PASSING DIM 7TH CHORDS

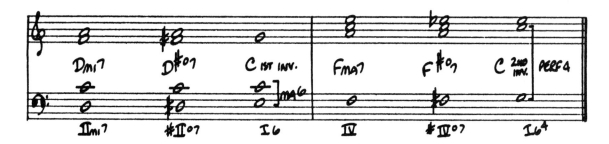

b. Secondary Dominant:

Actually functions like a dominant-tonic cadence (V7 to I):

II min.7 - #II°7 - III min.7 is really

II min.7 - V7(♭9)/III - III min.7

or

D min.7 - D#°7 - E min.7 is really

D min.7 - B7(♭9)/D# - E min.7

See Example 121b.

EXAMPLE 121B: SECONDARY DOMINANT DIM 7TH CHORDS

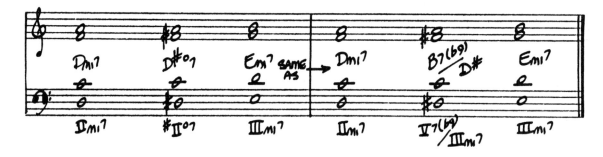

This relationship becomes very important in re-harmonization, which we will discuss later.

4. Deceptive Cadence

In general, this is a cadence which resolves in a way not quite predicted--hence it is deceptive. In this type of cadence, some other chord is substituted for the expected resolution. So instead of V7-I, we might try V7-VI min.7, which is by far the most common. The deceptive resolution is a very useful compositional device and is used to sustain musical interest, for extended ideas, etc.

The following deceptive resolutions are the most common and should be learned in all keys. V7 to I is the expected cadence. The progression examples that follow the deceptive cadences are not the only possibilities. They are just examples that suggest how the deceptive resolution might be used. Feel free to create your own--the possibilities are endless!

V7(G7)

to a. VI min.7 (A min.7) etc., e.g.,
G7 - A min.7 - D7 - D min.7 - G7 - C maj.7

to b. III min.7 (E min.7) etc., e.g.,
G7 - E min.7 - E♭°7 - D min.7 - G7 - C maj.7

to c. III min.7♭5 (E min.7♭5) etc., e.g.,
G7 - E min.7(♭5) - A7 - D min.7 - G7 - C maj.7

to d. V7 of VI (E7) etc., e.g.,
G7 - E7 - A min.7 - D min.7 - G7 - C maj.7

to e. sub V7/VI (B♭7), etc., e.g.,
G7 - B♭7 - A min.7 - D min.7 - G7 - C maj.7

to f. ♭III maj.7 (E♭ maj.7), etc., e.g.,
G7 - E♭ maj.7 - A♭ maj.7 - D♭ maj.7 - C maj.7

to g. ♭VI maj.7 (A♭ maj.7), etc., e.g.,
G7 - A♭ maj.7 - D♭ maj.7 - C maj.7

to h. ♭II maj.7 (D♭ maj.7), etc., e.g.
G7 - D♭ maj.7 - C maj.7

to i. ♯IV min.7♭5 (F♯ min.7♭5), etc., e.g.,
G7 - F♯ min.7(♭5) - F min.6 - E min.7 - E♭7 - D min.7 - G7 - C maj.7

to j. ♭VII maj.7 (B♭ maj.7), etc., e.g.,
G7 - B♭ maj.7 - E♭ maj.7 - A♭ maj.7 - D♭ maj.7 - C maj.7

to k. IV7(F7), etc., e.g.,
G7 - F7 - C/E - D min.7 - C7♯11

5.   Substitute Chords

These are chords that substitute for other chords because of certain musical phenomena. They are used to add variety to a composition. Because of the infinite possibilities, they are best understood grouped into categories:

Category A: Similar Function - Similar Notes

Usually means similar notes over a different root, which adds a slightly different musical effect without destroying the main musical idea.

Examples:

1.   Flat five substitutes
(Db7 for G7, etc.) (Example 122a)

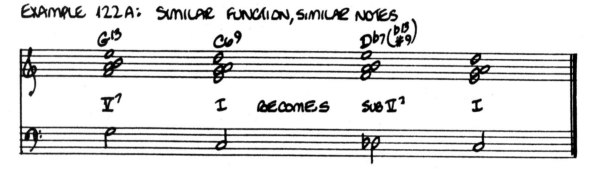

2.   bVII7 for IV min.6 or II min.7b5
(Bb7 for F min.6 or D min.7b5)
(Example 122b)

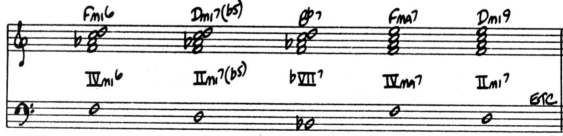

3. Secondary dominant diminished 7th chords that take the II min.7($\flat$5) - V7($\flat$9) substitute (Example 122c):

EXAMPLE 122C:

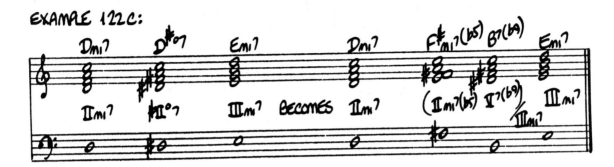

II min.7 - $\sharp$II°7 - III min.7 may be altered to II min.7 - (II min.7$\flat$5 - V7$\flat$9)/III min.7 - III min.7

or

D min.7 - D$\sharp$ min.7 - E min.7 may be altered to D min.7 - F$\sharp$ min.7($\flat$5) - B7($\flat$9) - E min.7

Explanation:

Since the target chord of the $\sharp$II°7 chord is E min.7, it is logical that we may precede the secondary dominant diminished 7th chord, which in fact actually is a V7$\flat$9 chord (B7$\flat$9), by its related II min.7$\flat$5 chord (F$\sharp$ min.7$\flat$5). This then sets up a II-V progression to the III min.7 chord and the result is F$\sharp$ min.7$\flat$5 - B7$\flat$9 - E min.7. Because of the symmetrical properties of the diminished chord, there are three other possible II-V substitutions, but they come under the next category.

Category B: Similar Function - Dissimilar Notes

This is where the "pole" system we discussed earlier comes into play--tonic, subdominant, subdominant minor, and dominant. The reason these poles exist is because of their similar function--and, in most cases, dissimilar notes (Example 123). It therefore follows that any chord from the same pole or family is interchangeable with another, the only contingencies being the melody, style, and musical taste. This is a great technique for reharmonizing a composition and will be taken up very shortly.

EXAMPLE 123: SIMILAR FUNCTION — DISSIMILAR NOTES

Also, as discussed in Category A, there are three alternate possible diminished chord substitutes.

For example, if you recall the II-#II°7-III progression, D min.7 - D#°7 - E min.7 became D min.7 - F# min.7(♭5) - B7(♭9) - E min.7. Using the symmetrical property of the diminished 7th chord, one soon discovers that D#°7, F#°7, A°7, and C°7 are basically the same chord. It follows, therefore, that D#°7 in this progression has four possible substitutions:

1. D#°7 = F# min.7♭5 - B7♭9
2. F#°7 = A min.7♭5 - D7♭9
3. A°7 = C min.7♭5 - F7♭9
4. C°7 = E♭ min.7♭5 - A♭7♭9

Number 1 is Category A (Similar Function - Similar Notes) and Number 2, 3, and 4 substitutions are Category B (Similar Function - Dissimilar Notes). Because of strong root motion, Number 1 is usually the best (root motion is a fifth), 3 is next (root motion is a half step), and then either 2 or 4 because of their weaker root motion of a whole step and a major third. Of course the melody of the composition will play a part in determining which substitutions, if any, will be used.

Category C: Dissimilar Function - Common Nondiatonic Note

For example, in the key of C, let's use the nondiatonic note D-sharp. The common reharmonization is V7#5 (G7#5). Any chord, therefore, which contains a D# could be considered a potential substitution. In Example 124, B7, F7, and C°7 are all potential substitutions. Again, one should consider root motion, melody, style, and musical taste to determine what works and what doesn't.

EXAMPLE 124: DISSIMILAR FUNCTION — COMMON NON DIATONIC NOTE

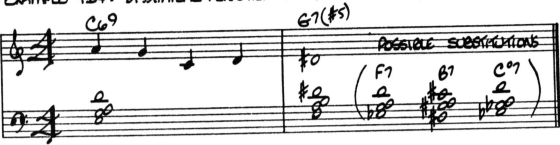

6. Additional Chords

This is the addition of one or more chords into an existing chord progression to give it more forward motion and variety. Example 125a is a simple twelve-bar blues. Notice the additional chords in measures 1,2,3,4,6,7 and 8. They help the forward motion and add variety without destroying the original progression's intent.

EXAMPLE 125A: ADDITIONAL CHORDS

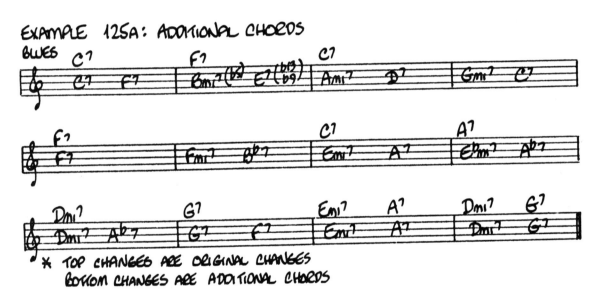

* TOP CHANGES ARE ORIGINAL CHANGES
  BOTTOM CHANGES ARE ADDITIONAL CHORDS

In Example 125b, notice the additional chords added between C min.7 and A♭ maj.7 and between A♭ maj.7 and F min.7. Again, this technique should be used tastefully with due regard to the melody, style, rhythm, etc. It can also be a valuable tool for the improviser, for it gives you more changes to create on!

EXAMPLE 125 B: ADDITIONAL CHORDS

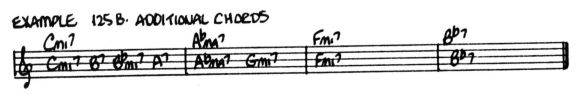

7.   Modal Interchange (M.I.)

Means interchanging one mode (scale) or chord color for another. The pitch axis or root remains the same but the mode or quality changes. For example, C maj.7 may become C min.7, C7, C min.7(♭5), C°7, etc.

    a.   <u>Picardy Third</u> - the use of a major third in the <u>final chord</u> of a composition in a minor mode. This qualifies as modal interchange, as the expected minor chord is changed to a different color--in this case, <u>major</u>.

    b.   <u>Other Uses</u> - In Example 126, an excerpt from "Body and Soul" and a simple blues progression are used to demonstrate some modal interchange possibilities. Play the examples so you can hear the difference.

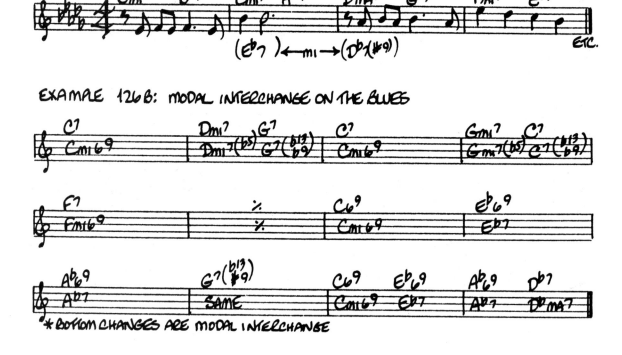

Modal interchange can be very useful in contemporary music, especially when that needed color or variety is sought.

Progression Analysis

Before going on with more harmonic phenomena, let's look at the progression analysis in Example 127, which demonstrates the harmonic concepts just discussed. This progression has been analyzed according to chord function. All II-V progressions as well as substitute II-V progressions are bracketed for easy recognition. All other chords are identified with appropriate Roman numerals as to their key and function. Special categories such as nonfunctioning dominant chords or modal interchange chords are indicated separately by their abbreviations. The four poles--tonic, subdominant, subdominant minor, and dominant--are also indicated below each chord.

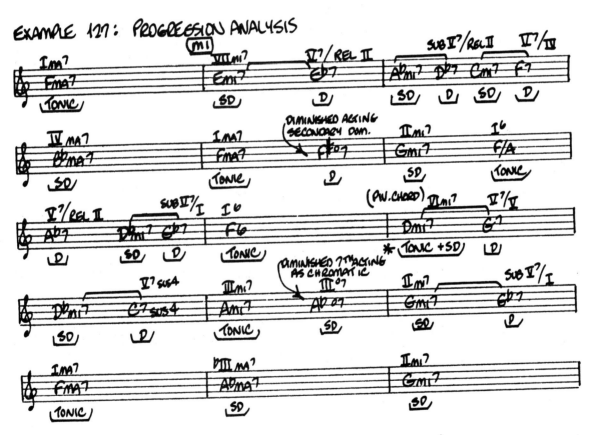

EXAMPLE 127: PROGRESSION ANALYSIS

* SINCE D7 IS A PIVOT CHORD, IT HAS A DUAL FUNCTION — TONIC IN KEY OF F AND SUBDOMINANT IN KEY OF C.

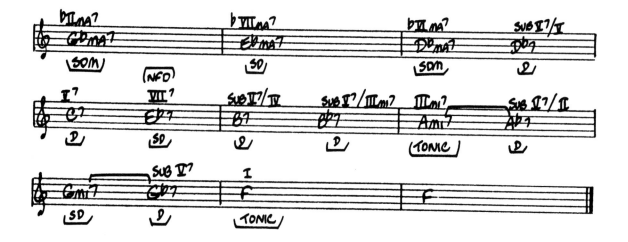

The following is a list of abbreviations used:

- SD   =   Subdominant
- SDM   =   Subdominant minor
- MI   =   Modal interchange
- NFD   =   Nonfunctioning dominant
- SEC DOM =   Secondary dominant

- V7/Rel II min.7 = V7 of the related II min.7 of a
  II-V progression (e.g., G7 is V7 of C min.7 in the
  II-V progression C min.7 - F7).

- Sub V7/Rel II min.7 = Sub V7 of the related II min.7
  of a II-V progression (e.g., Db7 is sub V7 of C min.7
  in the II-V progression C min.7 - F7).

- Piv. Ch. = Pivot Chord

Drill:

    Study the given analysis of the chord progres-
    sion in Example 127 until it is fully compre-
    hended. Look up any misunderstood or not-
    understood chord functions.

    The main benefit of chord analysis is an increased
harmonic awareness. This increased harmonic perception
will facilitate improvisation, arranging and composing,
reharmonization, and transposition. Actually, what we're
talking about here is better ears!

Let's continue on now with some further interesting harmonic phenomena.

8. Pedal Points

A pedal point is a note, usually but not necessarily in the bass voice, which is sustained while harmonic progressions, with which it may be discordant, continue above it. It's commonly referred to as simply a pedal. The pedal can be sustained, as in Johann Sebastian Bach's Fugue in C Minor (Example 128a), or rhythmic, as in Chick Corea's "No Mystery" (Example 128b). Although the above two examples occur at the tonic, pedal points are also common at the dominant: note the possible pedal on the first few bars of the bridge of Rodgers & Hart's "My Funny Valentine" (Example 128c). Actually, a pedal is valid wherever you can make it work, so feel free to experiment!

EXAMPLE 128A: FUGUE IN C MINOR   BACH

NO MYSTERY:
No Mystery by Chick Corea. © Litha Music. Used By Permission.

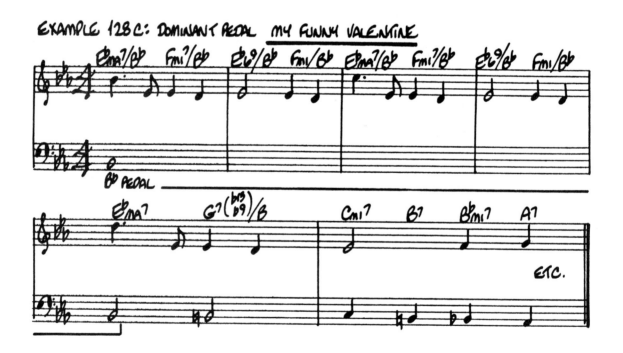

MY FUNNY VALENTINE:
By Rogers & Hart, © Hal Leonard Publishing. Used By Permission.

It's also not uncommon to have a "soprano" pedal or lead voice pedal sounding while the harmony changes underneath (Example 128d). In this example, D is common to all chords and produces a nice contrast while the harmony changes. Since the first four bars of the excerpt are in G minor, the D soprano pedal acts as a dominant pedal (D is the fifth of G minor). Since the next four bars are in B♭ major, the D soprano pedal acts as a <u>mediant</u> pedal, the name given to the third degree of a scale.

EXAMPLE 128 D: SOPRANO PEDAL

Pedals, as you can see, can create some interesting colors and tension. They work especially well in intros, bridges, and endings. Next time you listen to some music, be it commercial, jazz, classical, film scores, or whatever, see if you can hear any.

<u>Drill</u>:

Try and create some pedals in some familiar songs, either your own or other artists'.

9. Inversions

As discussed in Chapter 6, inversions are useful in creating stepwise bass motion, either ascending or descending. Although most of the motion is chromatic, whole steps may also occur. The resultant characteristic sonority of inversions, when used tastefully, can change a simple overused progression into a completely new and fresh sound (Example 129a). Notice the strong ascending chromatic line that was created by the use of two inversions (D♭/F - F♯°7 - C min./G). Try this same progression in all root positions, and notice the difference!

EXAMPLE 129A: INVERSIONS

Example 129b is an excerpt from a song entitled "America" that I co-wrote with my wife, Gloria. Notice the use of inversions and how they create a strong descending bass line. The bottom note of an inversion is almost without exception either the 3rd, 5th, or 7th. Tensions don't occur because the notes that are normally tensions now actually function as bass notes of other chords--usually some altered, modal, or hybrid (incomplete) structure (Examples 129c and d).

EXAMPLE 129 B: AMERICA   J. NOVELLO
G. RUSCH ©

EXAMPLE 129 C:

EXAMPLE 129 D:

Last, tensions are available in the upper voices of inversions, but are usually unnecessary because the inversion is already a rich, in-motion sound (Examples 129e and f).

EXAMPLE 129 E: EXAMPLE 129 F:

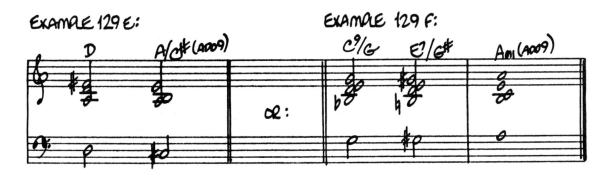

10. Incomplete or Hybrid Chords

These are four-part or five-part chords with the third omitted, creating a characteristic ambiguous sound.

In four-part hybrids, the upper three notes form an independent triad in any position (Example 130a). In five-part hybrids, the upper four notes form an independent seventh chord in any position (Example 130b). In order to maintain the characteristic sound of the hybrid chord, avoid using the third as a permanent melody note--otherwise you will complete the chord and destroy the hybrid. (No example.)

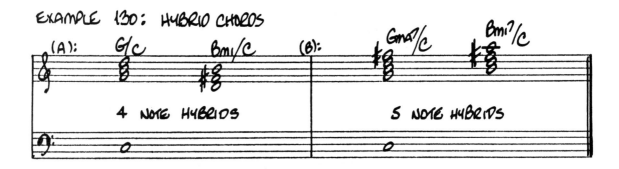

For improvisational purposes, however, you may ignore the incomplete chord, treat it as a complete chord and name it in the usual manner, from its root. Thus, Examples 130a and b are really C maj.7th chords. This makes things a lot easier for soloing.

All in all, the hybrid sound is fresh and contemporary and can add some needed ambiguity to standard chord voicings (Example 130c). Experiment on your own and try to incorporate these sounds in your writing or playing.

Drill:

>   Create as many hybrid structures as you can over the six chord qualities by eliminating the third and forming triads or tetrads over the root.

11. Constant Structures

A constant structure is a selected chord quality or structure that is simply transposed to various pitches for the purpose of harmonizing a given root progression or melody (Example 131a). This device may be used to generate a chord progression for introductions, interludes, etc. (Example 131b), or even for writing complete songs. Ron McClure's "Nimbus" consists of constant structures based on a diminished seventh chord root configuration--8 bars of C min.7, 8 bars of E♭ min.7, 8 bars of G♭ min.7 and 8 bars of A min.7 (C°7 = C - E♭ - G♭ - A). Compositionally, this is known as a four-tonic system because of its four different keys or tonics. This tonic system concept can be used with any created root configuration.

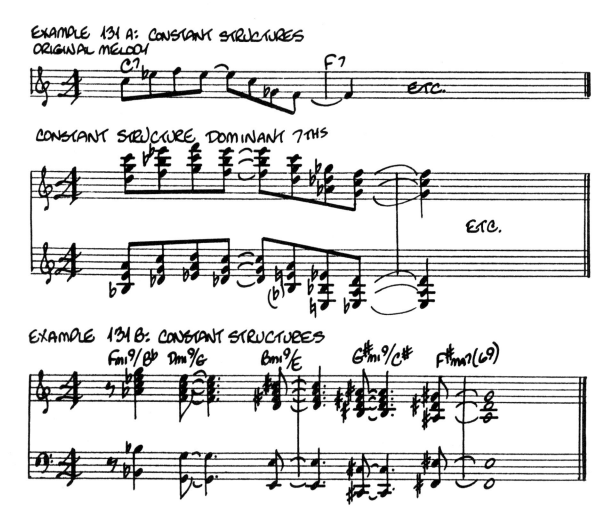

Examples:

1.   C - E♭ - G♯ = a three-tonic system
2.   C - F♯ = a two-tonic system
3.   C - D - E - G♭ - A♭ - B♭ = a six-tonic system

The root series may also be very complex, such as:

D-F-E-B♭-A-C-B-F-E-G-G♭-C

If you haven't figured out the pattern, here it is:

1.   up a minor third
2.   down a half step
3.   up a flat fifth
4.   down a half step
5.   continue steps 1 through 4

Get the idea?

12. Modulation

Simply stated, modulation is a change of key, or movement from one tonality to another. It is the harmonic and/or melodic technique of making a transition from one key to another.

There are two types of modulation:

a. Cadential
b. Deceptive

The first type of cadential modulation, given in Example 132a, is one in which the original melody is not changed, but a compatible progression or turnaround is written to set up the new key--in this case D --a half step up.

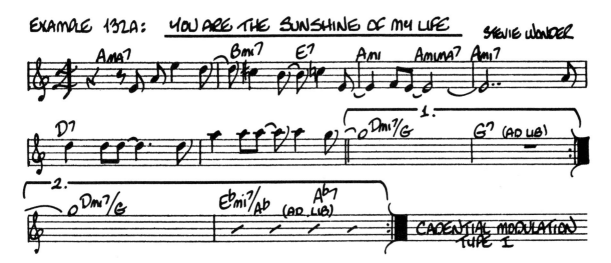

EXAMPLE 132A: YOU ARE THE SUNSHINE OF MY LIFE   STEVIE WONDER

The second type of cadential modulation, given in Example 132b, is one in which the melody is actually changed or altered--usually to fit a preconceived harmonic progression--in this case, a half step downward!

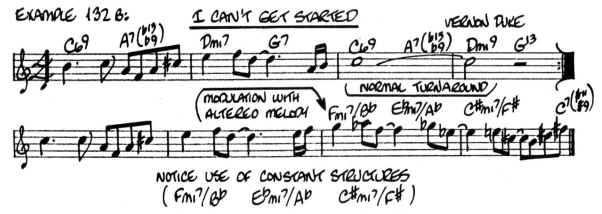

Type one is best suited for singers, while type two is ideal for instrumentals--although they both work either way. When using cadential modulation, the song is either left intact as to form, or lengthened to accommodate the transitional progression to the new key. It is more common to leave the form intact.

The deceptive modulation is exactly what it says-- deceptive and usually very sudden. It uses a pivot chord, which of course functions in the original key and the target key simultaneously. This usually results in a shortened form and is consequently used a lot in instrumental music, as the melody is cut short. (Cutting lyrics is tricky business!) This technique is therefore ideal for use in film scores and medleys because of all the deceptive and sudden changes demanded. Example 132c demonstrates a deceptive modulation between "Yesterday" and "Michelle." Although the modulation is unexpected and abrupt, it nevertheless works quite well!

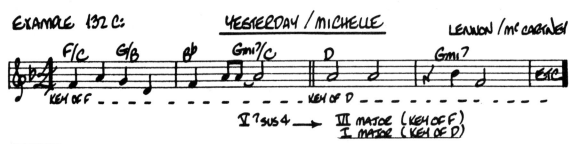

13. Transposition

Transposition is defined in The New College Encyclopedia of Music as "the performance or writing down of music at another pitch and therefore in a different key from that in which it is originally written." Because of the well-tempered system, which divides the octave into twelve equal parts called semitones (half steps), all keys are mathematically equal. It is this equality or symmetry of keys which makes transposition possible. Any melody or harmonic progression can be transposed to any other (Example 133). All keyboardists should acquire expertise at transposing, especially if they are working with singers!

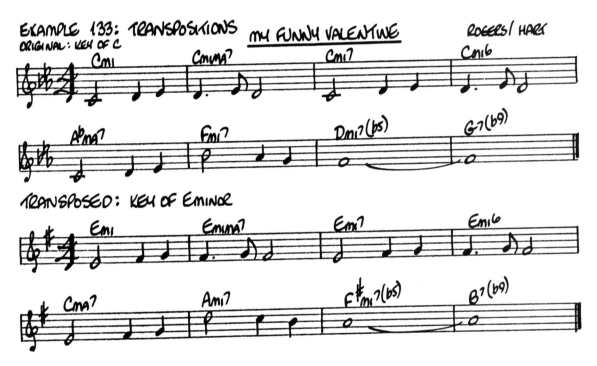

The following are two workable standard procedures that you can use as aids to transposing:

a. Intellectual Transposition

This means determining the interval separating the original key and the new key and then transposing all chords and melodies using that interval. In Example 133, the interval between C minor and E minor is a major third. Thus, all changes and melodies are raised a major third.

Standard Procedure:

(1) Figure out the interval between original and new key.

(2) If the song has a key signature, write in the signature of the new key.

(3) If the song has chord symbols, transpose all chord symbols.

(4) Next, transpose all written-out notes.

(5) Double check your written-out transposition by playing it.

b.   Ear Transposition

Simply means playing the song or phrase in the new key with little or no "thinkingness"--just doing it by ear!

Standard Procedure:

(Note: It is assumed that one knows the song or phrase to be transposed fairly well already; otherwise this type of on-the-spot transposition can be extremely difficult. The only exception would be musicians, such as sax or trumpet players, who have practiced transposing certain intervals on the spot. The theory here is that the ear cannot take over unless it knows the song or phrase to be transposed!)

(1) Quickly analyze the composition, noticing any standard harmonic progressions or groupings that may facilitate transposition.

(2) Note what degree of the scale the melody starts on (i.e., a third, fifth, etc).

(3) Last, rely totally on your ear and simply go for it, intellectualizing whenever you get into trouble.

My advice is to use whatever works the best for you. The logical thing to do is to use your ear _and_ your mind as necessary, depending on the degree of difficulty of the composition.

Transposition is one of those abilities that only gets better by _constant_ practice--otherwise it definitely gets rusty.

Drills:

1.   Take about ten tunes or more that you know well and do an intellectual transposition in all keys (written out), and then play them.

2.   Sit at the piano and play melodies _you know well_ in many keys, preferably ones that you can sing, like nursery rhymes, etc. Play the melody with both hands by just arbitrarily dropping your fingers on any note and then playing the intended melody by ear.

The secret is to confront, confront, and confront until you can do it, okay? Go for it!

Here are two additional terms you should know:

Transposing Instrument, an instrument whose natural key is not C. For example, a clarinet in B♭, which is a whole step below C, would have to play a written D in order to sound a C. The transposition, therefore, is up a whole step. This can be accomplished in two ways: the player either transposes on the spot, playing every written note up a whole step (any good player is capable of this), or the composer or arranger simply writes the music up a whole step. The latter is by far the most efficient.

Concert Pitch, means standard international pitch: A above middle C is fixed at 440 cycles per second. This means the _written pitch_ is the same as the _sounding pitch_! The piano is an example of a concert pitched instrument--its

written A 440 sounds as A 440. For more information on the various instruments and their
ranges, one should study arranging and composition. Check out the "Recommended Reading" at
the end of the book if you are interested in
this area.

14. Approach Chords

These are chords or structures that embellish or
serve as an approach to preexisting chords. Their purpose
is to add color and variety to the basic chord changes.
There are three basic types of approaches:

a. Constant Structure

All voices or notes approach the target chord in
parallel motion from the same interval. Although the most used intervallic approach is the
chromatic from above or below, any interval may
be used (whole step, minor third, etc.) (Example
134).

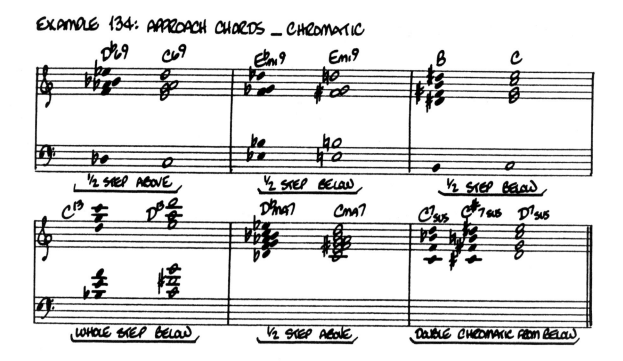

EXAMPLE 134: APPROACH CHORDS — CHROMATIC

b. Dominant Approach

This uses the basic V-I relationship or its sub
V-I (♭II-I). Notice that the voices do not move
in parallel motion (Example 135).

EXAMPLE 135: DOMINANT APPROACH

c. Independent Voices

Each voice of the chord may act completely independently and approach the target chord from any
interval. Chords resulting from this technique
are sometimes difficult to name, as the vertical
structures are not as important as the linear
motion (left to right movement) (Example 136).

EXAMPLE 136: INDEPENDENT VOICES APPROACH

VOICE 1 : UP AN AUGMENTED 4TH
VOICE 2 : UP A HALF-STEP
VOICE 3 : UP A WHOLE-STEP
VOICE 4 : UP A HALF-STEP
VOICE 5 : DOWN A HALF STEP

In summary, approach techniques add motion to harmonies and therefore are very useful to the player, arranger, and composer. Again, as always, you should experiment
on your own.

15. Reharmonization

Reharmonization is tastefully changing or altering
the existing harmony of a song or composition or part of a
song or composition through the use of substitute chords,
additional chords, modal interchange, hybrid structures,

and/or whatever. Although it is a chance to be creative, reharmonization is usually done for practical musical reasons such as these:

1. Creating custom arrangements for a particular artist (vocal or instrumental)

2. Film and TV scoring

3. Writing medleys

4. Adding variety or a fresh sound to old material

Example 137 is one possible musical reharmonization of "Green Dolphin Street." I have put the original and the reharmonized versions together so you can compare. Each reharmonization is numbered and explained as follows:

GREEN DOLPHIN STREET.

Reharmonization of "Green Dolphin Street"

1-2. <u>Constant Structures and Additive Chords</u> - Since the note C is common to all major seventh chords, these two techniques work well by creating rhythmic and harmonic variety. Notice how the rhythm of the melody is slightly altered.

3. <u>Modal Interchange</u> - D7, the secondary dominant, which is already a modal interchange (D min.7 to D7), is changed back to D min.7 and the pedal point is discarded to create good root motion from the previous measure.

4. <u>Additive Chords</u> - Since D min.7 is the target chord, a strong chromatic bass line was added to create more motion and variety. The progression is thus analyzed as follows:

I maj.7 - VII min.7$^{\flat}$5 - $\flat$VII min.7 - V7/II min.7 - II min.7, etc.

Again, care was taken to make sure the chords were compatible with the melody note G.

5. Deceptive Modulation - A compatible II-V-I-IV progression was used to reharmonize this section. (Modulation was from C to E♭.)

6. II-V Box Theory and Modal Interchange - Since we're headed toward F minor, a II-V to F minor is the strongest progression possible in this style (G min.7♭5 to C7 altered). By using the possible substitutes we come up with D♭ min.7 to C7 or D♭7 to C7, which is fine, but since we're already on a roll with the previous two major 7 chords, we keep the circle of fifths and constant major seventh structures going by the use of modal interchange (D♭7 to D♭ maj.7). Notice how the melody was changed to accommodate the C7 altered chord (A♭ on beats 3 and 4).

7-8. Sub V7 Dominant Approach - These dominant approaches from a half step above work very well. Technically, they're sub V7 dominant approaches.

9. Constant Structures and Additive Chords - Simply a string of major seventh chords that are compatible with the melody.

10. Hybrid Chords - Although F♯/B is technically a major seventh chord, it is treated separately because it functions as a hybrid--the third is omitted, thus creating an ambiguous fresh sound. For improvisational purposes, one treats it as a B maj.7th.

11-13. More sub V7 dominant approaches to add tighter voice movement, if desired (C7♭9 to B min.7♭5, F13 to E7♭9, and B♭7♯11 to A min.11).

14. Constant Parallel Structures - Parallel minor sevenths with the eleventh in the lead.

15. Dominant Approach - Sub V7 to E min.7 (F7 to E min.7).

16. Modal Interchange - E min.7 to A7 is simply a II-V progression. By changing A7 to its sub V7(E♭7), and then changing E♭7 to E♭maj.7 by use of modal interchange, a nice color is created. Try E♭7, it works great too.

17. <u>Deceptive Resolution</u> - The second-to-last measure sets up the I chord because it is a II-V. By going to the ♭VI maj.7 (D♭ maj.7), however, we are guilty of deceiving the listener. The effect created is a "suspended" feeling. Notice that the melody note G is the sharp 11 of the reharmonization chord, D♭maj.7.

You should now play through this reharmonization in order to <u>hear</u> the new sounds. Although a lot more are possible, I did only what I thought was necessary to be creative but still musical and communicative.

The following is a procedure for reharmonizing a song or progression. It can also be used as an inspiration for writing, especially when you're at a loss for "that particular" chord or progression.

<u>Reharmonization Procedure</u>

1. Analyze the entire tune harmonically as to function (II-V-I, etc.), and then as to poles (tonic, dominant, subdominant, subdominant minor). Be sure to bracket all II-V progressions.

2. Mark off the melody according to its existing harmonic rhythm (or its <u>potential</u> harmonic rhythm if you're writing your own song and it doesn't yet have chords). This is done simply for closer scrutiny of the melody.

3. In order to inspire yourself with the possibilities, create columns to the left which include titles of all the various reharmonization techniques discussed above.

4. Experiment with various techniques until you settle on a <u>musical</u> reharmonization. Sometimes the original composition is so good that it defies reharmonization.

Example 138 is a model of how one might go about using the above reharmonization technique. Notice how I simply filled in some of the options. The rest is your creative choice. Use your ear to keep everything flowing and musical. Remember, techniques exist only to aid and inspire. When you know or already hear what you want, forget the technique and just do it! Whatever works for you, use it!

Example 138: GREEN DOLPHIN STREET (LAST 4 BARS)

POLES		Em7	A7	Dm7	G7	Cma7	Dm7 G7
	TONIC					Em7 Am7	
	SUB-DOM.	Em7 Cma7	C#m7(b5)	Fma7	Bm7(b5)		Fma7 Bm7(b5)
	DOMINANT						
	SUB. DOM. MINOR						
APPROACH CHORD					Db7	Cma7	
MODAL INTERCHANGE			Ebma7	Dm7(b5)			
SUB V7 OR BOX THEORY		Em7 Em7 Bbm7 Bbm7	A7 Eb7 Eb7 A7	Dm7 Dm7 Abm7 Abm7	G7 Db7 G7 Db6		
DECEPTIVE RESOLUTIONS						Dbma7 Abma7	Dbma7
INVERSIONS							
HYBRID CHORDS		D/E				G/C Bb/Eb	Eb/Ab Ab/Db
PEDAL						G	
ADDITIONAL CHORDS							
CONSTANT STRUCTURES						Cma7 Ebma7	Abma7 Dma7

NONTERTIAL VOICINGS

All the harmony discussed so far has been <u>tertial</u> harmony (harmony in thirds--<u>tertius</u> is the Latin word for third). Just recall the four basic triads and six basic tetrads and notice the "stacked" thirds (Example 139). Even the tensions are just <u>upper structures</u> made of stacked thirds (Example 140).

EXAMPLE 139:

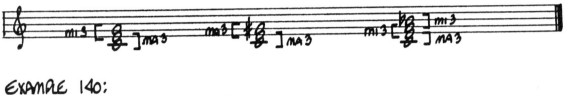

EXAMPLE 140:

There are, however, other intervallic relationships possible within the basic chord system discussed thus far. These relationships may be called <u>nontertial</u> and include voicings in fourths, fifths, clusters, and modal voicings. The nature of these voicings is discussed below.

A. <u>Voicings in Fourths</u> - "sonorities" in which the <u>predominant</u> interval between adjacent notes is a fourth (perfect or augmented). Other intervals may exist, but the predominant interval must be a fourth (Example 141).

EXAMPLE 141:

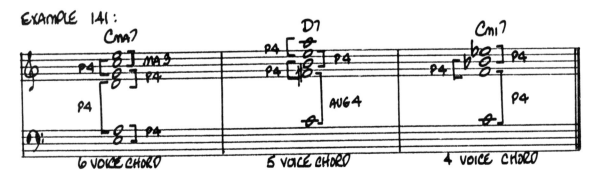

Because the interval of a fourth is not really pre-dominantly found in the harmonic series (Example 142), voicings built in fourths tend to be ambiguous and less resonant* than voicings in thirds--less resonant because their voices are in a less direct relationship with the harmonics (overtones) of the root or fundamental, thus less reinforced by them, and ambiguous because quartal voicings may imply more than one chord quality (major 7th, minor 7th, domi-nant 7th, etc.) (Example 143).

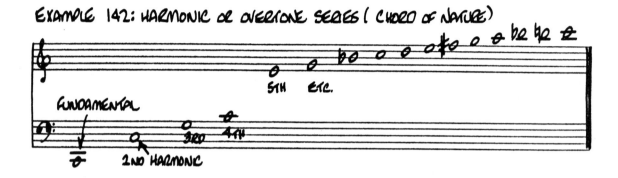

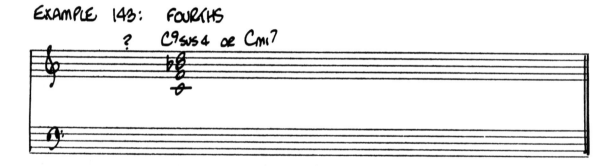

Many contemporary players and composers have taken advantage of these characteristics and created some very interesting sounds (for example, Debussy, Scriabin, Chick Corea, Herbie Hancock, McCoy Tyner).

---

* resonance, the creation, by a vibrating body, of vibrations in another body.

B. <u>Voicings in Fifths</u> - "sonorities" in which the predominant interval between adjacent notes is the
perfect fifth. Again, other intervals may exist as
long as the predominant interval is a perfect fifth
(Example 144). Now since the interval of a fifth is
the second interval in the harmonic series (referred
to as the third harmonic), it is a very strong,
stable sound in contrast to its intervallic cousin
the fourth (a fifth inverted is a fourth). In every
musical era from Baroque to Rock, the perfect fifth
has been used to create stable, powerful, almost
primitive sounds. Fifths are very flexible voicings!

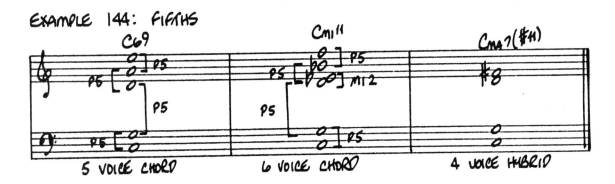

C. <u>Voicings in Clusters</u> - "sonorities" in which the predominant interval between adjacent notes is a second
(major or minor). Again, other intervals may be
found in clusters as long as the predominant interval
remains the second (Example 145). Used sparingly and
with discretion, clusters can add that extra bit of
color to your harmonic repertoire. Listen to works
by Aaron Copland, Bela Bartok, Stravinsky, Charles
Ives, Thelonius Monk, and Cecil Taylor, to name but a
few.

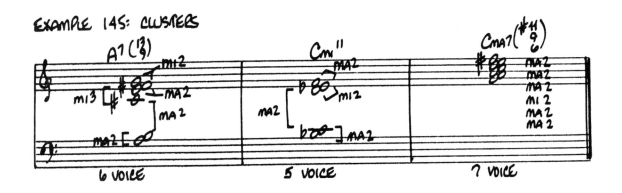

D. <u>Modal Voicings</u> - "sonorities" which use some or all scale tones of a particular mode or scale (for example, Lydian, Ionian, whole tone, etc). The intervallic composition of these voicings can be thirds, fourths, fifths, clusters, or any combination of these. In modal voicings there are no rules about what notes can and cannot be used (no "avoid" notes), as there are when voicing traditional chord qualities. Anything goes! (Example 146).

EXAMPLE 146: MODAL VOICING

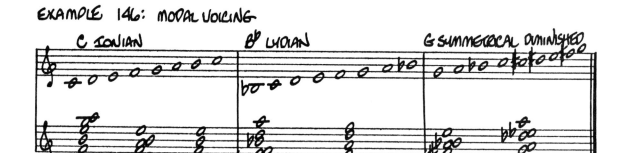

In Examples 147a-c, however, notice how some notes should be avoided when voicing traditional chords. The reason is that they tend to destroy the basic quality or color when used in a vertical structure.

EXAMPLE 147A: C MAJOR

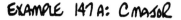

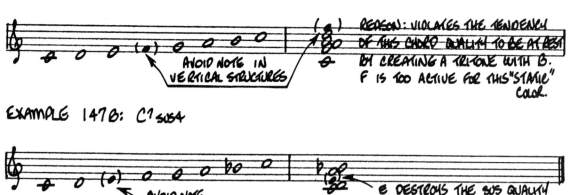

EXAMPLE 147B: C⁷ SUS4

In Example 147a, F is an avoid note because it creates a tritone with B, thus violating this chord's tendency to be at rest. F is too active a tone and should be avoided in a traditional framework. In Example 147b, E destroys the suspended ("sus") color and should also be avoided. There is a way around this problem--the "crazy 17th." In this voicing, the E actually functions as a tension 17 instead of a third! The sus sound is therefore not destroyed. In the scale in Example 147c (Lydian flat 7), there is no avoid note--all scale tones may be used.

E.   Atonal Chords - "sonorities" that create their own intrinsic color or quality. Their intervallic structures and use of chromatic tones defy categorization within tonal music and are thus usually referred to as atonal (meaning "not tonal," or lacking traditional key centers). In my opinion, the words atonal and atonality are inaccurate and impart a negative connotation which isn't necessarily correct. Contemporary, free, or just different would be more appropriate. In Example 148, all the structures defy traditional categorization. Play them--they're really refreshing and very usable. Try creating your own!

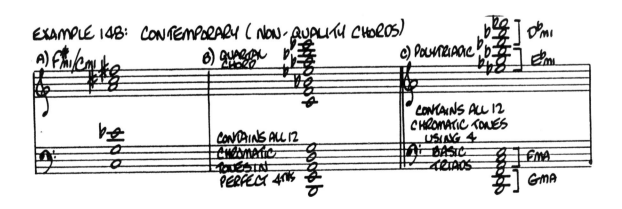

Question: Can these nontertial voicings be applied to normal, traditional progressions?

Answer: Yes. Check out Example 149, a simple progression that I revoiced using the various concepts just discussed.

As you can see, harmony can be a vast subject. I hope that these techniques have helped put it into perspective as well as inspired you to come up with your own ideas.

256

Chapter 12
ASERIGNMENTS

ASSIGNMENTS

_____ 1. Define:

a. harmonic progression
b. voice leading

_____ 2. In a harmonic progression, what's more important, the chord quality or the root progression? Why?

_____ 3. Arrange the following root progressions in order from strongest to weakest:

a. up by scale step
b. down a fourth
c. up in thirds
d. downwards in fifths

_____ 4. Describe in your own words why vertical structures such as chords tend to move or stay at rest.

_____ 5. What's the relationship between the II-V-I progression and the three categories tonic, subdominant, and dominant?

_____ 6. Define cadence and give examples of the following types:

a. perfect
b. imperfect
c. plagal
d. deceptive

_____ 7. Explain, using examples, why the flat five dominant 7th substitute works (Db7 for G7).

_____ 8. Write out the V7 of I box relationships in all keys and play the six possible resulting chord progressions, using standard A-B voicings.

_____ 9. Write out the V7 of V to V7 of I box relationships as indicated in all keys, using A-B voicings.

_____ 10. Write out the V7 of II min.7 to V7 of I box relationships as indicated in all keys, using A-B voicings.

_____ 11. Do the II min.7 - V7 drill as indicated (Steps 1, 2 and 3) in all keys.

_____ 12. Define tonic, subdominant, subdominant minor, and dominant, relative to tension and release. List in the key of A the chords contained in each category. What might be the advantage of these groupings?

_____ 13. Define and give examples of the following:

    a. Nonfunctioning dominant chords
    b. Pivot chords
    c. Passing diminished chords
    d. Secondary dominant diminished chords
    e. Deceptive cadence (give all possible examples in the key of B)

_____ 14. What are substitute chords? Give examples of the three categories:

    a. similar function - similar notes
    b. similar function - dissimilar notes
    c. Dissimilar function - common nondiatonic note

_____ 15. How can additional chords give variety and motion to a progression? Give an example.

_____ 16. What is modal interchange? Give an example.

_____ 17. Study Example 127 until you fully understand what's going on. Review anything that's unclear.

_____ 18. What is a pedal point? Create a pedal point in a song of your choice. What is a soprano pedal?

_____ 19. Demonstrate the use of inversions.

_____ 20. What are hybrid chords? Create as many hybrid structures as you can over the six chord qualities by eliminating the third and forming triads or tetrads over the root.

_____ 21. Demonstrate by example the use of constant structures.

_____ 22. Define <u>modulation</u> and give an example of each type:

     a. cadential
     b. deceptive

_____ 23. What is <u>transposition</u>? Is it important to be able to <u>do</u> it? Do the transposition drill as indicated in the chapter.

_____ 24. What is the relationship of <u>concert pitch</u> to <u>transposing instruments</u>?

_____ 25. Define approach chords and give examples of the three types:

     a. constant structure
     b. dominant approach
     c. independent voices

_____ 26. What is <u>reharmonization</u>? After studying the reharmonization of "Green Dolphin Street," do a reharmonization of your own choice, any style. Use the procedure outlined in the chapter and illustrated in Example 138 for best results.

_____ 27. What are <u>tertial voicings</u>? What are <u>nontertial voicings</u>? Give examples of each.

_____ 28. Explain <u>modal voicings</u>. How do they differ from traditional chord quality voicings?

_____ 29. What are <u>atonal chord voicings</u>? Give examples.

SUGGESTED READING

Dallin, Leo. <u>Techniques of Twentieth Century Composition</u>. 2d ed. Dubuque, Iowa: Wm. C. Brown Co. Publishers, 1964.

Machlis, Joseph. <u>Introduction to Contemporary Music</u>. New York: W. W. Norton & Company, 1961.

Piston, Walter. <u>Harmony</u>. New York: W. W. Norton & Company, 1969.

Russo, William. <u>Jazz Composition and Orchestration</u>. London: University of Chicago Press, 1968.

Sebesky, Don. <u>The Contemporary Arranger</u>. Sherman Oaks, Cal.: Alfred Publishing Co., 1974.

Chapter 13

Voicings and Comping

Now that you have a pretty good grasp of tertial and nontertial chord structures, it's time to acquire some facility using them in progressions. This is called accompaniment, or comping for short. Comping is an art all to itself. It is actually very close to composing, as one is expected to harmonize melodies, voice chords from chord symbols in the correct style, create counterlines, and add rhythmic variety--all pretty much spontaneously!

You should spend a lot of time listening to various artists comp as well as solo in many styles. Here are some of the exceptional ones:

            Chick Corea - jazz and fusion
            Stanley Cowell - jazz
            Denny Zeitlen - jazz and fusion
            Oscar Peterson - jazz
            Herbie Hancock - jazz, fusion, and funk
            McCoy Tyner - jazz
            Richard Tee - gospel, funk, and rhythm & blues
            Keith Emerson - rock and fusion
            Jerry Lee Lewis - rock & roll
            Nicky Hopkins - rock and blues
            Jimmy Smith - jazz and blues
            Dr. John - blues
            Bob James - fusion
            Keith Jarrett - jazz

...to name but a few!

Since there are literally thousands of voicings, an organized approach is best. We will therefore assume the arranger's point of view of the subject, since the arranger's gig demands excellent familiarity and facility with voicings. We will start with tertial voicings and go through each chord quality and its available tensions with any note in the lead (soprano voice). We will use four-note chords in close position (four-way close) as our basis and expand from there. These chord breakdowns are called the "Melodic Comping Exercises."

MELODIC COMPING EXERCISES

EXAMPLE 150 - QUALITY ONE:

The Major 7th or Major 6th Family (Tonic Major) (C Maj.7)

Scale: Lydian, since F in C Ionian (major scale) is an avoid note and would destroy or contradict this quality.

Tension Substitutions:

9 for 1, ♯11 or 13 for 5 (in a four-note voicing, only one may be used); 7 and 6 are interchangeable as long as the 6 functions as a 6 and not a 13. When there is a 13, the 5 is not present in a four-way close voicing. When there is a 7 in the voicing, the 6 is really a 13. Get it?

Practice Procedure:

1. Play each voicing in the circle of fifths and chromatically, as indicated.

2. Harmonize the scale using the George Shearing comp--four-way close with doubled lead voice an octave below. Use the voicings with the "X" marked over them, although you may experiment with all of them. George Shearing popularized this technique, commonly referred to as blocked chords. With much practice, one can become proficient at soloing in this manner. Check out Oscar Peterson's blocked chord solo on "Girl Talk" (found on the album Exclusively For My Friends).

3. Solo/Comp Exercise:

    a. Using any voicings from the major 7th family, write at least a sixteen-bar chord progression. Then write a solo, using only notes from the scale.

    b. While playing the left hand voicings, improvise a solo over your progression until you feel comfortable.

c. Now freely improvise a chord progression
and solo simultaneously. You may use voicings from the major 7 family and any notes
from the scale. If Bach and Mozart could
do it, you can!

EXAMPLE 150:

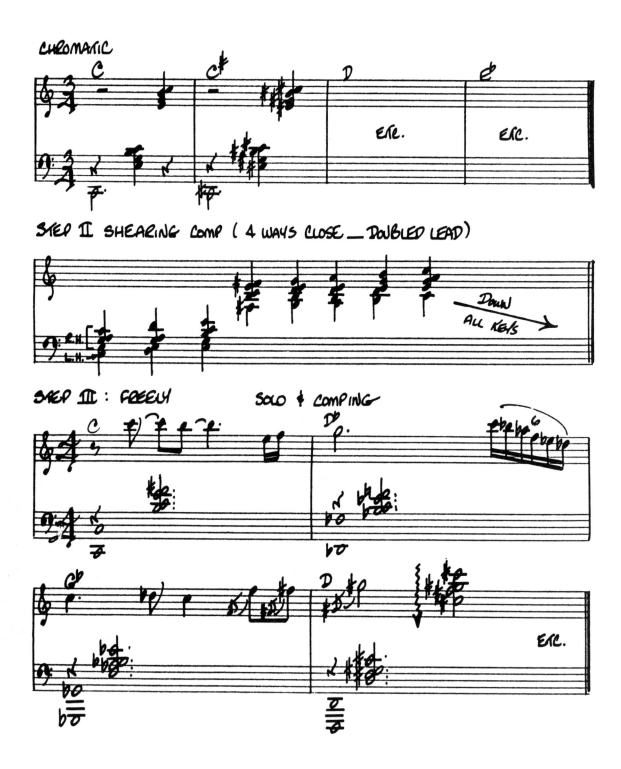

EXAMPLE 151 - QUALITY TWO:

The Minor 7th Family (C Min.7)

    Scale: Dorian (♭3 and ♭7)

Tension Substitutions:

    9 for 1, 11 or 13 for 5.

Practice Procedure:

    Same as with Major 7th Family, Steps 1, 2 and 3.

EXAMPLE 151:

EXAMPLE 152a - QUALITY THREE:

The Dominant 7th Family (C7)

    Scale: Mixolydian plus all available tensions.

Tension Substitutions:

$\flat$9 or 9 or $\sharp$9 for 1, 11 for 3 (this substitution actually changes the dominant 7 quality to the sus quality), $\sharp$11 or $\flat$13 and $\natural$13 for 5.

Practice Procedure:

Same as before (Steps 1, 2 and 3).

Step 4:

Try substituting sus 4 for all major 3rds, except where $\sharp$9 or $\sharp$11 are present in the voicing, the reason being that the resultant voicings sound as minor 7ths instead of dominant 7ths.

Substituting the sus 4 is actually equivalent to superimposing all possible minor 7th voicings over the dominant (e.g., G min.7/C) (Example 152b).

EXAMPLE 152B: SUS 4 FOR 3

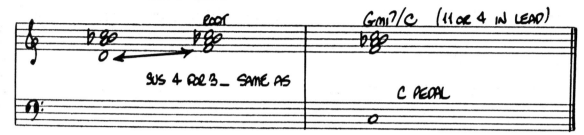

EXAMPLE 153 - QUALITY FOUR:

The Minor 7th(♭5) Family (C Min.7♭5)

Scale: Locrian plus ♮ 9.

Tension Substitutions:

♭9 for 1 (rarely used because of the harsh sound of the ♭9 interval in tonal music. If resolved properly, however, it sounds fine--use your own discretion), 9 for 1, 11 for 1, ♭13 for 1.

Note that in this family, in order to have a complete four-way close voicing, the tensions must all replace the 1 (the root).

Practice Procedure:

Same as before (Steps 1, 2 and 3).

EXAMPLE 153:

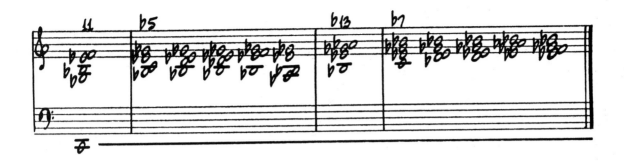

EXAMPLE 154 - QUALITY FIVE:

The Diminished 7th Family (C Dim.7)

Scale: Symmetrical Diminished (whole step-half step)

Tension Substitutions:

9 for 1, 11 for 1, ♭13 for 1, ♭15 for 1. Again, as in the minor 7(♭5) family, all tension substitutions are for 1 so as to create a complete four-way close voicing. You may find that some of these voicings take getting used to as compared to the traditional diminished 7th sound, so open your ears.

Practice Procedure:

As before (Steps 1, 2 and 3).

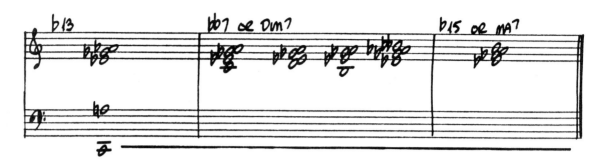

EXAMPLE 155 - QUALITY SIX:

The Minor Major 7th Family (Tonic Minor)

Scale: Melodic minor ascending (Jazz Minor)

Tension Substitutions:

9 for 1, 11, #11 or 13 for 5, maj.7 and maj.6
are interchangeable.

Practice Procedure:

As before (Steps 1, 2 and 3).

EXAMPLE 155:

Although this covers the six basic chord qualities, there is a variation of the major 7th quality that I'd like to cover--the major 7th augmented 5th family:

EXAMPLE 156 - QUALITY SEVEN:

The Major 7th ♯5 Family

 Scale: Lydian raised 5.

 Tension Substitutions:

  9 for 1, ♯11 for 1, 13 for 1.

 Practice Procedure:

  As before (Steps 1, 2 and 3).

After you have completed Steps 1, 2 and 3 for all the Examples above, Step 4 will be to write a mixed-bag etude which uses voicings from all qualities so far discussed. You should also improvise over the written chord changes until you acquire flexibility in moving four-way close chords around with any note in the lead voice. Write as many etudes as are necessary to achieve this ability. Remember, it takes as long as it takes! (Example 157.)

Another application of the melodic comping technique is the harmonization of any melody with four-way close blocked chords. Example 158 is one possible four-part harmonization I did of Coltrane's "Giant Steps." Play through this exercise in order to hear how full the resultant sound is.

EXAMPLE 158: GIANT STEPS

Melodic Comping Improvisational Procedure

Melodic comping can also be a powerful improvisational tool. Do the following procedure in order to gain reality on how it can function in this manner (Example 159):

1. Write a simple "guide line" through a set of changes. For purposes of this exercise, the guide line should move up or down in half or whole steps, although in reality it can move or leap anywhere by any interval.

2. Harmonize the guide line using four-way close techniques.

3. Write an improvisation which incorporates the guide line, preferably on the first or second note of the chord.

4. Practice soloing, using the guide line as a guide through the changes.

5. Do this exercise in all keys for maximum results.

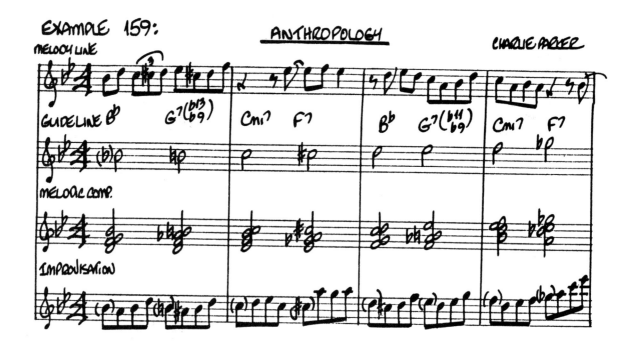

This technique is used, often unknowingly, by many
great players as they play. Although their solos sound
monstrously complex, they're usually thinking of a simple
melody, and embellishing it (theme and variations).

By the way, Example 159, "Anthropology," is a famous
rhythm change tune written by Charlie Parker. It is
called a rhythm change tune as it is based on the changes
of the famous Gershwin standard, "I Got Rhythm." Every
player should be able to improvise over a rhythm change in
any key. Since most rhythm changes move at fast tempos,
the melodic comp technique helps glue everything together.
Rhythm changes and the blues are two famous forms from the
past that are still popular vehicles for expression--espe-
cially for jamming!

OPEN VOICINGS

Before we move on to nontertial voicings, there is still a lot of mileage to be gotten from these basic four-way close chords, i.e., opening them up and voicing them in different ways. The three main categories of open voicings may be described as follows:

1. Drop 2 voicings:

    The second voice or note from the top is transposed down an octave (Example 160a).

2. Drop 2 & 4 voicings:

    The second and fourth voices from the top are both transposed down an octave (Example 160b).

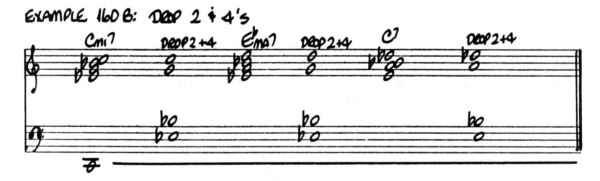

3. Drop 3 voicings:

    The third voice from the top is transposed down an octave (Example 160c).

EXAMPLE 160 C: DROP 3's

An organized approach to learning these voicings would be to convert all the previous four-way close chord qualities to drop 2's, 3's, and 2 & 4's and then practice them in all keys. You'll discover that some voicings work great while others don't. The ones you like should become part of your chord vocabulary. Although this assignment may take some time, it's worth it (Example 161).

EXAMPLE 161: Cmi7 FAMILY DROP 2's

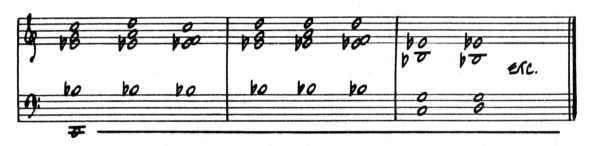

SPREADS

Spread voicings categorically describe voicings which simply have the root in the bass while the other notes or voices are spread out (not four-way close). Spreads may contain four, five, six or more notes and can also be tertial or nontertial (Example 162).

EXAMPLE 162: SPREADS

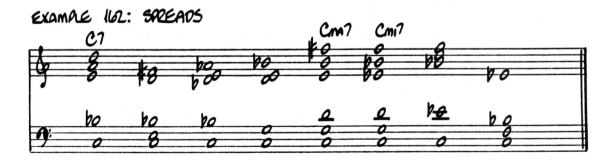

If the root was missing in Example 162, these voicings wouldn't be spreads. They would be drop 2's, 2 & 4's, voicings in fourths, fifths, etc. Spreads are used when an open and full sound is desired, and usually at slow to medium tempos, as they are a bit cumbersome.

VOICINGS IN FOURTHS

The Modal Fourth Exercise (Examples 163a-d)

The purpose of this drill is to develop facility in moving fourths around on the various modes and scales.

Example 163a - Three-Note Fourths:

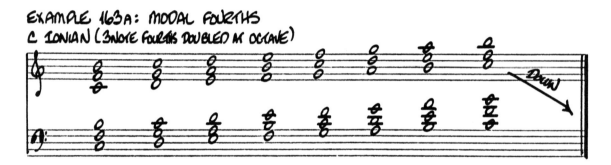

Both hands play the same voicing one or two octaves apart.

Example 163b - Four-Note Fourths:

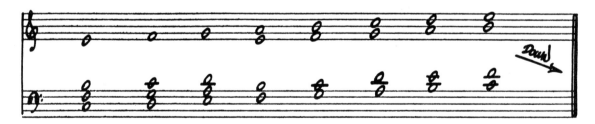

May be played in three ways:

1. Left hand plays bottom three notes, right hand plays top note.

2. Left hand plays bottom two notes, right hand plays top two notes.

3. Left hand plays bottom note, right hand plays top three notes.

<u>Example 163c - Five-Note Fourths:</u>

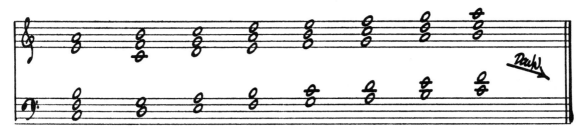

EXAMPLE 163C: 5 NOTE FOURTHS

May be played in two ways:

1. Left hand plays bottom three notes, right hand plays top two notes.

2. Left hand plays bottom two notes, right hand plays top three notes.

<u>Example 163d - Six-Note Fourths:</u>

EXAMPLE 163 D: 6 NOTE FOURTHS

Left hand plays bottom three, right hand plays top three.

By doing this exercise in all keys, you will actually acquire some flexibility moving fourths around in all the modes, since the rest of the modes are simply displaced major scales (e.g., D Dorian has the exact same notes as C Ionian, E Phrygian, F Lydian, etc).

After this preparatory exercise is mastered, it will be time to look at a standard procedure for voicing any chord in fourths regardless of its quality or number of notes:

Procedure for Voicing Fourths in Traditional Harmony

1. Determine the quality of the chord and its respective chord scale (refer to Chapter 11, "Advanced Improvisation").

2. Voice down from the desired melody note, using scale notes in intervals of fourths (perfect or augmented). If necessary, you may use an interval other than a fourth, as long as the predominant interval is a fourth.

3. Avoid adjacent non-fourth intervals (thirds, fifths, etc), as they will destroy the desired quartal sound.

4. Avoid ♭9 intervals between any two tones of the voicing. This interval's harsh characteristic sound will tend to destroy the quartal sound. In more contemporary music, however, this sound may be desired, so use your ears!

5. Be sure to include the tritone in all dominant seventh voicings, or the quality will be vague. (But this is fine, if intended.)

EXAMPLE 164:

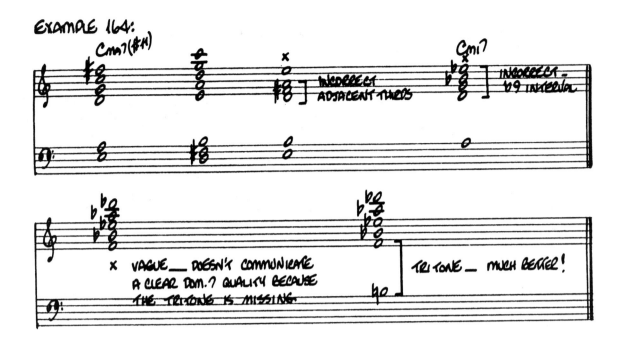

In Example 165 I have written <u>some</u> typical quartal voicings on each chord quality, using this exact procedure. I suggest you familiarize your ear with these voicings by playing them in the circle of fifths and also chromatically up and down. Some you will like, others not. Also, it should be noted that in any voicing with four, five, six or more parts, not all the voices are necessary. You may drop out one or two notes and still have a good three-part or four-part quartal voicing.

EXAMPLE 165:   QUALITY FOUR/4 VOICINGS
MAJOR 7TH QUALITY — Cma7

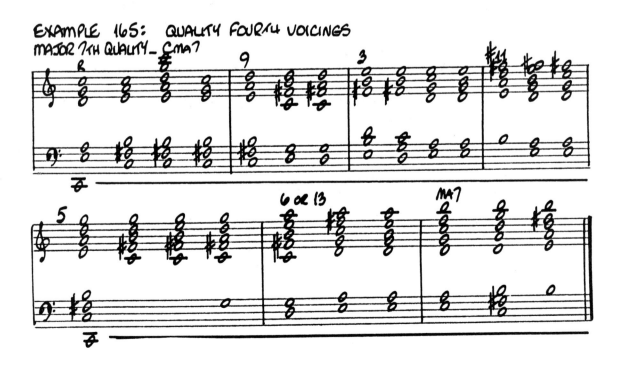

THE CONTEMPORARY KEYBOARDIST

282

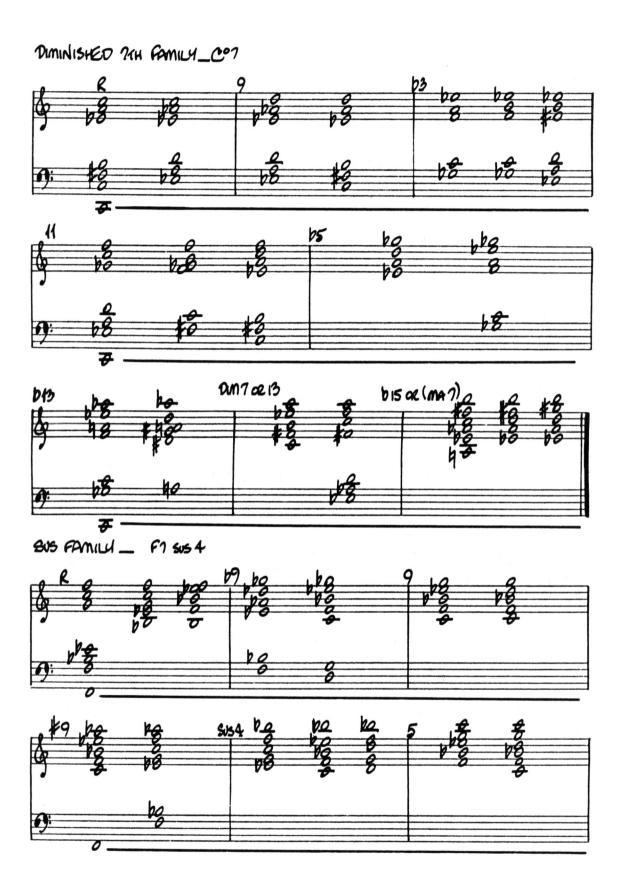

Left-Hand Comping Fourths

Now that we have seen how fourths are voiced, it's time to look at the various three-note left-hand voicings in fourths that are ideal for comping. For organizational purposes, we will again look at each quality (Example 166).

I have marked an "X" over the voicings most used. These define the chord quality, whereas the unmarked ones are ambiguous. The decision of which ones to use depends on the desired musical effect.

<u>Drill</u>:

Practice these voicings in all keys in the circle of fifths and chromatically.

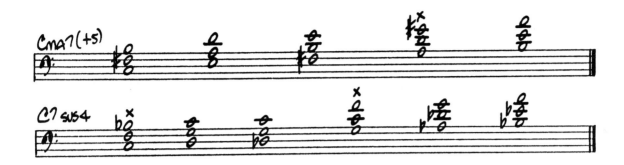

VOICINGS IN FIFTHS

Fifths are much more stable than fourths because of the nature of the harmonic series. Although root-five (perfect fifth) is one of the most common intervals in music, voicings in fifths of three, four or more notes are less frequent than voicings in fourths. They are nevertheless very useful.

The Modal Fifth Exercise (Examples 167a-d)

The purpose of this drill is to develop facility in moving fifths around on the various modes and scales.

Example 167a - Three-Note Fifths:

1. Left hand plays bottom note, right hand plays top two notes.

2. Left hand plays bottom two notes, right hand plays top note.

3. Both hands play all three notes one or two octaves apart.

EXAMPLE 167: MODAL FIFTHS

A: C IONIAN — 3 NOTE 5THS

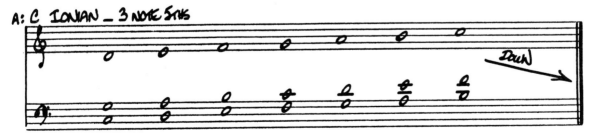

Example 167b - Four-Note Fifths:

1. Left hand plays bottom two notes, right hand plays top two notes.

2. Left hand plays bottom three notes, right hand plays top note.

3. Left hand plays bottom note, right hand plays top three notes.

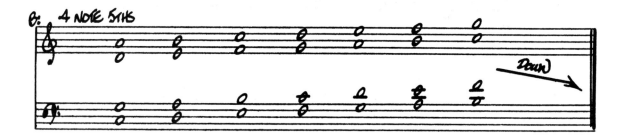

Example 167c - Five-Note Fifths:

1. Left hand plays bottom two notes, right hand plays top three notes.

2. Left hand plays bottom three notes, right hand plays top two notes.

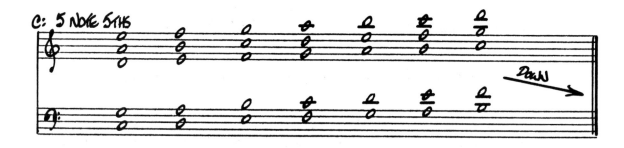

Example 167d - Six-Note Fifths:

Left hand plays bottom three notes, right hand plays top three notes.

Drill:

Do all the above exercises in all keys to gain maximum facility in moving fifths.

Procedure for Voicing Fifths in Traditional Harmony

1. Determine chord quality and respective chord scale (see Chapter 11).

2. Voice down from the desired melody note, using scale notes in fifths.

3. Intervals other than fifths may be used as long as the predominant interval is still a fifth.

4. Avoid adjacent non-fifth intervals (e.g., thirds, fourths, etc).

5. Avoid ♭9 intervals, as before, between any two tones of the voicing.

6. Be sure to include the tritone in all dominant seventh voicings or the quality will be vague (which, again, is fine if intended).

Example 168 shows some typical voicings in fifths on each of the chord qualities. As before, play all voicings in all keys using the circle of fifths and chromatic pattern.

EXAMPLE 16B: QUALITY FIFTH VOICINGS
MAJOR 7TH FAMILY

MINOR 7TH FAMILY

DOMINANT 7TH FAMILY

(DEBATABLE)

(AMBIGUOUS — NO TRI-TONE)

(DEBATABLE)

(AMBIGUOUS NO THIRD)

MINOR 7bs FAMILY

b9 MAY BE TOO HARSH FOR YOUR EARS

DIMINISHED 7TH FAMILY

NOTE: BECAUSE OF ITS "STACKED MINOR THIRDS", THE DIMINISHED FAMILY DOES NOT LEND ITSELF TO PERFECT FIFTH VOICINGS. HOWEVER, THE VOICINGS I HAVE WRITTEN DOWN QUALIFY AS FIFTH VOICINGS. (PERFECT, DIM. AND AUG. 5THS)

MAJOR 7 (+5) FAMILY

Left Hand Comping Fifths

As with the left-hand voicings in fourths, I have written down various left-hand voicings in fifths and marked an "X" over the ones most frequently used (Example 169). Now remember, in all these three-note left-hand comp voicings there exists some intended ambiguity. The right hand or soloist usually adds the missing notes!

EXAMPLE 169: LEFT HAND FIFTHS

VOICINGS IN CLUSTERS

Definition:

      Clusters are "sonorities" that predominant-ly contain major and minor seconds.

The Modal Cluster Exercise (Example 170)

      The purpose of this drill is to enable you to develop some facility in moving clusters around the various modes and scales.

    a.   Three-note clusters

        Right hand plays all three notes first, using finger pattern 1-2-3, while left hand does the same an octave lower. Then do the same with finger patterns 2-3-4 and 3-4-5.

b. Four-note clusters

Practice as in Exercise (a) above, using the two sets of indicated finger patterns.

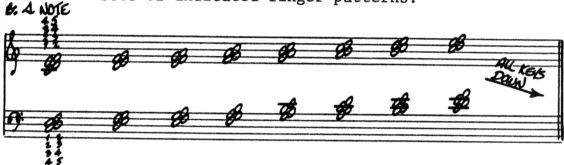

c. Five-note clusters

As above, except use one set of finger patterns.

d. Six-note clusters

Right hand takes the top three notes while the left hand takes the bottom three notes. Use three different sets of fingerings.

e. Seven-note clusters

Right hand plays top four notes while left hand plays bottom three. I suggest the indicated fingering, although there are obviously other possibilities.

f.   Eight-note clusters

Called <u>doubled lead</u> because the melody and bass
notes are in octaves. Although it appears un-
musical, give it a listen. You'll soon hear the
doubled lead and get a lot of ideas about color-
ing melodies with clusters.

Procedure for Voicing Clusters in Traditional Harmony

1. Determine proper chord quality and respective chord
   scale (refer to Chapter 11).

2. Voice down from the desired melody note, using scale
   notes predominantly in major or minor seconds.

3. Avoid adjacent non-second intervals in order to avoid
   destroying the overall cluster sound.

4. If a clear melody is desired, separate the melody
   note by a third or fourth.

5. Include the tritone in all dominant seventh voicings
   if a distinct dominant sound is intended. If you
   desire ambiguity, leave the tritone out.

Example 171 shows some of the possible clusters on each of
the chord qualities. Again, practice all voicings chromatically and in the circle of fifths.

EXAMPLE 171: VOICING CLUSTERS

MAJOR 7 (+5) FAMILY

MIXED-BAG VOICINGS

Open voicings that span more than an octave, have more than four notes, and usually don't contain a predominant interval can be considered mixed-bag voicings. They may or may not contain the root. Example 172a shows mixed-bag voicings with roots, while Example 172b shows mixed-bag voicings without roots. Mixed-bag voicings can be of any intervallic composition.

EXAMPLE 172A:

EXAMPLE 172B:

Since there are far too many combinations of these types of voicings to cover here, I have, as before, written down some of the common ones on each chord quality. Again, practice all chromatically and in the circle of fifths (Example 173).

EXAMPLE 173: MIXED BAG VOICINGS _ (PRACTICE ALL KEYS)

Cma7 family

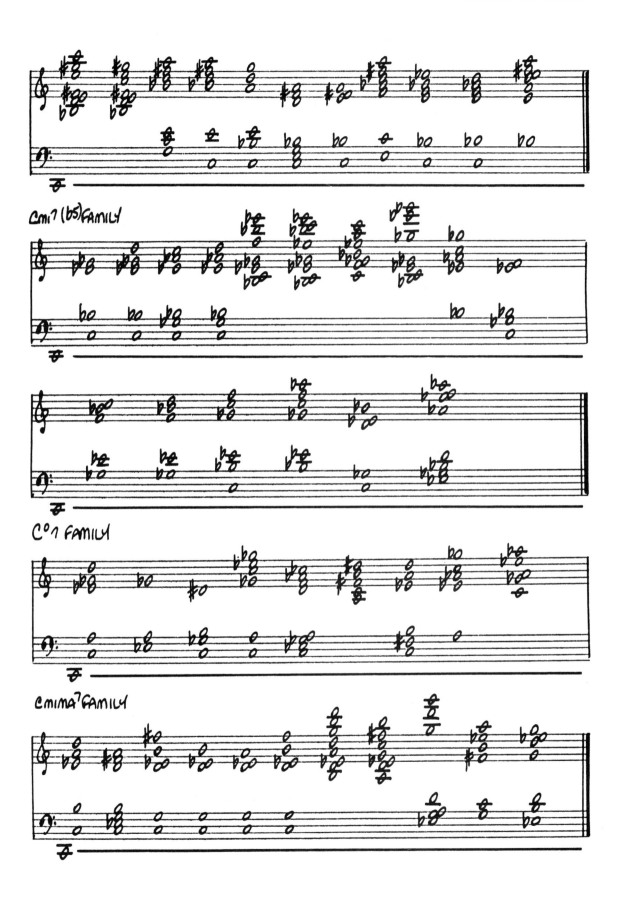

Cmi7 (b5) FAMILY

C°7 FAMILY

Cmima7 FAMILY

Once you get the idea, try creating your own voicings. Learn and use the ones you like. Bill Evans was
actually noted for his creativity in the area of harmony
and voicings.

Mixed-bag voicings are best suited for the acoustic
piano. When transferring these or any voicings to other
instruments such as strings, brass, woodwinds, synthesizers, guitars, etc., you should realize that the timbre
and range of these other instruments will tend to change
the voicings' overall sound. Some will sound better, some
barely satisfactory, and some won't work at all. These
considerations, however, fall under the heading of arranging and orchestration, and taking them up is outside the
scope of this manual. I strongly suggest, though, that
every contemporary keyboardist spend some time studying
these subjects, as they will enhance every aspect of his
or her career.

VOICE LEADING

Now, just as regular tetrads and A-B voicings can be
"voice led," so also can clusters, spreads, fourths,
fifths, etc. The exercises which follow in Examples
174a-i should be practiced in all keys to start you off.

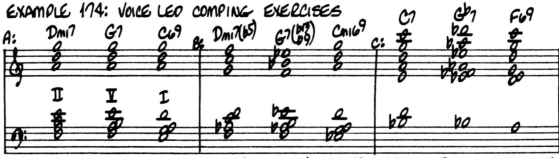

UPPER STRUCTURE TRIADS

Definition:

Upper Structure Triads, simply triads (especially major or minor) that are superimposed over basic chord qualities. The top three notes of a spread voicing are arranged in such a way as to form basic close position triads. Since they retain their own intrinsic triadic sound, they are especially sonorous, as they imply polytonality (Example 175a).

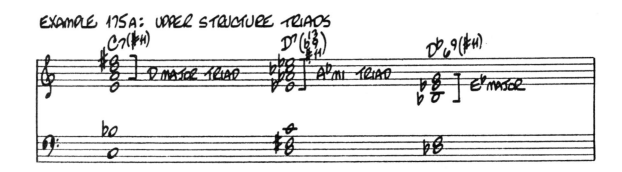

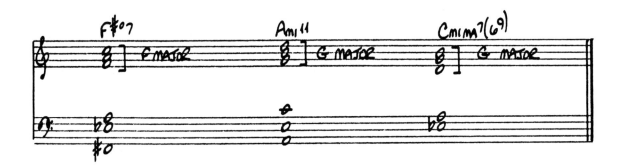

Each triad should contain at least one available tension from the basic chord quality to obtain an optimum polytonal effect. It should also be supported by the basic chord sound or the polytonal effect will turn into a hybrid or incomplete sound--which again is fine if intended (Example 175b). Recall that a complete basic chord sound should contain at least the third and seventh of the chord and in some cases the fifth (refer to Chapter 12).

EXAMPLE 175B:

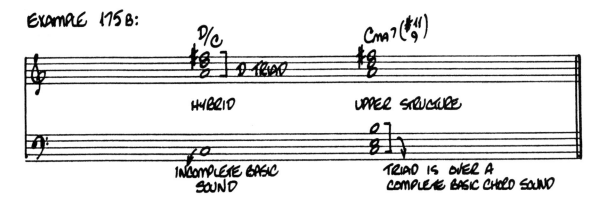

Procedure for Voicing Upper Structure Triads Over Basic Chord Qualities

1. Determine basic chord quality and respective chord scale.

2. Make the desired melody note (scale tone) either a root, three, or five of any triad. Although any of the four basic triads work, major and minor work the best.

3. Select an upper structure triad that contains at least one or more tensions.

4. Superimpose this structure over a complete basic chord. The root of the chord may or may not be present.

Example 176 shows <u>some</u> examples of upper structure triads on the different chord qualities. They should be practiced chromatically and with the circle of fifths. Try creating your own.

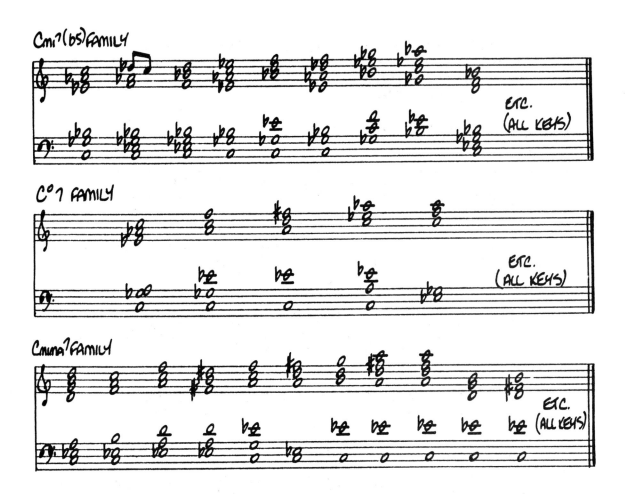

Example 177 shows some special applications of these triads:

a.   Whole-tone augmented triads

The augmented triad works best here because of the whole-tone scale.

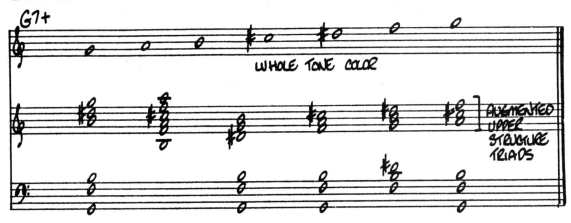

WHOLE TONE AUGMENTED TRIADS

G PEDAL

b.   Arpeggiated upper-structure triads

When a melody forms the notes of an upper-structure triad, the triad may harmonize it.

EXAMPLE 177 B: ARPEGGIATED UPPER STRUCTURE TRIADS

c.   Scales harmonized with upper-structure triads

This excerpt from Edgar Winter's composition, "Fire And Ice," from his first album, Entrance, demonstrates a symmetrical diminished scale harmonized in upper-structure triads superimposed over dominant seventh chords ascending intervallically in minor thirds.

EXAMPLE 177C: FIRE & ICE BY EDGAR WINTER

    d.   <u>Upper-structure triads ascending in minor thirds and superimposed over a dominant seventh chord--G7♭9♮13</u>

EXAMPLE 177 D: UPPER STRUCTURE TRIADS IN ASCENDING MINOR 3RDS

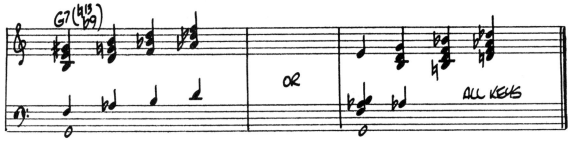

    e.   <u>Descending upper-structure triads in minor thirds superimposed over a dominant seventh chord--C7♭9♮13--with the melody doubled an octave below (doubled lead)</u>

EXAMPLE 177 E: DOUBLED LEAD WITH DESCENDING UPPER STRUCTURE TRIADS

    f.   <u>Upper-structure triads over basic triads</u>

In this case, we simply have augmented triads superimposed in whole tones up and down. Actually, these structures are augmented dominant seventh chords. But after you play this drill a few times, your ear will tell you that they are simply augmented triads in whole steps! I have labeled them both ways so you can see the difference.

EXAMPLE 177 F: SUPERIMPOSED AUGMENTED TRIADS (WHOLE-TONE SCALE)

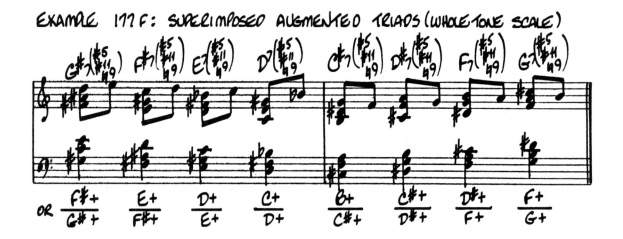

I hope these examples have stimulated your imagination as well as shown you some possible applications. Try creating your own voicings--these were meant as food for thought!

OPEN TRIADS

Yes, that's right--I saved the simplest for last! By opening up triads and doubling certain pitches, triads can take on new sonorities. In Example 178 I have voiced some of the most often-used open triads. Transpose them to all keys. In Example 179 I have written an arpeggiated left-hand piano part to demonstrate how triads can sound, properly voice-led and opened. Fredric Chopin was the master at this type of writing. You may want to check his compositions out if you desire flexibility in this style!

EXAMPLE 178: OPEN TRIADS

COMPING BASICS

A. Solo Piano Plus One Instrument (voice, sax, flute, etc.)

1. Find out, either by asking or listening, if the soloist desires you to lead or follow. Leading means the soloist is cueing off your harmony, melody, or rhythm; following means you are cueing off the soloist.

    Statements from the soloist such as "don't rush me," "slow down," "relax," etc., probably mean you're leading too much. In this case, try following. Statements such as "I can't hear my note," "you're dragging," etc., mean that you probably need to lead the soloist more. Listening is always the secret, for the situation may change at any time.

2. Accompany means to enhance, embellish, support, complement, etc.--not show off, overplay, solo, etc. A workable datum here is the following:

    THE MORE COMPLEX THE PART THE SOLOIST IS PERFORMING, THE SIMPLER YOUR PART CAN BE.

    Now, although there are some exceptions to this, it usually holds true. Give the soloist the spotlight and fill in competently during the spaces, and he or she will love you!

B.   Ensemble Comping

This usually refers to rhythm section playing (guitar, keyboards, bass and drums). Although the points
just covered on solo comping still apply, the
"comper" can usually be a lot more active, depending
on the style.

In jazz and fusion, the comper is expected to make
the changes come alive. Chick Corea is one of the
best in this area, so give his comping a good listen.
A good rhythmic and melodic sense are the required
tools!

In commercial music the "comp" part is again very
important. It is usually worked out beforehand, as
it's imperative it locks in with the rest of the
song--like we're talking hits man!

My advice is this: Your gig is to play the gig!
This means to perceive what the gig or session calls
for either by listening or asking, and then do it.
You'll get a lot of work if you can pull this off!

The real secret to all playing is that there is no
secret! Just play! Extrovert your attention to the total
scene (other players, audience, the physical space you're
performing in, etc). Don't listen just to yourself. Listen to the whole sound and blend with it. Play to communicate. If you have nothing to say, say nothing. (When in
doubt, lay out!) Always play what you "hear." Contribute
to the total sound and you'll soon be cooking.

Chapter 13
ASSIGNMENTS

_____ 1. Do the Melodic Comping exercise (all three
            steps) as indicated over the <u>seven</u> chord
            qualities (Examples 150-156).

_____ 2. Write as many <u>mixed-bag</u> etudes as necessary
            for you to achieve flexibility at moving
            four-way close voicings around with any note
            in the lead. The purpose of this drill is to
            break away from the A-B voicings (Example
            157).

_____ 3. Learn the four-way close block harmonization
            of "Giant Steps" up to tempo ($\quad$ = 256).

_____ 4. Do the melodic comp improvisational guide-
            line exercise on at least ten tunes, or until
            you have the idea! (Example 159.)

_____ 5. What are open voicings? Give some examples
            of the following open voicings:

            a. Drop 2's
            b. Drop 3's
            c. Drop 2 & 4's

_____ 6. Convert all the previous four-way close voic-
            ings to drop 2's, 3's, and 2 & 4's. Use
            Example 161 as a reference to get started.
            Do one quality at a time and practice chro-
            matically and in the circle of fifths.

_____ 7. What are spread voicings? Give some examples
            of your own.

_____ 8. Do the modal fourth exercise in all keys as
            indicated (Examples 163a-d).

_____ 9. What is the step-by-step procedure for voic-
            ing fourths in traditional harmony?

_____ 10. Do the voicings in fourths exercise on all
            the chord qualities in all keys as indicated
            (Example 165).

_____ 11. Do the left-hand "comp" drill using fourths
            (Example 166).

_____ 12. Repeat Assignments 8, 9, 10 and 11 above with voicings in fifths and clusters. (Except note there is no No. 11--left-hand comp drill--for clusters.)

_____ 13. What is meant by a <u>mixed-bag</u> voicing? Give some examples. What is the intervallic composition of these voicings? Drill Example 173 as indicated. If you are feeling overwhelmed, it's because you're trying to retain all the voicings. These exercises are simply a way of getting familiar in an organized way with all these potential voicings. They'll become second nature once you begin applying them to real musical situations!

_____ 14. Drill the voice leading exercises (Example 174a-i) as indicated. These are intended as food for thought.

_____ 15. What are <u>upper-structure triads</u>? What is the procedure for voicing these structures?

_____ 16. Drill Example 176 as indicated in order to get acquainted with upper-structure triads.

_____ 17. Drill Examples 177a-f in order to train your ear and mind to some possible applications.

_____ 18. Do the <u>open triad</u> drill (Example 178) to familiarize yourself with these structures.

_____ 19. What is the difference between solo and ensemble comping?

_____ 20. Do record copies of several of your favorite artists, paying particular attention to the comping, not the soloing. The way a player comps tells a lot about how that player thinks. These record copies can and should be from several musical styles (gospel, rock, fusion, Latin, etc).

SUGGESTED READING

Stuart, Walter. <u>Innovations in Full Chord Technique</u>. New York: Chas. Colin, 1956.

Chapter 14

Modality

Modes are simply scales. More exactly, the ancient Greeks called their scales modes. Later, the early Christian church adapted them and they became the Ecclesiastical Modes.

The modes of today differ from the modes of those early times in two main ways. The first has to do with the fact that the well-tempered system of tuning had not yet been created. Thus the modes we play and hear today are slightly different than the originals. But this fact hasn't at all diminished their usefulness.

The second point of difference is in our use of the modes. Early modal church music was vocal (therefore melodic). Thus the modes' unexhausted harmonic possibilities offered 20th century composers a valuable means of freeing music from what Bela Bartok called the "tyrannical rule of the major-minor keys" (tonality)!

So let's put this into perspective:

1. Greek or Church Modes:

    Basis of music in the Middle Ages and Renaissance (Gregorian Chants to Palestrina).

2. Major-Minor System:

    Rigid harmonic system of the Baroque Era (Bach, Handel); Classical Era (Mozart, Haydn, Beethoven); and Romantic Era (Schubert, Chopin, Liszt, Brahms, and early Wagner).

3. <u>Chromaticism and Resurgence of Modes</u>:

Late 19th to 20th century (late Wagner, Debussy, Scriabin, Bartok, Ives, Stravinsky, Schoenberg, Werben, etc).

Today there seem to exist three main "dynamics" or tendencies in music:

1. Folk elements organized into all types of structures with a mostly <u>tonal</u> base. Includes straight-ahead jazz and commercial music.

2. Continuous extension of proven musical practices of the past (Baroque, Classical, and Romantic musical forms).

3. Evolution of new musical styles not colored by tonality (12-tone or serial music, contemporary modality, electronic music realizations, etc).

As far as the future goes, I'll predict this much--computers and synthesizers will play a very important role--but they'll always need <u>operators</u>--musicians!

THEORY AND APPLICATION

Although the modes do not make available any sound not also possible in the major-minor system, it is the relationship of these sounds and their functions which offer new musical flavoring to the composer. Let's now take a look at these relationships as they might apply to the contemporary keyboardist.

Example 180 shows all the modes as they appear in the key of C. Notice where the half steps occur. Most beginners use this method to learn the modes, e.g., Dorian is a C major scale starting on D; Aeolian is a C major scale starting on A, etc. To graduate from beginner, however, one must learn the modes as individual entities instead of continuing to do this two-step associative thinking (knowing something by relating it to something else).

EXAMPLE 180: MODES (C TONALITY)

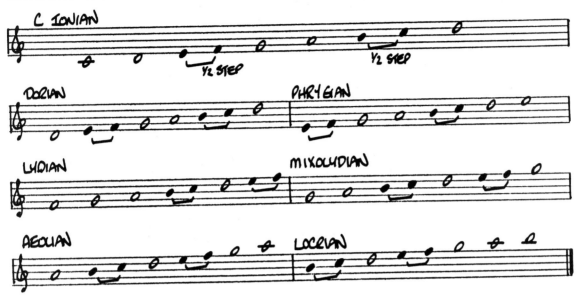

Example 181 shows all the modes built from the same primary axis (root or starting point). The pitch axis or key center of each mode is different. Also shown are the characteristic notes of each mode, which help clearly define it.

EXAMPLE 181:

Drill:

Learn the modes, as in Example 181, in all keys.
You should know them as individual entities, not
by relating them to their fundamental key. In
other words, D Lydian is D Lydian, not an A
major scale starting on D--just as you're you,
not just Mr. and Mrs. X's son or daughter--okay?

MODAL HARMONY

Just as the major-minor system has evolved its rigid
triadic and tetradic structures and harmonic progressions,
modes also have their own structures and harmonic progressions, each mode different than the next. Example 182 is
a chart that gives the qualities of both triads and
tetrads in each of the modes, using traditional tertial
harmony (harmony in thirds).

Modal Chart
(Example 182)

Mode	I	II	III	IV	V	VI	VII	
Ionian	maj. maj.7	min. min.7	min. min.7	maj. maj.7	maj. dom.7	min. min.7	dim. min.7($\flat$5)	- Triads - Tetrads
Dorian	min. min.7	min. min.7	maj. maj.7	maj. dom.7	min. min.7	dim. min.7($\flat$5)	maj. maj.7	- Triads - Tetrads
Phrygian	min. min.7	maj. maj.7	maj. dom.7	min. min.7	dim. min.7($\flat$5)	maj. maj.7	min. min.7	- Triads - Tetrads
Lydian	maj. maj.7	maj. dom.7	min. min.7	dim. min.7($\flat$5)	maj. maj.7	min. min.7	min. min.7	- Triads - Tetrads
Mixolydian	maj. dom.7	min. min.7	dim. min.7($\flat$5)	maj. maj.7	min. min.7	min. min.7	maj. maj.7	- Triads - Tetrads
Aeolian	min. min.7	dim. min.7($\flat$5)	maj. maj.7	min. min.7	min. min.7	maj. maj.7	maj. dom.7	- Triads - Tetrads
Locrian	dim. min.7($\flat$5)	maj. maj.7	min. min.7	min. min.7	maj. maj.7	maj. dom.7	min. min.7	- Triads - Tetrads

As you can see, each mode offers a different set of chord qualities. This immediately increases the subtle harmonic relationships possible without resorting to chromatic alterations and traditional restrictions. The dominant-tonic relationship of the major-minor system is for the most part destroyed because of the V chord either being a minor dominant (modes: Dorian, Mixolydian, Aeolian) or the dominant function occurring on a scale degree other than the fifth (modes: Locrian--6th degree; Dorian--4th degree, etc).

Example 183 shows some of the common types of cadences in each mode. These cadences are derived by noting the resolution of each mode's characteristic notes. With these fundamentals, one can compose melodies in any mode and harmonize them with the available modal structures. The only restrictions or guidelines would be the following:

EXAMPLE 183:

SPECIAL NOTE: BECAUSE OF THE I CHORD BEING DIMINISHED, IT IS DIFFICULT TO CONSTRUCT HARMONIC PROGRESSIONS. MELODIC EXAMPLES ARE EASIER.

Melodic Guidelines

1. Emphasize the primary axis (the root) by frequency (number of times played), by duration, and by melodic cadence (7 to 1, 2 to 1, etc).

2. Use all notes in the mode or the mode may not be clearly defined. If some notes are left out, however, they may be included in the harmony.

3. Place secondary importance on the characteristic notes of the mode--primary emphasis is, of course, on the tonic or root of the mode.

4. Use nonmodal notes sparingly or the modal effect will be lost. Occasional approach notes are fine, however.

Harmonic Guidelines

1. All harmony should be predominantly derived from the mode or you will lose the modal sound.

2. Harmony may be tertial (thirds) or nontertial (fourths, fifths, clusters, modal).

3. Although you may name each modal chord as in the major-minor system, it is sometimes easier to simply say C Dorian or F Phrygian, etc. When in doubt, write it out.

4. Modal voicings, if you will remember, have no avoid notes, and consequently create no obligation to define particular chord qualities. Some or all notes of the mode may be voiced, and this may be done in any manner possible (see Chapter 13, "Voicings and Comping").

    Example 184 is an 8-bar phrase I wrote to demonstrate a modal melody and accompanying harmony. The melody and harmony are derived from C Phrygian. I have also written the suggested harmonic changes so you can see both viewpoints--harmonic (vertical) and modal (horizontal). Both viewpoints were considered, as well as my ear, of course, when composing this example.

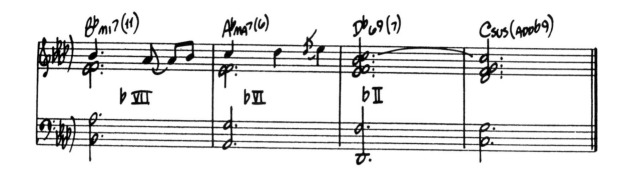

Drill:

    Write modal melodies in all the different modes
and harmonize them using modal voicings (tertial
or nontertial).

    Now, just as in the major-minor system there are
different key centers within the main key, a modal composition can have a variety of modes, both from a horizontal
and a vertical viewpoint. There are consequently five
possibilities of interaction between the primary axis
(root), pitch axis (key), and type of mode. I would like
to acknowledge Ray Santisi for this method of modal
organization (Categories 1-5).

1.   Common Primary Axis - Different Pitch Axis - Differ-
     ent Modes

    Same starting note, different key centers and differ-
ent modes.

    Examples: C Dorian   C Phrygian   C Lydian
                  8 bars   4 bars   4 bars
                  Key of Bb   Key of Ab   Key of G

2.   Unimodal - Unitonal

    Same mode and same key. Example 184 was in one key
(Ab) and used one mode, C Phrygian. This phrase is
therefore analyzed as unimodal - unitonal.

    Example: C Phrygian
                  8 bars
                  Key of Ab

3. <u>Unitonal - Polymodal</u>

    Same key but different modes.

    <u>Examples:</u>   G Mixolydian   D Dorian   F Lydian
                       4 bars   4 bars   4 bars
                       Key of C   Key of C   Key of C

4. <u>Polytonal - Unimodal</u>

    Different keys but same mode.

    <u>Examples:</u>   C Phrygian   D Phrygian   A Phrygian
                       4 bars   4 bars   4 bars
                       Key of A♭   Key of B♭   Key of F

5. <u>Polytonal - Polymodal</u>

    Different key and different mode.

    <u>Examples:</u>   C Ionian   D Lydian   F Aeolian
                       6 bars   3 bars   3 bars
                       Key of C   Key of A   Key of A♭

    Here are some modal selections to listen to and learn:

    1. <u>Impressions</u> - John Coltrane
    2. <u>Little Sunflower</u> - Freddie Hubbard
    3. <u>Guijira</u> - Chick Corea
    4. <u>Boston Marathon</u> - Gary Burton
    5. <u>Freedom Jazz Dance</u> - Eddie Harris
    6. <u>Passion Dance</u> - McCoy Tyner
    7. <u>So What</u> - Miles Davis

There are many more in all styles, serious to commercial. Modality can be applied to any style. Try writing some compositions in your favorite style using modes!

One may also mix the major-minor system with the modal system with the chromatic system with any system-- as you can see, the possibilities are infinite, which makes for a great game. Here are some examples of compositions that mix musical systems:

1. Litha - Chick Corea

2. Inner Urge - Joe Henderson

3. The Rite of Spring - Igor Stravinsky

4. Anna Maria - Wayne Shorter

5. Birdland - Weather Report

6. The Sunken Cathedral - Debussy.

POLYTONALITY AND POLYMODALITY

Whereas tonality implies the supremacy of a single key center at a time and modality implies the supremacy of a single mode at a time, polytonality and polymodality imply the existence of two or more keys or modes simultaneously. The result is a heightened friction between the keys or modes. Since most listeners can only assimilate two key centers at a time, the use of bitonality (two keys) or bimodality (two modes) is still the most effective. For this technique to work, each plane of harmony must be clearly rooted in its respective key.

Example 185 is an 8-bar excerpt from No. 148 of Microkosmos--a six-volume piano instruction course by Bela Bartok. Notice how Bartok uses the two modes, E Ionian and E Phrygian, against one another to create a kind of third key center or bimodality. Charles Ives, Igor Stravinsky, and other 20th century composers have not only used polytonality and polymodality, but often have juxtaposed two or more rhythms against one another--polyrhythms! Although frequent use of these techniques is a bit much for most listeners to digest, a little here and there may add that contemporary sound when needed.

EXAMPLE 185:   # 148 MIKROKOSMOS   BELA BARTOK

MODAL PLAN | E IONIAN | E PHRYGIAN |
           | E PHRYGIAN | E IONIAN | ETC.

MODAL IMPROVISATION

Now that you have a basic background in the modes, you'll find it a lot easier using them for improvisation. In order to gain some facility and experience permuting the modes, as well as other scales (whole tone, altered dominant, symmetrical diminished, etc), do the exercises in Example 186. Section (a) deals with major modes and scales, while (b) deals with minor modes and scales. The left hand comp pattern is simply a voicing in modal fourths (notes derived from the mode). While comping with

the left hand, explore various permutations of the mode or
scale with your right hand. After a while you should be
able to create some good lines using just the notes in the
modes and scales. Don't forget to apply the intervallic
techniques you learned in Chapter 11, "Advanced Improvisation." Also, while soloing, remember the melodic guidelines discussed earlier in this chapter, as they will help
guide you towards that "modal sound."

EXAMPLE 186B: MINOR MODES OR SCALES

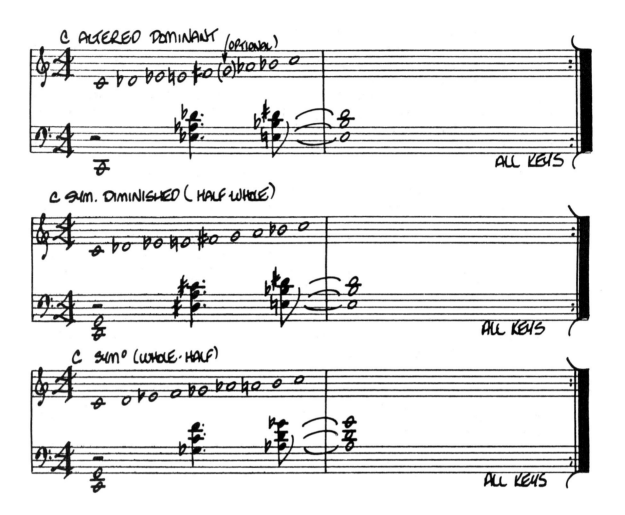

Note: Don't worry about the perfect fifth in the left hand relative to the modes and scales containing flat fifths. Because of the overtone series, the ear accepts this sound, even though the perfect fifth is not diatonic to the scale!

PENTATONIC SCALE STUDIES

Pentatonic scales (five-note scales) are very popular in many musical styles. They can readily be found in the works of Debussy, Bartok, and Stravinsky; in those of Chick Corea, McCoy Tyner, and Oscar Peterson; and in those of rock guitarists such as Jimi Hendrix, Van Halen, etc. The only difference from style to style is in how they're used. The main reason for this popularity is that they are natural for the human voice to duplicate and sing-- they've been around for a long time!

The reason I've waited until now to discuss them is because they are best understood after certain fundamentals are locked in (chord families, tensions, chord scales, approach notes, etc). Pentatonic scales are obviously two notes short of a regular seven-note scale and thus don't indicate the complete possible chord sound or color. Many beginning musicians learn certain easy pentatonic scale patterns over some basic changes and that's all they play. But being this limited in what they can play puts them at <u>effect</u> rather than <u>cause</u>. Now that we have a broader viewpoint of the game, devices such as pentatonic scales and blues scales will be frosting on the cake!

Although there are many five-note scales, the two used most are those I call the <u>tonic major</u> and <u>tonic minor</u> (Example 187). The same two scales, starting on their respective fifth degrees (in both cases A), give us two other important pentatonic scales, which when combined form the famous blues scale. I refer to these two other scales as the <u>relative minor</u> pentatonics. Example 188 shows the construction of the relative minor and relative minor flat fifth pentatonic scales, and Example 189 shows the blues scale, which can be derived from adding both relative minor pentatonics together. I'm not saying the blues scale was historically formed this way, but it is interesting. We'll explore this in more detail in the next chapter, "The Blues."

Drill:

Practice the seven permutations in Example 190a (major pentatonic) and in 190b (minor pentatonic). Since the relative minor pentatonic scales are actually permutations of the major and minor pentatonic scales--each starting on a different degree--you'll be learning all four scales by practicing the indicated exercises in all keys. For now, use C♭9 and C min.♭9 as the left-hand comp for the major and minor scales respectively. Use your own fingerings--ones that work for you.

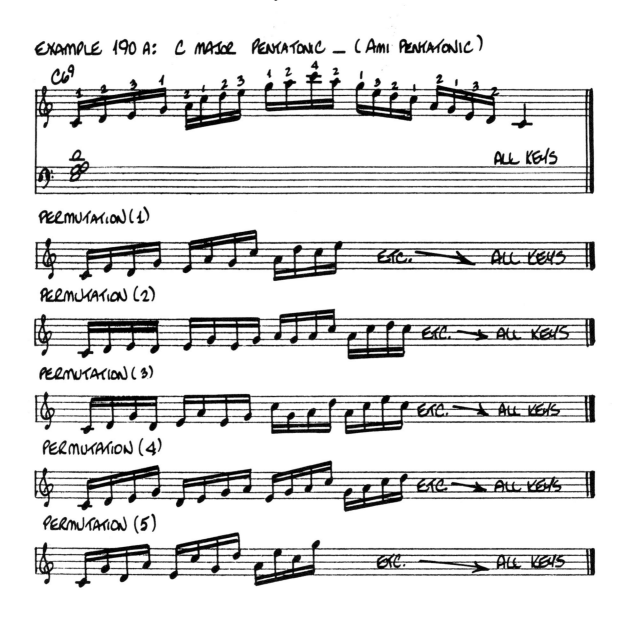

EXAMPLE 190 A: C MAJOR PENTATONIC — (AMI PENTATONIC)

PERMUTATION (1)

PERMUTATION (2)

PERMUTATION (3)

PERMUTATION (4)

PERMUTATION (5)

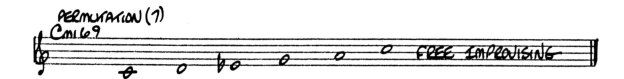

PERMUTATION (7)
Cmi69 ... FREE IMPROVISING

A device that players love to use is superimposing these scales over other chord qualities to create various colors. I have written down some of the possibilities relative to each pentatonic scale. Some really work-- others are ambiguous. Those most used are underlined--but again, use your ear! Practice the ones you like in all keys.

	C Major Pentatonic Scale	C Minor Pentatonic Scale
	(C,D,E,G,A,C)	(C,D,E$\flat$,G,A,C)
Possible Chords:	C maj.7	C min.(maj.7)
	F maj.7	F7
	A min.7	A min.7($\flat$5)
	B$\flat$ maj.7	A7$^{\sharp 9}_{\flat 13}$
	D min.7	D7($\flat$9)
	E min.7($\flat$5)	C min.7
	E min.7	E$\flat$ maj.7
	D7 sus.4	B7$^{\flat 9}_{\flat 13}$
	F$\sharp$ min.7($\flat$5)	F$\sharp$°7
	G7 sus.4	
	B min.7($\flat$5)	
	C7	

This juxtapositioning concept also works with the modes. When one wishes to make the mode a little ambiguous, playing "pentatonically" may add just the right touch. The following pentatonic scales may function with these various modes:

	C Major Pentatonic	C Minor Pentatonic
	Scale	Scale
	(C,D,E,G,A,C)	(C,D,E♭,G,A,C)

Possible
Modes:

C Ionian   C Dorian

C Lydian   F Mixolydian

A Aeolian   A Locrian

D Dorian   E♭ Lydian

G Mixolydian   B altered dominant

C Mixolydian

D Mixolydian

B♭ Lydian

F♯ Locrian

E Locrian

E Phrygian

F Lydian

F Ionian

See if you can think of more possibilities!

Now take a look at Example 191a for an example of pentatonic scales applied to changes and Example 191b for pentatonic scales applied to the modes. In 191a, Phrase 1 is derived from an E♭ major pentatonic starting on the fifth degree, or C minor relative pentatonic. Phrase 2 is derived from a B♭ major pentatonic starting on the fifth degree, or G relative minor pentatonic.

EXAMPLE 191 A:

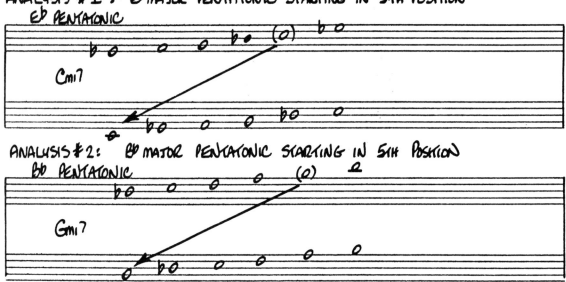

ANALYSIS #1: Eb MAJOR PENTATONIC STARTING IN 5TH POSITION

Eb PENTATONIC

Cmi7

ANALYSIS #2: Bb MAJOR PENTATONIC STARTING IN 5TH POSITION

Bb PENTATONIC

Gmi7

In Example 191b, the pentatonic scale used is derived from C major, starting on the fifth degree, or A relative minor pentatonic. The F in parentheses is the only note actually not in the pentatonic scale. Nevertheless, it is part of the A Phrygian scale and so is available.

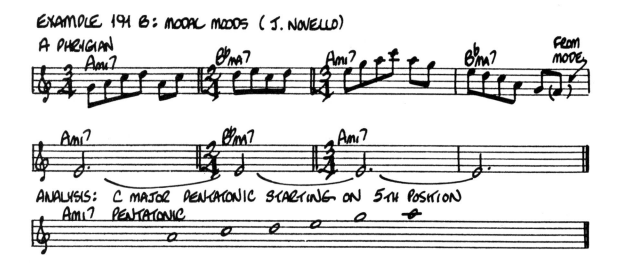

EXAMPLE 191 B: MODAL MOODS (J. NOVELLO)

A PHRYGIAN

Ami7   Bbma7   Ami7   Bbma7   FROM MODE

Ami7   Bbma7   Ami7

ANALYSIS: C MAJOR PENTATONIC STARTING ON 5TH POSITION

Ami7 PENTATONIC

To summarize, pentatonic scales can add a nice flavor to solos, especially if you use the permutations and juxtapositions just discussed and your imagination. Remember, though, pentatonic scales are not the complete picture. When you really want to "make the changes" or play clearly in the mode, you must include the other notes, tensions, approach notes, characteristic modal notes, etc.

338

"OUTSIDE" MODAL TECHNIQUES

Just as tonality can be stretched by the addition of tensions and nondiatonic notes (chromaticism), modality can be stretched by the use of free modal interchange (polymodality from a horizontal relationship) and by the superpositioning of modes against each other (polymodality from a vertical relationship).

In free modal playing, one simply emphasizes one main mode while taking temporary excursions to other modes. These excursions can be radical--like F Mixolydian to F♯ Lydian, where almost all the notes are different--or they can be subtle, like F Mixolydian to F Lydian, where only two notes are different. Also, in this type of playing, the left hand closely follows the right hand as to mode. In other words, if the right hand goes to F♯ Lydian, the left hand comp also goes to F♯ Lydian, and so on.

In Example 192, the initial solo mode is simply F Mixolydian. However, in this case, I took a few modal excursions to G♭ Lydian, to G Lydian ♭7, to A♭ Mixolydian, to G♭ Lydian ♭7, and back home to F Mixolydian. Notice that the left hand comps in the same mode as the right!

Drill:

> Practice spontaneously transitioning to any mode while maintaining one overall basic mode. For this exercise, be sure your left hand is always comping in the same mode that your right hand is.

In polymodal playing (vertical relationship), the same thing as above happens, only the right and left hands can be in different modes simultaneously. This produces a polymodal vertical effect. There are two such possibilities:

1. Left hand stays in one mode, usually the original, while the right hand makes a transition to another mode or modes, and eventually returns (tension and release). See Example 193a, which is the same as Example 192 except left hand stays in F Mixolydian!

EXAMPLE 193 A: POLYMODAL PLAYING

2. Left hand makes a transition to another mode or modes, while the right hand continues to improvise in the original mode (Example 193b).

EXAMPLE 193 B:

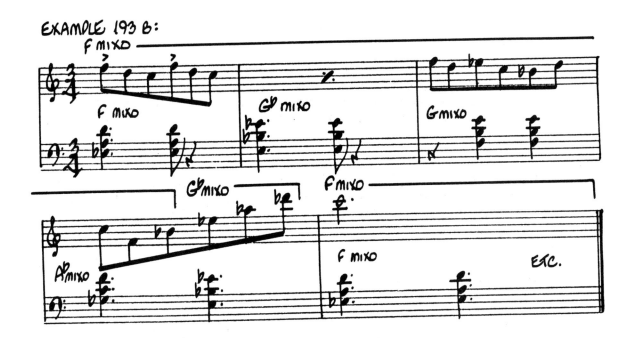

Now, by combining free modal playing with polymodal playing, we can create a musical system similar to chromaticism in the major-minor system, but much less restricted. I highly suggest doing record copies of the following two tunes in order to get a greater understanding of these concepts:

1. <u>Passion Dance</u> - McCoy Tyner

2. <u>Guijira</u> - Chick Corea

I hope this chapter has given you an insight into the modes and some of their possible applications.

Chapter 14
ASSIGNMENTS

_____ 1. What are the modes? Define <u>primary axis</u> and <u>pitch axis</u> as they relate to modes.

_____ 2. Write out all the modes in all keys as per Example 181. Memorize each mode's formula (e.g., Dorian is ♭3 and ♭7).

_____ 3. How does modal harmony differ from diatonic major-minor harmony with respect to the basic triad and tetrad qualities? How does this difference affect traditional harmonic progressions? Give some examples.

_____ 4. Using the melodic and harmonic guidelines in this chapter, compose at least two modal melodies in each mode and harmonize them, using modal voicings (tertial or nontertial). They may be in any style you wish. Refer to Example 184.

_____ 5. What are the five possibilities of interaction between a mode and its primary axis and pitch axis? Define each interaction and give your own examples. How might these interactions be used to write compositions, versus writing compositions in the traditional major-minor system?

_____ 6. Define <u>polytonality</u> and <u>polymodality</u>. How do they differ from tonality and modality?

_____ 7. Do the Modal Drill, Examples 186a and b, as indicated and discussed in the chapter. I suggest taking one mode at a time and practicing it in all keys. Then move on to the next mode and continue. It takes as long as it takes!

_____ 8. What are pentatonic scales? Do the pentatonic drill as indicated in Examples 190a and b.

_____ 9. Practice playing superimposed major and minor pentatonic scales over different chord qualities. Do the same with the modes. Refer to Examples 191a and b.

_____ 10. What is "outside" modal playing? Define <u>free modal</u> and <u>polymodal</u> playing and give examples.

_____ 11. <u>Drill</u>:

While maintaining one overall basic mode, practice spontaneously transitioning to others. Do this in the following ways:

    a. Left hand and right hand are always in the same mode.

    b. Left hand stays in original mode while right hand takes excursions through other modes and then back to original.

    c. Left hand comps through different modes while the right hand improvises in the original mode.

    d. All of the above! Go for it!

_____ 12. Do a record copy of either "Passion Dance" (McCoy Tyner) or "Guijira" (Chick Corea)--or both, if you wish--making sure you duplicate the left hand as well as the right.

Chapter 15

The Blues

Jazz is an art form which is basically a blend of African rhythms and folk elements of our American culture--which, of course, has its roots in Europe. It seems to be a form of all forms in that it can include--and be included in--many other musical styles and genres: popular, classical, gospel, theatrical, rhythm and blues--you name it!

Its evolution began with forms such as work songs, rags, spirituals, dances, and blues. I believe that this art form would not have emerged had it not been for the Afro-American culture and the communications of its people.

One particular form, the 12-bar blues, has survived many decades and has been constantly revised to fit the rhythm and harmony of the time. Its simple structure has served as a vehicle for communication of the feelings of many artists of varied musical backgrounds (gospel, rock, jazz, etc). The blues has had such an impact on the music scene that if you're a player and can't cook on the blues, you're not happening, man! It's the unstated test of a "good player."

To any musician, trained or untrained, the blues means a fairly fixed set of harmonic changes; over the years, these changes have been reharmonized as needed and wanted. Let's now analyze the basic form and all of its permutations.

The basic harmonic structure involves simply the I, IV and V chord placed in the following manner:

Form 1: Stock Blues

/ I7	/ I7	/ I7	/ I7	/ -	4 bars
/ IV7	/ IV7	/ I7	/ I7	/ -	+4 bars
/ V7	/ IV7	/ I7	/ V7	/ -	+4 bars
					12 bars total

The last two bars of the 12-bar blues make up what is commonly referred to as the turnaround. The turnaround is the set of changes that turns the blues around to the beginning so it can start all over again--and again, and again!

Form 2: Jazz Blues

/ I7	/ IV7	/ I7	/ I7	/
/ IV7	/ IV7	/ I7	/ VI7	/
/ II min.7	/ V7	/ I7 VI7	/ II min.7 V7 /	

Notice that in this version the basic pivot chords are still there (bar 1--I7, bar 5--IV7), but the addition of the IV7 chord in bar 2 and the VI7 in bar 8, along with the II min.7 - V7 progression substitutes in bars 9 and 10, give this blues a new dimension without destroying its basic integrity. The reharmonizations and/or substitutions have been circled for your quick recognition. Notice the different turnaround.

Form 3: Gospel Blues

				(II-V/of IV)	
/ I7	I$^6_5$	/ IV7 #IV°7	/ I$^6_4$ I7	/ V min.7 I7	/
/ IV7		/ #IV°7	/ I$^6_4$ #V°7	/ VI7	/
/ II7		/ V7sus.4	/ I I$^7_{6\,5}$ IV^6 #IV°7	/ I$^6_{4\,3}$ $\flat$VI7 V7	/

Harmonic Rhythm

Figured bass key

$$I^6_4 = \text{Triad in 2nd inversion}$$

$$IV_6 = \text{Triad in 1st inversion}$$

$$I^6_5 = \text{Tetrad in 1st inversion}$$

$$I_{4\,3} = \text{Tetrad in 2nd inversion}$$

$$I_2 = \text{Tetrad in 3rd inversion}$$

The basic idea behind this blues is to create a more interesting bass line. Notice, therefore, measures 1 and 2, 5 and 6, and 7 and 8, as well as the turnaround. This bass movement was accomplished by the use of inversions and our friend, the passing diminished chord. Check out the II-V progression that was added to bar 4 to set up the IV chord better.

Form 4: Be-bop Blues or the "Charlie Parker Blues"

/ I7   (IV7) / VII min.7($\flat$5) III7 / VI min.7   II7 / V min.7   I7 /

/ IV7   / IV min.7 $\flat$VII7 / III min.7   / VI7   /

/ II min.7 / V7   / III min.7 $\flat$III7 / II min.7 $\flat$II7/

The first four measures consist simply of a sequence of II-V progressions based on the diatonic circle of fifths (I-IV-VII-III-VI-II-V-I). The IV chord in the first measure is optional. The rest of the blues is pretty stock except for some standard chord substitutions in bars 6 and 7 and the turnaround. Be-bop players love to solo on this form for obvious reasons.

Getting acquainted with these four standard blues forms will help you understand the many many permutations that have already evolved, as well as help you create your own through the use of basic chord substitutions and reharmonizations. (See Chapter 12, "Advanced Harmony.") Example 194 demonstrates these four blues forms and some of their possible permutations. The chords in parentheses are optional, but should be played so the ear can get used to them. There are literally an infinite number of possibilities! Once you finally "hear" the blues--or should I say, feel the blues, you'll realize that there is only one form--the blues!

EXAMPLE 194: BLUES PROGRESSIONS
Form #1

Also, these chords can be voiced in any manner--triads, clusters, fourths--whatever. The style determines the arrangement, but the blues is "da blues"!

These forms may also be interchanged with each other and, in fact, usually are. It's very common, for example, to start out, let's say, with Form 2 as the overall basic form, and in the middle of someone's solo, transition to Form 4 and then back to 2. Like I said earlier, they're all the blues, so it doesn't matter unless it's a very rigid style, such as a rock shuffle, which is usually Form 1 all the way through.

In order to become comfortable with the blues, do the following harmonic drills in all keys. The first one deals with comping with guide tones. These are the critical tones that actually point out or define the chord quality--which is why they are called guide tones. Without them the chord quality is ambiguous. Many players comp with guide tones as it leaves a lot of space for the soloist to play on the changes. Guide tone playing also helps one hear the "soul" of the particular harmonic progression. The second drill deals with comping with four-way close voicings. Try varying the tempo, groove, and time signature (e.g., slow funk groove in 3/4). (See Example 195):

Drills:

1. Guide tone drill

   Left hand plays the root or bass while the right hand plays the critical tones of each chord quality. These are known as guide tones.

2. A-B voicings drill

   Left hand plays root or bass while the right hand plays A-B voicings or any four-way close voicing.

The blues is, as you are seeing, a very flexible form. After you have mastered the guide tones and standard four-way close voicings, don't forget all the other types of voicings--fourths, fifths, clusters, modal, etc.

BLUES IMPROVISATION

With regard to soloing on the blues, all the improvisational techniques discussed so far obviously work and should be explored. However, there are certain techniques idiomatic to the blues that we should definitely get familiar with. These techniques, which make up the blues sound, are so strong that they permeate all styles of music, especially jazz.

The blues sound is basically composed of two elements:

1. The blues scale: R, ♭3, 4, ♯4, 5, ♭7, R

2. Blues tones: crushed, usually nondiatonic notes that approach scale tones, but most often chord tones.

Example 196 contains all the blues scales in two octaves and their suggested fingerings. For practice purposes, play a dominant 7th voicing with your left hand while you run the scale with your right hand. Acquaint yourself with some possible permutations as you did with the modes.

EXAMPLE 196: BLUES SCALES

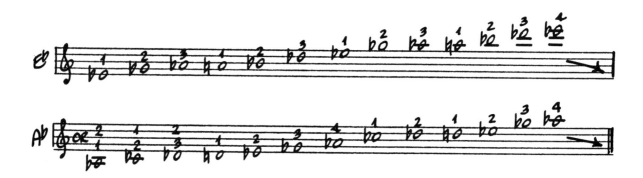

"Blue" notes are probably derived from archaic folk guitar, harmonica, and the human voice--all of which are capable of bending notes flat or sharp. This produces tension and release--hence the concept of "blue" (emotional) notes. On piano, blue tones are achieved by grace notes--the crushing of one or more notes into another or others (Example 197). With the advent of the synthesizer, however, keyboardists can now bend notes, if they so desire, as well as do many other incredible things. This bending technique will be discussed in Chapter 18, "Multi-keyboards." Yes, keyboards have definitely come a long way and are the happening instrument now and in the future!

EXAMPLE 197: CRUSHED NOTES *

So, to recapitulate, the blues can be said to be made up of the following:

1. Form: usually 12 bars which harmonically conform to one of the four patterns or their permutations.

2.   Melodic Content:

    a.   Idiomatic blues scale and blue (crushed) notes.

    b.   Conventional improvisational techniques.

I'd like to add that to really <u>feel</u> the blues emo- tionally, try playing or singing them when you're down or a little depressed (bluesy). Although this is not really necessary, it might help you duplicate a little of the original viewpoint that the early blues artists had, and might even answer why the 12-bar form is such a good vehicle for expression!

Examples 198 and 199 contain some traditional blues phrases, intros, and endings. They're all based on C7 and should of course be transposed to all keys. They by no means constitute all the possibilities. You may alter, extend, or shorten them, as well as create your own. They are simply food for thought--a way of helping you hear the blues sound.

EXAMPLE 199: CLICHE BLUES INTROS AND ENDINGS

Also, this blues sound does not just apply to the 12-bar blues. The blues in general is a substratum of jazz, gospel, R&B, rock, funk, fusion, country and western--you name it. So don't limit these sounds to the 12-bar blues only.

Now, by applying the data on improvising to the blues, we get the following:

1. Vertical Playing: "making the changes," be-bop, and outside techniques.

2. Tonal or Key Center Playing: use of blues scales and blue notes.

The use of both concepts is recommended to produce interesting lines, as playing only blues riffs can become very tiresome. In Example 200, the solo I've written uses predominantly key center riffs based on the C blues scale and C minor pentatonic scale, with the exception of bars 7 and 8 and bar 12, beats 3 and 4, which use the vertical concept of "making the changes." As you can see, changing back and forth between these two techniques makes for the most interesting blues improvisations, as long as you're "hearing" what you're playing!

EXAMPLE 200: BLUES SOLO

Drill:

Using both techniques, write your own solos over the various blues forms. You might also do some record copies of those of your favorite artists who incorporate the blues in their playing.

Here are some artists I suggest you listen to:

Ray Charles - vocals and piano
Dinah Washington - vocals
Ella Fitzgerald - vocals
B.B. King - guitar and vocals
Les McCann - keyboards and vocals
Dr. John - vocals and piano
Johnny Winter - guitar and vocals
Edgar Winter - vocals, sax, and keyboards
Stevie Wonder - vocals, harmonica, and keyboards
Jimmy Smith - organ
Oscar Peterson - piano
Charlie Parker - sax
John Coltrane - sax
Louis Armstrong - vocals and trumpet
Miles Davis - trumpet
Horace Silver - piano
Thelonius Monk - piano
Jerry Lee Lewis - piano
Otis Redding - vocals
Sam Cooke - vocals
Mike Bloomfield - guitar
Ramsey Lewis - piano
Muddy Waters - guitar and vocals
James Booker - vocals and keyboards

These are only a few to help orient you to the blues tradition. There are many more!

MINOR BLUES

Just as there is the 12-bar major blues, there is also the 12-bar minor blues. Although there are many versions of the minor blues, the following is standard and correct (Example 201). The only real change is the II-V of I in measure 2, which is much stronger than F min.7-- although F min.7 is still possible. The rest of the changes are just standard chord substitutions (e.g., E♭7 for A7 in bar 8, etc).

EXAMPLE 201: MINOR BLUES (C MINOR BLUES)

Although you now have enough data on improvisation to determine the available notes for improvising on the blues, I have nevertheless written out the appropriate chord scales for you to practice. A natural sign above a note means you have a choice (e.g., bar 8 A-flat or A-natural).

Conceptually, the minor blues is no different than the major blues. The use of blues scales and blue notes along with "making the changes" is still the way to travel.

Drill:

  Learn the changes of the minor blues in all keys!

Example 202, "Israel," is a unique tune by John Carisi which was made popular by the late Bill Evans (Example 202). The two cliche lines (5 - #5 - 6) in bars 1, 2, and 3 and bars 5 and 6, along with the modal interchange in bars 6, 7 and 8, make this a very interesting composition, especially to improvise on.

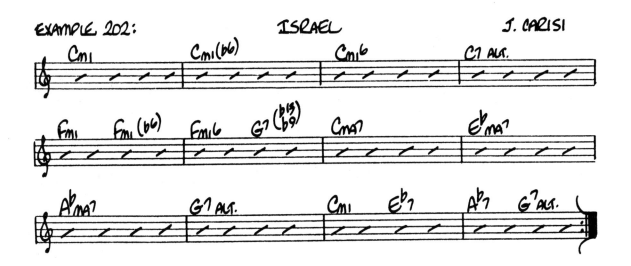

EXAMPLE 202:   ISRAEL   J. CARISI

OTHER BLUES FORMS

Over the years, composers have tampered with the basic 12-bar form and created all kinds of interesting departures. It is not uncommon to find 8, 16, or even 20-bar blues as well as a 12-bar blues for the A section of a tune and a non-blues form perhaps for the B section. Your imagination is your limit.

The following is a partial--and I mean <u>partial</u>--list of some famous blues I think you should get <u>familiar</u> with. They can usually be found in most good jazz fakebooks. Good hunting and keep cookin'!

"Billy's Bounce" . . . . .Bird (Charlie Parker)
"Au Privave" . . . . .Bird
"Bloomdido". . . . . .Bird
"Bud's Blues". . . . . .Bud Powell
"Blue Monk". . . . . .Monk
"Blues for Alice". . . . . . .Bird
"All Blues". . . . . .Miles Davis
"Eighty One" . . . . .Miles Davis
"Nostalgia in Times Square". .Charles Mingus
"Pfrancing (No Blues)" . . . .Miles Davis
"Straight No Chaser" . . . . .Monk
"Footprints" (minor blues) . .Wayne Shorter
"Blue Traine" (minor blues). .Train (John Coltrane)

Chapter 15
ASSIGNMENTS

_____ 1. Write out the changes to the four blues forms in all keys and then do the guide tone drill and A-B voicings drill as indicated (see Example 195).

_____ 2. What is a turnaround? Give at least four examples.

_____ 3. What is the blues sound basically composed of? Give musical examples as necessary.

_____ 4. Learn all the blues scales as indicated in Example 196.

_____ 5. Practice in all keys the traditional blues riffs and endings given in Examples 198 and 199.

_____ 6. Does the "blues sound" only apply to the 12-bar blues? Explain.

_____ 7. Describe the two improvisational concepts-- vertical playing and key center playing--as they relate to the blues.

_____ 8. Write at least two improvisations on each blues form, using the above two techniques.

_____ 9. Listen to as many blues artists as possible. Use the suggested list to get you started. Do record copies of your favorite solos.

_____ 10. Learn the minor blues, as indicated, in all keys. Use the guide tone and A-B voicings drills, as you did for the major blues.

_____ 11. When you're in a position to jam with other musicians, play a lot of blues for openers. The blues can only be really learned from doing--not studying!

Chapter 16
Sight Reading

Definitions:

      Reading, the ability to translate all musical symbols and markings into music. This may not necessarily be on the first reading. One may have to "shed" the more difficult passages in order to produce a proper rendition.

      Sight Reading, reading upon sight! The ability to read a music score from beginning to end, without stopping, as competently and musically as possible.

In other words, a great sight reader is also a great reader, but not necessarily vice versa! There are many levels of competence attainable in sight reading. The level you reach depends not only on consistent sight reading practice, but on your current level of playing expertise. Now, although the ability to sight read isn't necessary in order for someone to "make it," it can be very costly, especially to a keyboard player, not to have it. Sight reading opens the doors not only to the vast literature written for keyboards, but also to work of all types. And that means survival! Album, demo, film score, and commercial gigs, and jobs as rehearsal pianist, accompanist, and musical director--all require sight reading to a greater or lesser degree. So increase your odds for success! The rewards greatly outweigh the pains of learning this skill.

      The real secret of sight reading is that there is no secret! Seventy percent of learning how to sight read is simply sight reading every day, gradually confronting progressively more difficult music. Simply doing this will enable you to make steady improvement. The other thirty percent can be attacked through a discipline that I'm about to give you--so if you're ready, here goes!

1. **Quick-Study the Score**

   This means look over the score and note the following:

   a. **Tempo**

      The tempo marking ultimately helps one determine the speed, style, and groove, as well as the level of difficulty, of the composition.

   b. **Time Signature**

      Important for determining the basic time and rhythm of the composition. Be sure to note whether there are any changes of time signature within the composition, as they can be potential stumbling blocks.

   c. **Key Signature**

      When present, indicates the basic tonality of the composition as well as any major changes within. Its absence could indicate the use of accidentals only, so be alert!

   d. **Clef Signs**

      Clef signs help place the pitch of the tones in relation to your instrument. Note any changes of clef signs immediately!

   e. **The Road Map**

      This is the mapped-out journey through the score. It includes repeat sections, returning to the top of the score (D.C.), returning to the sign (D.S.), jumping to codas, first and second endings, etc. This is extremely important when doing studio work such as films, commercials, and album dates. Losing your place during a cooking performance because you didn't check out the "road map" first is inexcusable!

f. Worry Spots

These are areas that your attention gets stuck on when you glance through the score. In other words, you say "oh-oh!" Check these areas out before reading the score. They are usually fast passages, unfamiliar chords, wide arpeggios, tricky rhythms, solos, etc. <u>Axiom:</u> <u>The more worry spots you find, the more sight reading practice you need!</u> You may also be in over your head!

2. <u>Correct Tempo</u>

This only applies when one is <u>practicing</u> sight reading, not when one is sight reading, as on a gig. The correct practice tempo for sight reading is obtained by finding the tempo that allows you to play the entire composition all the way through without stopping and with few mistakes. If there are too many stops and mistakes, the tempo is definitely too fast, and maybe the piece is even too difficult for your level of expertise. The solution is to either slow the piece down considerably, or pick a less challenging one. <u>Sight reading</u> is <u>continuity</u> practice--therefore, <u>no stopping!</u> (In contrast, woodshedding is reiterative practice--difficult areas done repeatedly until they are learned!)

3. <u>Eyes On Score</u>

Although this should be obvious, it is the <u>fundamental</u>--and I mean <u>the</u> fundamental--most violated! The <u>compulsion</u> to take your eyes away from the score and look at the keys to find them disrupts the sight reading process. It also slows you down, because the mind's eye (you) is much quicker than the body's eye! There's also less of a tendency to stop when you watch the score, because you're too busy <u>sight reading</u>. Check out blind pianists. They find <u>their</u> way around pretty well, don't they?

4.   Keyboard Communication

Physical contact with the keyboard is a form of com-
munication--tactile, to be exact. By keeping one's
hands in physical contact with the keys, even when
they are temporarily not in use, the visual image of
the score is more easily translated into an aural
image and thus into music. The communication lines
go like this:

MUSICAL SCORE to BODY'S EYES to BRAIN (body's coordination center) to MIND'S EYE (YOU, the cat in
charge), who in turn sends instructions to the BRAIN,
which coordinates the BODY'S PLAYING MACHINERY in
order to reproduce the score. (Example 203.)

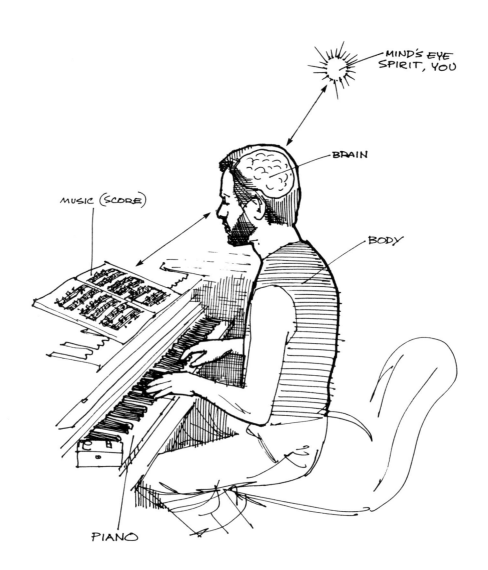

(An interesting thought here is that if we could raise our awareness to higher plateaus, we might be able to communicate music, concepts, etc., telepathically! It's kind of a drag that it takes so long to learn how to play well. Training bodies seems like an archaic way to communicate!)

So not keeping contact with the keyboard tends to break the tactile communication line, which enforces the desire to look (another form of communication) at the keys. Again, we can learn from the blind. Notice how a blind piano player is never at home until seated in front of the piano and touching (in communication with) it!

5. Chords

Chords are confronted a lot more easily if they're read from the bottom up in each hand. The ear and eye seem to work better as a team if this technique is used. Try it and see for yourself, though. Whatever works for you is what's right.

6. Musical Knowledge

The greater one's actual understanding of music, the easier it is to duplicate other composers' compositions. The ability to recognize fundamental scale passages and chords, compositional devices, styles, etc., definitely facilitates the sight reading process. Need I say more?

ON-THE-GIG SIGHT READING

On-the-gig sight reading has this added pressure: To get paid and called back for more work, you can't mess up! Sight reading for fun is one thing, but sight reading for a living is quite another. Gigs calling for sight reading are lucrative, and the competition for them is heavy. Following is a program I put together to enhance your success using this valuable skill:

1. Sight read every day--everything and anything you can: chord charts, classical, commercial, theatrical--all styles.

2. Always remember to quick study any music you receive at sessions. Reading it blind is the mark of an amateur.

3. If there is time before you have to play, woodshed very quietly all difficult areas--even if you just lightly touch the tops of the keys. You'll be surprised what one can do in a few minutes with optimum concentration.

4. Relax! Do the best job you can. If you fail, you'll have gained some <u>valuable</u> experience for the next time--so go home and practice!

In Chapter 19, "Studio vs. Live Performance," session playing will be discussed in more detail.

I hope the data in this chapter helps you confront and conquer sight reading. Remember, it's no magical skill--it just takes experience and practice! So do it!

Chapter 16
ASSIGNMENTS

_____ 1. What is the difference between reading and sight reading?

_____ 2. What does <u>quick study</u> a score mean and why is it important?

_____ 3. When practicing sight reading, what does <u>correct tempo</u> mean?

_____ 4. What do keeping your eyes on the score and hands on the keyboard at all times have to do with good sight reading?

_____ 5. What is the best way to sight read chords?

_____ 6. What is the relationship of musical training to sight reading?

_____ 7. Do the following basic sight reading program:

     a. Sight read short simple pieces every day for at least one-half hour. Use the metronome, count out loud in the beginning, and apply all the data in this chapter (e.g., no stopping, keep eyes on score, etc). Gradually move on to more difficult pieces after you feel more confident. The following is a list of books and selections that you can use for this purpose.

        1. Bela Bartok. <u>Microkosmos</u>, 6 vols. London: Boosey and Hawkes, 1980.

        2. Vincent Persichetti. <u>The Little Piano Book</u>. Bryn Mawr, Pa.: Elkan-Vogel, 1954.

        3. J. S. Bach. <u>Selections from Anna Magdalena's Notebook</u>. Sherman Oaks, Ca.: Alfred Publishing Co., 1969.

        4. Chick Corea. <u>Complete Children's Pieces</u>. Los Angeles: Litha Music, 1981.

5. W. Mozart. Easy Selections for Piano. Sherman Oaks, Ca.: Alfred Publishing Co., 1976.

6. F. Chopin. Easy Selections for Piano. Sherman Oaks, Ca.: Alfred Publishing Co., 1976.

7. B. Bartok. Easy Selections for Piano. Sherman Oaks, Ca.: Alfred Publishing Co., 1976.

8. J. S. Bach. Album of 21 Pieces. New York: G.S. Schirmer, 1898.

9. J. S. Bach. Two and Three Part Inventions. New York: Edwin F. Kalmus, 1943.

10. F. Chopin. Preludes. New York: G.S. Schirmer, 1943.

11. J. S. Bach. 101 Chorales. Minneapolis: Hall and McCreary Co., 1952.

Supplement the above with your favorite artists' works and compositions (jazz, rock, pop, etc).

b. After sight reading a selection, you should learn it well so you acquire associative faculties that are helpful in sight reading.

c. In short, sight read and learn selections of all types and styles until it becomes second nature. The pleasure finally outweighs the pain. Again, it takes as long as it takes.

SUGGESTED READING

Everhart, Powell. The Pianist's Art. Atlanta: Powell Everhart, 962 Myrtle Street, Northeast, Atlanta 9, Georgia, 1958. chaps.14-15.

Hubbard, L. Ron. Dianetics 55! Los Angeles: The American St. Hill Organization, 1968. chaps.7-9.

Chapter 17

Technique

A musician conceives of a sound or an organization of sounds in his universe. Then, if he· so wishes, he decides to communicate this creation to somebody in the physical universe. The mechanics or "doingnesses" involved in pulling this stunt off come under the heading of technique. The type and amount of technique an artist may need, therefore, is directly proportional to the demands of his mental creation! The music, for example, that Chopin heard when he created his famous piano etudes is much more challenging from a technique standpoint than his Waltz in C♯ Minor. But it is not necessarily true that a work is better than another if its technique is more demanding. The resulting product is all that matters to the listener. As a matter of fact, a difficult composition performed with technique that reveals great effort will not communicate as well as a simpler one performed with effortless technique!

So if the performer still has attention on his technique, the listener, no matter how uneducated, will know something just isn't quite right. Now, this is important stuff here! So let's review. Technique is really the act of producing music--your music or your interpretation of another artist's music. You have enough technique when you can communicate your creations effortlessly and flawlessly. If the music you're hearing is not very demanding, then you may very well be through with the technique phase of development and should get on with the business of creating and performing. If one day you create something beyond your present technical development, then you might need to improve your technique. Get it? Of course, you can always hire someone else to perform it--but that's a cop-out if you have a goal to perform it!

The point here is that one should never put attention on mechanics unless they're a problem. Music is a joy to create, perform, and listen to. Don't make it a task by unnecessarily putting your attention on technique. Put your attention and intention on the communication of your product or message or whatever and you'll eventually develop the technique needed. Honest! Now, I'm not saying that practicing technique is unnecessary--I'm just putting it into proper perspective.

MECHANICS

All <u>keyboard</u> technique, whether for acoustic piano, electric piano, harpsichord, clavinet, organ, synthesizer, celeste, harmonium, accordion, or whatever, involves <u>key depression</u>--the application of force to a key in order to depress it. Although keyboards vary as to the amount of resistance and depth of each key (the distance the key moves when pressed down to the keybed), two ounces resistance and a depth of about three-eighths of an inch are pretty average.

The problem is not the act of pressing the key down--that's easy. The real difficulty lies in the constant positioning and repositioning of the hand by the <u>playing machinery</u> over the notes to be played. Once this positioning ability is achieved, lesser problems such as finger coordination, hand independence, velocity, touch, and dynamics can be more easily handled. The playing machinery is actually made up of a series of levers that are hinged together. From largest to smallest, they are as follows:

1. Torso - hinged at the hips
2. Upper Arm - hinged at the shoulder
3. Forearm - hinged at the elbow
4. Hand - hinged at the wrist
5. Fingers - hinged at the knuckles

The coordination of all these levers to produce a desired sound constitutes the mechanics of technique as related to keyboards. (If someone invents a different type of keyboard that catches on widely, then the whole school of technique might have to be revised and re-learned.) Although the finger presses the key down with a perpendicular force, it does not act or reach independently from the rest of the playing mechanism. The upper arm, assisted by the torso, is really the initiator of movement, with the fingers simply pressing the keys down when they are in position. If the upper arm is not permitted to cover position, the smaller levers (hands and fingers) are forced to do it, resulting in limited coverage and unnecessary reaching for the keys. A movement of one or two inches by the upper arm causes a movement of three to four times that at the periphery of movement (the fingers). If you ever get a chance to watch a classical pianist play an extremely difficult composition (such as a Chopin or Liszt etude, etc), notice how quickly he or she shifts the hand into proper playing position. This allows the hand and fingers to do <u>their</u> thing--press the keys down.

So the playing mechanism consists of big levers and small levers, all connected to one another and all having different functions. Here are some basic laws concerning these levers:

1. The bigger the lever, the more potential keyboard coverage, the more potential intensity (volume), and the less potential velocity.

2. The smaller the lever, the less potential keyboard coverage, the less potential intensity, and the more potential velocity.

Translated into English, this means the <u>faster</u> the musical passage, the smaller the lever usually used for key depression (fingers). <u>Slower</u> passages that demand a lot of intensity can be assisted by the upper arm and maybe even the torso when it comes to key depression. Of course, the intensity law doesn't apply to keyboards with volume pedals (Hammond organ, electric piano, synthesizers, etc). With these keyboards, you can play, if you so desire, loud and fast at the same time. I have found, however, that the faster the musical passage, the better it is to adhere to this tendency toward less intensity--as loud volumes can distort quick runs!

For a more detailed discussion of technique, I highly recommend the following books:

1. Schultz, Arnold. The Riddle of the Pianist's Finger. New York: Carl Fisher, 1964.

2. Whiteside, Abby. Indispensables of Piano Playing. New York: Charles Scribner's Sons, 1961.

3. Whiteside, Abby. Mastering the Chopin Etudes and Other Essays. New York: Charles Scribner's Sons, 1969.

4. Everhart, Powell. The Pianist's Art. Atlanta: Powell Everhart, 962 Myrtle Street, Northeast, Atlanta 9, Georgia, 1958.

5. Corea, Chick. Music Poetry. Los Angeles: Litha Music, 1980.

6. Bonpensiere, Luigi. New Pathways to Piano Technique. New York: The Philosophical Library, 1953.

With the background data in this chapter and in the above books, you are now ready to confront some of the better technical studies available for the piano. The books marked with asterisks are highly recommended, although they are all excellent for broadening and improving your technique.

*1. Von Dohnanyi, Ernst. Essential Finger Exercises.

*2. Joseffy, Rafael. School of Advanced Piano.

*3. Pishna, J. Sixty Progressive Exercises.

*4. Clementi, M. Gradus Ad Parnassum (100 exercises).

*5. Beringer, Oscar. Daily Technical Studies for the Pianoforte.

6. Philipp, Isidor. Complete School of Technique for the Piano.

7. Hannon, C.L. The Virtuoso Pianist.

8. Sorel, Claudette. Compendium of Piano Technique.

9. Cramer, J.B. Eighty-four Studies.

There are also studies by Czerny, Brahms, Liszt, Tausig, Moscheles, Hummel, Duvernoy, Heller, and many, many more. All in all, the serious keyboardist has an incredible reservoir of knowledge and information from which to draw in order to improve technique ("chops")!

Besides raw technical studies such as those just listed, I suggest you study some of the works of great artists, such as Bach's Two-Part and Three-Part Inventions and The Well-tempered Clavier; the Chopin Etudes, Impromptus, Waltzes, and Preludes; and works by--

Mozart	Stockhausen
Beethoven	Boulez
Liszt	Ives
Rachmaninoff	Copland
Debussy	Dello Joio
Scriabin	Villa Lobos
Stravinsky	Barber
Ravel	Hindemith
Bartok	Gershwin
Prokofiev	Carter
Schoenberg	John Cage

--just to name a few of the greats!

In the jazz area, listening to and learning some works by the following wouldn't hurt either!

Teddy Wilson	Keith Jarrett
Art Tatum	Bill Evans
George Shearing	Thelonius Monk
Bud Powell	Lennie Tristano
Horace Silver	Jimmy Smith
Oscar Peterson	Stanley Cowell
Hampton Hawes	McCoy Tyner
Chick Corea	Cecil Taylor
Herbie Hancock	Joseph Zawinul

In the commercial world, check out recordings by:

Keith Emerson	Rick Wakeman
Jan Hammer	Tony Banks
Bryan Auger	Jerry Lee Lewis
Nicky Hopkins	John Lord
Dr. John	Edgar Winter
Mark Stein	Stevie Wonder
Elton John	Roger Powell
Billy Joel	Paul Shaffer
Gary Booker	David Foster
Michael Omartian	Greg Phillinganes

Don't be overwhelmed by all these technical manuals and great artists. Simply listen to the artists you like, extract what is right for you, disregard what's not right, and continue developing your own bag! I have found that just knowing some of the accomplishments of other artists on your instrument speeds up your entire development, as long as you maintain the right viewpoint. Likewise, use whichever exercises help you achieve your goals.

Remember, technique is necessary to you and your communications. In his book Music Poetry, Chick Corea says it very nicely:

> The ability to superimpose one's own thought and conception on and through the body and instrument is the goal of technique.

In the next chapter, "Multikeyboards," I discuss the different technique problems related to electronic keyboards--which, of course, weren't around when the masters wrote their technique books. So stay with me!

Chapter 17
ASSIGNMENTS

_____ 1. Define <u>technique</u> in your own words. What is its function and just how important is it? Give examples.

_____ 2. Describe the <u>levers</u> that make up the playing machinery of the body as to their function. What are some of the basic laws that govern these levers?

_____ 3. Check out the following books:

a. Schultz, Arnold. <u>The Riddle of the Pianist's Finger</u>. New York: Carl Fisher, 1964.

b. Whiteside, Abby. <u>Indispensables of Piano Playing</u>. New York: Charles Scribner's Sons, 1961.

c. Whiteside, Abby. <u>Mastering the Chopin Etudes and Other Essays</u>. New York: Charles Scribner's Sons, 1969.

d. Everhart, Powell. <u>The Pianist's Art</u>. Atlanta: Powell Everhart, 962 Myrtle Street, Northeast, Atlanta 9, Georgia, 1958.

e. Corea, Chick. <u>Music Poetry</u>. Los Angeles: Litha Music, 1980.

f. Bonpensiere, Luigi. <u>New Pathways to Piano Technique</u>. New York: The Philosophical Library, 1953.

_____ 4. Locate a <u>competent</u> and <u>reputable</u> classical teacher in your area or close by and study some classical music to help develop your "chops" and "musicality." Although this is not necessarily the way to go for everybody, I have found this kind of study invaluable--a good foundation or stepping stone to other areas. The length of time you pursue this depends on you!

_____   5. Listen as much as possible to great musicians
               of your choice. This is the best, and per-
               haps the only, way of actually acquiring or
               absorbing "potential technique"--for the ear,
               in the end, regulates technique!

Chapter 18

MulTikeyboards

Although some keyboardists specialize in one particular keyboard, the contemporary keyboardist is most successful in command of many (multikeyboards). The ability to play many keyboards well (acoustic piano, organ, synthesizers, etc.) increases your potential worth as a working musician a thousandfold, whether the work is live, on stage, or in the studio.

Now the only sane way to acquire what are commonly referred to as "multikeyboard chops" is to know cold the differences and similarities between any and all keyboards, and then put some serious playing time in! The following explanations of fundamental keyboard characteristics and variables will aid you in developing multikeyboard chops.

1. <u>Range</u>

   This is the extent of pitch within the capacity of the keyboard. The acoustic piano, for example, has a range of just over seven octaves, whereas some keyboards only have a range of three to five octaves (e.g., small organs, some synthesizers, etc).

2. <u>Type of Keyboard</u>

   At present there are two main categories:

   a. <u>Mechanical</u>

      Sound is produced by a hammer or some other object striking a string or reed, or by the escape, through pipes, of pressurized air generated by a pump, as in the case of a pipe organ.

   b. <u>Electronic</u>

      The key simply acts as a switch, completing a circuit when it is pressed.

Note that any keyboard is simply a control device whose conformation is arbitrary--any device could work. One of the most interesting and creative controllers yet involves the use of lasers. By shortening and lengthening narrow laser beams with one's hand, the pitch changes through the help of monitoring computers. As you can imagine, this is visually very exciting for both audience and performer.

3. Keyboard Sensitivity

When certain sound and playing parameters* such as vibrato, attack, release, timbre, pitch (and many others) can be controlled via the keyboard by the fingers, the keyboard is touch sensitive. At the time of this writing, these parameters can be controlled through touch sensitivity in two ways-- through velocity and through pressure.

4. Key Return

This is the rate or velocity at which a key returns to the before-playing position after it is released by the finger. This parameter is a determining factor as to whether the keyboard is fast or sluggish, and can usually be adjusted to meet your requirements.

5. Key Resistance

This is the amount of force required to actually press and hold down a key (usually about two ounces). A keyboard with light action has less resistance than one with heavy action.

Key resistance and key return are very important to the way a keyboard feels and responds. A light, fast action means minimal resistance and quick key return (e.g., Hammond organ, many synthesizers). In comparison, acoustic pianos and electric pianos usually have a slower, heavier action, which explains why synthesists, organists, and anyone who hasn't had

---

* parameters, defining or variable specifications or limits.

much acoustic piano training usually feels lacking or incompetent with regard to technique when playing these heavier-action "axes" (instruments). Conversely, players who have acquired a solid technical foundation on the acoustic piano often have even better technical facility on the lighter-action instruments, once they've gotten used to them. Logical, eh?

6. Sound Flexibility

This refers to whether the actual sound of the instrument can be changed, and if so, how radically. For example, the acoustic piano, though capable of many nuances, basically has one sound, or program, and it can only be altered by volume and touch contrasts. The organ and synthesizer, on the other hand, have many potential sounds or programs. So in order to compose for or play the latter instruments competently, one should be fully aware of all their sound capabilities. This is very similar to writing for an orchestra, isn't it!

7. Voice Capability

This refers to how many notes or keys (voices) can be pressed down simultaneously and still sound! A keyboard is said to be totally polyphonic (having many voices) if all its voices can sound when depressed simultaneously. If only eight of its voices work simultaneously, the instrument is referred to as an eight-voice polyphonic instrument; four notes would be a four-voice polyphonic instrument and two notes would be a two-note, or duophonic, instrument. An instrument that can only play one note at a time is referred to as monophonic.

It's important to know this data because it affects how you can play. With limited voice capability you have to construct chords very economically or some of the notes won't sound. (For example, a six-note voicing on a Prophet V synthesizer will only sound five notes.) It is interesting to note that the acoustic piano is totally polyphonic and touch sensitive with regard to volume. Think that has anything to do with its continued popularity over the centuries?

8. <u>Interface Capabilities</u>

This refers to the capability of a keyboard to communicate to other intelligent terminals (computers,
drum machines, sequencers, other keyboards, etc).
This is pretty much standard hardware on new synthesizers. In fact, acoustic and electric pianos,
organs, guitars, wind instruments, etc., can be
retrofitted with an interface called MIDI (Musical
Instrument Digital Interface) to enable them to communicate intelligently with other MIDI instruments.
For example, interfacing an acoustic piano with a
couple of synthesizers can greatly enhance its sound.

9. <u>Reliability and Serviceability</u>

These terms refer to how prone the keyboard is to
breaking down and how easily it can be serviced.
It's no good having an incredible keyboard that constantly breaks down and then is difficult to get
repaired.

10. <u>Performance Expectancy</u>

This is probably the most important point, because it
encompasses all the others! Does the keyboard satisfy <u>your</u> playing and/or composing demands? If it
doesn't, then don't buy it, no matter how good everybody else says it is. You're you and that's that!

In addition to the variables listed above, there is
the problem of how many keyboards to have in your setup.
Should it be one incredible synthesizer that's supposed to
do everything, or many different ones that you like for
different reasons? Well, I'll tell you, even though keyboard technology is evolving at an incredible rate, there
is no one axe, in my opinion, that does it all. So in
order to help you determine <u>your</u> setup, I have put together the following guidelines based on the needs of
different keyboardists:

<u>Studio Musician</u>

You should either own or have access to many keyboards, especially the current popular ones that
producers like. Although you may specialize on
acoustic piano, electric piano, or some other instrument, the more versatile you can be, the better!

Live Performer

You only need what the gig calls for. Sometimes,
however, you won't even receive a call if you don't
own or have access to the required instruments. A
good electric piano and state-of-the-art polyphonic
synthesizer are the least you should expect to get
away with--provided you can play! You may even be
able to do away with the piano if your synthesizer
can duplicate it <u>properly</u>.

Original Artist

If you primarily write and play your own material,
you only need to own the specific equipment that will
help you create your sounds. For some artists, that
may simply be an acoustic piano; for others it may be
ten keyboards, a vocoder, a sequencer, drum machine,
and sophisticated outboard gear (echo devices,
flangers, etc). For yet others it may be custom-
built instruments. Chick Corea, for example, has a
different setup for almost every project he does.
It's not unusual to see him playing only acoustic
piano on one tour and then be surrounded with six
keyboards of various types on another.

So, to recapitulate: In order to choose the keyboards that best suit you, determine which ones best help
you communicate! This could involve many hours of re-
search--going to keyboard conventions and music shows,
reading magazines, etc. When doing research, remember to
keep the keyboard characteristics we've just talked about
in mind and you'll have a much easier time of it.

For instance, when an acoustic piano player tries to
play a synthesizer or organ, the fundamental he should be
aware of is what type of keyboard it is--mechanical or
electronic. If the "synth" is not touch sensitive, playing hard won't do anything but give him sore fingers and
probably damage the plastic keys! Likewise, an organ or
synth player who attempts to play the acoustic piano usually has a tough time because he's not used to "digging
in"--one plays very lightly on electronic keyboards and
thus doesn't have the strength to tackle the acoustic
piano. The answer in either case is <u>not</u> to decide you
shouldn't tackle the new keyboard, for each has a solution: The organist-synthesist should simply take some
acoustic piano lessons--especially technique studies--
while the acoustic piano player should simply lighten up

his touch and put in many, many hours playing and getting used to the new technique. In both cases--as I've already said a number of times--it takes as long as it takes! But it is well worth it if it helps you along your chosen musical path.

So the contemporary keyboardist should really be a multikeyboardist. He or she must be able to play many different keyboards competently. And this means keeping up with the technology--so stay alert and open to change. Your survival may depend on it!

MULTIKEYBOARD SETUPS

This usually refers to how you set up your keyboards for a live performance. If you have more than one or two keyboards, their placement can be extremely important. Do you stack all five keyboards on top of one another? Do you have some on your right and some on your left? Do you play standing up or sitting down, or both? What system (speakers, amps, mixers, effects, etc), will best reproduce your keyboard sound? Well, here again are some guidelines:

Geometric Setup

Decide what keyboard you do the most playing on and then set up your other keyboards around that one. After many hours of trial and error, you'll come up with the right setup. This, of course, is subject to change as you get more or different keyboards.

The most basic is the single stack setup. This simply consists of all keyboards stacked upon each other in some fashion, facing any direction you want. (No diagram.) One of my favorites is the right angle setup, because I'm either facing the band or the audience. The parallel setup that Keith Emerson used is also great, as the audience can see everything you're doing! (See Example 204.) These are the setups most used, but there are many possibilities--so feel free to experiment. It's a matter of personal preference.

With regard to how to stack your keyboards, there are many companies that make racks just for multikeyboards. If you're low on funds, just prop them up on each other as best you can. It's how you play that really counts!

Example 204

Right Angle Setup

Parallel Setup

Sound Reinforcement

State-of-the-art keyboards deserve state-of-the-art sound reinforcement. A complete keyboard system should include a stereo mixer, an amplifier, effects (echo, reverb, chorus, etc), and two speakers (stage right and stage left). The mixer, amplifier, and effects are commonly referred to as the brain and should be rack mountable for durability.

The amplifier should put out at least 200 watts per channel and the speaker cabinets should at the very least be a two-way system (15 inch speaker and high frequency horn). The reason for a complete system is that the dynamic range of keyboards is very wide (about 30 to 15,000 hertz, a hertz being a cycle per second of a wave form), and a complete hi-fidelity system is the only sure way of reproducing decent sound. Putting your expensive keyboards through a guitar amp defeats the whole idea of hi-fidelity sound--unless, of course, you're trying to get that guitarlike distortion from your synthesizers that Jan Hammer and Tom Costa sometimes do--but that's the exception!

As to which speakers, amplifiers, mixers, digital delays, equalizers, etc., to purchase, that's a subjective thing that you'll have to put a lot of research into. Again, whatever equipment communicates your sound the best is valid. For example, if you play a lot of low frequencies (synthesized bass, etc.) simultaneously with mid or high frequencies, you'll want to graduate to a bi-amped system. This simply means a separate amplifier for the low and high frequencies, which results in clarity even at high volumes.

Since it is not the intention of this chapter to get heavily into electronics and sound reinforcement, suffice it to say that the more you know about these areas, the more control you'll have over your live sound. To play and not be heard properly is very frustrating and is indicative of incompetence in the area of sound reinforcement, acoustics, and musical dynamics!

SPECIALIZED MULTIKEYBOARD TECHNIQUES

The following techniques deserve special attention:

1.   Note Bending

Although natural for guitar players, harmonica players, singers, etc., this technique is relatively new
for keyboard players. It was made possible by the
introduction of pitch control devices such as levers,
wheels, ribbons, and touch-sensitive keys. The
secret of bending a note on a synthesizer lies in
hitting the wrong note and then, with one or more of
these devices, bending the pitch to the intended
note.

At first this can be very difficult to get used to.
The most common bends to practice initially are whole
steps, half steps, minor thirds, and octaves. Once
you get used to the sensitivity of the bending device
(usually adjustable), all that's left is simply hours
of practice! I suggest you listen a lot to the natural bending techniques of guitarists, vocalists, and
wind players to get familiar with the sounds. George
Duke, Chick Corea, and Jan Hammer are definitely
worth checking out, as they have much expertise in
this area. But remember, some players bend, some
don't! You have to prehear it to pull it off.

2.   Instrument Duplication

Although the ability of the synthesizer to duplicate
other instruments is becoming quite remarkable, one
must really duplicate the entire viewpoint of how the
original instrument is played in order to make it
sound authentic. In other words, if you don't play
string parts like string players would play them,
your great string sound won't sound so great. So
your concept of the duplicated strings must be correct in order to communicate the feeling of real
strings. The solution is to listen to real strings
until you get the hang of what they're doing and then
duplicate their sound and concept as closely as
possible. The basic datum here is that authenticity
is communicated to the degree the player understands
the nature and function of the original sound--and
that's all of that!

3. Keyboard Shifting

This refers to the ability to accurately and competently shift your hands from keyboard to keyboard, sometimes playing two keyboards at a time in order to produce different colors in the sound. This may also involve pressing different switches for different programs as well as using your feet to control a variety of parameters (volume, effects, timbre, etc). Add to this the differences between your instruments, such as keyboard touch and response, range, different formats, etc., and you can see that without a lot of practice one can easily become overwhelmed!

4. Portable Keyboards

These are lightweight keyboards that usually hang on a strap over one's shoulders like a guitar. They enable the keyboardist to be mobile on the stage. Getting used to the technique of playing a keyboard in this manner can take some time because its position in relation to the hands and body is different than with stationary keyboards. So experiment and find what works for you.

5. Programming

This refers to the ability to create different sounds for synthesizers in accordance with the needs of any particular gig. These sounds may be intentional duplicates of other instruments' sounds, or completely new sounds or special effects. Some people now actually specialize in programming synthesizers for movie and TV scores, albums, and live performances. This ability involves a complete understanding of synthesizers as well as the ability to recognize and differentiate between various types of sounds.

6. Multikeyboard Reading

The use of many keyboards compounds the normal sight-reading task. While doing a film score, for example, it is not uncommon to have to read a music cue for from four to six keyboards. A player literally has to jump from keyboard to keyboard and still keep his or her eyes predominantly on the score.

SUMMARY

Although keyboard technology is advancing at an incredible rate, there is no substitute for great playing! And although I strongly advise keeping abreast of all the new developments in keyboard technology (computer interfaces, sequencers, etc), good playing is still at a premium. A poor player with $100,000 of state-of-the-art keyboards is much worse off than a good player on an acoustic piano! Put the two together--good playing and state-of-the-art keyboards--and look out!

With regard to where this keyboard evolution will take us, I can say this much--computers will play a heavy role. The ultimate keyboard to me would be one that can receive telepathic transmissions from the artist and reproduce these sounds from his or her mind with no need for playing or programming. In other words, you would conceive of a sound, hear it clearly mentally, and then this particular synthesizer or computer, which probably wouldn't have to be a keyboard at all, would produce the sound for you without any physical activity on your part. But then why use the via of a synthesizer or a computer at all? Why not create your own sounds mentally and communicate them, telepathically, directly to your audience?

When possibilities like these are realized, of course, they will not only involve advanced computer technology, but advanced spiritual awareness--with a consequent interface of both worlds!

Chapter 18
ASSIGNMENTS

_____ 1. What is meant by multikeyboard chops?

_____ 2. Of what importance are variables and characteristics such as range, type of keyboard,
key resistance and return, keyboard sensitivity, sound flexibility, number of voices,
etc., to the multikeyboardist and how does
understanding them improve multikeyboard
chops?

_____ 3. Why is it important to put your keyboards
through a good sound system? What basic
components should a good keyboard system
consist of?

_____ 4. What specialized techniques have to be mastered when playing multikeyboards?

_____ 5. Do the following multikeyboard program:

a. Research all available keyboards to
determine which ones are best suited to
your needs. This can be done by:

(1) Going to music stores.

(2) Going to keyboard shows, clinics and
music conventions.

(3) Going to concerts to hear the top
multikeyboardists of your style.

(4) Reading and subscribing to technical
magazines that contain pertinent data
on synthesizers, speakers, amplifiers, mixers, computers, etc.

b. Mock up mentally or on paper the keyboard
setup you think you want and then decide
to get it however you can (one piece at a
time, or whatever). You must invest some
time and money into yourself and your
craft in order to succeed!

c. Once you have most of your setup, spend many hours figuring out the geometric layout, getting used to the keyboards and their potentials, playing with your effects (echo, chorus, etc), and playing actual gigs.

d. Do Step (c) until you are satisfied with your setup. This might mean adding or subtracting equipment, more research--whatever!

e. Finally, burn! Play! Communicate! "Play your melody," as Chick Corea says.

_____ 6. Stay up to date with computers, for they are playing an increasingly important role in many areas of the music industry.

_____ 7. Keep shedding your basics! There is no substitute for great playing--not even a thousand keyboards.

SUGGESTED READING

Crombie, David. The Complete Synthesizer. Chester, N.Y.: Omnibus Press, 1982.

Keyboard Magazine, comp. Synthesizer Basics. Vol. 1. Milwaukee, Wis.: Hal Leonard Publishing Corp., 1984.

Keyboard Magazine, comp. Synthesizer Technique. Vol. 2. Milwaukee, Wis.: Hal Leonard Publishing Corp., 1984.

Keyboard Magazine, comp. Synthesizers and Computers. Vol. 3. Milwaukee, Wis.: Hal Leonard Publishing Corp., 1985.

Keyboard Magazine, comp. The Art of Electronic Music. Milwaukee, Wis.: Hal Leonard Publishing Corp., 1985.

Martin, George. Making Music, the Guide to Writing, Performing, & Recording. Quill, N.Y.: Shockburg Reynolds, 1983.

Schrader, Barry. Introduction to Electro-Acoustic Music. Englewood Cliffs, N.J.: Prentice-Hall, 1984.

Tonus, Inc. Owner's Manual: The ARP Synthesizer Series 2600. Newton Highlands, Mass.: Tonus, Inc., 1971.

Yelton, Geary. The Rock Synthesizer Manual. Woodstock, Ga.: Rock Tech Publications, 1980.

Chapter 19
Studio vs. Live Performance

Although there are many differences between studio playing and live performances, the simple truth is that once one becomes used to these differences, <u>playing is playing</u>. Professional musicians consistently play their best no matter what the conditions, whereas amateurs allow certain conditions to affect their playing adversely. To help you reach this professional standard in both arenas, let's analyze the different possible situations and their ramifications.

LIVE PERFORMANCE

Live performance means any situation in which there is some kind of live audience. This may include live concerts, TV shows which have live audiences, "casuals" or general business gigs (parties, weddings, and so on), club gigs, etc. Since the most important item on your check-list of things to do is <u>communicate</u> to the audience, you should make sure that everything possible is done to insure this communication happens. This would include the following:

1. <u>Intending</u> to really communicate to your audience.

2. Knowing your music.

3. Knowing your instrument or instruments.

4. Making sure all equipment (instruments, speakers, microphones, monitors, effects, etc.) is functioning properly.

5. Being in good communication with the other members of the band.

In other words, do whatever works. As long as it gets you and keeps you in communication with your audience, it's valid.

The tendency for most musicians is to criticize and complain about audiences that don't respond. That's a cop-out! If there is any audience, you have a responsibility to communicate to them on some level. Why else would you be there? One can play to himself at home! The most successful artists are the ones who have figured this out. Communication is so potent, that when it clicks, such things as current trends, styles, mistakes, PR, chops, management, instruments--whatever--become secondary--just not very important. However, incredible communication coupled with good management, PR, technical expertise, expert marketing, good sound, etc., will produce incredible success--witness Bach, the Beatles, Miles Davis, Chick Corea, Journey, Stevie Wonder, etc.

<u>Live</u> also means <u>one chance</u>! There is really no chance to try it again if you blow it. So you must be prepared to go for it, mistakes and all. Also, the audience is watching, as well as listening, which means that how you look and the emotional content of your performance, in addition to how you sound, can be critical! So don't overlook these factors. "To be or not to be?"-- that was Shakespeare's question. The answer is, "to communicate or not to communicate"! Which will it be-- success or failure?

STUDIO OR SESSION PLAYING

Session playing refers to any situation where what you are playing is being recorded in some way. It may be video as well as audio. It includes gigs such as album dates, film scores, commercial jingles, demos, etc. Since a recording will usually be played many times, the audience--in this case the purchaser of the recording--will tend to be more critical. Your performance is therefore more crucial--which is where all the imagined pressure comes from for the amateur studio musician. In actual fact, playing in the studio offers many more luxuries than live performance does! They are--

1. The chance to do it over until it's exactly right--within budget limits, of course.

2. More control over sound due to state-of-the-art studio equipment and techniques, e.g., multi-tracking, special effects, overdubbing, better sound equalization, etc.

3. The opportunity to hear your performance back immediately, which is great for improving your playing.

About the only drawback is that there is no live audience to inspire you. Once you get used to this, however, you'll love recording. If you use your imagination and simply pretend there's an audience, you'll do just fine. After all, there will be, just as soon as someone listens to what you've just played!

The Studio Musician

A musician who makes a living predominantly in the studio (albums, demos, jingles, film scores) is said to be a studio musician. A top studio musician may average a couple hundred thousand dollars a year or more. If you're interested, here are the requirements:

1. Good sight reading ability.

2. Extremely good ears!

3. Versatility. The more versatile you are as to styles and types of keyboards you play, the more potential work there is. If you specialize in one style, or on one instrument, you'd better be one of the best.

4. The ability to be punctual, pleasant to work with, and able to take instructions from producers, artists, arrangers, etc.

5. A knack for playing the right thing, when nobody else knows what they want.

6. Good time and groove ("feel").

7. Competence and efficiency.

8. Extreme confidence.

These abilities are usually developed by doing a lot of playing, both live and in the studio. Practice definitely makes perfect in this case. Besides a good solid musical background, most session players have listened to a lot of music and duplicated it (by taking licks off records, etc). So, to reiterate--having a solid musical background and listening to a lot of music are essential in becoming a top-line session player.

In the end, if you can really play, almost any musical situation can be conquered, once you get used to it. Until you're comfortable, however, use the following procedure as a guideline when doing sessions:

1. <u>Be cause, not effect</u>.

   Find out in advance as much about the session as possible. This data is very important, as it could determine what keyboards you'll need or be expected to play and in what style or styles; if the session is in your league or over your head; who the producer is, etc. In other words, the fewer curves thrown at you, the better. Good session players are cause over the session, not effect! They do anything and everything necessary to remain at cause (in control) during the session, for they know that's the only way to get good results.

2. <u>Get into good communication</u>.

   Upon arrival at the studio, you should get into good communication with all the people you will be working directly with (producer, engineer, other artists, etc). This allows for better working conditions, less pressure and an overall clearer picture of what's needed from you. This is so important that I know many producers who won't hire certain musicians--not because they can't play, but because they are hard to work with!

3. <u>Quick study anything you need to</u>.

   In a studio situation, this just means <u>quickly</u> shed (practice) anything you're a little uncertain about. This could be a difficult part of the chart, a solo, your expected take over an unfamiliar chord progression, a tricky rhythm or feel--whatever. Jumping into unfamiliar terrain without preparation is the mark of an amateur.

4. Tune your instrument.

    This only applies if you're playing tunable keyboards like synthesizers. You must make sure that you are in tune with the track (previously recorded material that you are about to play to) or with the agreed-upon fixed pitch for the session--usually A = 440 hertz (440 cycles per second). This is usually done by using a strobe tuner or some fixed-pitch instrument like an acoustic piano. Not being able to quickly tune your axe is a dead giveaway that you are inexperienced.

5. Get the mix right.

    This refers to how all the instruments and vocals, if any, sound through the studio headphones or monitor speakers. This is literally crucial, because if you can't hear yourself and/or certain key instruments, your chances of performing great are slim. Don't be afraid to communicate to the engineer until you get the right sound that is best for you. Remember, you are the performer, not the engineer. The engineer is there to record and assist you so you can give your best performance. Don't allow yourself to be intimidated. At the same time, no studio is perfect. Sometimes you must perform your best under difficult circumstances. The ability to do this marks the difference between the amateur and the seasoned professional. One can't blame the studio and engineer for all of one's errors. Responsibility is with everybody. The whole team of artists--producer, session player, and engineer--have to be working together and competently for best results.

6. While recording--play!

    This simply means do your best, don't worry about mistakes, and don't stop the session! That's the producer's job. If you're taping multitrack (many separate tape tracks), there's a good chance you can fix your mistakes later by a technique called "punching-in." This means the engineer actually locates the mistakes and literally punches the "record" button in, you replay your part hopefully correctly (or until you get it right), and then he punches you out (stops the recording)! If you panic and stop during recording, you may ruin a perfectly good take--in which case the producer would be furious.

If, however, you are not doing multitrack recording, but a live mix recording (direct to 2-track or disk), it's probably best you stop the session if you make a major mistake, because you'll hear it back very shortly!

7.   Have a "go-for-it" attitude.

Fear of the tape is a common amateur symptom. It tends to make a player conservative about his or her playing through fear of making a mistake. Consequently, the keyboardist's playing will lack life and will not be good enough to record, let alone listen to over and over again. You must develop the "go-for-it" attitude of live concerts in order to capture that magic moment. This is what makes you play your best! Besides, this is supposed to be fun--not scary. If you blow it, just do it again--get it?

8.   Learn from your mistakes.

Anything that you had difficulty with in the session should be practiced so that it doesn't happen again. Whether it was a difficult chart, a tricky rhythm, an unfamiliar style--whatever--figure out a way to practice it so that you'll be prepared next time. By constantly doing this, you'll become a seasoned professional in no time, provided that's your goal!

In conclusion, session work can be a very profitable career, provided you're prepared. Each session you do is your PR. If you're happening, the word will get out very quickly and soon you will be doing all kinds of sessions. You must have patience and persistence because it usually doesn't happen overnight. Don't be selective in the beginning--play anything and everything! You'll need the experience and the exposure. Once you're in demand the law of supply and demand takes over and you can be more choosy, make more, and have a ball! Until then--keep cookin'!

Chapter 19
ASSIGNMENTS

_____ 1. Explain the basic difference between live playing and studio playing.

_____ 2. What luxuries does studio playing offer that live playing doesn't? Vice versa?

_____ 3. What are the requirements of a good studio musician? How can one best acquire these abilities?

_____ 4. If you ever did any recording sessions, recall the ones you failed on and note why.

Next, recall the ones you did well on and note why. Begin working on your weak points and strengthening your strong points. Good luck!

_____ 5. Play as many live gigs and studio sessions as possible. Keep at it until you feel very confident. At the same time, keep practicing and listening to other good players. It takes as long as it takes!

Part Three

THE BUSINESS SCENE

Chapter 20
Advice

The purpose of this chapter is to give you some valuable information in what I believe are crucial areas of the game. As most teachers, schools, and books only discuss mechanics, theory, etc., the following areas are usually learned, if at all, from the school of hard knocks. I hope my viewpoint in these areas will help cushion these knocks.

POWER

With so many interesting paths to choose, the contemporary keyboardist may easily get confused. The secret, of course, lies within you. Doing what you like to do is where your power lies--not what others tell you to do or what just makes the most money. If you like playing avante-garde jazz, then do it. If you are also good at it, your problem is solved. What you like and do best is where your power to communicate comes from, and communication is what it is all about!

SUCCESS

Definition: Making a good living doing exactly what you like! (Heaven)

FAILURE

Definition: Making a good living doing exactly what you hate! (Hell)

SUPPRESSION

Being suppressed is--by whatever means--being held back or stopped, being made continually wrong, not being permitted to advance or do your best (for example, a greedy manager not allowing an artist to do what the artist likes, but what the manager thinks best). Advice is one thing--suppression is quite another. The solution to any suppression is don't agree with it. Do what you like! If the whole world tells you that your song will never make it, but you believe in it, then do it. You must develop your own viewpoint and stick to it. Allowing yourself to be suppressed produces unhappiness, frustration, sickness, and failure.

MANAGERS

Managers are people who work for artists. A manager is your employee--not employer. A manager's hat (job) is to manage the business so you can continue being an artist. A manager represents you, the artist. He handles your business and gives you advice. You need a manager only when your creations (products) are so in demand that you can't handle the business yourself. Managers can be very valuable people, but remember--they work for you, not you for them! The latter can produce insanity!

POLITICS AND PR

Just being good is only half the game. The other half is, unfortunately, political. What I mean by being "political" is being "shrewdly tactful"! Who you know, how you get along with people, how well you and your services and/or products are publicized and promoted--all can have a bearing on your success or failure. So unless you are an absolute monster at what you do, be prepared to play the game: Hang out at top clubs, go to important parties, hire a publicist--and, of course, most importantly, be a professional at what you do. For remember, all the politics in the world are useless if you can't back it up. In fact, over-PR can backfire if you can't deliver what you've promised.

So here's the whole picture:

1. Find out what you like <u>and</u> are the most talented in.

2. Develop that area.

3. Once you're beginning to happen, speed up the game by actually playing the game! Being a genius in your living room won't do anybody any good.

4. Once you're a winner, have succeeded at the game and achieved your goals, you might find it's time to choose a new game (e.g., studio musician turns producer).

<u>DRUGS</u>

Wrong direction! Foolish! Possible quick demise! Lower, not higher, awareness! Waste of hard-earned money! Temporary highs and permanent lows! Don't be afraid to say no when people offer you dope. Just politely refuse and get on with your business. In the end, you'll be more respected. Like don't be a <u>dope</u>! You can <u>burn</u> without drugs. Honest!

<u>THE BIG BREAK</u>

Never <u>wait</u> for the big break! You must <u>create</u> your breaks. Continually doing what you do best is how you create your big break. In order to survive, though, while you create your pie in the sky, I strongly recommend versatility. The more "hats" you can wear as a contemporary keyboardist, the more potential work there is. The more you work, the better you'll become and the more comfortable you'll be--mentally as well as financially. This will allow you a safe and secure space from which to operate and create. Achieve this, and look out!

The following is a list of some possible gigs a versatile keyboardist could do:

1. Live performance:

    a. Casuals, general business gigs
    b. Top 40 club gigs
    c. Shows
    d. Concerts

2. Studio work:

    a. Records and demos
    b. TV and film
    c. Jingles
    d. Muzak

3. Lead sheets--writing lead sheets for song-writers, etc.

4. Rehearsal pianist--for dancers, shows, etc.

5. Musical director, conductor.

6. Synthesist, synthesizer programmer.

7. Composer, arranger.

8. Songwriter.

9. Teacher (private or group instructor, seminars, clinics, etc).

10. Salesman (musical equipment--especially keyboards, etc).

11. Producer.

12. Actor (musician-type parts).

So if you know your stuff, there's a lot of opportunity!

UNIONS

In general, the unions are okay. In order to do most of the top work, you'll have to be a member--so don't suppress yourself. Play the game, expand. Unions can be very helpful in many areas of the business--especially the setting and collecting of wages, etc. The musicians union is probably the first union you should join, and each city has its own local. Dues are usually reasonable, and in return the union provides rehearsal space, potential work leads, enforcing of contracts, legal advice, etc. If you're not happy with your particular union, then go to the meetings and change it!

GO WHERE THE ACTION IS!

If you do not live in New York, Los Angeles, or some other major city, your work possibilities may be limited to clubs, weddings and parties, and original bands. So if you want to make music your career, I suggest you move to where the action is--L.A. or N.Y. especially. Since all the major record labels, movie production companies, producers, managers, studio musicians, etc., are pretty much based in these two cities, you will have increased your odds, not only for making a living, but for actually "making it"!

CON ARTISTS

You should never be so hungry to make it that you get careless. No matter what somebody offers you, always make the following procedure a habit:

1. Question the person or persons about their past business dealings. Observe how willingly or unwillingly they give you information about themselves. Their past ventures will shed much light on your present deal.

2. Check out the person even further by asking around. You might be surprised what you uncover! If it's all good, then great--but if it's all bad, you'll be glad you checked around.

3. Forget verbal agreements! The ethics in today's music industry, I'm sorry to say, have to be fully policed. Get everything in writing and take everything to a reputable lawyer before you sign it. Never be in a hurry to sign "big deals." If "they" really want you or your products, they'll stay around and negotiate, that's for sure! When in doubt, lay out! Con artists are simply smart criminals!

AUDITIONS

Preparation is the key here. Find out before the audition what is ideally needed and wanted and then see if you can really produce it. If you're not sure, do the audition anyway, as the experience will be invaluable for the next one.

Research the potential gig as much as possible, because the better you're prepared, the more in control and "at cause" you'll be at the audition! When you are uncertain about things, you are to that degree "at effect" and do not usually perform as well as when you are confident and at cause.

STYLES

Listening to records and tapes and live artists whenever possible is the best way to absorb a particular style (gospel, funk, blues, rock, jazz, etc). Once you have a lot of affinity for a particular style, begin analyzing it, using all the fundamentals you've studied. Play along with the records, buy books on the style if available, and even talk directly with the artists, if possible.

Remember, a style is just the particular viewpoint of some other artist or group of artists. If you like that particular viewpoint, try to duplicate it and use it in your own way to fuel your viewpoint. Once you have developed your style or viewpoint, you may or may not be interested in other viewpoints. In his book, Music Poetry, Chick Corea states it like this:

> The World of Artists:
>   Each one makes his melodies
>   his own way
>   Each one creates the beauty
>   he sees
> With your own genuine interest
>   receive their beauties
> You like what you like
> You don't what you don't
>   Only you know

So, to recapitulate: learn from others, share with others, but don't become others--be yourself. Create your style! It doesn't have to be totally unique. It just has to be you!

ON THE ROAD

Literally, this means packing your bags and leaving home in order to work. Before doing this, however, there are a few things you should be aware of.

1. Determine if the gig is first, second, or third-rate!

First Rate

- Top salary--$1,500 and up per week.

- Per diem (expense account)--at least $35 and up per day.

- Private rooms at top hotels provided.

- Class transportation while on tour (limos, private buses, first class travel on planes, etc).

- All shows catered properly.

- Salary guarantee if tour is cancelled.

- Expert road crew to set up all equipment, etc.

- Top, experienced management, not a Mickey-Mouse operation--sorry, Mickey!

Second Rate

- Lower salary ($750 to $1,450 per week).

- Per diem--$25 to $30.

- Possibly shared rooms (bummer no matter how you look at it).

- Possibly rented cars, coach travel on planes.

- Meager catering of gigs.

- No salary guarantee if tour is cancelled.

- Satisfactory crew.

- Satisfactory management.

Third Rate ...Don't do it unless you're hungry!

- Salary--$250 to $700 per week.

- Minimal or no per diem.

- Shared rooms for sure (two to three per room).

- Low rent motels.

- Low rent transportation (uncomfortable buses, long rides between gigs, musicians doing a lot of the driving, etc).

- No catering of gigs.

- No salary guarantee--no anything guarantee!

- Little if any crew (probably set up your own equipment).

- Management pretty much useless and in the way.

2. <u>Weigh going on the road with staying in town</u>. Consider the following when comparing:

    a. <u>Location</u>: If you're already living where the action is (New York, Los Angeles, etc), you should only take first or second rate tours, for obvious reasons. If you're not where the action is (small town), getting on the road even on a third-rate tour might be very important--your chance to be seen and heard.

    b. <u>Salary</u>: Your on-the-road salary should be one and one-half to two times your in-town salary. This is because of your on-the-road overhead (high-priced food, entertainment to handle boredom, etc.) and the extra reserves you'll need when you get back in town and try to find work all over again! It always takes a while for people to realize you're back and available for work.

    c. <u>Career positioning</u>: This is basically politics! If it's a prestigious gig (top, well-known act), it may be a worthwhile investment to your overall career to do the gig. The work that can sometimes be generated from such a gig, due to the wide exposure, is not to be underestimated. One gig leads to another, and another, and then albums, endorsements, etc. People tend to hire known, already-working artists!

    d. <u>Potential in-town work</u>: If big things are happening for you in town, it could be foolish to go on the road and miss the action. Getting established in town and only going on the road with first rate gigs is the goal to shoot for!

    e. <u>Affinity for gig</u>: Being on the road can be boring and lonely. Add to this a dislike for the music you're playing, and you'll begin asking yourself why you became a musician in the first place. That's right, it's supposed to be fun playing and creating--remember? So, unless you're desperate, take a pass on projects you don't like. You'll find better gigs only by looking for them, believe me!

f. <u>Goals</u>: Examine your musical goals. If you want to be a studio musician, limit your road activity to top gigs and try to stay active in town. If you dig live performance, go for the road. Get it?

3. <u>Group member vs. sideman</u>. If you have a chance of actually being a royalty member of a top act, by all means go for it! That's a whole different ball game. Any time you can participate in a major group's profits (records, publishing, tour profits, etc), go for it. You could be talking mega-bucks!

4. <u>Off the road</u>. Once off the tour, begin promoting yourself immediately! Use the phone, hang out at clubs, and play every chance you can in order to let people know that you're back and available for work. Being with a top act can sometimes work against you. People assume you're not interested because you're rich and famous, or they assume you're too expensive to hire--or that it would be useless to call because you're getting ready to go back on the road again. The solution is to keep promoting until everybody realizes you're available for work again. Communication is the key, as always!

5. <u>Insurance</u>. All musicians, especially keyboardists, should invest in equipment insurance. If you travel on the road a lot, I'd say it's a must! The road is very rough on equipment. It would be foolish to take ten to twenty thousand dollars worth of keyboards on the road uninsured. If something happened, you might actually be in the red after the tour instead of the black! Also, you should get flight cases for all equipment. Although they are expensive, they're the only way to protect your equipment.

6. <u>Personal Ethics</u>. Going on the road is hard enough on relationships without adding promiscuity! Besides picking up strange diseases, I can guarantee a corrosion of your in-town relationship. So if you value your relationship, why do things that work against it? Even if you manage to keep road affairs a secret, <u>you</u> know--and that's enough: it'll never be the same. As to doing drugs--don't! I've seen more than one artist blow his whole salary on drugs, not

to mention his health, and sometimes his life. It's definitely not worth it. To sum up, personal ethics are the secret to peace of mind--good karma, as some people put it. Some people create their own little hell on earth with their lack of personal ethics! If you don't believe me, then I guess you'll have to find out the hard way!

BUSINESS CHOPS

There's no way one can expand in an "earthling" society without at some point taking care of business. You can justify cheating the government in many ways, but in the end you're only causing yourself to stay small. The best way to expand is to come out of hiding. Report all your earnings! Your gross income is your production and you should be proud of it. It will help you in the long run get credit, etc. Sure, you now have to develop some business chops! Go visit an accountant. Find out how to keep accurate records of all your income and expenses so you can beat the system at its own game! Unless you play this game all the way, you lose. It's rigged that way. If you try and cheat on your tax returns, you will eventually either get caught or you will simply stay small because you'll be afraid of getting caught. If you don't learn how to manage your finances, you'll pay too much to Uncle Sam. So seek competent financial advice, keep your business straight, and in the end you'll expand. Expansion takes responsibility. Staying small on this planet is easy. Winning takes the ability to confront! So go for it! Produce like crazy! Prosper! It's your right!

Chapter 20
ASSIGNMENTS

_____ 1. Explain in writing the relationship of power, communication, suppression, and personal ethics to your success or failure in the music game.

_____ 2. Read Introduction to Scientology Ethics, by L. Ron Hubbard. (4th ed. Los Angeles: The American Saint Hill Organization, 1973). pp.7-36.

_____ 3. Explain the role of personal managers.

_____ 4. How do "politics" in the entertainment industry relate to the contemporary musician?

_____ 5. Discuss some of the harmful effects of drugs, both short and long range. Are drugs really necessary to be able to create?

_____ 6. List all the gigs you are presently qualified for as a keyboardist. (Refer to the section entitled "The Big Break.") Decide which ones you wouldn't mind doing and begin promoting yourself in those areas. Continue until you're actually earning a living doing those gigs. Then, having become a professional, direct your energies toward that big break if that's your goal. Remember, it takes as long as it takes!

_____ 7. What does the phrase "go where the action is" have to do with your chances of success?

_____ 8. What is a con artist? How can you protect yourself from these degraded beings?

_____ 9. How can one be more prepared and thus at cause on auditions?

_____ 10. What is a "style"? How do you go about learning a particular musical style you like? Since there were no records, tape recorders or TV's when Bach, Mozart, and Haydn lived, how do you imagine they learned and studied other artists' styles?

_____ 11. Describe in essay form all the points to consider when accepting a road gig.

_____ 12. Is equipment insurance necessary for the contemporary keyboardist? If so, why? Give examples.

_____ 13. Read Chick Corea's <u>Music Poetry</u>, if you haven't already! (Los Angeles: Litha Music, 1980).

Part Four

INTERVIEWS

Introduction

It has always been my contention that the most valuable viewpoints come from those who "do," not from those who "don't"! It would be logical to assume, therefore, that any keyboardist who has achieved success in his or her field has done something very right. Now whether or not they can intelligently communicate their concepts is another topic all to itself. Generally speaking, those busy "doing" or creating are not very interested in--or, for that matter, even aware of--step-by-step procedures or details--except, perhaps, in hindsight. The challenge, then, was to slow these great artists down enough to get them to look into this area of "whys."

Thus my purpose in conducting the following interviews was to try and communicate to you in the best possible way the actions and concepts that lie behind each of these artist's achievements and success. I have purposely chosen successful keyboardists in different fields to help you get an overall picture of the contemporary scene.

I also wish to acknowledge that the philosophies and methods presented in the preceding sections of this manual are those of the author and not necessarily those of the keyboardists interviewed. Many artists take different paths to get to the same place, all of which are valid if they actually help them arrive.

It is also important to note that the successful actions of one or another of these artists may not readily work for you--there are too many variables for all methods to work for everyone. But this book was put together with that in mind: The inclusion of philosophic concepts, raw musical data based on my own experience and training, hard-learned business advice, and viewpoints from a number of successful keyboardists should provide you with a wealth of methods, solutions and means to get you where you're going. So choose what works for you and disregard what doesn't. Enjoy the interviews!

Chick Corea
composer/bandleader/keyboardist

CHICK COREA

JOHN: Often people just beginning their careers as musicians have a hard time finding a teacher who can really communicate with them and supply them with the information they need. One solution would be to go to a successful artist--someone who's made it in the field they're interested in. What are your thoughts on that?

CHICK: I'll tell you, I've been in very few one-on-one teaching situations myself. For a while, in the early 70's, I had some students. And then I discovered something: when you ask a professional how he does something, he can't always tell you, because the fact that a person can do something well isn't always the result of having thought about it. So, in my case, I had the experience of being asked very specifically how I do certain things that I and others know I do, and being stumped for an answer. I realized that I never did sit down and work out how I arrived at them, you see, because you can just go right to certain things.

So the professionals in an area are still not necessarily the best ones to ask about it. And I find this to be especially true with artistic and similar high skills, as opposed to mechanical subjects like bridge building or nuclear physics. You have to know how to arrive at a bridge so it can be planned out and constructed step by step. So this is why a differentiation between an educator and the subject he's educating about is necessary: you have people who can educate and communicate about music, and then you have people who can play music. That's not to say you can't have them both in the same person--but if you're asking someone how he creates art, and he himself hasn't thought about it, but just does it, you might get some wild stuff. For instance, I recently tried to read a series of interviews in which Stravinsky talked about music. I love Stravinsky's music, but if I hadn't been told who was answering those questions, I would never have been able to associate him with the Stravinsky I know from music.

And that's probably an appropriate prelude to this interview, or any discussion of this type. So anyone reading this should perhaps take it with about 20,000 grains of salt!

JOHN: That's right in line with an incident that occurred when I was in Boston. A friend and I were at a club in the Village where Dexter Gordon was playing. He had just come out of retirement from Europe and he was burning on this one song, "Stella By Starlight." My roommate, who was attending Berklee, was really into sax and he said, "Look, there's Dexter leaning against the wall, I gotta go up and talk to him." So I said, "What are you going to ask him, man?" And he said, "I'm gonna ask him what he thought about when he did that last solo-- it was incredible." I said, "Don't ask him that--not now, not between sets." But he went up, and I stood off to the side, and he said, all excited, "Dexter, that was great! That was great! I got to know what you were thinking about when you did that last solo." And Dexter was smoking a cigarette with a drink in his hand, leaning against the wall, waiting to go on again. So he looked over to my friend a little bit antagonistically and said, "You wanna know what? You wanna know what? I'll tell you what. I said: 'Here goes!'"

That was it! I laughed so hard.

CHICK: And that's probably the pure truth.

JOHN: Do you practice or work out everything you do in advance, or do you sometimes just do it?

CHICK: I think the usual way people achieve an ability or improve a skill is to work at it, and there's nothing wrong with that--doing that is part of life. But the reason I promote this next idea is because it's not thought about a lot, and it's even considered kind of frivolous. However, what I'm talking about is actually a natural, native ability a person has: the ability to just conceive of something and do it, without going through anything. And, as a matter of fact, I think when a person doesn't realize that he's chosen to do something, but just does it, it happens more easily.

JOHN: Than if he had thought about it in advance?

CHICK: Yes. In fact, if he just does it without even noticing, someone else might even have to point it out to him and help him realize he can now do something he couldn't do before--and that he didn't have to practice to be able to do it.

JOHN: Would you agree, though, that this phenomenon tends to occur more after one becomes more accomplished in an area? Don't you think that, in the beginning, when you're 14 years old and you're trying to develop physical chops on the piano, you need to get into it more as a step-by-step procedure?

CHICK: Well, when I refer to thinking of something and then just doing it, I'm not really talking about something as broad or general as "think of becoming a great pianist and then just do it." Rather, I'm talking about the things that you might have to achieve step by step. In the process of accomplishment there are lots of little steps. Rather than working 18 hours on this particular little step, if you didn't think about it, but could just conceive the result, you might just do it. I don't think it matters a whole lot whether you're at the beginning of the development of something or at the end of it--that potential of having an ability simply by conceiving of it is always there. I think once you notice the phenomenon and begin to understand it, and you become easy with it and actually enjoy it and see it not as something that's frivolous but, rather, as something that's quite deep, you can start becoming more causative with it.

JOHN: Would this be an example of what you're talking about? Say you're not hearing a particular group of changes as you would like to; you don't feel at home soloing over them. Usually at that point you would try to work with them a little bit and get something going, perhaps run some scales over them or play through the song and see if you hear something. Do you mean that instead of needing to do that, someone might just say, "Well, I want to solo over this and I'm just going to solo." And then simply do it?

CHICK: That could be an example. But the phenomenon I'm talking about usually occurs more on a conceptual level than that. It would happen more like this: Say you have some chord changes--D, G, C, E, A, D, cycle of fifths, and you're very familiar with them--you've heard them a lot and you've played them a lot. But then someone writes a tune that has some chord movement that has nothing to do with that, and all of a sudden you're on unfamiliar ground. But you have an attraction to it. That already means that you know something, even if you think you don't.

So one person might listen to it and think, "Gee, that's nice, but I don't know anything about that." Well, this musician might just end up going through life saying to his friends, "You know, this kind of music sounds so good when someone else does it, but I never can feel comfortable doing it myself, it's always seemed so awkward." What he's actually done is set himself up nicely with a barrier--the barrier of "I can never feel comfortable doing it." And a person might have that barrier there for quite a while.

Another guy might sit down and take a week or two and stumble a little bit--but then it starts to come for him.

But someone else might just sit right down with this stuff and think: "Well, here's this sound, and then here's this sound. Now if I play a scale through this sound that fits with this sound, and then I play a scale through this sound that fits with that sound, that sort of makes it. But playing scales that fit with each sound only goes with the old way of doing things. And there's something else that I'm missing here." So then he thinks, "Oh, well, melodically, the notes that go on top of these sounds have to be dealt with differently, too. There's a new thought process here. Let me try skating around a little bit and not actually playing, scalewise, what fits traditionally into these triads." And so forth. And you know, there could be the breakthrough. For the guy might start skating melodically, and then discover, "Gee, skating's real easy for me to do, I can skate like hell." And as soon as he starts skating, and applying it to this thing that he thought he couldn't do, then all of a sudden, in about a second, he sounds good on this thing that a few moments ago was a big drag.

So what I'm speaking of is more on that level. There are awarenesses that you could practice a lot to get around to, but if you achieve a conceptual understanding of something, all of a sudden you can do it.

JOHN: It's obvious that you are musically literate as compared to someone who plays entirely by ear. What did your musical education consist of, and what things were most valuable to you in helping you develop your abilities and build your career?

CHICK: One thing I did a lot when I was learning to play the piano and coming to understand the subject of music and jazz was transcription from records. From very early on I somehow had a natural grasp of the fact that, no matter how complex a record was, I could always start with the simple parts and get it gradually, little by little by little by little. I would listen to the record through and pick out a very simple thing to begin to transcribe, and pick at it until I got it. I would kind of find my way into that world by picking at it.

And through that process I actually learned almost everything I know about notating and reading music and recognizing sounds. It was a tool that I used to an incredible extent. And, using that concept, at any point since then that I've wanted to delve a little more deeply into something, I've simply slowed my life down enough to inspect it. For instance, if I didn't quite understand how to notate something I had heard, I would just break that thing down slower and slower and slower and more minute until I got to a point where I could understand it--and then build it from there.

JOHN: Do you mean that, whatever it took, you did it--whether it meant reading a book on notation or studying from somebody?

CHICK: Yes, whatever it took. If I had to open a book or study with someone, I did it. To tell you the truth, though, formal lessons in music were more of a pain than anything--but I had a few. I studied with Salvatore Sullo, a fine classical pianist, for a few years. He was very gentle as a teacher; he didn't lecture me or overload me with data, but I learned a lot. It was like a music appreciation class. He would assign me a piece of music to take home and learn. He'd play it through once and I'd watch him, and he'd tell me to take it up to a certain point and then bring it back to him. Then he'd send me home. I'd play it for him the next week and he'd make a few comments--nothing very critical, and not too much praise either. Then he'd go on and give me the next few pages in the same manner. He showed me a lot of things about fingering. Actually, he wasn't into jazz--this was classical music. He gave me Bach and Beethoven and then, eventually, most of the well-known composers. So I studied with him for about three or four years, and I enjoyed him because he was very easy-going.

On the other hand, I had gone once or twice to some other jazz people to try and learn something about jazz in a private teaching situation, but it was awful. So I decided instead to actually seek out the musicians that I liked and learn from them by listening to them and getting their records, and just staying home and working it out by myself.

JOHN: So it was one-on-one, via the artists' records. And that was your main teacher--especially in jazz.

CHICK: That was my main teacher. And then, second to that, the best learning experience I had--and continue to have--was playing with other musicians. And the greater the musician I played with, the more I learned. Especially if it was music that I really wanted to play. And a lot of the musicians I worked with were musicians I had decided I wanted to play with because I wanted to be around them enough to learn from them. I didn't want to ask them anything--I just wanted to play with them. As a matter of fact, I feel the best way of actually passing something along to another musician, technically and musically, aside from just encouragement and friendship-- which are very valuable in any case--is to work with him on a piece of music, in an actual situation, for an actual performance.

JOHN: The real thing.

CHICK: Yes. For instance, I have an idea for a music workshop. By means of auditions, some of the best students around would be chosen to put together a 30-piece band. I would write a suitelike piece of music for the band and spend four days rehearsing it. And then on the fifth day we'd do a public performance. And that would be the workshop.

JOHN: So instead of the usual concept of a workshop, which is to break down what you're doing, you'd go through the actual process that anybody would have to in preparing for a real performance: on-the-job training.

CHICK: Exactly!

JOHN: So, when you were starting out, you went right from listening to records and playing at home to forming little trios, playing out and experimenting--then you got into a couple of bigger bands and moved up from there. Was that the route?

CHICK: Well yes, but very, very gradually. I played for my father and mother and then I played for my uncles and aunts. Then I started doing some performing in grade school--not very often from a stage--and then I started playing some bar rooms around my neighborhood, even before high school, when I was still in grade school. I'd go into a place and take my fakebook.

426

JOHN: When you were older, who were some of the people you first played with?

CHICK: I played with some really good musicians in Boston, even before I went to New York. I worked with Herb Pomeroy once or twice.

JOHN: Did you go to Berklee College of Music?

CHICK: No, but I used to hang around a little bit and jam, and I worked with Jimmy Mosher in Boston--that was a nice experience--and Paul Fontaine. I played a couple of times with Tony Williams before he worked with Miles. And then, in the early 60s, when I moved to New York, I played with some great musicians. I worked with Mongo Santamaria for a while, Kenny Dorham a little bit, Pete La Roca, Steve Swallow--I jobbed around with different guys.

JOHN: How did you get those gigs? A lot of people wonder if they should go out and PR themselves, or let their playing do it for them.

CHICK: My opinion is that the greatest public relations is a great performance, and just service. You go on a gig and you do the gig. And don't just _do_ the gig. Even when I was playing commercial gigs that I didn't enjoy nearly as much as creative music gigs, my own personal attitude was always, "This is a gig." I'd do everything I could to make sure that things were right. I would get there early, tend to the piano, make sure it was all right and its position correct, and learn what I could about the repertoire of the person I was going to be working with. And then I would just try and play great and serve this guy. Whatever he was trying to do, I would try and get into that groove and do it and make him happy. Never to a compromise of my own professional ethics, though. So I believe that idea of service is the best promotion. As a matter of fact, early on I would do that naturally, and sometimes I would think, well, maybe to be very creative I ought to be a little harsh and angry. Maybe I should be a little bit ornery--maybe I'm too nice. You know, "Nice people don't get along very well." But then these guys would call me back for another gig, and I realized that what I was doing felt right. Now, as a band leader, I have incredibly high standards for someone working with me. For instance, if I ask someone to work with me and he even just has a second thought about whether or not he should, I don't want to work with him. I like to work with someone who totally knows that that's what he wants to do at that moment. And is going to be there an hour early for the gig and is going to practice a whole lot and prepare. And that's the way to go through life.

JOHN: If you're going to do it, do it like a professional.

CHICK: If you're going to do it, just really, really, really do it. Do it completely--give it everything. Every shot is the shot. And I think that's how you build yourself a reputation, because building a reputation should never be your goal in life. That's a false, backwards thing. A good reputation is just the result of good service. How others regard you is the result of how you deliver something.

JOHN: So you played with all those guys in New York and eventually hit up with Miles. Was Miles's the last band you played with before you went out on your own as a leader?

CHICK: Miles was my last gig as a sideman, for all intents and purposes. Then I formed a band with Dave Holland--my first real leader band--and then there was Return to Forever.

JOHN: What about the album Inner Space?

CHICK: That was just a record date. It was the only time I played with those particular guys. In fact, we had one rehearsal, I think, and then went in and did it in one day.

JOHN: How did that one come about, though? Did somebody just hear you play and ask you to do some tracks?

CHICK: I had a gig with Herbie Mann at the time, and Atlantic Records had given him a label called Vortex to produce young musicians on. So while I was working with him, Herbie asked me--several times--to do a solo record. He wanted me to use some timbales and do some Latin music. But I didn't want to do Latin music then. Finally one time he said, well, look, do whatever you want. So I wrote some music and did that album.

JOHN: So from then on you seemed to have done your own music.

CHICK: Yes, I got more and more into being a composer. And more and more I came to love just creating bands and writing music for them--just trying to find that unexplainable balance between the musician that you work with and the music that you write. They're inextricable sometimes, if you view the result as a whole finished product. What I mean is that if the finished product is the music--which is played by the band, which is experienced by people, which creates an effect on the world-- then it's actually hard to draw a line sometimes between the musician and the composition that's written. And when I view it like that, there's an infinite game there for me that I really love.

JOHN: Well, then, were you at all shocked at the success of the later Return to Forever when it took off?

CHICK: Man! The first Return to Forever was the thing that shocked me, because that band created a really beautiful effect on people--a kind of effect I had always dreamed of creating. I never placed much emphasis on communicating to large numbers of people. I like doing it, but it's not the important thing. I never thought about it one way or the other. I wanted to create a certain kind of effect, and if I could create it on one person or a small audience, I felt like I was succeeding. So the first Return to Forever band just started creating this effect that I wanted with audiences at the Vanguard. Our first gig there was as an opening band for Roy Haynes' group. But we jobbed and gigged around mostly in clubs, with a very occasional concert, and then we recorded Return to Forever for Manfred Eicher in New York on ECM.

JOHN: Did he hear you jobbing and offer you a deal?

CHICK: No, I had already been recording with Manfred. I had done Circle Records with him, I had done my piano solo records with him, and I think we had already done Crystal Silence with Gary Burton. And we were the greatest of friends. So he was willing to record whatever I put together. In fact, as I remember it, he didn't particularly love everything we did on that first record right away. The record wasn't even released in the United States initially--nobody wanted to take it on.

But then, almost overnight, like within a month or two, it became a hit record in Japan, selling thousands and thousands of copies. So we were offered a tour there--and this was only after that band had been playing for eight or nine months or so--and we went to Japan. It was the first time I had ever experienced thousands of people thronging into concert halls to hear the band. Not

only that, but we had just come out of clubs, playing long
sets and long solos, and had taken the original material
we'd developed in New York and really quite abstracted it
in performance. We weren't playing just straight melody
or things that were easy to follow. And the audience for
some reason went crazy. They just loved it. So we continued to create that kind of effect with that band, and I
know it's because there was a kind of purity in the way we
played the music--a kind of lightness, and nobody in the
band thought anything about what we were doing, except
just loved it.

JOHN: Is there anything else you feel helped you and
contributed to your success?

CHICK: In addition to this idea of giving service
when you play, I have to mention my other successful
action, which has been using Scientology. You see, once
you tune yourself up to the wavelength of making a piece
of art, and making music, you immediately become aware
that there's a kind of equilibrium that you have to maintain. You have to maintain this equilibrium in order to
keep the channel open on which you can start to flow your
creation out through your body and fingers and instrument
into life. And for a composer or pianist or keyboard
player, for instance, who's learning his instrument and
putting his craft together, there's also the aspect of the
discipline of getting through that process or procedure of
creation. Once you begin composing or practicing and you
tune yourself up to that point and hook onto it, all
that's necessary is to continue until you really reach
something. And this is why Scientology has been so helpful. One of the things that used to bug me--and I know
bugs a lot of people--is how difficult it is sometimes to
concentrate. There are so many things that call your
attention away, from just maybe the ill health or ill tone
of the body through to the biggest offender of all, which
is what in Scientology we call the reactive mind. What
I'm talking about is when the mind just starts yapping at
you without your wanting it to. And that was the thing
I knew, way before I read anything by L. Ron Hubbard, I
wanted to get out of the way--because I knew concentration
for long periods of time was a key thing.

You see, a snowball effect occurs when you can concentrate for long periods. At first it takes a while to
tune yourself to that creative wavelength. It may take
some things such as making your work place quiet, or it
might take you doing a whole bunch of business for a few
days until you can get your scene clean enough to start

practicing. Really, it's whatever you might have to do to be able to sit down at your instrument and begin your creation. Then, once you do tune yourself and start putting it together, and you start making some notes and making some progress, a snowball phenomenon occurs. And then you're in there and you're going. But when you are in there and it's going, the only thing to do is to continue to go, see? That's really all you have to do-- unless the mind isn't quiet enough for you to do that. People end up inventing all sorts of strange habits and methods to get the mind out of their way. And any artist knows that the channels that have to be opened to get your creation out have to be free so that you're not thinking about every little thing that you do, or thinking about other things that have nothing to do with what you're doing. Well, I don't have those problems any more, and Scientology was the key. It's been a very, very success- ful endeavor that didn't really have anything to do with the study of music, but had to do with the study of the mind.

JOHN: You made a key point regarding interruptions and trying to get your creative juices flowing so you can really get into the meat of what you want to do. Do you actually set aside a specific time period and control your environment such that, when you go to work on a project, you know there will be no phone calls and no one knocking on your door?

CHICK: That is really a very practical and sure road to your work, and yes, I do that--especially if I have a target to deliver something quite meaty, such as an entire repertoire for a new band. Or if I have an intensive week or two ahead of me in the recording studio and know that I have to bring to that recording finished compositions, finished arrangements, rehearsed bands, and that sort of thing. Then I organize my environment such that my daily life is free for me to be a kind of phantom within life-- nobody knows I'm around. I have to do that.

But lately I've been going back to an earlier method of operating which may appear spontaneous and impulsive, but really is based on the fact that if I have enough of my life organized that I'm not in danger of falling apart, I have the liberty to have many, many projects going at one time. Rather than sitting around spending a lot of time scheduling out how many hours I'm going to spend with one project and how many hours I'm going to spend with the other, I'll let one play off the other. For instance, right now I have two completely diverse projects going on during the course of a day. One is the organization of my filing cabinets, and the other is the composition and arrangement of some new pieces I'm putting together for a performance this weekend. So I'm sort of letting them play off each other, and they fit in very nicely together. I may go for a day and a half at one, and then spend a few hours on the other, and then come back to the first. So I don't have a set plan. But I do have targets and I know that I have to accomplish certain things by certain times.

JOHN: The reason I asked is that a lot of people get distracted by the physical universe games that go on out there. Say someone's got the TV going and you're in the next room and hear something interesting--next thing you know you're opening the door and looking, and you've interrupted your thoughts for a minute. Many people don't even realize that things like that are half the reason they don't get what they want done. Do you make sure you will be free of interruptions before you get into projects such as those you've mentioned?

CHICK: Well, this is the concept--it's easy to show it for a musician or a painter. If you're a painter and you want to paint something, the very first thing you need is a blank canvas. The most horrible thing to do is to try to start a painting with something already painted on the canvas. And it's the same way if you're going to compose music, practice music, or make music--you have to start with silence. And I'm not talking about something like scientifically produced silence. I mean you have to start with an environment you're in control of.

JOHN: That's a good point. Turning now to your recent involvements--over the last few years, you've been delving heavily into the world of classical music. Why does a successful jazz musician and composer such as yourself suddenly branch out like this?

CHICK: Well, I don't know how common this is to other musicians, but I always held classical music at a distance from me, and never conceived making it a part of my professional life. I always thought playing classical music was such a different activity that it took a whole different lifestyle and approach. Therefore, I used classical music mainly as a reference point. I always knew it was a great source of inspiration for new ideas as well as just pure enjoyment. As the years went on, though, the incredible wealth of music in the classical area became more and more apparent to me. Most music written with what is unfortunately usually called "seri-

432

ous" musical intent ends up in classical music. I say unfortunately, because what is usually referred to as "serious" music, as opposed to music that isn't considered "serious," is music that's created just out of the joy of making music! But I think what that finally comes down to is simply the culture's agreement on the concept of seriousness.

JOHN: So you're comparing serious music with commercial music, since society seems to use those terms?

CHICK: Yes. But you do sense a unique integrity when you listen to classical music. Normally, when you listen to classical music--and especially the music of those composers agreed to be the masters, such as Bach, Beethoven, Mozart, and others of course--you do get a different sense and communication and feel than you get from most other music you might hear on the radio. Not all other music, but most other music. There is a sense of effortlessness and serenity and peacefulness--a communication of music that's not asserted. It's an easy communication, so its beauty can more readily be felt than that of some commercial music. Whatever multiple intents go into the makeup of commercial music, one of the things that differentiates it from classical music to me is that its intent seems to be a frantic "I must communicate! I must get this record done and put this communication out!"

So I never considered that classical music was a part of my life in a professional sense. But more and more over the past six years, as I would pull out some Mozart or Bach between tours and practice, it became apparent to me that I really felt a part of this culture of classical music and would like to do something within it. The point of change for me was when I started to write some music for the Leprechaun album in 1974 or '75 and had to enlist the help of some classical musicians--a string quartet. I loved the degree of professionalism and competence they had with their craft. This attracted me to work with them further just purely as musicians, not even considering the type of music they played. I was encouraged to write more music for string quartet because I enjoyed it so much. So I did in Madhatter and Spanish Heart, and included a string quartet on one of my tours. And that was the beginning.

The actual crossover point, however, was getting a commission from Fred Cherry, the cellist, through the Chamber Music Society, to write the five movement work Septet. Septet was premiered in a completely classical environment with all classical musicians, and was completely written-out--the first I had written out to that extent. It was very attractive to me--I had such a good time. I then wrote a piece called "Lyric Suite for Sextet" that included my jazz duet with Gary Burton. We took that around the world and made a record, and that was another great experience working with the string quartet, but more in a jazz environment. So working with the string quartet was kind of my way in, until I finally accepted the invitation of Friedrich Gulda to play Mozart's Double Piano Concerto. That was straight into the teeth of the incredibly rich classical repertoire, rather than my own music.

JOHN: What effect has playing classical music had on your own compositions and playing?

CHICK: That's probably best related by talking about the fineness of classical music. They do call it a fine art. The term is well chosen if fine means incredible attention to detail. I find that when more and more detail is tended to in art, it becomes finer and finer. So it's a taste you have for a communication that is more or less fine. Well, one of the senses that playing Mozart and Bach has given me--a sense that I'm excited to bring back to my own music--is this fineness: the quality of the sound, the detail one tends to the composition, the detail one tends to the blend and balance of the rendition--and also the fineness of the intention: the reason the music is made, what is expected of the listener, and all of that. My contact with classical music has just heightened my awareness of all those questions and my desire is to bring what I feel I'm beginning to learn about that into my own music. I cannot stop desiring it now that I'm beginning to experience it. It's a delicacy and an attention to group playing and lyricism and the integrity of making a good performance that I want to bring into my music.

JOHN: How might you think playing classical music would benefit other musicians?

CHICK: The ways other musicians might want to involve themselves and what they might want to get out of it, of course, are personal choices. I would think, though, because it is such a rich source of music, that any musician's study of the subject of music would be a little bit incomplete without some knowledge or appreciation of classical music, even as a listener if not a player. The extent to which someone would get involved

is, of course, a very personal thing. I would suggest
that a musician get into classical music or any music just
because he feels he should. It should be chosen because
of a real desire and intent. Basically what I'm saying
here is that there's an incredibly rich body of spirit and
culture and great creation in classical music, and at some
point you've got to check it out.

JOHN: Has studying classical music helped your technique with your own music, or is it so different that it's
not applicable?

CHICK: Technique is an after-the-fact thing, of
course: technique is actually created out of the necessity to make music. Those who write this kind of music
require a pianistic technique that is probably the most
demanding there is for the instrument. So just through my
involvement with Bach and Mozart, and spending hours with
the music, my pure command over the instrument has increased without question.

JOHN: Well, to pull it all together, the common
thread that seems to have run through your entire career
and life has been a really strong love of music and a
great desire to play it and create it and be around it.

CHICK: How can you attack that? Let me give you the
last concept of this talk, the coda, because concepts
string all things together. I've actually been playing
around with this the past few days, and this is a heavy
one.

Many people think that in order to become something,
or do something, or accomplish something, it takes talent,
or something like that. And a lot of people think it
takes a lot of hard work. Well, that's true, but there's
something else here that's very interesting to me, and
it concerns someone's decision to do something. You know,
nowhere can it scientifically or otherwise be predicted or
shown how or why a person decides to do something. In
fact, even in defining what a person or a spirit is, it's
one thing you never get taped, simply because the one who
decides is the person himself.

So the way I evaluate people and what they do is not
so much by their talents as by their thrust and their
decision and their involvement in what they're doing.
Their basic intent. And, you know, it's nothing more than
a decision. And you can't force someone to make a decision. Somehow or other, as any individual really knows,

you have the freedom to make whatever decision you want, at whatever degree of thrust you decide. Basically, when you take everything else away, it's up to you to decide. Because nothing's going to happen until you do. And there's nothing more that can be said about that. So maybe if people knew that they have that power within them--they'd get into trying it out, and decide, instead of waiting for something to happen.

You know, I often try to figure out why this person's doing one thing and not another, or why that person's doing what he's doing. You can come up with a lot of reasons. You can even talk about a person's mental state, and this and that. But basically what it comes down to is that that person made a decision at some point and is walking the road of that decision, even if he no longer remembers that he made it--even if he isn't sure why he's doing what he's doing.

JOHN: Yes, and what's interesting is that if you simply get someone to change their decision or consideration about something, you can see the result almost instantaneously. One minute they're doing this--next thing you know they're doing that. When you ask what happened, they say, "Oh, I just decided to do this."

CHICK: Exactly.

JOHN: So obviously you made a decision early on about creating and enjoying and playing and disseminating music, and that's been a big thrust in your life for a long time. But that brings me to my next question. There are a lot of musicians out there playing the music game. But the majority of them could be viewed as just servants to a commercial machine. I'm not saying, necessarily, that that's right or wrong. But then there are a few in every era who really have a message or a concept that they want to express and who seem to push through and create either their own music or their own style, or something that they contribute to their particular field. It's interesting to compare them with those who are perhaps quite good composers and good players, but who don't carry it any farther. Do you think it's because they get side-tracked, or aren't strong enough to push through, or just never rise to that level of conceptual operation that we've been talking about?

CHICK: I think there are probably a lot of factors that enter in, not just one. For instance--getting back to making decisions--I've observed that sometimes it seems

to take a heavy experience for someone to come around to
making a heavy decision. But then, sometimes it doesn't.
Sometimes it takes the opposite--a long period of peace-
fulness--before a person finally comes around to a reali-
zation that he wants to do something. So that's why I say
that it's hard to predict how and why someone makes a
decision. And this is true no matter what mental or
spiritual condition a person might be in. Just because
someone is in excellent shape doesn't ensure that he will
make one decision and not another. Does a person decide
not to go the standard route, but do something he really
wants to do--or does he decide to be part of the commercial machine? You mentioned that could be either right or
wrong. I'm just fascinated by that because, for instance,
I see people who are part of the commercial machine who
aren't being innovators in anything particularly, yet who
I think could be.

JOHN: I brought that up because, in the world of
jazz composition, you're probably one of the least compro-
mising composers--yet you're successful. I'm contrasting
that with a lot of guys who have gone to the hit syndrome,
along the lines of "I'm going to have to write a hit now
because the record company's gonna drop me," or "I'm going
to have to jump on the thing that's happening now"--which
may be a particular funk groove--or "I have to do this for
airplay." You can see them fluctuate back and forth from
one project to the next, doing what they think will make
them more successful. And this involves the artist and
his integrity, to an extent, and the question that people
have probably been debating for centuries: "Should I sell
part of my soul to go open some doors and then, if I do,
will I get it back and be able to do what I want to do?
Or should I right now just keep on pushing with what I
want to do?" It seems to me you've never thought this
way. When you do albums and compositions, they're the
songs that you wanted to write, for whatever reason you
wanted to write them. When you want them on an album,
they go on the album--and if the album sells and it's a
success, it's fine, but if it doesn't, that doesn't
matter.

CHICK: That's a great compliment for you to have
even noticed that, because, actually, that's probably my
greatest pride and joy--knowing that and living that way.
But I've learned this the easy way and I've learned it the
hard way, and it always proves 5,000% true to me: for
better or worse, if I don't follow my own vision, if I
don't keep my own counsel and do what I see to do, I do
less well--a little bit poorer, a little worse. And,

consequently, things around me get little bit poorer, a little worse. So, no matter what others might be thinking, no matter what other master plan or philosophy is presented to me by whatever great person--if I can't see it, and if it's not a way that feels right for me to go, I can't go that way.

JOHN: So in that situation you actually make a decision <u>not</u> to do whatever it is?

CHICK: Right. Several times I even tried doing something that wasn't really what I wanted to do. And I can't tell you what suffering I had. Worse than the worst physical pain you could ever imagine. It isn't physical pain; it isn't even mental pain--it's spiritual anguish. There's no word in the language to describe this kind of pain.

JOHN: Like being an enemy to yourself?

CHICK: Yes, it's an incredible, horrible kind of suffering. Even if I do that just a little, especially in the line of music and art, I feel it very strongly. So instead I use this clear insight I have regarding my music and art and do what I know is right for me. And now I'm trying to expand myself and apply this concept to other parts of life. Because it works. You see, I've always had the dream, ever since I can remember, that all of life's experience can be artful--every moment of it. So that's what I'm trying to do.

JOHN: Thanks very much, Chick.

Herbie Hancock
keyboardist/composer

HERBIE HANCOCK

JOHN: Looking at your career in retrospect, can you single out any important elements that directly contributed to your success?

HERBIE: The fact that I basically took the training route: I studied classical music from age seven to about 20. First it was just private lessons--in college I started out studying engineering--but then later I switched to a music composition major. I studied harmony, theory, sight singing, orchestration and composition while continuing my study of the classics. I played Chopin Etudes and Preludes, Bach Inventions and Fugues, etc. When I was about 13 I got into jazz on my own, just by listening to all the happening players and analyzing what they did.

JOHN: Did you do record copies?

HERBIE: Yes. To understand why a soloist did what he did in a certain part of the music, I'd try to write it out. I started to see that there were definite musical relationships between chords, like common tones and so on, and that helped me actually figure out harmony before I formally studied it. So by the time I got to college I already had a rudimentary understanding of harmony and theory. The formal training validated the basics I had already learned and added some valuable tools like counterpoint and orchestration.

JOHN: When did you start applying all this training and begin playing live gigs?

HERBIE: When I was in college--I decided to put on a jazz concert and try my hand at arranging. So I got some records and, like I had done with improvising, I listened to the arrangements and tried to figure out what each instrument's parts were. I listened to guys like Neil Hefti, Count Basie, Frank Foster, and so on. Doing it the hard way like that really developed my ear. That was also actually when I changed my major to music, because I realized that was what I really wanted to do. I then studied a course called Instrumental Techniques which was really helpful in teaching me all about other instruments--

ranges, fingerings, arranging techniques, terminology--the whole works.

JOHN: Who were some of your major jazz influences?

HERBIE: Originally it was George Shearing, Oscar Peterson, Earl Garner, Dave Brubeck.   Then Art Blakey's group, Horace Silver, Miles Davis, and then Bill Evans. But I have actually been more influenced by non-piano players, with the exception of Bill Evans for harmony. Most of my harmonic stuff comes from listening, for example, to the Hi Lo's, and in particular, Clare Fisher's arrangements, which I heard in college.   I learned about harmony from Clare's arrangements.   Also I used to listen to one particular mood music orchestra--Robert Farnon's. His harmonic sense was incredible, even though it was only background music.   Quincy Jones, Dizzy Gillespie, J. J. Johnson, Lalo Schifrin and Donald Byrd are all into him.

JOHN: Did you ever study jazz with anybody?

HERBIE: Yes, I studied with a local Chicago piano player named Chris Anderson for about two weeks.   I was a fast learner.   I heard him play a solo piece one night that literally brought tears to my eyes.   The harmonies were so gorgeous and the heart that went into it was so fantastic that I just knew I had to study with him.   So I did.   I was really into learning.   I used to dig taking a ballad and changing all the chords around and adding modulations and counterpoint, etc.   And this was even before I heard Bill Evans, who of course was really into that kind of thing.

JOHN: What was your first big break?

HERBIE: Donald Byrd was the guy you could say discovered me when I was about 21.   He had been passing through Chicago on his way to Milwaukee to do a concert, but his piano player somehow got stranded in a snowstorm. So Donald called a local club owner who was a good friend--John Court--and said he needed a piano player. John recommended me, and I sat in with the band for the weekend.   They liked me, so Donald brought me to New York and introduced me to the scene.   Donald also turned me on to some of the contemporary serious composers like Boulez, Varese, Messiaen, Penderecki, Stravinsky and Ravel.   And I learned a lot from listening to another composer hardly anyone knows about--Lily Boulanger, Nadia Boulanger's sister.   She did incredible things with harmonies and modulations.

JOHN: What was your next big break?

HERBIE: Playing with Miles Davis was the next step after Donald Byrd. Donald introduced me to Miles by bringing me over to his house one night. I played a ballad or something and Miles said "Nice touch!" Everybody was telling me that Miles was going to call me, though I really didn't think he would. But he did, so I left Donald and went to Miles in May of 1963, which of course shot me more in the public eye. But a year earlier, in '62, I had actually made my first album for Blue Note Records. Donald, who was like a big brother to me, told me it was time to do my own record. He told me to call the owners of Blue Note, Alfred Lyon and Frank Wolf, and tell them that I was being drafted into the army and I wanted to do an album before I left. Donald also told me not to give up my publishing to Blue Note. I didn't know anything about publishing, but I took Donald's advice. So when I went to Blue Note to discuss business, sure enough they wanted the publishing on any original tunes I wrote for the album.

JOHN: The moment of truth for Herbie Hancock?

HERBIE: That's exactly right. I took Donald's advice reluctantly, because I knew I might lose the record deal, and told them that my original tunes had already been published by my own publishing company--which of course wasn't true. They said they couldn't make the record under those conditions, so I said I was sorry and started to walk out the door. Then all of a sudden they said okay, all right--you keep your publishing. Now, of course, that made a big difference, because "Watermelon Man" was one of the tunes and became a big hit!

JOHN: So was that the beginning of your commercial career?

HERBIE: Yes. There I was, just after I had joined Miles--who represented the epitomy of jazz at that time-- and I concurrently had a top ten hit pop tune--which had originally just been aimed at a larger jazz audience I thought would be into the funkier side of jazz!

JOHN: You seem to have found a formula for communicating your art no matter what the style--jazz, avant-garde, funk, pop, film scores. Looking back, is it possible to explain your success in such a wide musical panorama?

THE CONTEMPORARY KEYBOARDIST

HERBIE: Well, part of the idea is communication. I love people. I've always been into people. The other part is that I love those different kinds of music. And I felt I would be a coward if I didn't pursue what I liked.

JOHN: That's very interesting, because a lot of critics think you gave up your personal musical integrity when you switched from the serious jazz world to the commercial world. But in actual fact, for you, keeping your musical integrity meant playing the types of music that you liked.

HERBIE: That's exactly right. The ability to change makes you a bigger person. By doing that, you get more respect from those who count, as well as feel more respect for yourself.

JOHN: Do you still find time to keep your jazz and classical chops up? Is it important, or even necessary?

HERBIE: Well if I'm not doing jazz 24 hours a day, I'm bound to get a little rusty--which means I have to work harder when I'm getting ready to do a jazz record or performance. But because of my versatility, my playing is actually getting fresher and more creative, and my overall concept is more well rounded. So that's the plus factor.

JOHN: Has allowing yourself this freedom to be versatile opened doors that would otherwise have remained closed?

HERBIE: It has. When I was preparing to do Headhunters, I decided that I wouldn't use a guitar for the funk stuff, but a clavinet. So I played rhythm figures on it and developed a whole style of playing that was largely my own, even though, of course, it was influenced by other people. It was based on using both hands independently in rhythmic playing, like a drummer. I can now draw from this ability when I'm playing the acoustic piano--even when I'm not playing R&B or funk. It's like playing the drums but using harmonic structure.

JOHN: Were there any influences in the R&B world who led you out of the jazz elite viewpoint and into all these other changes?

HERBIE: The first time I paid any attention to R&B since I had been a kid was in the mid-60's, when I heard "Papa's Got A Brand New Bag," by James Brown. His syncopated feel and sense of rhythmic space was dynamic. Then

I did a record with Stanley Turrentine and got a chance to play a tune by Curtis Mayfield that had that double-time feel, and I really liked it. Then I was further exposed to R&B when Bill Cosby asked me to do the music for the TV cartoon series, Fat Albert. I did a lot of listening research in order to write some authentic R&B for the show. In fact, I ultimately got my record deal with Warner Brothers after they heard the music from the show.

But the artist who really tripped me out was Sly Stone, with his record, "Thank You For Lettin' Me Be Myself." I could envision having created other forms of R&B, but Sly's music--never! I had been a musician all my life, had all this training, played with all these great players, but I knew I could never have created that. And if I can't do it, something is missing--I have to find out how to do it! I've always been like that when I've heard something I liked but couldn't do. That's how I got into jazz. I heard this guy playing at a variety show in high school, and I knew that he knew what he was doing, and he was doing it on my instrument--but I had no idea of what was going on. So I wanted to learn how to do it. That's what got me started.

JOHN: So you've developed the ability to know when you don't know something. Therefore, you're able to continue to learn and change.

HERBIE: That's right! And that's very important, you see, because I later concluded that most jazz musicians didn't know the first thing about funk. They thought it was easy to play, and thus really knew only the periphery of it. Actually they didn't have a clue as to what was going on, and you could tell it from the way they played it. I didn't want to be that kind of jazz musician. I wanted to find out what the real deal was. In order to do that, to put it back into your own words and to intelligently do the necessary research, you have to know that you don't know.

JOHN: Otherwise you're clouded by your ego or a know-it-all viewpoint.

HERBIE: Right. I've never really been like that. If I can't do something, but I really like it, I know something is missing. Around 1973, after I broke up the New Mwandishi Band, I really didn't know what musical direction to take--whether to be a studio musician, do more films and commercials, continue doing my own recordings, or what. I had started studying Buddhism at that time, and one day when I was chanting, trying to seek an answer to this confusion, I started humming Sly Stone's tune "Thank You For Lettin' Me Be Myself" mentally and at the same time thinking how much I liked that kind of music. I asked myself, "Do you like that kind of music?" The answer was yes! "Are you curious about it?" Yes! "Do you realize you might lose all of your present jazz audience?" Yes! "Do you know that you could maybe gain a whole new bigger audience that you never had?" Yes! And I started thinking, "I'll learn something new, it'll be a challenge, and how can I call myself a musician if I can't play this type of music that I like?" In other words, I saw the handwriting on the wall. I even realized that I might not be able to do it well, because it's like starting all over again. But one thing I had learned from Buddhism is whatever you decide to do, do the best you can. Don't half-do anything. It doesn't even really matter if it's any good or not. As long as you do the best you can, you can walk tall!

JOHN: Sounds like more personal integrity!

HERBIE: Right! You have to follow your own path. That's how I developed my particular style of music. At the time I really started to develop my style, I was simply trying to do a funk album because I liked the music. But with my jazz background and limited knowledge of the funk style, something different came out. And since I liked what I heard, I said well, let's just keep doing this. One of the tunes that came out of this was "Chameleon." It wasn't funk, it wasn't jazz, it wasn't jazz rock like everybody else was doing--it was its own thing. From there it just kept evolving into a R&B trip, Herbie Hancock style--which was what I originally set out to do when I did the Headhunters album. Then, once I had done that to my satisfaction, it was time to move on.

JOHN: Is this when you began getting more heavily into synthesizers, computers, drum machines and so on?

HERBIE: Well, yes. For years my method had been to work with two or three other writers. I wanted to do something completely on my own, so I began experimenting. At first I threw a lot of music away, because I just wasn't happy with anything I was creating. But then Tony Meilandt, who I originally hired just to help run my office, started doing a lot of research on the new music scene. He kept me up with the current scene while I was creating and searching.

Then Tony told me about these guys in New York, called Material, who do a lot of different kinds of music and producing. He felt that if I got together with them and did a couple of tunes, something great would happen. So they started preparing some tracks in New York as a starting point, and about a week before we were supposed to meet in L.A. to start collaborating, I heard my first scratch record, called "Buffalo Gal," by Malcolm Mclaren. It really blew me away. It sounded avant-garde. Yes, it was dance music, but the idea of someone using that sound as a rhythm was out and I really dug it. Even the way it was performed--a guy playing a turntable--completely fascinated me. The way those sounds were zooming in and out of the track reminded me of Stockhausen, even though the medium in this case was dance music.

Thus I was prepared to tell the guys from Material-- Bill Glaswell and Michael Beinhorn--that this was the kind of thing I wanted to do. So they came to L.A. and played me their tracks--and it was the same kind of thing! I freaked! They already had the drums, bass line and the scratchin', and I added the melody and all the other overdubs. That track was, of course, "Rocket." We did a great video, which got on MTV, and the video and song were a smash and we went on to win a Grammy! And there was another goal of mine realized--to be more visible. Now there are tons of new things happening--TV and film acting, more film scores and commercials, TV talk shows-- you name it.

JOHN: That's a great story! What advice might you give to an aspiring keyboardist who wants to know what to study? Is it still valid to study classical, jazz, harmony, arranging and orchestration, and possibly let the whole electronic technology pass you by? Or should you do everything?

HERBIE: I don't think you can stop a person from playing around with something he likes. But I would still suggest that even someone who likes playing and programming synthesizers get into classical music, because it's a great springboard into other areas. In other words, it's a healthy place to start, because all the basics are contained in it--fingering, technique, dynamics, composition, etc. And I recommend jazz because it includes all the same basics plus adding the art of improvisation-- which all the great masters were great at. But if someone likes synthesizers, commercial music--whatever--there's no reason he can't do it all to get a good foundation, and then specialize. I don't believe in suppressing anything

constructive. Even if it's destructive, it should be
dealt with! That's why for me, Buddhism has been very
valuable. It has helped me deal with things when I needed
to deal with them and thus allowed me to be more in the
place I physically am, 24 hours a day--or at least approach that. It's allowed me to improve myself. And the
more you improve yourself, the more your environment
reflects that improvement.

Ralph Grierson
studio keyboardist/composer

RALPH GRIERSON

JOHN: Let's begin with a little musical autobiography--when you first became interested in music, things you studied that are indispensable to what you're doing now, and so on.

RALPH: I discovered music when I was about three. At that time my father was occasionally writing arrangements for a 17-piece rehearsal band, and one night he took me to one of the rehearsals. The energy of that experience had an incredible effect on me. At first I wanted to be a drummer, but later, when I was about five, I began classical piano lessons. The idea then, of course, was that no matter what you wanted to play, you needed to get a classical background because you had to know what you were doing if you wanted to get anywhere. So I continued those lessons, and when I was 12 or 13, I went to Vancouver, British Columbia--we lived in a suburb--and studied with one of the best teachers in town. He gave lessons on a beautiful concert grand Steinway, which was a great incentive.

In addition to the classical lessons, I also began learning commercial music. My dad used to play casuals with a quintet, playing private parties, working in a supper club a couple nights a week, and so on. So he would pick the piano player's brains and come home and teach me chord changes. That was when I was about 10. When I was 13 I started working with him, subbing for the Hammond organist. Eventually I got the job as pianist. At the same time I began playing rehearsal piano for the chorus line at the Cave Supper Club in Vancouver. I would go to Vancouver after school every day and rehearse for a few hours with them, which got me sketching things. Then I would get together with the arranger so we could do the arrangement for the band. When I was 19 I took over the job of piano player in that band and did that for a year and a half before going to USC to study.

In addition to all that, I played weddings and bar mitzvahs, fashion shows, school projects, rehearsal piano for ballet classes, operettas. I also played clarinet in the school band. By the time I got out of high school I was also beginning to do radio and television work with the Canadian Broadcasting Corporation--live radio shows, television variety shows. During the two-year period before I went to USC, I did everything it was possible to do musically in Vancouver--I was the busiest guy in town. But I was working around the clock and only making about $12,500 a year, and I thought, wait a minute, there's got to be more than this! And I knew there was. I had always planned on attending Juilliard so I could study seriously. I had saved the money and was all ready to go, but a woman I had been studying theory and composition privately with, who was going down to USC during the summer to work on her doctorate in composition, started telling me about the people who were there: Ingolf Dahl; John Crown, who I later studied with; Lillian Steuber; Alice Ehlers, a baroque specialist; Eudice Shapiro; Jascha Heifitz; Gregor Piatigorsky. At that time it was really the golden age of music at USC. So I decided to go there instead.

I'd planned to study without having to work, but after almost a year costs escalated and I began needing things. So I started connecting with people, doing a few fashion shows and casuals, and the whole pattern started over again. Soon I was playing every kind of music again, and that's primarily how I put myself through school.

JOHN: So having that wide range of experience helped you make a living.

RALPH: Yes. It was do whatever I had to do to get myself heard. I also got involved in a lot of contemporary classical music through the Monday evening concerts in Los Angeles. I got a chance to work with Pierre Boulez, playing the music of Stravinsky, Varese, Stockhausen, Boulez himself, and a lot of other contemporary composers under really super conditions. Michael Tilson Thomas and I were in some of the same classes and became friends. We did some two-piano music together, played some concerts and ended up recording the two-piano version of the Rite of Spring. So, between Monday evening concerts, Ojai Festivals, and traveling on the road with the King Family doing their television specials during the summers, I was busy. I even spent my honeymoon on the road with the King Family!

JOHN: Do you presently do mostly studio work?

RALPH: Yes, that's my bread and butter. Back when I was at USC, my work with the King Family led to some television shows. At the same time I connected with the Ojai Festival, where I played some Edgar Varese pieces with

Boulez and Stravinsky's "Les Noces." A percussionist there named Ken Watson was beginning to work with Lalo Schifrin and told him about me. Lalo came to some of the rehearsals and subsequently hired me to do some television and motion picture work. Then, while doing a picture for Lalo, I met Artie Kane, who at that time was the king of keyboard players in film and freelance studio business. He was like a mentor to me--he was really supportive and got me more work. Also, around that time I played a Monday evening concert of chamber music for soprano, electronics, and nine-piece chamber orchestra written by Leonard Rosenman. Leonard was then also doing Marcus Welby, M.D. at Universal and started calling me for that, which put me in touch with the contractor there. So it was through those two composers and some players I met along the way that I began to be heard and consequently got work! By the time I finished my Masters at USC I was already working enough that it was basically a smooth transition into full-time studio work. There were a few lean years in the beginning, but by the early 70's I was working as much as I wanted to.

JOHN: You were obviously cutting the gig very well, as they were calling you back!

RALPH: Well, I guess I made a good impression. Two of the records I did--the Rite of Spring and some Cage prepared piano music--also helped a lot in getting me heard. I had a reputation for doing a lot of the "unplay-able" contemporary piano music. I had gotten into that because a teacher I had at USC very wisely--and in opposi-tion to a lot of teachers--felt it was really important for the performers to connect with the composers within the university. So he would see to that by encouraging his students to play works of young composers. And you did it under really trying conditions--the guy would write a piece and you'd have to have it ready for his recital in two weeks. Being faced with challenges like that and having to make it got me to realize that there was no big mystery to learning that type of difficult music--it just meant incredible hours at the piano and dissecting every-thing. And that was when I realized that, basically, I could probably do whatever I wanted, musically--it was just a matter of how much energy I was willing to put into it.

I also recorded a couple of albums of Scott Joplin music, which got some attention, and produced an album of my own that got some good reviews. I got bitten by the composition bug some time ago, so in the last few years

I've been experimenting with improvisational things. I'd always played commercial jazz and improvised very easily. I have perfect pitch and it was no problem for me to imitate sounds I heard and sound like any number of people--which, by the way, is what Hollywood needs. You know--can you sound like Oscar Peterson today?

JOHN: Did you actually do transcriptions to develop that ability?

RALPH: Almost never. I think the closest I ever came to transcribing anything was on two or three occasions when I transcribed some Andre Previn solos I needed for a radio show. But that was about it. The rest of it was just done by listening a lot and playing a lot.

JOHN: So are you now, as we say in Hollywood, the first call cat?

RALPH: Yes. There are half a dozen really first rate keyboard players who are called first.

JOHN: Are they all variety like yourself, or specialists?

RALPH: The most successful of us are those who can do almost anything. You can go from one extreme to the other within a three-hour session.

JOHN: Even as well as you play, would the work be limited if you didn't play multikeyboards?

RALPH: Yes. I was very fortunate in that I started when the Rhodes electric piano, the Baldwin electric harpsichord, the old Yamaha organs, the Hammond, the Novachord, etc., were just coming out. It was really exciting. I would go to work and not really know what keyboard I was going to play. It might even be an instrument I hadn't seen before. And the first object was to discover how to turn it on! So it was a real learn-while-you-earn situation--which I've always believed in anyway. As the keyboard scene expanded, so did I. I've always been interested in new things--new music and new sounds. So I kept up with the instruments, programming, and I also listened to other players, especially Ian Underwood, Mike Boddiker, and Pete Robinson, who were the big three synthesizer players in town. I'm still learning, to this day!

454

JOHN: With so many sessions a day, how do you get all this complex equipment around quickly still working properly?

RALPH: I have a good cartage company that comes to my studio and picks up all the equipment I know I'll need for the week. It's their job to get it to its destination on time, set it up and then tear it down and get it to the next place. At present, the synthesizers I use most are the Jupiter, Chroma, and the Yamaha DX's. Except very occasionally, the Buchla never moves.

JOHN: Do you have to do much quick advance programming when you get a score, or do you just handle it as it comes up?

RALPH: I do it as the cue comes up. Usually when you turn open the music there are instructions for the synthesist. If you're really lucky, the composer might come over and offer some suggestions! Usually, though, you just get some basic ideas and work them out as you rehearse the cue.

JOHN: So you have a good, adaptable library of sounds that you know handle most occasions?

RALPH: Right--sounds I can quickly modify. That's why analog synthesizers like the Jupiter, Oberheim and Prophet work well. With them you can modify a sound very quickly to make it work.

JOHN: Do you have your own signal processing gear or do you play directly into the studio board?

RALPH: I have my own rack of signal processing gear that I bring to all my dates to enhance my sounds. The reason I do is that in TV and films, unlike record dates, time is at a premium. You have to be able to produce whatever the composer wants quickly and efficiently. I have a tuner plugged into all my keyboards so I can constantly monitor my pitch. I have a separate volume control for my monitor sound so I can turn it off when I have to do quiet programming; otherwise, since everyone wears headphones, the rest of the musicians would hear me working on new sounds, which is very distracting! When we're ready to tape, I flip the switch and send the sound to the engineer for recording. I also have a ton of effects to enhance my sounds--analog delays, digital delays, a vocoder, compressor-limiter, stereo chorus, parametric equalizer, phasers,--whatever they need. I also have a complete patch bay, with everything normaled (patched) the way I usually use it. But I can patch the effects any way--series or parallel. I can even have one set of effects left channel and a separate set on the right. And in some cases that may even be separate instruments, so there can be a separate feed for each two instruments.

JOHN: It sounds as though you've used your experience and hard-won knowledge to build yourself a setup that helps you produce high quality work very quickly and efficiently.

RALPH: Yes, because it has to--that's the only way one's going to survive in this business. But about half the time I'll go to a date and it'll be piano concerto time, so I won't have any instruments there.

JOHN: With the incredible variety of a music scene today that's exploding in so many directions, a beginning keyboardist has the problem of deciding which way to go and how to prepare. Is it necessary to spend fifteen to twenty years and really learn the keyboard? Because they can get into bands so quickly, keyboardists today can end up in the glib situation of having all this expensive gear, yet never having really studied the art of playing. What advice would you give somebody trying to make a living today?

RALPH: I would suggest definitely developing keyboard technique, one way or another. At this time the black and white keyboard is the most common way of creating through synthesizers. It's certainly not the only one available--in years to come the electronics will be available for every section of the orchestra, so someone into electronic music won't necessarily have to become a pianist or develop keyboard technique. But now it certainly would help, since keyboards are the most common and advanced controllers. To do that, you can study classical music and techniques, and different methods of building up the musculature and developing digital coordination. Digital coordination is important, whether it be on a black and white keyboard or a computer keyboard. I would also say you've got to be computer literate, because music is going to be connected to computers from now on, as is everything else.

I'm also convinced that a complete keyboardist couldn't expect to really make it now without being able to play all keyboards. As a keyboardist you can still specialize, as many have already--you can still play just the piano or harpsichord, or be just a synthesist or a programmer. But if we're talking in terms of a working keyboardist, I think you have to familiarize yourself with the happening instruments. You see, in any period there are instruments that are the most successful, and all the others are in some way derivative of them--they're basically just different manufacturers' versions, based on the same technologies. So if you can play them, you can translate that knowledge to all the others.

JOHN: Sight reading is a bug for a lot of keyboardists. In your field it's a necessity. How did you develop that ability?

RALPH: There's no mystery to much of it. We have to keep things in perspective here, because my own view of myself has always been that I'm not that good a reader-- yet I have a reputation for being a great sight reader. So the reality must lie somewhere in between. I've always felt that a better term would be quick study, and that's what Artie Kane also used to say to me. Given the nature of the work, there's usually always some time to skim and find the tricky spots. The key is to be able to look ahead, recognize problems instantly and work them out in your mind before you even start playing. I will silently finger something ahead of time. And the other thing is that you just have to do it--you have to read and read and read music. It's like when you start reading as a kid. If you don't read books, your reading skills won't develop. It's only by plodding through--looking up the word in the dictionary--that you improve. So you have to plod through, note by note sometimes. There's no shortcut.

JOHN: Would you say that a good knowledge of harmony and theory facilitates the process?

RALPH: Of course. All the knowledge you accumulate when you study music is indispensable.

JOHN: So we're back to getting a good solid background in technique, reading through the literature, learning some repertoire, playing a lot of different types of music.

RALPH: Absorb everything you can. Do as much as you can--do all the dumb jobs you can, because you never know where you're going to get experience that's really going to be valuable.

JOHN: What's an example of a problem a keyboardist might have to solve using an earlier experience?

RALPH: Say you're working on source music for television and pictures--you might have to do the music for
a scene in a bar. That's the most common kind of thing.

JOHN: Cocktail pianist?

RALPH: Sure. If you haven't worked in a variety of
different cocktail piano situations, there's no way you
can call up a quick identifying aural image that will
reinforce the visual one. Take a restaurant with a guy
playing the piano. It's going to be different depending
on what kind of restaurant it is--whether it's a dive, a
moderate place, or an expensive sophisticated club. To be
able to recreate the kinds of music and the caliber of
playing you hear in all those different places, you need
to have done it, or at least been there and then tried to
recreate the kinds of sounds that you heard. You have to
keep your ears open. Some of the off-the-wall, terrible
musicians you hear in remote places become real character
studies. You've got to get yourself into that charac-
ter--it's like being a character actor. You may only have
a lead line and chord changes, and it's up to you to be
able to translate that and make it fit the needed image.

JOHN: Have you ever gotten some cue so difficult
that it would have been impossible to try to do it in real
time?

RALPH: Yes I have. You have to know what's essential, what's important. Just as with sight reading, you
grab what's essential the first time through, and then you
add to that. There are times when it may be necessary to
change a part without even discussing it with anybody.
You're in an industry where time is very expensive--any
question you ask takes up a lot of someone else's time.
So the faster you can make those decisions, the better.
You see, basically it's a partnership between you and the
composer. He's there to try to write the notes that will
make the music happen, but occasionally he's confused
about what the producer wants or how to make the music cue
work. Your job is to make him look good, regardless--and
yourself in the process.

Another situation that can be really nightmarish is
when they call you in advance for something when it really
isn't necessary and then, when you arrive at that date,
you find something else there, twice as hard, that they
never even considered mentioning. I've come across Chopin
waltzes, things I've never played. I call it the "Oh by
the way" syndrome--"Oh, by the way, we've got the second

movement of a Chopin piano concerto, but we never found
out about it until an hour ago, and we have to do it--can
you do it on your lunch hour maybe?" That's where the
adrenaline is--that's the sheer terror part of the job.
And it's challenging--everything gets going at once. You
burn into it, you give it your best shot, and it works--or
you hope that they can cut it properly if you don't make
it!

There are also logistical problems. Often composers
don't know synthesizers--they don't know the piano, basically, let alone electric keyboards. So they'll write
impossible segues from one instrument to another. We used
to have to run from one instrument to another. Now we get
setups in L shapes, but it's still one hand here, one hand
over here, and the next part you should play with your
nose, you know--and you have to try to make all the pedals
and the switches. And they don't want to hear that you
can't do it. It's the kind of business where if, more
than a few times, you don't make it, pretty soon somebody
is there who is making it. So that's where the adrenaline
is, and that's the fun part. I like working under those
kinds of conditions--it keeps you from being bored. The
boredom is much more deadly than the occasional bouts of
high anxiety.

JOHN. What are your feelings about film and TV work
in comparison with album and studio dates?

RALPH: I always like a balance of all those situations. Sometimes you'll get a date where you might not
have that much that's musically challenging to read, but
you have a chance to create a part, contribute your own
ideas and work in a more intimate setting--maybe in a
studio with just a rhythm section, doing a basic track.
Then you have time to focus, perhaps spend a three-hour
session on two or three tunes. On the other hand, doing a
jingle is a real challenge, too, because everything has to
be done in an hour. It's just get in, do it, and get out.
A big budget picture is great in that there's time to pay
attention to details at all levels--from the underscore or
classical type of score to the source music. But, again,
in films, so much time and attention is put on the details
that sometimes it doesn't move fast enough for me. I like
to be able to balance that type of work with a television
show where you've got to do five minutes of music an hour.
It's a four-hour call and you're going to do twenty minutes of music, bang--rehearse it, record it, rehearse it,
record it--and sometimes not even rehearse it, if things
get tight due to technical problems or something. So it's
the variety that makes this work attractive to me.

JOHN: So you do all those things?

RALPH: Yes, although I'd say 75% of my work now is films and television. The other 25% is jingles and records. Whether you want to or not, you get type-cast as a certain kind of player. Fortunately, I was type-cast in the right area, so in spite of the way the record business has been for musicians, I've been able to buy a couple months a year just for myself.

JOHN: Do you find yourself getting into other areas musically, in your own time, that aren't directly related to your bread-and-butter work?

RALPH: Yes--I don't expect too many people to give me money for some of the outrageous things I want to do myself. You always hope that eventually the work that you want to do more than anything else will be supported to the extent that you can devote most of your time to it. I haven't reached that point yet, and I don't know if I ever will, because my musical tastes are pretty eclectic and there isn't a big audience for a lot of things I'm interested in. But it doesn't make them any less worthwhile for me. I feel that if you're going to serve music, you have to be prepared to put energy into things that there is no guaranteed return from--for the simple reason that it's important to do them. I can't tell you the number of Monday evening and other kinds of concerts I've practiced six months and rehearsed probably 35 or 40 times for--all to play a piece of music once, and never again. But it all pays off eventually in terms of the techniques you've developed and the increased facility in reading virtually impossible music. All of a sudden, going in and reading the score to a picture they expect to record in one day is much easier. Although the challenges are different, it helps you maintain a high standard for yourself from which everything else emanates. So I think the important thing is to discover your musical desires or tastes and then be true to them and support them by doing whatever you have to. I'd sooner play a bar mitzvah than sell shoes. I'd sooner work in a club: at least it's music. I'll do anything musical. I've never had any kind of snobbishness about it, because I've always liked all kinds of music.

JOHN: A lot of people will try to get a straight job and study music on the side in hopes of eventually dropping the straight job and becoming a professional musician. You're saying that it would be better for them to try to make a living musically, even it it's not playing

what they're most interested in. At least they're being a
musician and learning.

RALPH: A professional musician makes music. And the
more you can do that, the better off you are, because
you're receiving all that training for whatever you're
going to do later. And it's a lifetime study. Some music
is great, and some of it is not so great, but it's all
music, and somebody's going to get off on it somewhere! I
think it's important we educate people who are getting
into the field of music that whatever they do musically,
making music is the act--that's the thing, that's the joy
of it, whether it be a career in an orchestra, playing in
a club somewhere, doing studio work, or actually doing
their own solo projects. They'll find their own level
based on what energy they put into it, what kind of breaks
they get, who hears them and everything that happens. But
at any stage along the way, it's valid. Basically you go
for what you can do. I always tell people to get heard as
much as they can--just do it. It's not complicated. It's
like anything else--if you want to be anything, you put
the time and the energy into it. You don't worry about
whether you're doing it right or learning all the right
techniques--you just trust that if you're doing it, you'll
learn more and you'll be continually refining your skills
and abilities.

JOHN: That brings up another point. A lot of musicians tend to neglect the business and promotional aspect
of music--they'd rather just be creative. But nowadays,
knowing how to do your taxes and balance your books, do
PR and form a corporation if you need it, are all very
important to your survival. What are your comments on
this?

RALPH: Fortunately, because I was able to work with
Artie Kane and some of the others who fought really hard
in the pioneering days to improve conditions for musicians, I have adopted the attitude that, basically, everyone is responsible for themselves. For a musician to be
disdainful of the practical and business end is mostly
laziness.

Although I myself find those things difficult, there
is a certain challenge in, for example, looking for ways
to support oneself as an artist. And if we're talking
about being an artist--the keyboard player as a keyboard
artist--then we're opening up far more than just the
ability to play the instruments, know all of the material
and be able to read. Like I tell players who come to

town, we _assume_ you're a mother. You wouldn't be stupid enough to try and get into a business where there are a lot of heavyweight players unless you thought you were pretty good. Or if you don't have all the needed skills, you're at least working on getting them and you're out there doing it. So we _start_ with that assumption. But there are also so many extra-musical aspects to this: we're talking about a complete person and a complete career. When you're talking about complicated, big-budget motion pictures, television shows and record albums, you're talking about a lot of money that corporations are spending. This creates the requirement that things move-- It's the Hollywood machinery. The technicians and craftsmen have to be there to do their jobs. And part of that is simple responsibility--being able to show up on time, stay in good health--being able to perform the function. I don't care who you are--if the red light goes on and you don't make it, you're not going to last.

And that responsibility even extends down to the simple fact of keeping books. Everybody has to do it in the beginning. You learn enough about it to take care of it; then hopefully you soon get to a point where you can pay someone else to do it. But you still have to stay on top of it and make sure it's being done right. That's a part of the game you're playing, so you accept the responsibility.

And we're also talking about being able to relate to a lot of different people--able to do whatever is required of you to coexist with your fellow human beings with as little friction as possible. Because if you can't, someone else will.

JOHN: So someone can be a great player, but if they can't make it in one of those areas, they can still blow it all.

RALPH: Right, because we're talking about instant creative abilities--turn on the switch and let's have your best show, bang, right now. And you may be working with a hundred-piece orchestra for a movie, such as when I worked with John Williams and a hundred-and-two-piece orchestra doing _Indiana Jones_ for Stephen Spielberg. All it takes is someone who's off somewhere--technically, mentally, or just in terms of some negative energy. You're talking about a lot of sensitive, highly trained musicians together in a room. They immediately pick up if something's weird, and it gets really uncomfortable.

JOHN: Not to mention how the conductor or composer feels about it.

RALPH: Sure. So this all becomes much more important than most people are aware of. With an orchestra of that size, every second means money out of someone's pocket, and it becomes really apparent who fits in and who doesn't. Often the people who don't make it are the first to proclaim how cliquish everything is--perhaps for the simple reason that they were unable to fit in. It's absolutely necessary that the group is really compatible. I've found that, for the most part, good players are received with open arms everywhere, by everybody. Anybody who's worked as hard as those people have to get where they are in the business has to respect talent and good players. First of all, there's nothing you can do to stop them anyway--good talent always gets heard eventually. Maybe you could stop somebody or slow them down a little bit, but not for long--so all you can do is support everyone. A lot of people approach me who want me to consult with them and want to show me what they can do, or they want to come on a date with me and see what it's like. I'd love to find someone I felt was really dynamite, because I'd be able to recommend them, and that makes me look good.

JOHN: That's very interesting, because it contradicts what you tend to hear a lot. Turning to another controversial subject, what are your feelings about drug use and how it affects the musician?

RALPH: I've been around it since I was a kid--when I started playing night clubs there were musicians who drank, and I was kind of a joke because I didn't. I was a cigarette smoker and it's only been recently that I've let go of even that--nicotine's been a big hook for me and I consider it a powerful drug. There are times when people utilize drugs, I think, for creative things, and it's acceptable. I don't presume to tell anybody what to do. But having worked with a lot of people who have used heavy drugs, I've observed that it's an eventual burnout situation. It starts out as a little crutch to get them over certain things, you know, and it's okay--it can be controlled. In moderation it's like anything else--coffee, tea, a drink, or a cigarette--it'll work. But I think continued use has a debilitating effect. I haven't seen any exceptions. There's just no way to sustain intense concentration and alertness and be on top of everything if your mind is in any way getting a distorted image of reality.

JOHN: So in your profession--especially when you're doing films and TV and jingles--you don't very often see people coming in loaded or stoned.

RALPH: Not for long, no. Not even record date players. Every once in a while there'll be a series of hot players who'll come through who might be into some sophisticated drugs. But I haven't seen any that have survived! It's like, all right, "next!" They end up dying really young.

JOHN: So you don't necessarily have to be high to be creative--it's possible to do it just by being very aware, on your own.

RALPH: Well, I think you can get high without drugs. See, I think you do have to be high to be creative--but I think the state of mind that "high" describes might not actually be "high"--it might be really introspective. Whatever it is, it's going to be really intense, and yes, you have to be there. But you have to be able to get there naturally, or eventually you'll become drug dependent, and things will go downhill from there. It's that simple. If sometime an experience with a drug can maybe help someone--hey, under controlled conditions, why not? But I haven't seen it work for anybody. I know it doesn't work for me. I play much better when I don't smoke anything and when I'm not drinking coffee. If I have a drink, I can feel the coordination in my hands lessen. Why should I work hard to build up a tolerance to it when I can very clearly see, hey, this isn't good!

JOHN: Any final overall word of advice?

RALPH: Just don't be discouraged. If you really love music--if you're really into it--there's got to be a place for you somewhere. And if you're not, then there still might be--but it won't be as intimate a place. I think everyone has to find what it is for themselves. Music can be enjoyed and perceived on so many levels that it doesn't matter. You need listeners, you need players, people who play for a hobby, people who are really into it. But anyone who can experience joy and all the other emotions through music is definitely enriched. And if that's what you want to do, do it. Don't be discouraged.

Henry Mancini
composer/arranger/conductor

HENRY MANCINI

JOHN: Would you elaborate a little on your early
musical background--how you got started, what you studied,
where you played?

HENRY: I started flute at the age of eight--piccolo,
actually--and then at about thirteen I began playing piano
and studying classical music. I continued those studies
until I went to Juilliard, which I attended for about a
year before being drafted into the service. I was in the
service for about three years and during that time I
played a lot of piano. I was actually an invaluable
asset, because not only did I play piano, but of course
flute and piccolo as well, and I could also arrange. So I
played for the officer's club dances and those types of
things. Then, when I got out of the service in 1946, I
went with the Tex Beneke Orchestra as arranger-pianist.

JOHN: When did you move out to California, and why?

HENRY: I came out here in 1947 to be married. My
wife, whose professional name was Ginny O'Connor, was
singing lead with the Mellowlarks, who were with Tex
Beneke. It worked out pretty well, because it put me
where I wanted to be for work. Up to that point, the only
thing I had done professionally was play piano and write
arrangements for Tex Beneke. When I got here, I sustained
myself mainly by playing gigs. Then I started writing
arrangements--not composing, but just doing charts--for
Jerry Gray, who had the Club 15 radio show. I first
started composing for Harry Zimmerman. He was musical
director for The Mutual Network on radio, and since he had
a lot of shows, he used to let me do some family theater.
He was very good to me. David Rose was also very nice. I
composed for some of his radio shows and at the same time
kept gigging to support myself.

JOHN: Where did you learn arranging and composing?
On your own, or did you study privately?

HENRY: I started on my own. You must realize,
though, we're talking 1937-38 and there really were no
teachers. There was literally no place to study commercial
arranging--there was just Frank Skinner's book. Of

course, I studied the legitimate books available at the time--Forsythe's book, etc.--but that was about it. Then, up until I went to Juilliard, I studied arranging with Max Adkins in Pittsburgh. He was an excellent musician and arranger who had the pit band at the Stanley Theater. At Juilliard I studied theory, ear training, harmony, piano--mostly traditional things. I didn't really get heavily into composition until after the war when I moved out to L.A. Out here, at different times, I studied with Mario Tedesco, Ernst Krenek, and Dr. Alfred Sendrey, who had been one of Bartok's classmates, I believe. I also did a lot on my own by studying scores, listening to records, and things like that. Whatever it took to learn, I did it.

JOHN: How did you promote yourself as an arranger and composer?

HENRY: Through a lot of personal contacts--I knew Jerry Gray very well; I met Harry Zimmerman after he had heard some of the arrangements I had done; David Rose heard some things he liked, and so on.

JOHN: So, in other words, the best PR was the product.

HENRY: Definitely. But I didn't crack the studio scene on piano. That was too much for me! I just wasn't cut out to be a piano player. I didn't start recording for RCA until Peter Gunn happened in the 1958-59 season--that's what really got me going. Before that I had been at Universal for six years, from 1952 to 1958, as a staff writer.

JOHN: How did you get that staff writer job?

HENRY: I was arranging and Ginny decided she had had it with the road and the cold, so she came back to California. Then her group, the Mellowlarks, came back. Around town there were a whole bunch of self-contained singing groups, such as the Skylarks and others, that were acts in themselves. Each group had its own arranger, and I was the Mellowlarks' arranger--although I wasn't getting paid too much because they weren't working very often. Now, all the bands that played the Palladium--all the great bands--would go over to Universal to film their hits of the day. They would pull out their library and with no rehearsal make a prerecord and then go and shoot their number. So the Mellowlarks went in to do this. I went with them as their arranger, and we did the short with

Jimmy Dorsey's Orchestra. The head of the department there, Joe Gershenson, and his assistant, Milt Rosen, liked the chart I did with the vocal group. They were looking for what I like to call a "token young person" for the music department. You see, at that time all the hot arrangers were over at MGM, and Universal didn't do that many musical pictures--they did a lot of different kinds of things. So I just happened to be in the right place at the right time. I came in to do an Abbott and Costello and some other arrangements. I went in for two weeks and before you knew it I had been there for six years. It was a nine-to-five job, arranging and composing. So that's how I did it.

JOHN: What got you into playing piano on your own records when you had such great players on all your albums from Peter Gunn on?

HENRY: That's an interesting story. When I went to Universal, my piano playing days were basically over. Johnny Williams was the first pianist--on the Peter Gunn album. When he decided to quit playing and do more writing, I got Jimmy Rowles in there. After him there was a whole succession of players who did my records over the years. I had never played piano on record, but in 1969 I came upon that love theme from Romeo and Juliet. Now this was such a nice melody, you know--it was very simple--and I said hell, I can play this! And the album, which was called A Warm Shade of Ivory, went gold. So I created this pianistic style in which, of course, melody was the king. But I also got a chance to open it up on transitional things and improvise on specific changes, and it developed into a very listenable recording style. I basically still use it today in my live concerts. Now I don't apologize for only playing "so good." I'm playing at the top of my form and there's a communication there with people--and it's a very personal kind of thing.

JOHN: So it all boils down to communication!

HENRY: That's exactly right. So since that album I've done a lot of things on piano. But I have to practice before I go in to record, because I get stiff from writing--I guess it's the way one's fingers hold the pencil or something. So I always practice scales, etc., because you can't fool that red light. It picks up everything!

JOHN: Do you have a rehearsal regimen?

HENRY: I use the Pischna Technical Studies, Hanon in all keys, not just C--technical things like that. Also, I practice pieces, because actual performances are different than technical studies. So I do both before I record or play live.

JOHN: What's the secret to the successful Mancini sound? If you had to analyze what you do, what would you say is probably the key to your success as an arranger-composer?

HENRY: I use my inner ear. That's something you develop from listening to records a lot and noting the things that really interest you--instrumental combinations and so on. I've always been able to hear these things in my inner ear and use them when I need them. The real key, though, is editing. You have to be able to edit your material so that in the end it all comes together. Some writers, especially good keyboardists, tend to get too "notey." The key is to edit the music so it communicates and does the job. That's why I love to listen to jazz keyboardists--especially solo piano. Imagine all that stuff being created on the spot! I guess jazz could be called instant editing in one's mind. I think the thing that makes guys swing at whatever they're out to do is inherently knowing how to do a line and knowing where they're going without getting all tied up and stepping on themselves.

JOHN: When you compose or arrange, do you rely heavily on the piano and try everything out as you write it, or do you just use the piano for your basic pitch and write from your inner ear?

HENRY: Well, it can be done both ways. It depends on what I'm doing. Sometimes, depending on the nature of what I'm doing, I don't even use a piano--I just score it all out.

JOHN: Do you have perfect pitch or perfect relative pitch?

HENRY: I don't have perfect pitch, like A-440, but ever since I can remember I've had good key sense. So it's a perfect relative pitch kind of thing. When I'm scoring on the piano, I basically don't even hear it as a piano--I always hear what the group I'm writing for sounds like.

JOHN: When you compose, how do you work? Do you stick to a rigid schedule? Do you work for long stretches at a time?

HENRY: If I'm doing something that has a deadline, say a film, I like to get right at it in the morning. I get more done between 8:30 and 11:00 than during the rest of the day because I find that in the morning 1 can really zero in on things better than at other times of the day.

I usually don't work for really long stretches, and I rarely work way into the night--but again, it depends on the project. I don't follow any strict rules. If I'm forced to put in more hours because of the nature of what I'm doing, I can break from it, then come back and do more. I hate to leave a sequence in the middle, though, no matter how long it is. Once I sit down, I'll always at least figure it out as to form, melody, harmony so I know where I'm going and how it's going to end. That's just something about me--if I can at least think or sketch it out, I can walk away happy.

But, on the other hand, if I can't come up with something, I will walk away. Either that or I'll go to something I can do. I write at my home studio, and when I need to get away, I like to come to my office for one or two hours, relax, and maybe take care of some business. This is where I have my library, secretary and everything else.

JOHN: What are your feelings about synthesizers--do you use them? How do you think of them in relation to the usual orchestral colors?

HENRY: I use them when I feel it's necessary--usually as an adjunct to the orchestra. I don't think of a synthesizer that sounds like a string section, for example, as replacing a real string section. Most of the time I use synthesizers and such for their own characteristics and colors--for sounds not already available in the orchestra.

JOHN: How does someone get started in today's scene?

HENRY: It can be done in different ways. But no matter what you do, you've got to do it. Get with somebody, whether it's a rock group going on the road that you can play keyboards with, or whatever--do it. Because I've found that nine times out of ten, the people you're working with will bring whoever's playing with them into the studio. And this is how countless people get known. So you have to pay some dues out there. You have to go out on the road. You have to be with these people because these people are a first link to what's going to happen to you from here on out. Also, in the meantime, you're getting paid--which isn't a bad reason for working--and you're meeting other people. Look how many rock people actually get into film scoring nowadays as a result of their success. It does, however, take a certain amount of aggressive action on your part. You can't be passive unless you have some very good friends. For example, when I went to Universal, I made myself known to the people I was working for and with. I would go to Guild meetings, etc., get to know them and let them know me on another level.

JOHN: You mean other than on just a business level?

HENRY: Yeah! It's easier in a semi-social setting to say, "Hey, could you take a listen to this?" For instance, look at all these cassettes lying around here-- they've all been sent so I can listen to them. Now, although it's one way to do it, I have no attachment to any of these because I don't know the people who sent them. To recommend someone just on what you hear can be risky. I like to know the person, his demeanor--and I don't mean how he dresses or anything like that. Because sometimes you can recommend someone to a very good friend and then afterwards you get "Where the hell did you get that guy?" You see, people have to be able to be comfortable with someone's personality traits. You're not just recommending a pencil--you're recommending a person, and sometimes it happens that someone just does not have the personality to know how to fit in. It's a big point.

JOHN: So, in other words, one has to have his "life chops" as well as his artistic chops together!

HENRY: Yes, that's a great point. Take a film: The keyboard player is working for me, I'm working for the director, the director is working for the producer, and so on. The lower you are on the totem pole, the less you can afford to have personality problems. I mean, sometimes I don't give artistic credibility that many points. If you want to be credible artistically, book yourself at Carnegie Hall where that's what it's all about. If you're working for a commercial purpose, you have to realize that and "play the gig"! Most of the guys in L.A. know this, and if they don't, they soon find out.

JOHN: What are your thoughts on integrity and how it applies to your profession? How do you produce what the people you work for want and at the same time satisfy your own creative goals?

HENRY: Integrity is being faithful to the job that you're doing. A plumber can have integrity. I mean, who's to say whether or not he put a new float in your toilet? He might have put a used one in and charged you for a new one. But some people would never cheat on a thing like that. That's the integrity of the job.

JOHN: That's also ethics.

HENRY: Yes, there is a connection between integrity and ethics. I don't know if you could have one without the other. For instance, if I take a television theme, I don't talk to the producer of that television show any differently than I talk to the producer of a major movie that I do. If I accept a commercial gig, I operate at the same level of integrity. It's all in that attitude and it's all in your own Christian way of dealing with other people. Now I'm not a church-going person, but there are certain Christian values that make us civilized and allow us to live together, as long as we're here. So it's how you feel inside. It's your attitude toward your players, your fellow writers, and so on. It's really a religion! And in that area, I'm more honest and more religious than many people who go to church and then go home and beat their wives.

Regarding integrity to yourself, you have to know the level that you go in at. I'm basically a commercially-oriented person--and when I say commercial, I mean the best of it and the worst of it. In our business you can have the best cast, the best director, the best writers, and the first week at the box office the studio writes it off and the computer says stop. So you have to learn how to roll with the punches. There have been a lot of things I've done for various pictures that I thought were very nice, but they didn't happen--they didn't have it. Everybody's got failures, no matter who they are--even those at the very top! I like to have an attitude based on a mixture of humor and acceptance of fate, knowing that my piece of music can be in the hands of one man in the dubbing room who says "Turn it off." One flick of a switch and you don't exist! When that happens, I accept it. I don't in that respect control my own destiny. Of course, I try to write the best that I can and in that way exercise some control. But in the commercial field, there's always that chance that they're going to flick the switch on you.

JOHN: What are your feelings about drugs and alcohol?

HENRY: I cannot function in any professional capacity under any kind of stimulant or drug whatsoever. I can't do it--even on stage, where you'd think you could have some fun. But in my situation--say at these pops concerts where I have over a hundred musicians in the orchestra and only one rehearsal--well, they're really depending on you to cue and guide them when you're supposed to. And of course, on the other side, you have the audience. Believe me, they'll let you know if they pick up that maybe you're not all there. So I don't think there is anything to be gained by it. Now, I can't speak for the rock groups and such, but I would think the situation would be the same. You're still up there in front of everyone, and erratic behavior is less acceptable nowadays, especially because of the high ticket prices. If someone cuts a show short or does this or that, the audience will turn on you as quick as you can shake a stick. If you're not functioning at the level they think you should for the money they paid, they'll let you know.

JOHN: In your profession, how important are awards such as Grammys and Oscars? Are they what you strive for each year, or are they just byproducts of good products?

HENRY: Well, they are just byproducts. The best thing about awards is the moment when you go up to get them. That's the emotional high; that's where the adrenalin is--especially the Oscars. You have your emotional high, about a two-day trip, getting the wires and congratulations and so on. But once the adrenalin level is down again, it's "next case." It's what's coming up, what's new. You put the awards on your shelf and that's that. Now the Grammys can't really do that much for you with regard to work, but an Oscar is a good passport to other work--only because there are just so many people within ten miles of where we're sitting right now discussing who is going to do the music for this picture or that picture, and the high visibility of the recent Oscar winner is a big plus. Especially if it's a new artist and especially, I think, if it's in the area of dramatic scoring. An Oscar is usually a good passport to a lot of other work for songwriters.

JOHN: Is there any final advice you can give that might enhance the up-and-coming keyboardist's chances for success?

HENRY: Well, in my mind, there are two kinds of smarts--street smarts and school smarts. And I think that if you examine people who provide services like I do-- writing, etc., as opposed to performing--you find that you need them both. Too much of one or the other is no good. For example, some people have school smarts to spare, yet they do not know how to deal with people. So you need a good balance of both these smarts, both mentally and physically, and you need to remember that you're not alone and you have to deal with people. You really have to have both, I believe, because you can end up a hopeless babe in the woods without the school smarts, and you can be a fish out of water without the street smarts--no matter how smart you are.

Edgar Winter
composer/vocalist/saxaphonist/keyboardist

EDGAR WINTER

<u>JOHN</u>: When and how did you first get into music?

<u>EDGAR</u>: My earliest memories of music were of my mother sitting at the piano--I was just tall enough to look up in between her hands over the keyboard and start to associate the sound with what she was actually doing. My family was, and is, musical--I sang in the choir when I was about seven and my father played guitar, banjo and alto sax. The first thing my father ever showed me was how to play chords on the ukulele. We had two of them, so my brother, Johnny, and I played Everly Brothers type songs. When I was about 11, we won a talent contest for the local TV station. One of the prizes was a chance to make a record, which we did. From that point on I would say we were more or less hooked musically. About that time we started playing in a few clubs, which was unusual at that age.

<u>JOHN</u>: This was in Texas?

<u>EDGAR</u>: Right. The club owner and his wife were good friends of my family, and they looked after us when we played. And we did basically the same type of thing after the basketball games, sock hops, graduation proms. Very early on I listened a lot to blues records my brother had, and that covered a lot of area--he liked the authentic country blues, like Muddy Waters, Lightnin' Hopkins, and John Lee Hooker, but he also had B. B. King, Ray Charles, Bobby Bland and all the R&B artists, and that was the direction I took. I decided not to play guitar quite early, because Johnny had already fallen in love with it and I thought it would be better if I branched off into something else if we were going to play in bands together. We did play guitar together for a while, though. I also played drums, and for about three months filled in on bass when I had to. I was sort of the all-purpose musical arranger in all those early bands we had.

<u>JOHN</u>: Did you develop all those abilities just by listening and teaching yourself, or did you have formal training?

EDGAR: The only formal training I had, if you could call it formal, was piano lessons for about three years. I wanted to learn how to read music so I could write. I was playing in a big band and wanted to do some Ray Charles arrangements and get the voicings right. We had two trumpets, an alto and tenor, a bass trombone and a baritone sax. Although three of the guys in the band were theory majors in college and a few years older than me, I ended up doing a lot of the arrangements because I had the knack or ability to listen to those records and take all the voicings off them, even when they were big band arrangements. I was able to get a really good big-band spread sound, even with five horns. So my piano teacher showed me how to read, and it was very useful, along with what I learned from playing in that kind of band with theory majors. But although I played piano for two or three years, I never really thought of myself as a piano player. I heard Cannonball Aderly and fell in love with the saxophone. That's when I started to get intensely serious and love music a lot more. Before it was just a fun thing to do. So when I started playing saxophone, I formed my own group because it didn't really fit with what my brother was doing.

JOHN: How old were you when you got into the sax?

EDGAR: I was 15 by then. I'd been playing for quite a long time.

JOHN: In listening to you play sax, it sounds as though you've spent more time developing your technical chops on it than the piano. You mentioned that you had piano lessons. What kind of training did you have on the sax?

EDGAR: I never had any lessons at all--I picked it up myself. After I decided I wanted to play the saxophone, I practiced about 14 hours a day for three days and then played my first job. After just three days I didn't sound that great, but I was able to get through it. If you already have natural talent and ability, lack of formal study doesn't have to stop you. Certainly it's helpful to get all the knowledge you can from whatever sources, but I think that listening is a real key. If you have the talent to begin with and you keep listening to good music and trying to emulate it, you'll be in good shape. I came to understand a lot about chord theory in that way before I ever studied it. In fact, I was already using advanced chord voicings like flat 9's, raised 5's, 13's and all those things in my arrangements for the band, even though I didn't know their names. I would just listen to them on records, say "Oh, that's cool," and pick out the notes. So I used them, and found out about theory later.

JOHN: How did you first start getting out there and communicating to more people--was it your first album, or did you do other things prior to that that were never released?

EDGAR: Entrance was my first statement, first project.

JOHN: How old were you when you did it, and how were you able to do it?

EDGAR: I was 21. I had played on my brother's last two Columbia albums as well as toured the U.S. and Europe with him, playing keyboards, synthesizers and some drums. So when I met Johnny's manager in the process of doing those recordings, he suggested I come to New York so he could introduce me to some of the record executives and see about getting me my own record deal. It was something I hadn't even thought about--I felt I should continue to develop and learn to play better. I was really interested in jazz, and probably would have projected myself as being a starving jazz musician. I had no ideas of stardom. So it was quite a surprise to me when all of that happened. But when I realized that the opportunity was actually there, it changed my thinking a lot. One particular thing I wanted to do then was present some kind of music other than the formula you kept hearing--something that would try to go further and integrate more forms of music. I wanted to be able to blend jazz and classical forms into contemporary types of sounds.

JOHN: This was when you were getting ready to do your first album?

EDGAR: Yes, this was the concept I wanted to follow for the first project. I like that album because it was completely innocent--it wasn't calculated at all. I told the record company executives what I wanted to do and they agreed that I could have the freedom to do it--under the condition that if it wasn't monetarily successful, I would focus my efforts as well on more commercial music. That sounded fair to me, so I said okay. I would get a chance to put something out in the universe; I wouldn't be able to say I never got a chance to do what I wanted to. So that was what happened. I actually got the record deal by a live audition. I went to CBS, supposedly just to meet the president, Clive Davis, and three or four others. We went into a conference room with a long table and an up-right piano, and he said, "Let's hear what you can do."

JOHN: On the spot.

EDGAR: On the spot. I was totally unprepared for it.

JOHN: Do you remember what you played?

EDGAR: Yes. I'd already written parts of Entrance, so I played the "Entrance and Reentrance" theme. I also played "Tobacco Road," as something that would be impressive and show them I had a somewhat unique vocal style. It was also a good choice of a song because at that time a real blues revival was happening. So I got the record deal.

JOHN: Your first album didn't make money like they wanted. Did they actually get behind it, or did they think it was a bit heavy and just put it out because they had to?

EDGAR: I really don't know, but they didn't display a negative attitude toward it. You can usually tell when they're saying they're behind it but they don't really mean it. So I was really happy to have done it. After that I went more R&B with White Trash, which achieved a certain degree of success and got me my first gold album. After White Trash I put together the Edgar Winter Group. I wanted to have a hard winning, Number-1-in-the-nation American rock and roll band. We did extensive auditions-- we wanted to find people who had stage presence and could contribute to the writing.

JOHN: Your first album was jazz classical and R&B, but since then you've become progressively more and more commercial, as a seemingly calculated move. Were you thinking that because the first album wasn't successful you'd try hitting the nail from the other side with the idea that you might get back into that type of music later? Or did you just consider that to have been your first statement and decide to get into other areas?

EDGAR: There were two things. Regardless of the success of the first album, I wouldn't have wanted to do another one like it right afterwards. I wanted to form a group and capture that group feeling that is totally different than when you write and organize everything yourself and then have other people play it. I wanted to have that artistic interplay and energy that comes with the band. Second, I wanted to do something I liked. It was natural for me to do R&B, having grown up with it. The R&B was still not that commercial in intent, but I thought it would probably have a better chance than jazz and classical, which was a totally unheard-of concept. There was a lot of R&B being played, but mostly by black people, not white--so that was another innovation in its own way. There were also other horn bands at that time-- Blood, Sweat and Tears, and Chicago. Of the three, we had the only real rock and roll band. Our idea was to bring the excitement of R&B to people on a national level so you would always hear it in clubs as well as in gospel situa- tions. So my motivation was twofold--after having made a statement with _Entrance_, I did want to do something that would be more commercial, but I also wasn't ready to do something I didn't like.

I think it's always good to do what you really love. For example, "Frankenstein" was one song that was not calculated or designed to be a hit, yet ended up being one. So I think it's important to follow your instincts and do what you really feel is right. A certain amount of direction and focus is good--you shouldn't overlook those things altogether--but just make sure that along the way you don't lose your integrity, that you don't just do things because you think that's what's contemporary and what's going on. Don't leave _yourself_ out of it, in other words. You're trying to communicate with people, so of course you should have an understanding of who your audi- ence is going to be and what they are going to want to hear. But just make sure that you are saying something. Don't leave yourself out of it--don't try to make yourself into someone else.

JOHN: So your new direction wasn't for the negative reason of something not having worked--you had affinity for the new things you wrote and did it as a new game.

EDGAR: Yes, and when I subsequently put together the Edgar Winter Group, I was becoming more and more inter- ested in music as a form of communication, whereas before I had been mainly interested in music from an artistic point of view. That was my compulsion to be original, to try to come up with new ideas--and I was doing it with my own satisfaction in mind foremost and not really thinking of it in terms of the enjoyment of the audience. I was aware that the other musicians would certainly enjoy it, but that was as far as it went. But as I became more interested in music as a communication and fascinated with

how it worked, I began to see that other people were looking at it that way and playing with that in mind, and I
wanted to also.

JOHN: So prior to that you were more into art for
art's sake. But putting your attention on communicating
and the audience became a very successful action for you.

EDGAR: Do you want to be successful or do you want
to be an innovator? I'm not saying that one is any better
than the other--they are different approaches. I don't
think advances in music would be made if there weren't
people who were willing to make the sacrifice of research-
ing, knowing that it may not bear immediate fruit. It's
fun to do both things. After discovering the communication aspect of it, I started to enjoy it more and more and
went in that direction.

JOHN: This brings us to something very interesting--
the difference between mere playing and singing and really
communicating. It's always been this mysterious quality,
and most people, for lack of a better way to describe it,
just say this performer has it and that one doesn't.
Those who have "it" become known as very theatrical, dynamic performers. In your case, did it come as a result of
actual research and effort, or did you always have that
stage talent?

EDGAR: When I first started to play with Johnny, I
didn't move around at all. That was partly because I was
behind the B3 and had my feet and hands tied up and also
had a sax. But mostly it was because, coming from a jazz
background, it never even occurred to me then that people
would enjoy it more if you moved around, or that it might
be more fun for you to move around. But I watched the
kind of shows a lot of the groups we were playing with
were putting on and realized almost immediately that their
visual impact had a lot greater effect on the audience
than the music they played. It was a shock that a big
part of the audience's perception of those groups was
visual rather than musical. I always considered that the
groups were there to make music. Well, that's one of the
things they are there to do, but what the audience is
really going to like is a combination of good music and a
good visual show that helps them understand. The show
shouldn't, however, be just for the sake of the theatrics
involved.

So what I did was start developing a style of movement on stage that felt natural to me. I didn't decide I

should go take choreography lessons or something like
that; that didn't occur to me. I just said, well hey, I'm
going to loosen up a little bit here. So I started doing
that and observing the result. I did it more and more,
and finally developed the style I have, which is not
really very complex. I just started to put more feeling
and real energy into what I was doing. I found that the
more I put in, the more I got back from the audience, so I
continued to put in more and more. That was another great
experience for me--and I think it's generally true--that
the more you can let go, the more of the music and yourself will go out there. It's sort of a gamble each time,
and you should try to extend yourself to the furthest
possible limit. The more you're willing to take a chance
and give, the more you're likely to get back.

JOHN: So you're saying a "go for it" attitude is
more successful than a conservative one--as long as you
keep the quality of your music within professional standards.

EDGAR: Yes. You see, one way of looking at playing
and performing is that you're just there to play technically as well as you possibly can without really considering that an audience is there looking at you as well as
listening to you. You'll definitely play well and get
better the longer you do that, and I would say that's
actually a good starting point. Get that together so you
can get over the stage fright and play without making a
bunch of mistakes. After you reach that point, it will
happen to you naturally--you'll start looking for other
things to improve. "I've got my rhythm and my pitch and
my technique down okay--what else can I do?" So you try
to take it a step further and put more feeling or more
expression into it, or change it a little bit and do
something individual with it instead of just playing it
the same way you learned it. Try to play it better and
with more feeling each time. And ask yourself what you
can do to make the people actually feel it more. And if
the answer is an attitude, or a movement of some sort,
then do that.

JOHN: So observing the audience's reactions is a
very important thing for an artist to do, because you can
see if what you do works.

EDGAR: Right. I've seen it in countless group situations where, for example, somebody has a chance to do a
solo. We start talking about what a good solo is and how

it works--the fact that it should make a definite statement and have a beginning and a climax and an end, and a
whole middle area for improvisation. How long can it be?
What can you do to help it? So every time you play, you
should be aware that the audience is there, and watch
their reactions to what you do. And you'll find that the
more you can get them to react, the more fun it will start
to be for you. But never forget about playing well.

JOHN: Sometimes all you get after a solo--even if it
is a great solo--is "social" applause, where the audience
claps because they know they're supposed to when you're
done--it's a kind of protocol. And then you get the kind
of applause that happens right during your solo when you
do something that blows them away and they really freak
out. Afterwards you walk out and you think, "God, all I
did was bend that synthesizer note over and over again and
everybody freaked out, but before that I played 4,000
notes on the whole-tone diminished scale and nobody got
anything." Do you have any reaction to that?

EDGAR: I just think you should be able to cover all
those areas. For me it's not fun to watch somebody who's
a good showman and has a good act, but only does the thing
of involving the audience. I feel that as a musician you
have a certain responsibility to try to play music that's
on the highest technical level you can without diminishing
the audience's enjoyment of it--to play the best you possibly can and to feel, because really, if you don't feel,
if you're not really getting off on what you're doing,
you're going to find that they aren't, either. In other
words, if you leave yourself out of it, if you just look
at the audience and think, "Okay, when I bend the synthesizer note over and over everybody goes crazy," and start
doing it repetitively or mechanically, you'll find you
won't be enjoying it very much and neither will the audience. And you'll start to wonder why it worked so well
the first time you did it. Well, it's because your attitude in doing it is now different. At first you were
doing it with some kind of feeling, and you were experimenting. You were doing something that was really happening.

JOHN: Let's get into a subject that is controversial
for many musicians. Many start off thinking that getting
high is the way to experience and play music. What are
your experiences in this area and what advice might you
give a musician who's involved in drugs or having problems
with them?

EDGAR: It's definitely a hard thing to avoid--a lot of the people you'll be playing with are going to be involved with drugs. I don't want to preach to people and say what they should or shouldn't do--I would just like to say how it was for me. I quit four years ago. I've seen a lot of my friends and people I respected get into drugs and really lose themselves, and I've seen a lot of them die. I don't regret my own experience--I think it definitely, in some ways, developed a lot of my attitudes and my character. But I've come to the conclusion that drugs are a very negative influence and should be avoided if at all possible. It's a personal decision, and really all I can say about it is that as long as you really love your music, are really serious about it, and keep it the number one thing, you're not likely to get caught up in drugs. It won't become the most important aspect of your life as long as the music is. Just keep that in mind.

JOHN: Did something happen to cause you to change your mind?

EDGAR: Yes, a lot of things happened. My wife, Monique, and I jointly made the decision to stop. Our relationship is a very unique and special one and we share everything with one another. We're one of those rare couples who don't just live "with each other"--we really live together. The drug question really segues into many other areas.

You see, Monique and I both love philosophy and had studied a great many things such as Zen, objectivism, transcendental meditation, the Bible and so on, to name a few. About two years after we were married, Monique was introduced to Scientology through the Celebrity Centre in New York. I was very resistive to Scientology at first, thinking it was just another of those positive thinking self-help programs. It was then Monique decided to do something called the Purification Rundown at the organization in Clearwater, Florida. The results were amazing! She was like a new person. She was absolutely resolved to do no more drugs and in support of this I made up my mind to go drug free with her. It seemed like the perfect time.

It was also then that I finally started to read all the L. Ron Hubbard books on our bookshelf and I must explain what happened here, since it totally changed my life. I want to acknowledge my wife, Monique, as my greatest strength and source of inspiration. Without her love and understanding I might not be here at all.

Monique loved me as a person, for myself alone, having nothing to do with my music. This helped me to regain a sense of myself apart from my music and to realize I was going through something faced by many artists.

Say you start out playing music, as I did, just for the fun of it. You think--this is great! I love it! What could be more fun? Then you achieve a certain degree of success and you say "Wow! I'm actually doing what I love most and even getting paid for it. What could be better?" And then comes the pressure and responsibility of success. And, suddenly, maintaining that level of success becomes terribly important. This is where an artist may become confused, disoriented or disillusioned. It's as though you lose your sense of personal identity as it becomes submerged in that of your work. The work gets bigger than life--bigger than _you_ are. _It's_ what people see, not _you_. It's what you're constantly judged by--the measure of your self worth--and you may tend to forget that it's _you_ who created the _art_, and not the other way around.

JOHN: Are you saying that the _creator_ of something is always more important than the things he creates?

EDGAR: Yes. Scientology showed me this in terms of cause and effect. When you cause something, you feel good because you're in control. When you become the effect of something, you feel less certain. Even though you may have caused the effect yourself, you may come to view it as something outside your control.

Once I was struggling through a writer's slump and Monique said something like, "Why don't you try just writing what comes naturally without being concerned about what anyone may think of it? Just do the music you want to do instead of worrying about it." And I said, "But this could be the turning point of my career, or this could affect our whole future." Then I realized I was already projecting myself as the effect of something I hadn't even created yet, instead of simply being the cause and going about creating it.

There's another Scientology concept that expresses this same idea. It's easy to get this backwards. It concerns the conditions of "be," "have" and "do." People tend to think it's what you have and what you do that make you who you are. It's really the other way around. It's who you _are_ that allows you to determine what you do and what you have. In other words, it is your spiritual beingness--you--which is senior and controls the action of doingness toward the aim of havingness.

And Scientology really reinforced my personal convictions and feelings about music, as well as enhanced my ability to create and enjoy it. From the time I first played with jazz musicians and discovered the feeling of improvising a solo on the spot, I always thought of music as a spiritual experience. To me, it was on a very high, spiritual level of creativity. You're spiritually linked to the people you're playing with, and there's this dynamic interplay and creation and exchange of energy. It's a unique and incredible feeling.

I'd like to pass along another thing I learned through Scientology: don't impose any limitations on yourself in anything--whether in music or in life. Most of the difficulty we have doing things is a result either of some past experience we've had, or our lack of belief and confidence that we can do it, whatever it is. In reality, people have a limitless potential to do virtually anything, but we develop blocks about certain things. It's just like when you go to school and they give you an IQ test and say, "You're bad in math and you're better in this subject." So you start to look at yourself from that perspective and you say, "Well, I'll try to accentuate my strong points and I'm not going to worry about this other stuff over here because I can't do it."

JOHN: And forever afterwards you can't add.

EDGAR: Right. If, when you were a little kid trying to learn how to walk, somebody said "Oh, you can't do that, you better not try," and you gave up, where would you be? You have to fall down hundreds of times to be able to do it. Failing at something or apparently lacking the ability to do it is no reason to assume you can't do it. And it may look like it's hopeless--like it's impossible. "Oh, I did that a hundred times and I know without any doubt that I can't do it, I don't have the talent." Well, you're wrong--you can do it.

JOHN: So you can change those conditions if you don't agree with those limitations--whether imposed by yourself or someone else. That was reinforced by reading L. Ron Hubbard's writings?

EDGAR: Absolutely. Phrased simply, it would just be, "Go for it. Don't be afraid to try things!"

Michael Boddicker
composer/studio synthesist

MICHAEL BODDICKER

JOHN: Would you elaborate on your musical background, especially the things you feel were important to your present career?

MICHAEL: I was born into a musical family. My mother started playing records by my bed when I was two weeks old and didn't stop. Later she had me playing all sorts of different instruments, which essentially gave me an orchestrator's background. I played the trumpet and the guitar seriously while I was growing up, but for shorter periods I also played violin, trombone, woodwinds and the like. That really helped, because that's partly what I'm doing now--orchestration.

JOHN: How did you study those instruments?

MICHAEL: I studied mostly on my own, at home, by just picking up an instrument and learning it. None of them are that difficult as long as you know the basic mechanics of music--it's just different muscle control. I also studied things like orchestration and composition from age nine on. And I wrote songs constantly. I remember going through a period in which I wrote 200 songs in a year.

JOHN: Pop songs?

MICHAEL: Yes. You see, the high school and the college I went to were pretty advanced in the music area. In high school I could take a music harmony class, a jazz band class, a choral class, and a creative writing class all in the same day and get credit for it. So during that period I was writing all the time and pretty much turning out at least one song a day, every day. I'd get up in the morning, take my dog out for a walk, get an idea, write it down and expand on it a little. Then I'd come home and write the song, lyrics and all, copy it out, make out the copyright form and send it in. It was pretty expensive! I continued doing that and studying until I was 17 and old enough to get out of the house, get on the road and start making a living.

JOHN: When you went on the road, did you tour with any name acts?

MICHAEL: No, I went out with a sleaze night club act I played a trumpet with my right hand, kick bass with my left foot, and organ and piano with my left hand. It was terrible. The reason I got the gig was the guy I was replacing was going on to play with the Ides of March--which is now the band Survivor.

JOHN: You were already getting into the multikeyboard concept.

MICHAEL: Yes, and I hated it even then. I still don't like playing multiple keyboards. I like concentrating on playing one instrument at a time--I think you can play so much better. When you're being both a bass player and a soloist, you almost always have to work out both parts in advance, rather than being free to improvise--unless you're Chick Corea, Herbie Hancock or Keith Jarrett!

JOHN: Something in the music is compromised?

MICHAEL: Yes, so I stay away from that.

JOHN: What happened after that gig?

MICHAEL: I had a six-piece band called Westwood that played a lot in clubs and shared the bill with people like Kenny Rogers, Mongo Santa Maria, the Four Tops. We made three albums, but the band didn't go any further.

JOHN: What were you playing in that band?

MICHAEL: A B-3 Hammond, an Arp 2600, Arp soloist, and RMI electric piano. This was about 1973, which was the year I moved out to L.A.

JOHN: What made you move out here? Was it an actual shrewd decision to go where the business was?

MICHAEL: Yes. This is where the business is. I had come out a year before, prior to Westwood, and auditioned for White Trash, which Edgar Winter had just left. I actually rehearsed with the band for two weeks, but they let me go because I was 19 and too young to hang out. Then, after Westwood, I moved out to L.A. and met Bill Como, who started recommending me for gigs.

JOHN: How did you meet him?

MICHAEL: By showing up for auditions for touring bands like Laurie Lieberman's tour, Harriet Schock's tour, etc. Somehow I met Bill and he hooked me up with an audition for a hot prime-time TV gig. They were in a real time bind. Though I'd never professionally played piano before--I'd never actually even owned a piano--I went out, rented one, got up at six o'clock every morning, and transcribed all of Bill's licks. I wrote the whole show out, note for note. I walked in the day of the audition and I could play the show from top to bottom. And no mistakes. So that was how I got the gig. And that was basically how I started getting established as a session player. Through doing those shows I met Mike Post, who later started using me on The Rockford Files.

JOHN: Did you make the transition from live playing to studio recording easily?

MICHAEL: No. Actually, I had red light fever like crazy. Every time they turned on the red light to record with the orchestra I would just choke. I hated it. In live playing you get another chance the next night, but when you're going to play something in the studio for the red light, that's it! You don't have any more opportunities to correct it. Now, curiously enough, I feel 180 degrees the other way.

JOHN: How did you finally get over that problem with playing in the studio?

MICHAEL: Basically by just doing it again and again. Mike Post helped me a lot. He used to say you need a "fuck-you" attitude, like, "Fuck you, I'll play this anyway--I don't care whether the red light's on or who you are. Stand over my shoulder and look--I don't care, I'm gonna play it!" And that really helped.

JOHN: I think a lot of people play conservatively when the red light goes on because they don't want to make a mistake. But then there's never much magic in the performance. Then you get the guy who walks in and really burns, and even though he may have mistakes, the producer freaks out because there's magic there. And he'll work with the player until he gets it right. So you got over that problem by just continuing to play again and again until you were able to relax in that situation.

MICHAEL: Yes, it's a matter of just feeling comfortable.

JOHN: If you're doing a film score where there's just one rehearsal and you've got to get it right, do you then adopt that more conservative attitude, as contrasted with when you're doing an album and you have a lot of takes?

MICHAEL: You have to. There are adjustments to be made. But sometimes you don't have to adopt a conservative attitude at all, because the music's not that difficult. And other times the music's really difficult, or it's written wrong. For example, they'll tell the orchestrator to just combine three of the different sections and give it to the synthesizer player. And then he might not leave you any rests whatsoever in which to change instruments or sounds. Well, you just have to look at the part and scale it down, throw a lot of things out, keep what's important and allow yourself time to make changes. And almost always the composer will appreciate it because it will sound so much better than trying to cover everything and messing it all up.

JOHN: In other words, you have to be a problem solver as well.

MICHAEL: Definitely!

JOHN: So getting with Mike Post started your in-town career?

MICHAEL: Yes. He introduced me to a lot of the top studio players in L.A. I got to sit next to and play with guys like Mike Lang, Larry Muhoberac, Lincoln Meyorga, Artie Kane, and Ralph Grierson.

JOHN: Were you playing the second keyboard part?

MICHAEL: I played the easier part--although actually it was better for me, because they always got stuck on piano while I did all the doubles, having played celeste, harpsichord, two or three synthesizers, Hammond B-3, Yamaha organ, and so on. It was a great experience. Then, after playing The Mac Davis Show every Tuesday night for about a year and a half, Mike started using me on The Rockford Files, which introduced me to the Universal crowd. I did that five or six times a week out at Universal until I got written up in Keyboard Magazine as being the synthesizer player behind the Bionic Woman. Then I quit--that was it for those dates! You know--I had come out here to be a rock and roller. So I continued to be a session player, but I was just more particular about the sessions I played.

JOHN: How were your reading chops then?

MICHAEL: I was probably a somewhat better reader then than I am now. I'd been in high school and college and was practicing and reading a lot, whereas now I'm working most of the time.

JOHN: So you didn't run into the syndrome of blowing the gig because you couldn't read well enough?

MICHAEL: No. If they'd written a really difficult part--for example, the parts of four or five instruments that play one note at a time combined into one keyboard part--I might just take the melody line, or maybe just the important harmonies.

JOHN: And you'd get away with it most of the time?

MICHAEL: It wasn't a matter of getting away with it, because it just sounded better after it was orchestrated. There's a philosophy I picked up from Ray Parker. He would sit there and let everybody else read the music and get their stuff together. Then he'd pick out a one or two-note part that would fit in between all the others. The composer ended up not caring if he read the music or not, because Ray came up with his own parts that were great and it sounded wonderful.

JOHN: So the bottom line is really this--if it sounds good, the composer is pretty likely to accept it.

MICHAEL: That's the whole idea. There's another thing that Ray Parker hipped me to. One day at Studio 55, when I was trying to do exactly what the composer wanted, he took me aside and said, "You know, we have a responsibility to the composer, we have to help him out. If it sounds bad--even if you're playing what he wants--you have the responsibility to say 'No, I won't do that. Let me do this, it'll sound better.' Just try to say it a little more tactfully!" Ray gave me a lot of guidance in this area. Regarding self-confidence in that type of situation, he said, "Look, I might not have the chops of Jay Graydon, or the reading ability of Tommy Tedesco, but I do what I do, and it's very solid--and it's valuable." That really helped, because if I had tried to be a Ralph Grierson, forget it--I had started 20 years too late. I would've had to have played piano from the day I came from the womb to try to be that good! So I had to find my niche.

JOHN: Which brings us to the question of what that is nowadays. Define your niche, your forte--what sets you off from others in your field.

MICHAEL: Well, that's changing. For a while there it was the fact that I had learned synthesis classically. I really knew how to operate the synthesizer because I understood all the elements that were behind the knobs.

JOHN: So when you would create a sound, there was really no trial and error.

MICHAEL: Right, no trial and error at all. If somebody plays me a sound over the speakers, then I can analyze the elements and get that same sound, or improve upon it. If I just hear a sound in my head, I know how to go about getting it.

JOHN: On each instrument?

MICHAEL: Yes, because the mechanics of getting the sound up on each synthesizer are different--the controls or knobs may be placed in a slightly different arrangement, and some controllers are different than others. Actually, though, the basic theory behind synthesizers remains the same--you're still working with all the same elements. I couldn't afford to buy a synthesizer when I first wanted to, so my high school comp teacher turned me on to someone who taught me how to operate and to play a synthesizer--on paper! He didn't even have a synthesizer, but he had his doctorate in electronic music. I went to his place once a week for about half a year, and later went to college to study under him.

JOHN: So you got a lot of theory.

MICHAEL: Yes. So when I came into town, I was fast because I knew what I was doing. Also, I always prided myself on the fact that I didn't get cheap sounds--I refused to get all those boinky, "wah wah" types of sounds. I mean, again, "refused" is kind of a strong word, but I really shied away from that. I looked for different ways to get what was wanted. Instead of that boinking and wowing, I would think of different kinds of modulation to create colors that would stand out, yet not be cheap sounding.

JOHN: So your own musical integrity was developing at that time--you were able to please who you had to please and still please yourself.

MICHAEL: I pleased them even more than they had expected. You see, they "knew" that to get the synthesizer to stand out you had to put "wah wah" on it--yet I would then give them a better-sounding way to do it. So I worked in the background with a lot of different composers, arrangers, and keyboard players.

JOHN: So for a while your bread and butter was playing and programming synthesizers?

MICHAEL: Yes. Those were the kinds of gigs where they would call in the synthesizer right as they were doing the mix. So I'd come in for three or six hours and do an entire album.

JOHN: Just a little frosting.

MICHAEL: That's right. "The song is finished, but if you can come up with something that just sparkles it up a little bit..." If you could do that, you were a hero. Then I got more and more into films. For a long time I was booked up solidly two months in advance on films, and it made me nuts, because Quincy Jones or someone would call me up for a project and I wouldn't be able to do it because I was already booked doing some film that I'd go and read books on. I would sit there and read magazines and books all day and wind up playing two minutes worth of music for an entire day's work. So I had to consciously steer away from being that kind of a film musician. I still do film work now--my own film scores and other projects where the composer makes use of what I have to offer. I really enjoy the variety of writing, playing on records and doing jingles and films.

JOHN: So after the live gigs you did more TV and film, and then started doing more albums?

MICHAEL: Yes. At first I did a whole bunch of dates where it was show up, work three hours doing your few parts, and then leave. Then I'd go to another session and do three hours there. So I consciously began working my way into the type of dates where I was hired for nine-hour days so I could really be involved and not just do inconsequential parts,

JOHN: Did that lead you to more of what you're doing now?

MICHAEL: Absolutely--which is more composition. In fact, we won a Grammy for "Imagination," from Flashdance. I co-wrote that with Jerry Hey and Michael Sembello.

JOHN: So you're still keeping very active all the way around.

MICHAEL: I'm still doing 25 dates a week of various types; sometimes I do other people's dates all week. Sometimes I have to take off weeks to finish a film that I'm scoring.

JOHN: What are your basic work axes?

MICHAEL: My present setup consists of a modified Jupiter 8A, Jupiter 6, two DX-7's, PPG Wave 2.3 with wave term, and a modified Mini Moog that's modular--I can patch in and out of it, and it then patches into a modular Moog 55 system. I also use a Bode and Roland vocoder, the Emulators I and II with the Digidesign system, a Super Jupiter, a JX-8P, TX7, TX816 and a Bit-One.

JOHN: Are all your synths interfaced with each other?

MICHAEL: All of them can be hooked together via midi.

JOHN: What interface are you using?

MICHAEL: I'm using midi junction boxes that Roland makes and a 10 by 22 midi switcher by J.L. Cooper. Sometimes I run the HP-400 into a Roland MSQ sequencer and then the MSQ not only runs the piano itself, but all the other synthesizers. I can use this setup live as well as in the studio. So in fact, even though I do my basic or "temp" track live, it still sounds like I've overdubbed for days. This is really a great change from my old system, because before I had to deal with the fact that a synthesizer is basically an unfeeling axe that you have to program all the dynamics into. So in order to have dynamics on the basic part, I would always write and record my pieces on the electric piano or acoustic piano and then orchestrate them from there. But now with this midi setup, I can orchestrate all the dynamics into the basic synthesizer track live. But this is just for me to play my basic keyboard part on. I still do my overdubs on all the different synthesizers, especially the Emulator.

In fact, I have an assistant whose entire job is just to create stock sounds on my PPG Wave Term and Emulators.

JOHN: Sampling and creating sounds for you to use in your scores and so on?

MICHAEL: Yes. For example, there's a scene in a recent movie I scored where the aliens looked a lot like insects. So I had my assistant go around and sample insect noises. He'd combine all these bee and insect sounds and then I'd go over it and use what was musical.

JOHN: When you do something like that do you actually put the insects in a jar and tape them?

MICHAEL: We get them wherever we can!

JOHN: Do you improvise your film scores or write them out?

MICHAEL: The themes are always written out ahead of time, and when I work with other players it's almost always written out as well. On a film I did recently, I didn't have enough time to sit down and just improvise the parts at home while watching the film, which is the way I prefer to do it. I had the film and I knew essentially where we were going to start music and where there wouldn't be any. So I took those timings and, in the studio, while watching the film and playing the synthesizer, I decided what parts of the film I wanted to synchronize the music to (hit points) and figured out a click track* that worked. Then I took the click home and wrote out my chart and all the cue points on it.

JOHN: Do you use the Knudson tables** to figure out your click track and hit points?

---

* click track, a film metronome that can be locked in synchronization with the picture.

** Knudson tables, a computer-accurate book of charts showing the relationship between tempo, timing and beats, based on the speed of 35mm film, as standardized by the Academy of Motion Picture Arts and Sciences, at 90 feet per minute.

MICHAEL: Yes, and then I enter the information into my Apple IIe using the John Eidsvoog program. Then I figure out the kind of mood changes I want, write out a basic piano part and set about orchestrating it. With the midi system I have many different sounds available to choose from--if I play my master keyboard hard, it sounds completely different, because most of my synthesizers are touch sensitive. If I play fast I don't hear the strings at all, because they have a slow attack. If I play a soft slow part, all you hear is the strings.

JOHN: What advice might you give someone desiring to become a successful synthesizer session player?

MICHAEL: I would recommend that anybody who's a serious synthesizer student study in school with a good teacher--and there are plenty of them who aren't good teachers. I ran into several along the way who had weird attitudes--they believed that synthesizers were not meant for pop music. In fact, one manufacturer actually refused to sell me its synthesizers because I was playing them on commercial dates! They said their instruments were created for the sake of art, and not for the sake of making a living. Hopefully, I've been able to do both--make a living and make art. So I would advise someone to learn the basic theory of synthesizers. See, nowadays it seems so easy. When preprogrammed synthesizers first came out, any keyboard player who could rent a programmable synth all of a sudden thought he was a synthesist--until they asked him to change the attack. Then it might take him forever to figure out how to do a simple thing like that, or how to make the sound less buzzy. So those guys were really only as good as the preprogrammed sounds. And once they used up all those preprogrammed sounds and they couldn't get any new ones, they were to a large extent using the same things over and over again. So that was the situation in town for quite a long period. I would recommend that people not rely heavily on a synth's memory. I use it only to store sounds that I'm using on a given gig. For example, if I have a certain program for one scene and I know I'm going to use it later in the film, I just store it up for quick access.

JOHN: Does it take hours to create your sounds?

MICHAEL: Well, it never takes hours to get sounds-- it shouldn't.

JOHN: Not even when you're experimenting?

MICHAEL: That usually only occurs with overdubs on records, like when you do maybe 20 tracks of overdubs to see if you can get a certain sound. That happened when we did Wacky Dust for Manhattan Transfer and did 15 overdubs to create a horn ensemble. Nobody had ever done that. We hadn't done it. So we had to experiment a bit, and in a situation like that, as opposed to when you're working on only one sound, we would not know ahead of time if we had gotten the desired results or not. It took us about two days to do it. Nobody that I know in the business would ever give me hours to create sounds. It shouldn't be necessary--they're just not that complicated if you know synthesizers. Even if you have to go out and record a sound, and then sample it, and then process it, you're still talking about minutes, unless you have to drive someplace to do it.

JOHN: So if someone's at a gig and one of the synthesizers accidentally erases his programs and he has to sit there for an hour and a half trying to get his one string sound, then, obviously, he's got some missing programming tech.

MICHAEL: Most definitely--a lack of theory. I can get a string sound up without hearing it.

JOHN: So you can shut the audio of the synth off, get the sound up, and then turn it on and know almost exactly what's going to sound--on any of your axes?

MICHAEL: Any of them.

JOHN: That would be a good training drill to do with somebody.

MICHAEL: Yes--Clark Spangler used to do that with me.

JOHN: You studied with Clark?

MICHAEL: Sure--I studied with everybody I could get my hands on. I consider myself a permanent student.

JOHN: What are your views about business chops? That's an important area.

MICHAEL: Oh boy, is it! I'll tell you, as far as that's concerned, I always still believe in the business end of your karma. As long as you take care of your stuff and you're honest, then you will have good fortune with

your work. The thing you can't be responsible for is
other people's karma--there are people who will always try
to take advantage of you. I've run into more than my fair
share of them. Accurate recordkeeping and accounting are
important, and being able to keep up with it--and if you
can't do it yourself then hire somebody who can.

JOHN: So you should keep up with everything that
comes under that heading--your bookkeeping, your taxes,
any other kinds of recordkeeping, your contracts with
people when you're doing dates?

MICHAEL: Absolutely. In our business, except in
some areas like composing and arranging, it's still done
on a handshake basis instead of with contracts. People
hire you for a date, you usually discuss the amount of
money you get or they already know that, then you show up
and you turn in your bill. No contracts are signed
between anybody, and you just assume you're going to be
paid. And it's your responsibility to make sure. You
might think it's their responsibility to take care of you,
but it's actually yours to make sure you do get paid. It
took me a long time to learn all this, and I still hate
bookwork. But I've fortunately learned to farm out almost
everything I can of that nature.

JOHN: Whatever you can't do, you subcontract out?

MICHAEL: Which means I farm out everything! I would
much rather sit behind a synthesizer. Give me any excuse!

Nicky Hopkins
composer/studio keyboardist

NICKY HOPKINS

JOHN: I'm interested in knowing what sparked your
career and what some of the key elements were that contributed to your success as a studio musician and performer. Let's start with your musical background.

NICKY: I had a classical upbringing, taking lessons
from age six to sixteen, including four years at the Royal
Academy in London on Saturday mornings. The most important thing I learned at the Royal Academy was music theory. I became very adept at reading music and also at
writing down music as I listened to it. This last ability
is very important and has stood me in very good stead in
many sessions where there have been no charts. After one
or two passes through the song I'll just write out a chart
then and there--the basic changes, the lead line and the
rhythm figures. That way I don't have to spend the first
couple of hours just learning the song. Without this
skill I probably wouldn't have been that successful in the
early days--that and the ability to play rock and roll.

JOHN: How did you make the transition from classical
music to rock and roll?

NICKY: When I was eleven my sister brought home a 78
rpm Fats Domino record. I liked it, so I began listening
to Little Richard and a few of the other rock and roll
artists. I was in my first rock and roll band at the age
of sixteen. Then I heard Jerry Lee Lewis. I was quite
intrigued by his style--I'd never really heard anything
like it before. So I transcribed all his piano parts, his
solos--even the wrong notes! And I learned those wrong
notes, too! Then I decided to team up with an English
band called Cliff Bennett and the Rebel Rousers, because
Bennett sounded like Jerry Lee Lewis. It took two of us
to do it, and we lacked Lewis's showmanship, but goddamn
it, we sounded like Jerry Lee Lewis! In 1962 I got into a
very big blues band called Cyril Davies and the R&B All-
Stars. Cyril had played with Alexis Korner, who of course
had the first blues band in England. Korner's band had
been playing Chicago blues, but wasn't playing it really
authentically, so Cyril decided to form a band that played
this music the way it should be played. Cyril turned me
on to a lot of the early boogie piano records by Albert

Ammons, Meade "Lux" Lewis, Pete Johnson, old Cripple Clarence Lofton, and Cow Cow Davenport. I transcribed all those artists' albums. Big Maceo Merriweather was another one--I think Ray Charles based a lot of his piano and vocal style on his work.

JOHN: Most keyboardists today have never even heard of those artists.

NICKY: That's right--somebody has to turn you on to them. So, along with the classical, my background added up to all those influences--rock and roll, the old blues guys, the rhythm and blues people, and the blues and boogie piano players. All that training and exposure was invaluable with regard to my success with studio work. First, I was one of the few people in England who could play good rock and roll piano, and second, I could read fairly well and I could write very quickly. So I began doing studio work in 1965 and have continued right up to the present.

JOHN: Some people think if you study too much you'll get too mechanical and lose your soul. Yet at the same time, if you don't know what you're doing these days, you can lose out on a lot of work and options. What are your feelings about this?

NICKY: I've seen some people who have been able to do without it--who were brilliant musicians without any training at all. My personal view on that is that they've been around before and done it another lifetime. But by and large I think training is very important. I've seen the reverse side of the coin, too, where it's overdone. I imagine there are some classical musicians around who've been trained since the year dot who still can't play anything without music in front of them. Now that's over-emphasis on training. I think you should train with an open mind, familiarizing yourself with and analyzing other styles of playing. Then you can adapt them to your own use.

JOHN: So your most successful career actions consisted of first developing some technique and learning to sightread through your classical training, and then learning not only to play what you heard, but to write it out rapidly as well. And you developed this last skill by listening to many artists' records and transcribing their music. Is there anything you want to add regarding your musical background?

NICKY: In thinking back, there's a certain amount of classical influence in things I've written--especially ballads. So studying and playing classical are not just something I did in the past. I still enjoy it and the influence can definitely be heard in some of my work.

JOHN: Everyone who has studied classical music seems to have their favorite pieces or composers. Who influenced you a lot?

NICKY: I think Chopin was one of the most important composers for me in my formative years. I played as many of the Chopin Preludes as I could, as well as Brahms and the old Romanticists. But you've reminded me of something else I used to do: Every week I would borrow three, four or more classical music books from an excellent library that was near the Academy in London, bring them home and sightread the pieces. I discovered a lot of music doing that. Every now and again I'll hear something I've still never actually heard before but remember having played back then. And I'll realize, oh this is how it's supposed to sound! Sometimes I came close then and sometimes I didn't.

JOHN: Just being able to read through a piece can give you so many ideas, even if you never play it exactly right. It seems to seep into your playing subliminally.

NICKY: Yes, that's true.

JOHN: When you started doing session work, were there any key artists who helped you in forwarding your career?

NICKY: The Who were actually among the first people I recorded with, and their engineer, Glyn Johns, who was producing a lot in those days, got me work. So did Shel Talmy, the producer. And of course one thing led to another--because I was the only guy in town who could do that kind of work fast, I got all the dates and calls. Then I started working with the Stones in 1967, which of course was a big move in my career.

JOHN: Did you work with them in the studio first?

NICKY: Yes, and then I did three tours with them, in '71, '72 and '73. I had also toured with Jeff Beck in '68, and I was in his band for a few months. Then I joined a west coast group called Quicksilver and did a few other bits and pieces. Apart from that I've mostly done studio work.

JOHN: When you played with the Stones, did you and the guys learn everything just by jamming, or did they write out charts?

NICKY: Well, it went back even a step further than it did with most of the people I worked for, because there was often no song when we went into the studio. Keith would grab a guitar, sit down on the floor for a couple of hours, work out a chord change or pattern he liked, and then perhaps work out a chorus chord pattern. Then we'd go onto the floor and learn it, and it would continue to change while we were doing it. And often, of course, I would get to know the song just through playing it through so many times. But just as often Mick and Keith would walk in with a complete song, and then I would just write it out.

JOHN: That brings us up to the present. The music scene today is much more diverse than it was when you started. Now there are so many styles of music, along with the added complexity of the technology boom. Keyboard players sometimes have to play four and five keyboards, and have the choice of either playing live or in the studio. What might you do if you had to start out in today's scene?

NICKY: It's a tough question. As I already said, I listened to a lot of different styles when I was growing up. In a way it worked against me in that I was never able to stay with a live band for longer than a few months at a time because I got tired, not only of playing the same tunes every night, but of having to play in just one style. But that's the only negative point I can think of on being familiar with many sounds and styles. So I would suggest that anybody listen to as much music as they can. And you can extend that, of course, to learning different keyboards. If you like the sound of synthesizers and computers, go for it.

JOHN: So you recommend that someone starting out should acquire some versatility before specializing?

NICKY: Yes, although it depends to some extent on what that person's goals are. If he knew that all he wanted to do was be a rock and roll keyboard player in a rock and roll band, then fine. But if someone may not ever have listened to anything else, he may only think he knows what he wants. Only by listening to other music, and from that sorting out what he likes and wants to do

can he really make a sound decision. His first decision
<u>might</u> be right--but it's probable that it wouldn't be.

<u>JOHN</u>: Now that synthesizers and computers have
finally become easy to use and widely applicable to
playing situations, how do you think they will affect the
role of the contemporary keyboardist in the future?

<u>NICKY</u>: There's already some indication of what the
keyboardist's role might be: A lot of pop records I hear
today were obviously recorded with just a singer or two
and a keyboardist with a synthesizer, a drum machine and
some computers. It's obvious how important the technology
is becoming. Now that synthesizers and computers have
improved so much, anybody can learn them. Mick Jagger had
one of the first Moogs, and I remember sitting down with
him at his house one time for about three hours, trying to
get a sound out of it--we failed! So I lost interest
until recently. Now I'm very interested in synthesizers,
not just because they sound good and it's fairly easy to
get the sounds, but because they're obviously going to be
around for a long time. Of course the technology will
improve and they'll continue to change.

<u>JOHN</u>: So you feel that a keyboardist who has some
equipment, understands it and can program it--who can also
read, sightread and take things down from records--is
going to be in demand in the future?

<u>NICKY</u>: Yes, if he also has a good attitude. It
hasn't been something that I've forced, but I know it's
been a contributing factor in my own success. I've seen a
lot of people lose out on studio work because their attitudes weren't good.

<u>JOHN</u>: Could you elaborate?

<u>NICKY</u>: I've seen some people come in obviously
thinking the world owes them everything, or that they're
brilliant players and thus exempt from the normal rules
governing human decency and interrelationships. This
doesn't go down at all well. They're never used again.

<u>JOHN</u>: How important do you think communication is in
this game?

<u>NICKY</u>: Well, it's something I never thought about
because, apparently, I've always had the ability to communicate well. And I could never figure out what it was.
But it <u>is</u> the ability to communicate. Some people don't

inherently have it, and if that's the case, they'd better acquire it.

JOHN: How could they do this?

NICKY: I would recommend that they study what L. Ron Hubbard has written about communication in his works on Scientology.   By doing that I came to understand what communication was and to see that I did have a natural ability to communicate that I was often able to use.

JOHN: How important do you think it is for an art-ist--in this case a keyboardist, but actually for any musician--to understand the world of business?   If he's really good, does everything just get taken care of for him, or should he know what's going on?

NICKY: Interestingly enough, it did just get taken care of for me in the early days, but only because I was in a unique situation with unique skills.   What I was doing, actually, was promoting myself without even knowing it, just from session to session.   But, as I say, that was a unique time and one of those situations that don't often come up.   In more recent years I've done PR--I send out promotions in the form of a double-sided postcard contain-ing all my important statistics, such as the people I've worked for.   The main thing this does is keep your name out there.   I send this promotion to as many musicians and producers--mainly producers--as I think will need it. This has been very effective.   Now again, what I'm specif-ically using is L. Ron Hubbard's business and promotional technology.   He's written a lot on business, and I would advise anyone to learn it whether they're interested in Scientology or not, as it's very, very effective.

JOHN: How do you feel a musician should handle his money, books, and taxes?   Many people have a hard time confronting this area.

NICKY: They should be able to confront it--otherwise they're not going to remain solvent for very long.   And I've done it both ways.   I originally had an interest in keeping books tidy, and then I got into several years of drugs where I didn't give a damn about it.   And I got into a huge colossal muddle and wound up owing thousands of dollars.   So you should keep a check on your finances and know what you've got and what you haven't got.

JOHN: Do you think there is such a thing as a good manager?   And if there is, what makes him good?

NICKY: Yes, there is such a person. I personally haven't encountered too many of them, but there are a few! You need to get somebody who's a good businessman, yet who knows and understands the music business. To a certain extent he has to be a good salesman. But I think, over and above that, he has to have ethics. He has to be somebody you can really trust, not somebody who just puts on a good front, smiles a lot and <u>says</u> "you can trust me."

JOHN: Is there any final advice you'd like to give the up-and-coming keyboardist--or, for that matter, any musician?

NICKY: There are a couple of points. The first, to recapitulate slightly, would be to absorb as much music as you can in different styles. Also, get into a little band--it's important to learn to play with other people. Then you can take that into a studio situation.

The other thing I'd like to mention is the matter of drugs. I did drugs from 1968 to 1979 pretty much nonstop. For the first couple of years it seemed like it was the answer to everything, and my creativity did seem to come up a little bit. But what happens is that it's an artificial stimulus and it all starts to go downward. You get a rise first of all, but then you gradually go down--way, way down. With me it was to the point where I damn well nearly killed myself--it was about two months off. So I would tell any upcoming musician to stay away from drugs.

JOHN: Thanks a lot, Nicky.

Keith Emerson
composer/multikeyboardist

KEITH EMERSON

JOHN: How did you get started in music and what were some early musical influences?

KEITH: My father was a main influence; he played piano-accordion in an army band and I grew up listening to his jam sessions with his friends. These jam sessions were quite improvisational, based on the standards of the day, such as "Whispering," and all the old World War II army tunes. Now I could never really handle the piano-accordion, because it was too heavy, but when I was about seven we had a huge upright piano shipped in. I heard my father playing it and thought wow, that's incredible! So I started playing it when I came home from school every day. I seemed to learn pretty quickly, and my father built me extensions for the pedals with blocks of wood. He taught me various things to play in duet with him. Then he decided I should be taught properly and I began lessons--although as far as I was concerned, I was already playing properly. These were basically classical studies, theory, and some sight reading. I also entered some competitions that I did quite well in. But I was never really into this route--it was forced on me. However, while I was at school I was interested because I found that I gained a lot of friends through playing the piano. The music teacher would say, "Come on Emerson, give us a tune." I would then go up and play the hits of the day. This was really a bit before the Beatles, but in England at that time there were a few popular pianists who had hit records--so I used to play a sort of barrelhouse style patterned off guys like Russ Conway, Winifred Atwell and the like. It was very popular.

JOHN: Were you beginning to pick up on improvising yet at this stage?

KEITH: I was getting the left-hand stride and boogie woogie stuff together--tenths and so on. I couldn't reach tenths, but I rolled them. So at school I used to mess around with the pieces I had to do for my piano classes. I would do a bit of Tchaikovsky in the right hand and stride piano in the left. It got quite a few laughs, so I guess it worked out pretty well. Then, when I was 16 or 17, I joined a local swing orchestra whose repertoire consisted of a lot of Count Basie and Duke Ellington arrangements. I met up there with a lot of jazz purists of about my age. At first I played my rinky-dink stride piano--jazz with my right hand and this weird stride piano with my left, and they didn't quite match up. It was like playing from two different periods at the same time. It took me quite a while to learn that one comps with the left hand while improvising with the right--and you had a bass player to play the bass line. Then I formed a trio with some of the guys from this big band. The drummer was a very strict jazz purist who had all the really heavy Miles Davis, Wynton Kelly, Eric Dolphy albums. So I got into all that heavy jazz and it wasn't okay to play all the baby stuff I'd been playing any more. Now, the Beatles were just coming on the scene, but, being a purist, you had to ignore them. You had to model yourself after Miles Davis and be very Ivy League. We started going out and playing jazz dates, and because I was play-ing them on all these junk pianos, it became necessary to get my own instrument. Now around that time the jazz organ suddenly broke onto the scene--Jimmy Smith and "Walk On The Wild Side." But because that went commercial, it was ruled out here in England. Nevertheless, it became acceptable to use the organ in a jazz context. Our drum-mer told me to check out brother Jack MacDuff. I listened to his album, Rock Candy, and flipped right out--I thought it was absolutely amazing! So I saved for about two years to buy an organ, even though I didn't know what type he was playing.

JOHN: You didn't know it was a Hammond?

KEITH: No. I'd seen a local guy playing a Bird organ, which was very portable and had kind of a good sound to it, so I went to the Portsmouth organ center to buy it. I played it, but just before I was going to buy it the salesman suggested that I try out a Hammond L-100 he had in the back. I did, and that was the sound! It was a bit more money, so my father chipped in the rest and we shipped it back. I began taking it on some of my gigs, even though it was awkward to lug around.

Now, around 1966 or '67 I had a band called John Brown's Body. I was doing a day job and playing a club date in the evening. I had my Hammond L-100 hooked up to a big amplifier going through some whatnot speakers that really pumped it out.

JOHN: So you weren't using Leslie speakers yet?

KEITH: That's right. I couldn't afford them.

JOHN: How did the Keith Emerson Hammond sound develop?

KEITH: Well, as you probably recall, there was a fault with the Hammond's keyboard contacts. If you put on a lot of presence and top end when you hit a key, it sort of spit at you. And this, you see, was the sound I had heard coming from Jack MacDuff's organ with his version of Rock Candy. So when I zapped it through an amplifier I got that very tacky, spitty sound coming out of the speakers. It really spit at you, and I thought it was wild!

JOHN: What was your first big exposure to the music scene as it was then?

KEITH: A popular rhythm and blues band called the T-Bones heard my band play and asked me to join. I chucked my day job and moved to London. That was my first big exposure to the London music scene. But the T-Bones were still kind of jazz purists, and they got left behind when the Who, the Stones and the Beatles started to happen. I was still into my Miles Davis button-down Ivy League shirts, and all of a sudden you couldn't do that any more in London--it was old fashioned. The band couldn't adapt and fell apart. I left and joined a band called the VIP's that toured all over Europe. It was pretty awful--I was literally living in the band wagon.

JOHN: How did you get into doing your own thing?

KEITH: I was then asked to put a band together to back a singer, P. P. Arnold, who was from the Ike and Tina Turner Band. It was mostly soul music, but we were allowed to do our own thing out front before she came on, and that's really how it all started. The people used to say "what the hell is that?"

JOHN: What was the nature of the music you were doing?

KEITH: A bit of original stuff, some Charles Lloyd-- all sorts of weirdness. I was still playing my L-100 and getting all kinds of special effects out of it. For instance, I found out that if the instrument was jarred a bit, the reverb unit would crash. So I used it quite percussively. Also, if you got into the back of the organ and ran your thumb along the reverb spring, you got a kind of big twangy noise. It was quite an amazing instrument. It was heavy--it weighed about 300 pounds--but if you lifted it up and aimed it at a speaker, it would feed back like a guitar. So I started using it much the same way as Peter Townshend and Jimmy Hendrix were using their guitars, with feedback, howls, and so on.

JOHN: So it appears you were developing your theatrical side at this time. Was this in response to seeing the guitar players moving all around the stage?

KEITH: Yes--it was really because the guitar players were out there pulling all the girls, and as the keyboard player you'd sit there in the background unnoticed. It was always a big battle in those days between me and the guitarist. Because the organ was such a difficult instrument to amplify, it couldn't be heard well and I'd always have to yell across the stage and tell the guitar player to turn down. I felt I had a lot to say and I was fed up with being drowned out by some bloody guitar player who fancied himself as another Pete Townshend, so I began making so much noise on my own that there wasn't any point in having a guitarist in there any more.

Now I'll jump on a bit to the early days of the Nice. The original lineup was Brian Davison, Lee Jackson, David O. List, and myself. By doing quite well at the Windsor Jazz Festival we were offered a residency at the Marquee Club playing every Friday night. It was a very valuable gig to have because we were doing our own stuff. We then signed to Immediate Records, which was run in those days by the manager of the Rolling Stones. We were told to go into the studio and do what we wanted. The first thing I wrote was a five-four riff called "Asreal." Then we did an adaptation of "Blue Rondo A La Turk" called "Rondo," which seemed to go over quite well. We then said, oh hell, let's go for it. The whole soul music period of Sam and Dave, Wilson Pickett, and people like them, was dying out. But there was a very heavy underground movement in London at that time--all sorts of weirdness was really in! Bands like Soft Machine were doing quite well. What the Nice was doing then was really a mixed media--we were combining classical, way out visual shows and special effects. We did an arrangement of "America" which we played at Albert Hall to celebrate American Independence Day. Now, we used that particular piece of music to very great effect: we destroyed a replica of the American flag. That gained us quite a degree of notoriety--the press got hold of it and we were were announced as not being very "nice." So when we got into town for the next day's gig, we saw these great lines of people waiting and thought the Rolling Stones were playing. But in fact they were lining up for us. And that was really the beginning of it all. People came for the show aspect and then to listen to the music.

JOHN: What was the instrumentation of the band at this point?

KEITH: Well, by this time I had managed to push the keyboards to the front line! We said bye-bye to our guitar player because he was making a hell of a lot of noise but not doing anything constructive. I did try to replace him at one point with Steve Howe. It sounded great, but Steve wanted to get his own band together, so he left. From that point on I really couldn't see working with any other guitar player, so I left it as a trio. At that time I was still playing the L-100. Then around 1968 I managed to get hold of a C-3 Hammond, and I involved the piano in the act as well. But I was still looking for effects as well as new sounds from the instruments. Then, around 1968, I discovered the Moog synthesizer. I was in a record store and the owner, who knew me, had me listen to an arrangement of Bach's Brandenburg Concerto in G, played on the Moog by Walter Carlos. He knew I had done an arrangement of the same piece. I asked him what the hell that instrument was. He showed me a picture of it on the album cover and I was amazed. I started making inquiries around England and I located one of the early modular Moogs owned by Mike Vickers from Manfred Mann. I rented it for a concert at the Royal Festival Hall, and Mike programmed it while I played it. He'd bob up from behind the instrument occasionally to change the jacks, since at that time there was no such thing as a programmable synthesizer. It was a multimedia concert in which I used the London Philharmonic Orchestra; we did some arrangements of Stanley Kubrick's 2001 music and I featured the Moog a lot. It was at that concert that I realized the instrument's potential.

The Nice disbanded in 1969 and late that year I started to get ELP together. I thought if I was going to form a new group, I had to have that synthesizer. I somehow got hold of Bob Moog and told him I'd successfully used the Moog on stage and wanted to know if he could build me a programmable one that was easier to use in live performances. Now, although they were working on a preset Moog, they had decided that the Moog was strictly a studio instrument, as you couldn't rely on it to tour with. But I encouraged Bob to bring me over one of the first prototypes of the Moog modular system, which he did. The instrument cost me a lot. It arrived all packaged up and had no instructions. I unpacked it and couldn't even figure how to switch it on! So I called Mike Vickers, and he took it for a few days to try to put it together and get some sounds out of it. He called me back and said the preset box didn't do too much except control the filtering. We could alter the pitch with the oscillators and that was about it. But out of that we got about four or five different sounds, which I used with the early ELP band. It was a very temperamental instrument. At the first concert I used it in, the pitch went all haywire and it became unusable when the hall heated up. So I incorporated a cutoff switch and a frequency counter (tuner) that enabled me to check the tuning, when I was about to play it, without the audience hearing it. ELP then went over to New York, where Bob Moog heard us. He had never heard his instrument used in quite that way and we became pretty close after that--I became an informal consultant for him on the Moog's use in performances. So ELP did a number of gigs after that and things just took right off from there.

JOHN: How did you learn composition?

KEITH: I never had any formal instruction. Listening to lots of music, of course, helped a great deal, and my exposure to the classics gave me a lot of insight. I started reading about composition later on when I was with the Nice because I became interested in some other way of putting my music across. Counterpoint was interesting. I hated the idea of being just a one-handed keyboard player. I wanted to make the most out of both hands, and from that point of view, counterpoint was quite a demanding style. So I used it in the earlier days of the Nice.

JOHN: You were one of the first rock keyboardists to incorporate this countrapuntal style into your music. Sometimes you'd play a riff in five with your left hand on the synth while you took a screaming organ solo with your right hand. Most cats would have had the bass player do the bass riff. Did you really have to work at developing this linear independence so characteristic of the contrapuntal style, or did it come naturally?

KEITH: Well, I had to work at everything, really. But a lot of what I did with the left hand was like an ostinato figure.* I had dabbled with a lot of boogie woogie left-hand figures, and it was an offshoot of that.

----

* Ostinato, a figure repeated in the bass throughout a composition while the upper parts change.

516

JOHN: So you drew a lot from the boogie woogie style?

KEITH: The boogie-woogie figure is very much like an ostinato form anyway. Take, for example, the left hand figure of "Tarkus," with all those fourths. Once you get this pattern going in the left hand, which is almost like playing boogie, you keep it rolling and your right hand is quite free to do whatever you want. Now, I wouldn't say I'm one of those very skilled people who can sit down and improvise freely with the left and freely with the right. I have done it and been quite pleased with the results at times, but as many other times I've been horrified, because what I did didn't make all that much sense.

JOHN: Did you ever do much studio work?

KEITH: No, I never really got into doing sessions for other people. Besides a session I did with Rod Stewart and maybe a few others, I basically just did my own thing.

JOHN: During all of the ELP period you basically stuck to the classical rock fusion sound, mixing classics with rock and jazz. Why?

KEITH: Well, I had established that whole direction of music with the Nice: We did the Brandenberg in G and Tchaikovsky's Pathetique, as well as my own compositions. I was commissioned by the Newcastle Arts Council to compose the Five Bridges Suite, a bold attempt of mine to use a classical orchestra with an electronic group. So we developed this image of a classical rock. One might call it a type of fusion now, but in those days the term was mixed media. Then ELP followed on--Greg Lake and Carl Palmer were both interested in this aspect of the music. We did an arrangement of Bartok's "Allegro Barbaro" and one of Moussorgsky's Pictures at an Exhibition, and I would always be very strict and try to remain as faithful to the original composer as possible. My reason for playing the classics was I liked the music. It was a nice break to play music written by somebody else, rather than just our own original repertoire, and it was nice to do it in our own way. Rather than rocking or hamming something up, like some groups, I liked to choose a fairly obscure piece of classical music that ELP could use as a vehicle for branching out and getting a big grand sound at the same time.

JOHN: And doing it with just three guys!

KEITH: Right--it wasn't an easy job. After a while people said all we did was just rock out classical pieces, which of course wasn't right. We were doing our own pieces, like "Tarkus" and "Karnevil Nine," which had no relation at all to any classical piece ever written. Finally it was rebellion on my part to sit down and write a serious piano concerto in its strictest form. That came out on Works Volume One.

JOHN: What was your keyboard setup at this time?

KEITH: By that time I had the Moog modular system and it had grown so big, I couldn't reach the top. It had sequences, which was a big deal at that time. I'd send it back occasionally to Moog and they'd add the latest hardware updates, and then I used to rewire it and learn my way around the "spaghetti" patching. I also had two mini Moogs that were installed in drawers so they could be slid in and out and not obscure the audience's view. I had the Hammond C-3, the Hammond L-100--which was going through boosted-up Leslie speakers--the Yamaha Electric Grand, and the conventional nine-foot Steinway grand piano.

JOHN: What was your method of composing for ELP?

KEITH: I mostly wrote on the piano and then, once I had taught the composition to the rest of the band, I would experiment. For example, I'd try it on the organ, acoustic piano, Moog, etc. I'd try left hand on one instrument and right hand on another; different setting on one, different setting on another. I experimented like that until we took it into the studio, at which point, if I was still undecided about the actual balance of the instrumentation, we might do a few overdubs. That would spark other ideas, and so on. Then, having gotten the album together, I would go back and rehearse the band for the live performance version and program the synthesizers to match the overdubs I did on the album. So the whole arrangement took its shape that way. It was a question of a bit of composition done beforehand on the piano and a bit of studio composition.

JOHN: After you had become familiar with your own tendencies in orchestrating for the group, did you then just score everything out? For example, this is going to be on the Moog, this on the piano, this on the C-3, etc.?

KEITH: No, I never wrote the material out that way. In those early days, I really didn't have the time. I did, however, score everything out for the fugue on "The

Endless Enigma," because it was very strict. But with most of the material it was just a question of playing it over and over until we memorized it.

JOHN: When you do score music, do you have perfect pitch or perfect relative pitch, or do you rely on the keyboard?

KEITH: My pitch is okay once I'm established with the piece. But I couldn't sing A-440 right now if you wanted me to. So I guess that's perfect relative pitch. But I can tell if something is out of tune!

JOHN: Being a keyboardist, do you usually write at the piano?

KEITH: About 70% of the time I do write at the keyboard. But there have been times when I have written things without any keyboard in sight; I literally sat down with the manuscript and just thought it all out. Sometimes the keyboard is a bit restrictive. You know--you can sit there and think something is nice and be led astray. Composing away from the piano is a more thoughtful process--it's almost like meditating.

JOHN: Do you think, then, that there are advantages to sometimes composing away from your instrument?

KEITH: There are. You can sort of let your mind go--but you have to be in the right mood for it. Being at the instrument is a far more exciting occasion. But, because of the excitement of hearing it played back instantaneously, you can get a bit involved, and tend to do things you've done before or fall into the trap of doing something because it feels good rather than because that's how it should sound. If I ever feel that I'm being led in that direction, I'll halt the compositional process at that point and just put it on ice for a bit. If I find myself singing it the next day and it grows on me like fungus, then I'll say, well yeah, that's all right--I'll buy that. But it takes me a bit of time to buy it--to decide to accept it.

JOHN: So you try to be objective in what you're doing.

KEITH: Oh, absolutely! I'm very, very objective. There are a lot of things I've just thrown away. Something has to pass quite a few tests before I'll accept it. But once I accept it, I just love it. The difficult thing, then, is to relate it to other people. It's not, for instance, the easiest thing to get it across to a singer. But once you know the singer's abilities, it has to be possible. Now when you're dealing with people who don't read music, you have to have a lot of patience. I think I have that, really. I can sit down with somebody and literally go over and over and over something until they've got it, provided the interest is there.

JOHN: Do you think the word integrity exists in the music industry nowadays? Many artists seem content just trying to please the music industry machine rather than being artists and creating what they really feel. Is it very different now compared to when you were with ELP?

KEITH: Well, there are many ways of dealing with that question. Right now, in England, many interesting things are happening. The producer has the key say in the whole issue--he's quite a responsible figure, especially here in England. I find it a little bit disconcerting when the fashion element, the look, the attitude is the selling thing while the music is secondary. Because of that, the 80's have not seen many new soloists. There are good points and bad points connected with the 80's. The good points are that there is a lot of free expression for the performer, the instruments are programmable--there are lots of sequences--and using tape machines on the stage is not frowned at. And a lot of keyboard players in England don't disguise the fact that they just play the instrument with one finger. That's okay--it's not frowned on by the new generation. And while they're holding down a keyboard with one finger, they can also show off or present an attitude to the new generation. So it does leave a lot of freedom in that respect. But ultimately the whole sound is up to the producer, especially in England. In a lot of cases, he'll get the drummer to come in, have him whack a snare drum--okay, thank you, you can go home. Then the bass player--well, sample that. Okay, thank you--you can go home. And then he puts all this into a pot and mixes it all up and then finds the face, the singer, who can front that whole sound.

JOHN: So it's almost a formula at that point.

KEITH: Yes. These things are very short-lived. The records you buy are basically made by session musicians. The producer uses Synclaviers and Fairlights and whatever, and all of a sudden the band has to go out and play on its own and it's a disaster. Now, there are a few good bands and a few good soloists, but ultimately the whole scene is being overrun by A&R people, producers, etc.

JOHN: Do you think all this computerized, made-to-formula music is affecting up-and-coming good players? Should a player spend many years perfecting his instrument to then find out that the producer only wants him to play one note while the computer plays the whole sequence?

KEITH: Well, it does rile me, because it can be done today with very little effort, especially if you're sharp. You know, instant results without all the effort, as long as you dress up and look a bit weird. I suppose some of them have some kind of talent there somewhere, but, quite honestly, I don't really listen to that sort of stuff. However, I've been finding lately that people are getting a bit fed up with computerized rock and roll. They want to hear the real thing. They want to hear players. There is a demand for it. So I don't think it's anything to worry about.

JOHN: Considering that these are different times, what might you recommend to young keyboardists just starting out that might enhance their chances for success?

KEITH: First, become a good lawyer!

JOHN: In other words, get your business together.

KEITH: Yeah! But, unfortunately, you find it out the hard way. It's such a hard business, because ultimately the musician is a dreamer. You have to be that way--you float around. Now, the attitude required to create music doesn't match up with the attitude required for business. It's so hard to zap back and forth between these two attitudes, and of course the corporate rock and roll industry knows about this and they prey on it a lot. So you have to find the right people to take care of your business, people who are trustworthy enough to look after it for you--and they're really hard to find.

Besides having your business together, I think it's important to find a teacher who will listen to what you want to play, and be sympathetic and encouraging and know how to steer you in the right direction. I couldn't take Scott Joplin to my classical teacher and ask if I could learn it. He'd say no, that's ragtime--that's not music! So it's important to find a teacher with an open mind.

It's also important to get a good grounding in the fundamentals to help you do what you want to do. If you don't acquire what you need early on, it can become a hindrance later. I find, sometimes, that I have to practice an awful lot at certain things I want to do. If I'd have learned a bit more at a younger age, I may have been quicker at it. But then again--if I had spent too much time on my technique, maybe my musical ear wouldn't have developed as much as it did. So although you should get your chops together as much as possible, there's no reason to get discouraged, because you've always got your ear. With today's instruments, you can still make a living if you have a good sense of balance and musicality. Now if on top of all this you can find a different approach to communicate to the public and indeed do just that, you'll also be a winner. You don't always have to be that proficient a piano player. After all, Earl Garner couldn't read, but he played very well. Thelonius Monk had a totally weird style. He just had the courage of his convictions and went out and did it. So ultimately what it comes down to is that you have to believe in what you're doing. And if you really do love it, then you'll stick at it.

JOHN: What are your feelings and/or experiences as to how drugs affect the musician?

KEITH: Well, they can definitely alter the way you think, sometimes for better, sometimes for worse. But ultimately your health comes first, I think, because without that you can't play at all.

JOHN: Besides just a love for creating and playing music, is there any other reason you do it? Does Keith Emerson have a message, like to make people feel good, or something like that?

KEITH: Yes--to stir some sort of feeling is great. It's not just the surface level of relating a tune to somebody so he can hum it. Whatever I'm doing is a little deeper than that. Even people who don't understand music can get the effect. It's a basic kind of communication. If you hit on the right combination, there's an effect that people get, so that after they've listened to it, they sort of want to climb mountains or laugh or whatever. It's that emotional quality that is slightly below the surface that I'm going for.

JOHN: That's great. Thanks, Keith.

522

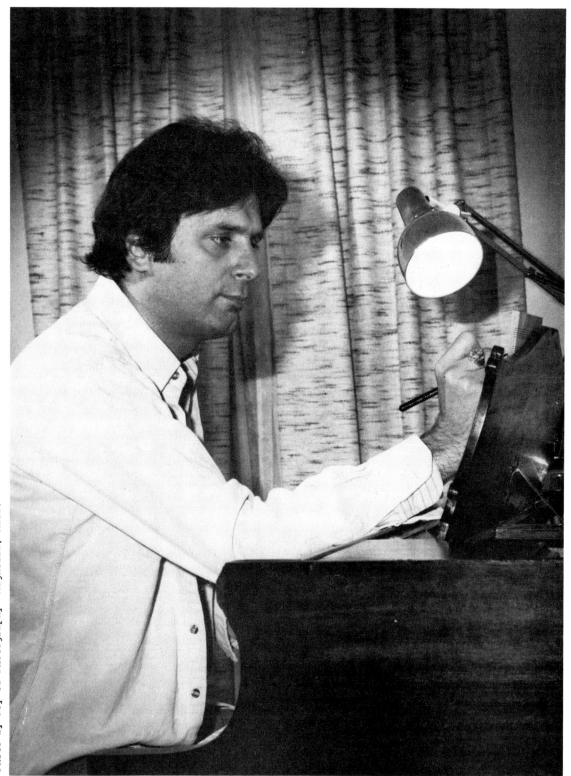

Charlie Banacos
pianist/composer/teacher/author

CHARLIE BANACOS

JOHN: How did you get into teaching improvisation, and what do you feel are the basic requirements needed to be a teacher of improvisation?

CHARLIE: I actually got into teaching when someone asked me a question about something I played. Teaching, for me, became and is totally effortless. As to the requirements to be a teacher of improvisation, the first is a thorough knowledge of the subject, both through personal experience and through listening to and studying other people's music. The second requirement would be that the teacher be able to do what he's teaching. The third would be the desire to have others do these things and hopefully go on to find their own paths. I myself can virtually "taste" this desire so strongly at times that I almost believe I want the student to be greater than the student himself wants to be! The fourth and perhaps final requirement is the ability to hear someone for the first time, and after only a short listening, intuitively know what to do with this particular student. I myself am graced with this ability, and I can remember having it even with my first student, 24 years ago. And I don't think it's changed at all in that period of time. Very strange but very wonderful!

JOHN: So it seems then, that you have no one particular method. You intuitively draw from your reservoir of knowledge and experience whatever you need to teach the student at hand.

CHARLIE: Exactly! There is no one method! Upon hearing each student, I immediately have a method that will work for that particular student and no other. But there are certain techniques of musical composition that all modern musicians need to know and be able to use, either in pre-composed settings or spontaneously. I might even use some of the same written exercises with more than one student, but explain them in a totally different way for each student. This is completely spontaneous and based on intuition, which to me seems like a fusion of knowledge and love and devotion to each student's needs at that particular time. Obviously, if a student wants to become a studio session player, that would affect when the study of the seven clefs would take place. Or, for another example, a student with a great love of mathematics might be introduced, if necessary, to the concepts of Joseph Shillinger earlier than someone else. I am making these and many other not-so-obvious decisions every split-second of the lesson. And because of all these variables, I don't really believe you can teach someone to teach. Let me tell you an interesting story relating to this if I may.

Bill Evans, the great jazz pianist, in a lecture at Harvard University not too long before he died, was asked if he taught. He answered that he couldn't teach because every time he tried it, he ended up teaching everything he knew in about an hour--so the student wouldn't learn anything. The audience roared with laughter, and I'm sure a great many of them thought he was joking. He then went on to say that a good teacher knew how to give information a bit at a time and in such a way that the student gained confidence and familiarity with the material until he or she could master it and then hopefully become a good craftsman or craftswoman and go on to become an artist. This story is fascinating to me because even though Bill knew what a good teacher had to do, he knew why he couldn't do it himself. Amazing! To me this shows that he was even a genius when it came to analyzing processes--to the point of such insight that he could discover that he shouldn't participate in them himself. Having been fortunate enough to have met and talked to Bill, I'm sure he was being totally sincere in those statements.

JOHN: Would you share a little of your music background--how you were inspired to get into music, who you listened to, how you studied?

CHARLIE: I was first inspired to become a musician at around age five, when listening to my father's record collection. It included Duke Ellington, Coleman Hawkins, Erroll Garner, Teddy Wilson, Earl Hines, "Fats" Waller, etc. I used to cop as many of their licks as possible, and this in turn gave me fast ears. I used to have a player piano and, of course, this helped me to hear all the old piano rolls and a lot of the masters who played them.

By the time I was eight, my father, who was a former big band singer, could see I had a thing for music and wanted me to learn to read. So he took me to my first "legit" teacher, who taught me the lines and spaces of the treble and bass clefs as well as some classical pieces. I eventually had about 14 different classical teachers, but the only one I still think back to with the fondness and respect I think worthy of a teacher is Joey Kahn, who I studied with in my early teens. He knew the names of all the things I had been copping for years, and he also played great be-bop piano. He would even take me to jazz clubs to see the cats who happened to be in town.

JOHN: What kind of playing experience did you have during this period?

CHARLIE: The Lowell, Massachusetts area had many wonderful musicians I jammed with. I also tried to do any kind of gig I could get--jazz, rock, country, funk (a la James Brown), bar mitzvahs, weddings--you name it and I tried to do it. I tried to learn as many standards as possible. That came easy for me, because if I could hear it mentally, I could play it. I would then force myself to transpose those tunes into all keys--a lot of old boppers would try to cut you by calling tunes in any key-- especially someone younger or the "new kid on the block."

JOHN: Did you have any formal training besides private instruction?

CHARLIE: Yes, I later went to a teacher's college, where I obtained a degree in Music Education. One of the few good experiences I had there was meeting some great friends and musicians like Gerry Bergonzi and John Donahue. We formed a group in 1965 with Harvie Swartz, Nick Goumas, and Jack Diefendorf. We were looked down on by most of the other people at the college for playing American music.

JOHN: Did you learn composition there?

CHARLIE: Not really. Because of the degree program I was in, composition wasn't stressed. So I learned a great deal on my own by studying scores and listening to recordings.

JOHN: How extensive was your study of classical repertoire and how did you go about learning it?

CHARLIE: Well, I did the same thing with piano pieces that I did with composition--I got a score, some records, and started woodshedding. When I could, I practiced about 14 hours a day--not only at the piano, but mentally too! As far as the repertoire goes, I've played all the Chopin Etudes, all of Bach's The Well-tempered

Clavier, plus the Goldberg Variations. I've at least read through all of the main classical and romantic repertoire--all the Beethoven Sonatas, etc. I've only worked up the ones I particularly enjoy. I love the "Les Six"* composers and Debussy and Ravel, but I still think a 12-bar blues line by Charlie Parker is worth more than all of these put together, so I guess that's why you'd call me a jazz musician, huh?

JOHN: Who are some of your main influences?

CHARLIE: One of my favorite all-time musician-composer-players is Jaki Byard, who I think is one of the most underrated players of all time. He was doing things in the 1950's that people are just starting to play now. Of course I love Herbie, Monk, Chick, Keith Jarrett, Bill Evans and McCoy and consider them all main influences on my playing and writing. But this perhaps doesn't say much, because I like every piano player and musician who can play, and try to learn from everyone.

This brings me to what I think is a very important point--I don't think that anyone really needs a teacher! That might sound like a strange thing for a teacher to state, but I really think that if a person wants to play, he'll learn by listening, imitating, and altering, and comparing, and creating. I think teachers have a purpose and that is basically to save the student a lot of time. For example, I can show someone something in five minutes that might take him five years to put together if he tried on his own. Literally!

JOHN: It has been said by some that improvisation is a very mystical thing and best left to a certain few talented players. What's your viewpoint on this?

---

* "Les Six," the name given by Henri Collet in 1920 to a group of six young French composers who were influenced by Erik Satie's emphasis on simplicity and by the artistic ideals of Jean Cocteau. These composers were Darius Milhaud, Louis Durey, Georges Auric, Arthur Honegger, Francis Poulenc, and Germaine Tailleferre.

CHARLIE: I don't believe in "talent"--only hard work--unless you want to call talent the ability to practice for long--and I mean long--periods of time at something you love. I think improvisation is like a conversation. We do it all day. Some of us are better at communicating our ideas quickly or with humor, or whatever. Not everyone is as great a speaker as Martin Luther King or John F. Kennedy, but this doesn't mean that no one else should talk or speak to one another! Some people used to quit playing after hearing Art Tatum or other players who just knocked them out. But I think it's important to remember that as heavy as any player is, you are the only one who knows your idea of what you want to say. Your job is to train yourself to state your ideas in the most individual manner possible. Be yourself! That's why Monk is one of my favorite jazz players. He's playing American music, which to me is going for the individual.

JOHN: Do you feel there are any basic requirements needed to be a student of improvisation?

CHARLIE: Yes, the desire to gain as much knowledge about music as you can and to be willing to spend every waking moment directed towards mastery of any element needed at that time for greater achievement in your chosen field, whether it be for the final goal of entertainment, or the uplifting of yourself and/or others.

JOHN: Transposition can haunt even the best of players. How does one get this area together?

CHARLIE: I think all students should learn all seven clefs to transpose written notes, do ear training to transpose mental sounds, and other exercises too difficult to mention in the context of an interview.

JOHN: Comping can be an art in itself--at least you would think so by listening to Chick Corea, Stanley Cowell, Oscar Peterson, and others. Voicings can be infinite! Where does one start?

CHARLIE: Comping is an art in itself. I think the student should check out Wynton Kelly, Hank Jones, Red Garland, Bill Evans, McCoy Tyner, etc., and actually transcribe some of their comping right off the record. You should do this for every possible singer's and player's accompanist heard in jazz, rock, pop and country--and all styles!

JOHN: Fingering can really hang someone up--some of the greatest lines aren't easily playable on the piano. How does one confront spontaneous finger problems?

CHARLIE: I believe that the student should never, unless playing an etude specifically designed for a certain digit, think of fingering. After a while, problems will cease to exist. Glenn Gould has also found this to be true, as have others.

JOHN: Do you have any thoughts on the type of technique needed to improvise? Does the ear govern all, or should one spend time acquiring independence of fingers, pearly scales and arpeggios? Abby Whiteside and Luigi Bonpensiere, in Idiokinetics, say no to scale and arpeggio drudgery, yet the Clementi and Czerny school seems to have turned out the greatest players!

CHARLIE: This question is too delicate to answer in this context, as every student should have his own technique. This, of course, presumes a thorough knowledge of scales, chords, embellishments, tensions, etc. If you watch McCoy and Chick Corea, you will see many similarities, but also many different ways they use their bodies, depending on the sound they want. The sound is all! With regard to using Whiteside or Czerny or Bonpensiere, or Hannon or Ortmann, I would have to see the student in question and his point of development. "Do-it-yourselfers" should perhaps use Whiteside.

JOHN: Most great players seem to have learned mostly from listening to other players and by doing record copies. Even though some of them have very extensive schooling, they say they learned more this way. Why is that?

CHARLIE: Most players say they learn more from doing record copies because it's the real situation of how to use some technique or other. Schooling and lessons, by their very nature, dissect and examine things in parts and not in a real situation. I think people need both or they might start to sound too much like someone else and not develop their own sound and voice.

JOHN: How much classical music should an aspiring jazz musician get into, or is it even necessary? Might it help in one area and hinder someone in another?

CHARLIE: Actually, I think the more types of music you play, the better off you are, as long as you go into it unprejudiced and with some knowledge of it.

JOHN: How can a player develop a good left hand?

CHARLIE: One thing that will help a lot of people get a good left hand--again, all students are different-- is to transcribe all of Oscar Peterson and Phineas Newborn, Jr.'s two-handed lines, and learn them top speed in all keys.

JOHN: How important is perfect pitch? Should one be able to hear a phrase or chord progression and immediately know what it is, and then be able to play it? Mozart was supposed to be a genius at this!

CHARLIE: I myself have perfect pitch only on the piano. People can develop perfect pitch using Pavlovian techniques--it takes most students about two years to acquire. All musicians should develop the ability to "hear" every tone being played at any musical moment. People like Art Tatum and Mozart had the extra ability to remember, for long periods of time, every tone played, in the exact order it was played in, just as a tape recorder does. This is the very rare ability of photographic memory applied to sounds. In 24 years of teaching, I have seen two people with this ability, and it is fascinating. When I asked them how they did it, they didn't know. Neither of these people pursued careers in music, so apparently the ability can be inherent in people with no real need to stay in musical careers.

JOHN: What's your opinion about drugs in relation to playing and creating music?

CHARLIE: People who do drugs are "dopes." Period!

JOHN: Competition in the music scene today can be so great that many players end up doing things they really aren't into just to pay the rent. What's your opinion on musical integrity?

CHARLIE: I honestly can't answer that question because I've never been in that situation--thank God!

Paul Shaffer
keyboardist/bandleader

PAUL SHAFFER

JOHN: How and when did you get interested in music?

PAUL: Well, rock and roll was a little late to hit Canada, but when it came on the radio there, it started to catch my ear. Those really basic records like "Hundred Pounds of Clay" by Gene McDaniels and "Good Timin'" really appealed to me. I started playing the piano by first just learning how to put my fingers on the keys, and right away I started playing by ear. I loved it immediately. First I played the songs I heard that had only three chords-- once I knew the three chords, I could play a lot of songs. I always played them in the key of C, single line melody in my right hand and simple chords in my left hand. I'd play them really loud and just get into it. When songs started to have that fourth chord, A minor, along with C, F and G, it was a revelation to me. After I learned how to play it, I could play a whole bunch more songs. I never bought records as a kid, I just learned to play them by ear from the radio. Although I had started taking private classical lessons about the same time, at age six, I didn't practice too much. Playing and expanding my repertoire of chords by ear were really the most important things to me. So this is what I did all through my youth, in addition to taking piano lessons up through grade 12 in school.

JOHN: Were those traditional classical lessons?

PAUL: Yes, in Canada they had something called the World Conservatory of Music. I took from a private teacher up where I lived in Thunder Bay, Ontario, and then the Conservatory in Toronto sent out examiners twice a year to give you an examination and grades. That way you could pass the different degrees of Conservatory training. So I did that and I also studied rudimentary theory and harmony up there. I played a little bit of everything. I can still play the Chopin "Revolutionary Etude"--at least the first half of it! I was pretty much of a dilettante, mainly concerned with playing rock and roll by ear.

JOHN: But you probably developed a lot of technique through those lessons.

<u>PAUL</u>: Yes, I got my technique together and then at about age 16 I started playing in a local Top 40 rock and roll cover band. In that high school band, which was called The Fabulous Fugutives, I learned the skills of putting together rock and roll rhythm section arrangements that I still use today.

<u>JOHN</u>: Were you playing organ?

<u>PAUL</u>: Yes, little portable organs. The first one I had was a Hohner. It sounded really silly. Then I graduated at about age 18 to a portable Yamaha that had variable stops almost like draw bars--so that was big. I always wanted a Vox Continental organ but could never afford one when I was younger. In fact, I only recently finally bought one--I located it and got it second hand from a kid in New Jersey--because it still has the greatest sound. The Animals, the Dave Clark Five and all those happening bands used it.

<u>JOHN</u>: Because of your early training and record copying, you were probably always the one in the band who was telling everybody, "No, this is how the part goes."

<u>PAUL</u>: Exactly. It's really an education to copy those arrangements from the records, because you're learning hit records--arrangements these guys came up with after trying them a lot of different ways. The best way became the record, and if it was really good, it became a hit.

So at age 18 I left Thunder Bay and went to the university in Toronto, where I took sociology and philosophy. I thought I was going to be an academic or lawyer or something, and I kind of gave up music for my first two years at school. However, I got very depressed during that time. I couldn't understand why, but it was really because I didn't have an outlet--I wasn't playing any more. Finally, in my third year I hooked up with a jazz guitarist named Munoz. I remember walking through Yorkville Village, which was like the Greenwich Village of Toronto, about 6 a.m. on my way home after an all-nighter, and a guy was sitting on the stairs of a building playing guitar modally. I really did a double take--I walked by, and I just walked right back and zeroed in on him, because he was playing some Coltranesque stuff I had never heard before. It just grabbed my ear. So he took me under his wing and we put a band together in which we were playing modal stuff. He taught me all about it--4th chords, introduced me to McCoy Tyner's style of playing, and opened me up to that kind of music. It was a big change, a big turning point in my life. I decided to try music for a while, so I made a deal with my parents--let me take a year off and do that. I took my arts degree after three years instead of going into an honors program. I could see how much happier I had been in my third year when I had a little jazz band to play with. So during my fourth year in Toronto, I played those gigs with Munoz. But I couldn't support myself with them, so for money I played lounges or anything I could--we used to call it jobbing. Weddings, topless gigs, whatever. I did that and played with Munoz for a couple of years in Toronto.

JOHN: So you didn't have any formal or private study in the area of jazz fusion--you learned it from Munoz and by ear?

PAUL: Yes, listening to records and the Toronto players, some of whom were schooled in that kind of music. There were some good keyboard players up there, like Don Thompson, who plays with a guy named Sonny Greenwich, another Coltranesque guitarist. Bernie Senensky is a great player, Ted Moses in Toronto, Doug Riley--I learned a lot from going and listening to these guys and then trying to emulate them and McCoy in my gigs with Munoz.

JOHN: Did your emulation go as far as actually doing note-for-note transcriptions--writing things down and learning them?

PAUL: I do that incessantly with rock and roll records and solos--I learn those, because they are licks. Rock and roll playing and soloing is lick playing, and when I play an old record that I love, it's important to see how those licks were put together into a solo, and recreate it. That's the fun for me. But Munoz taught me that that was the difference between pop and jazz--jazz is not supposed to be lick playing. Jazz is supposed to be improvising based on modes, scales or whatever you make use of. And so, in my own humble way, that's what I would do--learn the pentatonic scales, practice them and try to build solos that way. So I didn't actually learn jazz solos; I just tried to learn the rudiments and a little bit of improvising. Now I like to think of myself as a guy who can fake a number of different styles and sound pretty authentic in them. Thanks to Munoz, I can get close in that style.

JOHN: That's a good requirement for a being a session player these days, because of the variety of styles you're expected to do. Do you consider yourself a New York session player?

PAUL: Not as much now as I used to be. When I first got on <u>Saturday Night Live</u> as a pianist in the house band, I started to get a lot of calls for dates in New York. Of course, there were more records made there when I first arrived in the mid-70's. Not a lot are made in New York any more.

JOHN: Is it jingles now?

PAUL: Yes, it's jingles. If I get a call I'll go, because that's where you get to play with the good players of New York.

JOHN: After you got into jazz, did you move to New York?

PAUL: Well, the other thing I was doing was trying to get heard in any way I could in Toronto. It didn't look like I was ever going to crack the studio scene up there--those guys had it sewn up very tight, tighter than in this country. I guess that's because there's less work, so they really hold onto it. But one thing I used to do was play auditions for performers. They would come to me and maybe pay me $20 and I'd rehearse with them. Then I'd go play for their audition, even though there would be a house piano player at a show audition, because they'd have the advantage of having rehearsed with me.

So what happened was a performer up there called me and said she wanted to audition for a New York off-Broadway show called <u>Godspell</u> that was opening a Toronto company. She had me learn a song from the show for her to audition with. The composer, Steven Swartz, was up there in Toronto this day casting his show. I played the song for the audition and right afterwards he approached me. He dug the way I played the tune from his show and asked me if I could play the rest of the auditions. The piano player there didn't know a lot of rock and roll songs, and Swartz thought I probably did. Yes! So I played the rest of the auditions, and at the end of the day he said, "Can you put together a band for this show, <u>Godspell</u>?" Well, that was a real show business break for me, my first professional gig.

JOHN: So in a sense you created your own break--because of your love of rock you were actually ready for it.

PAUL: It's true, because this was a "rock musical" and people were coming in and asking the piano player if he knew this song or that, and he didn't. But I knew them all, even though I couldn't read very well. A lot of piano teachers discourage their students from playing by ear, and in retrospect, I've realized that it's because if you have a good ear you fake your way through your lessons. You listen to the teacher play it and then you play it back at her by ear and you never really learn how to sight read. That was the case with me. But having learned all those songs by ear was really worthwhile. I was band leader for the Toronto company of Godspell for one year, and that put me in the theatrical scene in Toronto and I started playing shows. I also made a lot of friends with actors and musical comedy performers there, a lot of whom are still my best friends--guys like Martin Short and Eugene Levy and Dave Thomas. They were the performers in Godspell, and now they're well known in the States. They influenced me a lot--I started to value a good laugh and their ability to be really funny.

The next thing that happened was that Steven Swartz was going to do The Magic Show on Broadway, so he got me my first visa and brought me into the country to play in the pit. That got me into New York, and I played The Magic Show for a year.

After that show, some Canadians arrived in New York to put together the Saturday Night Live show. Lorne Michaels, who was from Toronto, was the producer. I hadn't known him there, but just before leaving Toronto I had met Howard Shore, who was a Canadian who was to be the band leader on Saturday Night Live. I was the only piano player he knew in New York, so when he got into town to put together his band, he called me and I got to be in the house band on the show.

JOHN: Were you the arranger?

PAUL: I did some arrangements, but I was mainly the keyboard player. Then I became "writer of special musical material." I would write the funny musical stuff on the show. If there was a song in a skit, I probably wrote or co-wrote it with some of the show's writers.

JOHN: Had you been composing before that?

PAUL: I had done a little composing for a show in Toronto before I left town--that was the first time. The next writing I did was special material--parodies of rock tunes. That was when I was first starting in theater and doing revues and things. People would say "Let's do a 30's number," or "Let's do a 40's number," and that actually used to drive me crazy because although I'm familiar with standards and those types of tunes, they don't move me like rock and roll. I was always saying, "Can we not do 50's? Can't we do 60's?" Well, finally things started to change and I was one of the first people doing 60's parodies--girl group parodies--things like that. Now, of course, you can't get away from it--it's all 60's.

So I did _Saturday Night Live_ for the first five years and also built up my reputation in the studios during that period. Then I spent two years just doing freelance studio work, and then the Letterman show came up. I was hired on the basis of my work on _Saturday Night Live_. The rest is geography!

JOHN: You've done both live performance playing and studio playing, and now you're doing live TV. Do you have any tips based on your experience in any of these different playing situations?

PAUL: I think the trick to studio playing is to come up with a part that works really great--that is, if it's not already totally written out. It's coming up with a part, or a hook--something that will work with everybody else. In New York, sessions are so fast that you've got to come up with something very quickly. Sometimes you get a situation where all the players are being really careful--everybody is playing such subtle parts that you don't really have much body to the arrangement. It's because everybody knows they've got to come up with something very fast that's guaranteed to work.

JOHN: As opposed to an album date, where you'd have time to do it over and over again, going for the real heavy magic?

PAUL: Well, in this case the magic comes from the spontaneity of doing it quickly, of doing it under pressure, and then getting a great take. Everybody really knows it's going to be the second or third take that's going to work. That's another thing about it--trying to time it so you get your best take when everybody else does. So often the drummer's got it right away because he doesn't have to learn notes or anything. His first take is his best and then he's downhill from there. Meanwhile it takes the guitar players about four takes to get their parts together. So it's important to try to make the takes coincide.

JOHN: You've mentioned that your ear is stronger than your sight reading. How do you handle it if you get some charts that are a little too difficult to read easily on the spot? Rather than sweating it out, do you do a lot of quick studying, silently working things out if there are rough areas?

PAUL: Definitely. When I arrive at a session and see that the chart is a little difficult, I sit down right away with a pencil and start working on it--I start writing stuff into the chart that will help me. And no matter what anybody else is doing, I take every available moment to woodshed.

In my earlier days I was caught a couple of times and just couldn't cut it. When that happens, they just have to do it without you, and they send you home. It can be very embarrassing. I learned that honesty is certainly the best policy. It is a little easier for me to be honest now, though, having gained a bit of a reputation. People will let me get away with things. But I was still caught with a difficult chart a couple of months ago--so I told the arranger that I needed about five minutes with it. Because he was a friend of mine he told everyone to take five, and they went and got coffee. I worked intensely on it for five minutes and when they came back I had it and everything was fine. That's much better than not saying anything, and then the producer can't understand why the piano part isn't coming out. I've even gone as far as saying, "Do you have two tracks? Let me do it one stave at a time." I can only get away with it now because people know me, but I have laid down the treble clef on one track and the bass clef on the other track when I had to.

So what I learned from that type of experience was how to deal with it on the spot. How to be honest, how to negotiate my way through it. Then, also, you've got to learn to be able to spot which are the important parts of the arrangement--which are the parts that really need to be played as written.

JOHN: So you almost do your own editing.

PAUL: Yes. You realize, "there's a bar that he's really going to want to hear." So you just make sure you've got that bar. Maybe you can slide the bar after that a little.

JOHN: A lot of musicians have to deal with the problem of whether they should only play music they like, or take jobs playing music that isn't completely their thing to get heard more or because it pays better. Maybe they'll make some good connections, but maybe they'll get stuck in it. It can come down to a question of musical integrity. Did you ever have to deal with this problem? It seems as though you're doing what you love.

PAUL: Isn't that the bottom line, as they say? Yes, it's true, I love what I do. I have always been a guy who loved Top 40 radio. There have always been musicians around me who scorned it and said it's not happening. However, here I am playing Top 40 songs on TV--the same repertoire I was playing with the Fugitives in Thunder Bay. When I put "Louie Louie" into the Letterman band repertoire, it was as though 20 years might not even have passed, you know. But my idea for putting together the David Letterman Show band was to have the hippest kind of a late night band you could possibly discover in a lounge. I based it on a topless bar in Toronto called the Zanzibar, which used to be a very hip sitting-in scene in the afternoon. They had an organ attached to the top of the bar and different organ trios would slide into position there. So I modeled this band after that, and thought we would play R&B and soul music.

JOHN: So you had planned to do this material before the show even got started?

PAUL: It has slipped into more of a white rock and roll bag now, because that's what the musicians wanted to play. I wanted to play more Stax and Motown, they wanted to play Stones, Yardbirds--so that's where the repertoire has moved. And I don't write out very much for these guys because I think it's better not to, especially with this kind of music. Rather than reading it, we are all really playing simultaneously by ear. Sometimes I call tunes spontaneously. If it's simple enough and everybody thinks they remember it, we say yeah, let's try it, and we do it right on TV with no rehearsal. So I have this band of great players--each guy in the band is really better than I am--and we play these tunes great, and all of a sudden people are saying, "Jeez, those tunes were hip. I never realized." When Gary Burton did the Letterman show, I had him play "Stop In The Name Of Love" by the Supremes and recreate the vibe part, which is close to the melody. I wrote it out for him from the record, voiced in block chords. He really liked what we did and wrote me a letter saying he might like to do a little record in my style sometime.

So, going back to your question about choosing a gig for money or connections versus playing what you don't like--are we talking about integrity here or are we talking about career? Will Lee, my bass player, who played on the very first date I ever arranged in New York, taught me that integrity is really trying to play whatever music is put in front of you the best you can. So if somebody puts "My Baby Does The Hanky Panky" in front of you and you play it great and get a great take on it, to me that's where the integrity lies.

JOHN: So whatever you are doing as a musician, whether it's the Revolutionary Etude or "Louie Louie," make it like gold.

PAUL: That's right. And then you get a groove on "Louie Louie" and there's nothing like it--it's the greatest, and everybody digs it. McCoy Tyner called me for some shows after hearing me on Letterman. He was doing a couple of club dates in New York, promoting an album that had some vocals on it by Phyllis Hyman and some orchestrations. He wanted a synthesizer to orchestrate some of the things he was going to play. Apparently he tried out a few keyboard players, but they were intimidated by him and really couldn't get the hang of it. All they were required to do was big lush string pads and double some of the horn things with Gary Bartz and electric violin things with John Blake. So McCoy caught the Letterman show, thought maybe that kid could do it, and gave me a call. I got to play those four shows with him, and it was really the thrill of my life. McCoy didn't know at that time that I had studied with the Munoz Cosmic Experience, but when I got to play one solo in the show with a steel drum sound on the synthesizer--it was a calypso kind of thing--it was like full circle. I played some of those pentatonic scales back at him, and when I caught his eye on the stage, I could see that we had made contact--he knew that I knew. It was wonderful. Speaking of integrity, this guy has never compromised--but he digs my band, and that's a huge thrill for me. Even though we're playing Motown stuff he can hear the groove and that's important to him, too.

JOHN: He sees your integrity shine through in your vehicle.

PAUL: You can tell, when we play a song on the Letterman show, that the guys in the band are loving it. It's a lot different than just a TV band reading a chart. I've got guys who are not only great studio players with chops in all the different styles I like, but who also just love these tunes, too. Some of the players I've had previously in the band were too hip to be digging these tunes when they were kids, although they dig them now. But all the guys I have now played in bands when they were younger and learned these tunes--they liked them then and still like them now.

JOHN: You obviously have a lot of affinity for the Hammond. Who were some of your influences on it?

PAUL: Jimmy Smith first, of course; Groove Holmes; then moving into Felix Cavaliere from The Rascals, who really applied a Hammond organ to gospel pop and really knew how to work the draw bars. Billy Preston--and how could I not mention Booker T?

JOHN: On all those organ things, did you do record copying?

PAUL: Yes; also, in New York I've had opportunities to actually see in person what some of these Hammond players use for their stops. I've learned a lot of organ stuff from Paul Griffin, a marvelous studio player, and from Billy Preston and Richard Tee. With each of these guys, I waited until he had left the instrument and then sneaked in to see what draw bars he had used. With the Hammond, your basic settings for the different sounds is the first step, but then you really have to tune them in with the track, frequency-wise. You cut out the frequencies you don't need that are just thickening things up too much.

JOHN: Have you gotten into synthesizer programming?

PAUL: I resisted it for a long time and then finally learned the OBXA, which I still think is the best analog synthesizer--it's got a nice fat sound. That's about as far as I take it. I recently started using the Kurzweil on the show and learning it slowly. I've just produced the first record in which I extensively used synthesizers, drum machines, and sequencers, and I just loved it, especially because the time is perfect, and there's nothing like it. If I ever produce anything else I'm definitely going to do it with that method.

JOHN: What's the setup you use on the Letterman show?

PAUL: Hammond B3, the OBXA, the Kurzweil and the Yamaha grand piano. We've been out here in Hollywood, so I've rented the instruments. But just for a change I didn't bother calling Kurzweil to get an instrument out here--instead I rented a wonderful reconditioned old Wurlitzer electric piano that has the real authentic sound of Joe Zawinul's "Mercy Mercy" and the Staple Singers and "What I Say" by Ray Charles. I've been using that on the show just for fun.

JOHN: What instruments do you bring when you do sessions? Do you have your own setup?

PAUL: No--New York is a lot different from L.A., which is cartage heaven, with guys bringing their own setups. The synthesists in New York bring their own, but I don't--you have to rent instruments for me when I go. I'll bring my XA and the Kurzweil, but I don't own a lot of outboard equipment--I just use what's in the studio.

JOHN: Is there anything in particular that your experience with the Letterman show has taught you that musicians might benefit from?

PAUL: When I got the show, it was my first really important gig--I knew it was going to have a lot of exposure. At first I figured I would try to do something unbelievably hip and have a very new synthesizer band or do some other contemporary concept. But then I decided that doing the simplest or most obvious thing would be the best for me. I love Hammond organ and I've known how to play it since I was a kid, so I thought, let me build an act around it. I have a great knowledge of pop tunes--let me use that as my repertoire--what would come most naturally to me and what I can do the best. And what was easiest for me to do also turned out to be the best-- people related to it. And now, you know, I have a lot of heavy players sit in and perform with my band on the Letterman show, and I use the same philosophy. When Eric Clapton played with us, I said to him "You know, Eric, when you come on, we should do something by Cream. We've got to do 'Layla'--I've learned that the most obvious thing is the hippest." And he seemed to relate to that. So that's the philosophy I've learned: do the most natural thing--it's going to work out the best.

JOHN: Do you have any advice or suggestions for handling drug problems or the other pressures of the entertainment business?

PAUL: Just stay in control. What else can you say? I know some guys who are unbelievably talented musicians who have lost control, but I also know a lot of guys who bottomed out but then realized they had to get back in control. They did, and they're back. There's not much other advice than that. Basically you've got to show up for the gig--it doesn't matter how good you are, you've got to show up and be on time and be able to cut it, and all that stuff is of primary importance. Lifetime reputations can be blown in a month of being a little slack. Your reputation is on the line with every date you do. Word gets around.

JOHN: Whether it's a jingle or a heavy TV show, right?

PAUL: You blow a jingle and word gets around very quickly in New York City.

JOHN: So your product is your best PR?

PAUL: That's right, and something else that really applies is that you're only as big as your last hit.

JOHN: How do you handle the business scene? Do you have people to help you?

PAUL: I have an accountant and a lawyer, but I book my own schedule myself. I've almost reached the point where I might need somebody to do that for me, but I haven't made the transition yet.*

JOHN: Do you have anything in the way of personal philosophy or beliefs that have helped you that you'd like to pass along?

PAUL: I don't want to sound corny, but you have to be a good person in life, and your profession is one aspect of life. You don't want to screw anybody around. That happens a lot in this business, and if I attain any success at all, I really would like to try to show people that you can also still be an OK guy--you don't have to be an asshole when you're successful. Your ego doesn't have to carry you away.

----

* Since this interview, Paul has signed with the Gallin Morey Addis management company.

Coda

Coda, a passage, long or short, at the end of a piece or movement, which extends the ideas that have already received logical expression and brings the work to a satisfying conclusion.

The New College Encyclopedia of Music

Well, although we're at the end and playing the Coda, it's my hope that this entire book actually serves as but the Prelude--or maybe underscore--to a rewarding career, and provides you with enough usable knowledge and guidance to put the whole music game into proper perspective and help you achieve your musical goals.

Now by no means was the book intended to be all-inclusive. Subjects such as arranging, orchestration, film scoring, composition, styles, producing, etc., were purposely left out, either for lack of space or because there were already excellent books available on them. So I strongly suggest you check out the books listed in "Recommended Reading" at the end of this manual if any of these areas interest you.

I'd also like to reemphasize that if you as a keyboardist are to consider yourself "contemporary," you should stay abreast of all the latest developments relating to your particular path or direction. Attending special seminars and clinics, subscribing to pertinent publications, going to concerts, exchanging concepts with other artists, listening to records and tapes, and putting a lot of honest hours in, both practicing and playing, are all ways to improve your chances in this creative but competitive game.

If you plan to attend a music school, there are many fine ones specializing in different musical studies to choose from. However, I personally recommend Berklee College of Music in Boston as one of the best comprehensive and contemporary schools. At Berklee one becomes immersed in an intensive musical environment as well as exposed to an extensive curriculum covering all aspects of the music industry. But whatever route you choose-- school, private study, or self instruction using this manual--study diligently, honestly, and with patience--it really does take as long as it takes!

And last--remember, music is fun! It reminds us that we are spiritual beings with a native ability to create. Why else do you think it's referred to as the universal language? So, if it isn't fun...it isn't music!

Best of luck!

RECOMMENDED READING

Alexander, Peter L. *How To Stay Booked A Year In Advance*. Sepulveda, Cal.: Keefay Publishing, 1985.

Anderton, Craig. *Electronic Projects for Musicians*. Saratoga, Cal.: Guitar Player Books, 1980.

Bach, Karl Philipp Emanuel. *Essay on the True Art of Playing Keyboard Instruments*. New York: W. W. Norton & Company, 1949.

Backus, John. *The Acoustic Foundation of Music*. New York: W. W. Norton & Company, 1969.

Bailey, Derek. *Musical Improvisation*. Englewood Cliffs, N.J.: Prentice-Hall, 1980.

Banacos, Charles. *Voicings--Tonal Paralipsis*. Books 1 & 2. Dracut, Mass.: Charles Banacos, 1973.

Banacos, Charles. *Voicings in Fourths, Fifths, and Clusters*. Dracut, Mass.: Charles Banacos, 1973.

Bellson, Louis, and Gil Breines. *Odd Time Reading Text*. Melville, N.Y.: Belwin Mills Publishing Corp., 1968.

Boehm, Laszlo. *Modern Music Notation*. New York: G. Schirmer, 1961.

Bonpensiere, Luigi. *New Pathways to Piano Technique*. New York: The Philosophical Library, 1953.

Boretz, Benjamin, and Edward T. Cone, eds. *Perspectives on Notation and Performance*. New York: W. W. Norton & Company, 1976.

Chapin, Jim. *Advanced Techniques for the Modern Drummer*. New York: Jim Chapin, 1948.

Chowning, John. "The Synthesis of Complete Audio Spectra by Means of Frequency Modulation." *Journal of the Audio Engineering Society*, Vol. 21, No. 7 (1973). pp.526-534. Reprinted in *Computer Music Journal*, Vol. 1, No. 2 (1977). pp.46-54.

Cooke, James Francis. <u>Mastering the Scales and Arpeggios</u>. Bryn Mawr, Pa.: Theodore Presser Co., 1913.

Corea, Chick. <u>Music Poetry</u>. Los Angeles: Litha Music, 1980.

Crombie, David. <u>The Complete Synthesizer</u>. Chester, N.Y.: Omnibus Press, 1982.

Crombie, David. <u>The Synthesizer & Electronic Keyboard Handbook</u>. New York: Alfred A. Knopf, 1984.

Dallin, Leo. <u>Techniques of Twentieth Century Composition</u>. 2d ed. Dubuque, Iowa: Wm. C. Brown Co. Publishers, 1964.

Dawson, Alan. <u>A Manual for the Modern Drummer</u>. Boston: Berklee Press Publications, 1962.

Dearing, J. W. <u>Making Making Making Music</u>. Cincinnatti: Writer's Digest Books, 1979.

Edlund, Lars. <u>Modus Novus, Studies in Reading Atonal Melodies</u>. New York: Alexander Broude, 1963.

Everhart, Powell. <u>The Pianist's Art</u>. Atlanta: Powell Everhart, 962 Myrtle Street, Northeast, Atlanta 9, Georgia, 1958.

Ferand, Ernst. <u>Improvisation in Nine Centuries of Western Music</u>. Cologne: Arno Volk Verlag, Hans Gerig KG, 1961.

Fish, Arnold, and Norman Lloyd. <u>Fundamentals of Sight Singing and Ear Training</u>. New York and Toronto: Dodd, Mead & Company, 1972.

Hanson, Howard. <u>The Harmonic Materials of Modern Music</u>. New York: Appleton, 1960.

Hindemith, Paul. <u>The Craft of Musical Composition</u>. New York: Associated Music Publishers, 1941.

<u>Keyboard Magazine</u>, comp. <u>Synthesizer Basics</u>. Vol. 1. Milwaukee, Wis.: Hal Leonard Publishing Corp., 1984.

<u>Keyboard Magazine</u>, comp. <u>Synthesizer Technique</u>. Vol. 2. Milwaukee, Wis.: Hal Leonard Publishing Corp., 1984.

Keyboard Magazine, comp. Synthesizers and Computers. Vol. 3. Milwaukee, Wis.: Hal Leonard Publishing Corp., 1985.

Keyboard Magazine, comp. The Art of Electronic Music. Milwaukee, Wis.: Hal Leonard Publishing Corp., 1985.

Kasha, Al, and Joel Hirschhorn. If They Ask You, You Can Write A Song. New York: Simon & Schuster, 1979.

Machlis, Joseph. Introduction to Contemporary Music. New York: W. W. Norton & Company, 1961.

Magadini, Pete. Musicians Guide to Polyrhythms. Vols. 1 & 2. Hollywood, Cal.: Try Publishing Co., 1968.

Mancini, Henry. Sounds and Scores. Northridge, Cal.: Northridge Music, 1973.

Martin, George. Making Music, the Guide to Writing, Performing, & Recording. Quill, N.Y.: Shockburg Reynolds, 1983.

Mason, Thom David. Ear Training for the Improviser, A Total Approach. Studio City, Cal.: Dick Grove Publishing, 1981.

Mehegan, John. Jazz Improvisation 2--Jazz Rhythm and the Improvised Line. New York: Watson-Guptill Publications, 1962.

Monaco, Bob, and James Riordan. The Platinum Rainbow. Sherman Oaks, Cal.: Swordsman Press, 1980.

Nyman, Michael. Experimental Music. New York: Schirmer, 1981.

Piston, Walter. Harmony. New York: W. W. Norton & Company, 1969.

Piston, Walter. Orchestration. New York: W. W. Norton & Company, 1955.

Read, Gardner. Music Notation. London: Gollancz; New York: Taplinger/Crescendo, 1974.

Roads, Curtis, and John Strawn, eds. Foundations of Computer Music. Cambridge: MIT Press, 1985.

Runstein, Robert E. Modern Recording Techniques. New York: Howard W. Sams & Co., 1976.

Russell, George. The Lydian Chromatic Concept of Tonal Organization. New York: Concept Publishing Co., 1959.

Russo, William. Jazz Composition and Orchestration. London: University of Chicago Press, 1968.

Schrader, Barry. Introduction to Electro-Acoustic Music. Englewood Cliffs, N.J.: Prentice-Hall, 1984.

Schultz, Arnold. The Riddle of the Pianist's Finger. New York: Carl Fisher, 1964.

Searle, Humphrey. Twentieth Century Counterpoint: A Guide for Students. New York: John de Graff, 1954.

Sebesky, Don. The Contemporary Arranger. Sherman Oaks, Cal.: Alfred Publishing Co., 1974.

Shemel, Sidney, and M. William Krasilovsky. This Business of Music. New York: Billboard Publications, 1977.

Siegel, Alan H. Breaking Into the Music Business. Port Chester, N.Y.: Cherry Lane Books, 1978.

Slonimsky, Nicolas. Thesauras of Scales and Melodic Patterns. New York: Charles Scribner's Sons, 1947.

Stone, Kurt. Music Notation in the 20th Century. New York: W. W. Norton & Company, 1980.

Stuart, Walter. Innovations in Full Chord Technique. New York: Chas. Colin, 1956.

Tonus, Inc. Owner's Manual--The ARP Synthesizer Series 2600. Newton Highlands, Mass.: Tonus, Inc., 1971.

Whiteside, Abby. Indispensables of Piano Playing. New York: Charles Scribner's Sons, 1961.

Whiteside, Abby. Mastering the Chopin Etudes and Other Essays. New York: Charles Scribner's Sons, 1969.

Wilson, M. Emmett. How to Play by Ear. New York: Abelard-Schuman, 1955.

Yates, Peter. Twentieth Century Music. New York: Greenwood House, 1967.

Yelton, Geary. The Rock Synthesizer Manual. Woodstock, Ga.: Rock Tech Publications, 1980.

Books by L. Ron Hubbard*

Art Series. Los Angeles: Bridge Publications, 1983.

Dianetics and Scientology Technical Dictionary. Los Angeles: Publications Organization United States, 1975.

Dianetics 55! Los Angeles: The American St. Hill Organization, 1968.

Introduction to Scientology Ethics. 4th ed. Los Angeles: The American Saint Hill Organization, 1973.

The Management Series. 2 vols. Los Angeles: Bridge Publications, 1982-83.

The Problems of Work. Los Angeles: The American Saint Hill Organization, 1972.

"Dianetic Processing." Book 2 of Science of Survival. Los Angeles: Publications Organization World Wide, 1951. pp.1-14.

Scientology/A New Slant on Life. Los Angeles: Publications Organization United States, 1965.

Scientology, The Fundamentals of Thought. Los Angeles: Publications Organization United States, 1973.

Dictionaries and Encyclopedias

Ammer, Christine. Harpers Dictionary of Music. New York: Barnes & Noble, 1972.

Britannica Book of Music. New York: Encyclopedia Britannica, 1980.

Randel, Don. Harvard Concise Dictionary of Music. Cambridge: Harvard University Press, Belknap Press, 1978.

Westrup, J.A., and F. Harrison. The New College Encyclopedia of Music. New York: W. W. Norton & Company, 1960.

---

* For information on obtaining these or other books by L. Ron Hubbard, contact Bridge Publications, Inc., 1414 N. Catalina Street, Los Angeles, California 90027.